English Fundamentals

Form A

Eleventh Edition

Donald W. Emery
Late of University of Washington

John M. Kierzek
Late of Oregon State University

Peter Lindblom
Miami Dade Community College

Allyn and Bacon

Boston • London • Toronto • Sydney • Tokyo • Singapore

Vice President, Humanities: Joseph Opiela
Editorial Assistant: Kate Tolini
Editorial-Production Service: Omegatype Typography, Inc.
Marketing Manager: Lisa Kimball
Cover Coordinator: Suzanne Harbison
Composition Buyer: Linda Cox
Manufacturing Buyer: Suzanne Lareau
Production Coordinator: Deborah Brown

•

ISBN 0-205-27109-X

Printed in the United States of America

10 9 8 7 6 5 4 3 2 1   02 01 00 99 98 97

Contents

Preface

The eleventh edition of *English Fundamentals* continues a long-standing tradition of quality instruction in the use of English. That tradition has produced changes and improvements in each edition of the book without removing the tried and true qualities that have made the book a mainstay of English instruction for many years. This new book closely resembles the earlier editions, but it has changed significantly to make it work better for both teachers and students. The purpose and the audience, however, have not changed since the first edition. All students who want to improve their ability to use the language in writing and speaking can profit from working in this new eleventh edition.

Organization of the Text

Certain important qualities have always been characteristic of *English Fundamentals:* clear, effective instruction in the fundamental principles of English; carefully crafted exercises designed to illustrate those principles; and a comprehensive testing system to diagnose problems and measure progress. The first lessons introduce students to the basic system of the language and provide carefully chosen examples of verb connections, basic sentence patterns, and the internal workings of the sentence. Simplified presentations make the book accessible both for developmental students and for those who have advanced in their study of the language. Because the first sections are cumulative, building step by step a foundation in the operating principles of the language, these early lessons should be studied first. Once the foundation is laid, the order for studying the remaining units is flexible. Work on spelling and capitalization, for example, can be undertaken at almost any point, even during study of another unit.

Building on the foundation of the early lessons, subsequent lessons explore the more complex structures and relationships of the language. Students examine the function of various clauses and phrases, first learning to recognize their structures, and then learning to use them by practicing with sentence combining, and embedding and transformation drills. The drills are proven methods for helping students to develop flexibility and sophistication in their writing and to recognize effective, correct constructions when they revise.

The last instructional section surveys college writing. Students study the writing process, with special emphasis on techniques of invention, and then learn to apply that process to a wide range of writing assignments typical of college courses. These assignments range from personal essays to academic papers, with an additional focus on paragraph development. The section closes with an examination of essay tests and test-taking. The examples and exercises throughout the book come from a number of disciplines, including science and business, to accommodate the interests of a wide range of students.

The text concludes with a set of twenty Progress Tests and three appendixes. The first appendix discusses study skills and focuses on reading, note-taking, and time management. A dictionary usage section completes this appendix; explanations and exercises ask students to look at several excerpts from widely used desk dictionaries so that the students will learn how to use a dictionary to full advantage. The second appendix offers diagnostic tests to analyze students' abilities in spelling, punctuation, sentence structure, and usage. The third appendix contains the answer key to the Practice Sheets. The book concludes with an index to help students use the text for references to specific concepts.

New to This Edition

The instructional material in all lessons has been significantly rewritten to make the concepts more accessible to the students. Explanations have been simplified, and examples have been updated to accommodate a wider range of students.

The number of practice sheets and exercises requiring active production has been increased so that all important concepts are covered by drills that require recognition and production. These new drills use sentence-combining, embedding, transformation, and rewriting to encourage the students to use the concepts taught in each lesson.

Practice Sheets

The eleventh edition continues the use of Practice Sheets. After every lesson there is at least one easily understood worksheet that provides examples of and practice with the concept introduced in that lesson. The sentences in the Practice Sheets are usually shorter and somewhat simpler than those in the Exercise worksheets that follow. Thus the Practice Sheets provide a starter exercise, a warm-up for students to begin work on each new concept. The Practice Sheets also allow teachers to use the book with students whose reading levels might require simplified material.

Practice Sheets are followed in Appendix C by an answer key for every Practice Sheet, which allows students to use *English Fundamentals* independently as a drill and practice book. Students in composition classes who, for example, might need extra work on punctuation for compound sentences can find that section in the index, read the instruction and commentary, work through the Practice Sheets, and correct their work by referring to the answer key in Appendix C.

Variety in Exercises

In the minds of some, English texts that focus on the fundamentals of the language often limit student work to recognition, identification, and correction—a sort of fill-in-the-blanks scheme that doesn't require much actual writing. *English Fundamentals* requires such work as is necessary to build certain skills, but also incorporates a large number of exercises that require active production of sentences. Students will practice sentence combining and reducing independent clauses to various dependent clauses and phrases. They will learn to embed independent clauses in sentences and will rewrite sentences. They will transform active expressions to passive ones and vice versa, and change from direct to indirect quotation and from indirect to direct. They will write sentences to practice using various constructions. Research has shown, and we are convinced, that such active manipulation of the structures of language will greatly improve students' ability to write effectively and correctly.

Optional Testing Program

The eleventh edition, like the tenth, offers additional tests. The Optional Testing Program consists of thirty tests sent to instructors on request. These tests are printed in a separate volume with perforated pages. These tests differ from the Progress Tests in the text in that they generalize, focusing on major concepts (for example, introductory subordinate elements) rather than specific constructions. The tests first ask for recognition of correct forms, then ask for generation of the new structure out of the basic parts. There is an answer key provided with the tests so that, in addition to use in evaluation, they can be used as higher-level practice exercises.

Acknowledgments

Our thanks go to all those who offered advice and suggestions for improving this and previous editions: Edwin J. Blesch, Jr., Nassau Community College; Ladson W. Bright, Cape Fear Community College; Bernadine Brown, Nassau Community College; Kitty Chen Dean, Nassau Community College; Patricia Derby, Chabot College; Neil G. Dodd, East Los Angeles College; Loris D. Galford, McNeese State University; Harold J. Herman, University of Maryland; William T. Hope, Jefferson Technical College; Sue D. Hopke, Broward Community College; Clifford J. Houston, East Los Angeles College; George L. Ives, North Idaho College; Edward F. James, University of Maryland; Thomas Mast, Montgomery College; Walter Mullen, Mississippi Gulf Coast Community College; Mary E. Owens, Montgomery College; Crystal Reynolds, Indiana State University; Albert Schoenberg, East Los Angeles Community College; Ines Shaw, North Dakota State University; Barbara Stout, Montgomery College; and Robert S. Sweazy, Vincennes University Junior College.

P. L.

Basic Sentence Patterns

Lessons, Practice Sheets, and Exercises

Lesson 1   *The Simple Sentence; Subjects and Verbs*

It might be difficult to produce a satisfying definition, but you probably recognize that the sentence is a basic unit of written or oral expression.

Sentence: an orderly arrangement of words that makes sense.
Sentence: a self-contained grammatical unit, usually containing a subject and a verb, that conveys a meaningful statement, question, command, or exclamation.

You need to understand the basic construction of the sentence in order to write and speak effectively and correctly. In the first few lessons of this book, you'll be examining the parts that make up a sentence and the distinctive characteristics of a few types of sentences that serve as the basic structures of more complicated units.

To begin be sure you can recognize the two indispensable parts of a sentence:

1. The **subject:** the unit about which something is said.

2. The **predicate:** the unit that says something about the subject.

Although the predicate usually includes other modifying words and phrases, the indispensable part of a predicate is the **verb,** the word (or words) that says what the subject does or is. Here are a few things to remember about the subject-verb relationship:

1. In a sentence that reports a specific action taking place, the verb is easily recognized. For instance, to find the subject and verb in *The rusty bumper on the front of my truck rattles noisily,* ask the question, "What happens?" The answer, *rattles,* gives the verb. Then, by asking the question "Who or what rattles?" you come up with the subject, *bumper.* Notice that neither "front rattles" nor "truck rattles" makes the basic statement of the sentence.

2. Some sentences do not report an action. Instead, the sentence says something about the *condition* of the subject. It points out a descriptive quality of the subject or says that something else resembles or is the same thing as the subject. In this kind of sentence you must look for verbs like *is, are, was, were, seem,* and *become,* words that are almost

1

impossible to define because they lack the concrete exactness and action of verbs like *rattle, throw, smash,* and *explode.*

In this descriptive type of sentence, the subject usually reveals itself easily. For example, in "The long first chapter seemed particularly difficult," the verb is *seemed.* The question "Who or what seemed?" provides the subject, *chapter.* The other possible answers to the question—*long, first, particularly,* and *difficult*—do not make sense as answers to the question "Who or what seemed?".

3. Very often the subject has material between it and its verb:

The *price* of potatoes *is* high. [The subject is *price,* not *potatoes.*]
Each of my sisters *is* tall. [The subject is *each,* not *sisters.*]
Only *one* of these watches *works.* [The subject is *one,* not *watches.*]

4. Most modern English sentences place the subject before the verb, but in some sentences the verb precedes the subject:

Behind the house *stood* [verb] an old *mill* [subject].
Under the table *sat* [verb] a large *cat* [subject].

A very common type of sentence with the verb–subject arrangement uses *here* or *there* preceding the verb:

There *are* [verb] three willow *trees* [subject] in our yard.
Here *is* [verb] the *list* [subject] of candidates.

5. Casual, informal language often combines short verbs and subjects with apostrophes representing the omitted letters:

I'm (I am)   It's (It is)   You've (You have)   They're (They are)

For your first practice work you'll be using only one-word subjects. Within this limitation the subject is always a noun or a pronoun. Review a few facts about the *form* of nouns, pronouns, and verbs, so you can easily recognize them.

Nouns

A **noun** is a word that names something, such as a person, place, thing, quality, or idea. A noun is called a *common noun* and is not capitalized if it names just any member of a group or class:

man, city, school, relative

A noun is a *proper noun* and is capitalized if it refers to a particular individual in a group or class:

Albert Lawson, Toledo, Horace Mann Junior High School, Aunt Louise

Most nouns have two forms; they show whether the noun is naming one thing (singular number) or more than one thing (plural number, which adds *s* or *es* to the singular): one *coat,* two *coats;* a *lunch,* several *lunches.* Proper nouns are rarely pluralized, and some common nouns have no plural form, for example, *honesty, courage, ease,* and *hardness.* (Lesson 28 examines in detail the special spelling problems of plural nouns.)

Nouns often follow *the, a,* or *an,* words which are called **articles.** A descriptive word (an adjective) may come between the article and the noun, but the word that answers the question "What?" after an article is a noun:

Article	$\left(\begin{array}{c}\text{optional}\\\text{adjective}\end{array}\right)$	noun
A (or The)	happy	_____.

Another way to identify nouns is to recognize certain suffixes. (See Supplement 1.)* Here are some of the common suffixes found on hundreds of nouns:

age [break*age*]; ance, ence [resist*ance*, insist*ence*]; dom [king*dom*]; hood [child*hood*]; ion [prevent*ion*]; ism [national*ism*]; ment [move*ment*]; ness [firm*ness*]; or, er [invest*or*, los*er*]; ure [expos*ure*]

Pronouns

A **pronoun** is a word that substitutes for a noun. There are several classes of pronouns. (See Supplement 2.) The following classes can function as subjects in the basic sentences that you will be examining in these early lessons:

Personal pronouns substitute for definite persons or things: *I, you, he, she, it, we, they.*

Demonstrative pronouns substitute for things being pointed out: *this, that, these, those.*

Indefinite pronouns substitute for unknown or unspecified things: *each, either, neither, one, anyone, somebody, everything, all, few, many,* and so on.

Possessive pronouns substitute for things that are possessed: *mine, yours, his, hers, its, ours, theirs.*

Verbs

A **verb** is a word that expresses action, existence, or occurrence by combining with a subject to make a statement, to ask a question, or to give a command. One easy way to identify a word as a verb is to use the following test:

Let's _____

[action word]

---

*In some lessons of this book you will find notations referring you to a supplement that is appended at the end of the lesson. Read the supplement *after* you have thoroughly studied the lesson. The lesson contains the essential information that is vital to your understanding of subsequent lessons and exercises. The supplement presents material that has relevance to some points of the lesson but has only incidental application to the lessons and exercises that follow. The supplements at the end of this lesson are found on page 4.

Any word that will function in this position to complete the command is a verb: "Let's *leave.*" "Let's *buy* some popcorn." "Let's *be* quiet." This test works only with the basic present form of the verb, not with forms that have endings added to them or that show action taking place in the past: "Let's *paint* the car" (not "Let's *painted* the car").

Supplement 1

A **suffix** is a unit added to the end of a word or base, making a derived form. A similar unit added to the beginning of a word is called a **prefix.** Thus, to the adjective *kind,* we add a prefix to derive another adjective, *unkind,* and a suffix to derive the nouns *kindness* and *unkindness.* An awareness of how suffixes are used will do far more than aid you in your ability to recognize parts of speech: Your spelling will improve and your vocabulary will expand as well.

Hundreds of nouns have distinctive suffix endings. The definitions of some of these suffixes are rather difficult to formulate, but you can quite readily figure out the meanings of most of them: *ness,* for instance, means "quality or state of" (thus *firmness* means "the state or quality of being firm"); *or* and *er* show the agent or doer of something (an *investor* is "one who invests").

Supplement 2

Two classes of pronouns, the **interrogative** and the **relative,** are not listed here. Because they are used in questions and subordinate clauses but not in simple basic sentences, they will not be discussed until later lessons.

Another type of pronoun that you use regularly (but not as a true subject) is the **intensive** or **reflexive** pronoun, the "self" words used to add emphasis:

You *yourself* made the decision.

or to name the receiver of an action when the doer is the same as the receiver:

The boy fell and hurt *himself.*

The first example is the intensive use; the second is the reflexive. Pronouns used this way are *myself, yourself, himself* (not *hisself*), *herself, itself, ourselves, yourselves,* and *themselves* (not *themself, theirself,* or *theirselves*).

The "self" pronouns are properly used for only these two purposes. They should not be substituted for regular personal pronouns:

Mary and I [not myself] were invited to the dance.
Tom visited Eric and me [not myself] at our ranch.

Subjects and Verbs

NAME _____ SCORE _____

Directions: In the space at the left, copy the word that is the verb of the italicized subject.

_____ 1. The *explanation* for the mishap was not believable.

_____ 2. A *few* of the players were late yesterday.

_____ 3. The *team* selected a captain this morning.

_____ 4. *Three* of the kittens hid behind the couch.

_____ 5. *Those* are my three favorite movies.

_____ 6. There comes the *announcer* now.

_____ 7. Jane's new golf *clubs* arrived today.

_____ 8. Only *one* of my new teachers came to school today.

_____ 9. In her locker is the shortstop's new *glove*.

_____ 10. *Less* than ten dollars remains in my checking account.

_____ 11. From behind the high fence rumbled the *growl* of a very large dog.

_____ 12. *All* but two of the employees ride bikes to work.

_____ 13. There's a *sandwich* in the refrigerator for you.

_____ 14. The *list* of new parts disappeared from the screen.

_____ 15. *Neither* of the two girls helped with that project.

_____ 16. Only a few *members* missed the picnic.

_____ 17. A dense *fog* covered the road into the valley.

_____ 18. From the top of that building flies a large state *flag*.

_____ 19. A *teacher* from the Geology Department delivered a report to the college president.

_____ 20. *Some* of our problems seem less important now.

Directions: In the space at the left, copy the word that is the subject of the italicized verb.

———————————— 1. The shorter of those two books *is* quite popular with the students.

———————————— 2. Under the twisted branches *lay* a huge black snake.

———————————— 3. A package from my uncle *arrived* this morning.

———————————— 4. A friend of my sister *took* my locker key home with her.

———————————— 5. Even the weakest person in the class *lifted* that light weight.

———————————— 6. In the corner of the room *stood* Mary's new softball bat.

———————————— 7. Only the last question on the test *stumped* us.

———————————— 8. The two students in the back of the room *slept* through the lecture.

———————————— 9. Along the twisting pathway *walked* a tired hiker.

———————————— 10. Mary Anne's skill as a mathematician *earned* her a scholarship to the state university.

———————————— 11. A decrease in the price of gasoline *saved* the company a great deal of money.

———————————— 12. There *were* several members of the club on that earlier bus.

———————————— 13. Only a few of the students in the math class *failed* that test.

———————————— 14. The last of the tired boys *straggled* in about 3:00 P.M.

———————————— 15. All my sources, with only one exception, *came* from our college library.

———————————— 16. Out there in the field *stand* three tall sunflowers.

———————————— 17. Applications for that job at the campus radio station *came* from all over the state.

———————————— 18. My neighbor's car alarm *woke* me very early this morning.

———————————— 19. All the trophies from the football team's championship season *stand* in the display cases in the lobby.

———————————— 20. The research assistant in the chemistry lab in the basement of Allen Hall *injured* herself yesterday.

Exercise 1   *Subjects and Verbs*

NAME _____ SCORE _____

Directions: In the first space, copy the subject of the sentence. In the second space, copy the verb.

_____   1. Two of the faster runners on the team finished the race in record
_____   time.
_____   2. The closing bell sounds at 4:00 P.M.

_____   3. A low oil pressure reading in his car worries my brother.

_____   4. We're certainly not happy about this heat wave.

_____   5. There comes Jim with two other members of the baseball team.

_____   6. In her first week of work, Marge made two successful sales calls.

_____   7. None of the detectives spotted that important clue.

_____   8. During the afternoon my two younger sisters always go to the
_____   park for a run.
_____   9. Behind every cloud there's a silver lining.

_____ 10. At the end of a long day, Robert gratefully locked the office door.

_____ 11. The high-pitched call of the hawk pierced the afternoon's quiet.

_____ 12. In the attic late last night, Martha heard a strange rattling sound.

_____ 13. Each of our three telephones rings with a slightly different sound.

_____ 14. On the last page of that news magazine, Mark read a very con-
_____   troversial editorial.
_____ 15. That's the last picture in that series of pictures of professional
_____   musicians.
_____ 16. Seven recent graduates joined our class for its annual picnic.

_____ 17. On her third attempt at the competency test, Carol finally passed.

_____ 18. In a complicated program such as this one, there are always some
_____   minor problems.

_____ 19. Jan's time in the quarter mile dropped significantly in the past
_____ two weeks.

_____ 20. After twenty years an old car becomes an antique.

_____ 21. There are five qualified applicants for the director's job.

_____ 22. Yesterday Alice walked to class in a terrible rainstorm.

_____ 23. Most of the little kids watched a movie yesterday afternoon.

_____ 24. Two of the players missed practice yesterday because of a test.

_____ 25. There was an important announcement on my phone-mail this
_____ morning.

_____ 26. Hardly anyone in my class made less than a B on that paper.

_____ 27. In a back corner of the basement lay my father's old baseball
_____ glove.

_____ 28. Several of my friends had jobs in construction last summer.

_____ 29. On the corner of the professor's desk sat a manual typewriter.

_____ 30. A small group of angry students walked slowly toward the presi-
_____ dent's office.

_____ 31. Only one person knows the real reason for his resignation.

_____ 32. There's no answer at Janie's apartment.

_____ 33. Several members of my high school graduating class won schol-
_____ arships to college.

_____ 34. In the shade of the big oak tree in the back yard slept an old gray
_____ dog.

_____ 35. Our search for the lost boots ended in failure.

_____ 36. A few members of last year's debate team came to the champi-
_____ onship this year.

_____ 37. Sam's very unhappy with his new work schedule.

_____ 38. An apple with a huge worm hole in it sat on the top of the basket.

_____ 39. The new girl's radiant smile won her many new friends.

_____ 40. Last night during the late news, I fell asleep on the couch.

Lesson 2 *Verbs, Adjectives, Adverbs, and Prepositions*

In Lesson 1 you learned how to recognize a verb. The verb form that you examined there is called the **base** or **infinitive;** it is the form that "names" the verb. Verbs change their form according to various conditions, three of which are person, number, and tense. You should learn these forms because they occur in nearly every sentence that you speak or write.

Person specifies the person(s) speaking ("first" person: *I, we*); the person(s) spoken *to* ("second" person: *you*); and the person(s) or thing(s) spoken *about* ("third" person: *he, she, it, they*).

Number shows whether the reference is to *one* thing (*singular* number) or to more than one thing (*plural* number).

Tense refers to the time represented in the sentence, whether it applies to the present moment (I *believe* him) or to some other time (I *believed* him, I *will believe* him).

To demonstrate these changes in form, you can use a chart or arrangement called a *conjugation.* In the partial conjugation that follows, three verbs are used: *earn, grow,* and *be.* The personal pronoun subjects are included to show how the person and number of the subject affect the form of the verb.

Indicative Mood
Active Voice*

	Singular Number	*Plural Number*
	Present Tense	
1st Person	I earn, grow, am	We earn, grow, are
2nd Person	You earn, grow, are	You earn, grow, are
3rd Person	**He earns, grows, is	They earn, grow, are
	Past Tense	
1st Person	I earned, grew, was	We earned, grew, were
2nd Person	You earned, grew, were	You earned, grew, were
3rd Person	He earned, grew, was	They earned, grew, were
	Future Tense	
1st Person	I shall earn, grow, be	We shall earn, grow, be
2nd Person	You will earn, grow, be	You will earn, grow, be
3rd Person	He will earn, grow, be	They will earn, grow, be

Indicative mood indicates that the verb expresses a fact as opposed to a wish, command, or possibility. *Active voice* indicates that the subject of the verb is the *doer,* rather than the receiver, of the action of the verb.

**The pronoun *he* is arbitrarily used here to represent the third-person singular subject, which may be any singular pronoun (*she, it, who, nobody*); singular noun (*girl, neighbor, elephant, misunderstanding, Alice, Christopher Robert Klein III*); or word groups constituting certain types of phrases or clauses that will be studied in later lessons.

9

Present Perfect Tense

1st Person	I have earned, grown, been	We have earned, grown, been
2nd Person	You have earned, grown, been	You have earned, grown, been
3rd Person	He has earned, grown, been	They have earned, grown, been

Past Perfect Tense

1st Person	I had earned, grown, been	We had earned, grown, been
2nd Person	You had earned, grown, been	You had earned, grown, been
3rd Person	He had earned, grown, been	They had earned, grown, been

Future Perfect Tense

1st Person	I shall have earned, grown, been	We shall have earned, grown, been
2nd Person	You will have earned, grown, been	You will have earned, grown, been
3rd Person	She will have earned, grown, been	They will have earned, grown, been

Notice that in the past tense, *earn* adds an *ed* ending, but *grow* changes to *grew*. This difference illustrates **regular** and **irregular** verbs, the two groups into which all English verbs are classified. *Earn* is a regular verb, *grow* is an irregular verb. (Lesson 21 discusses irregular verbs in more detail.)

Notice also that some verb forms consist of more than one word *(will earn, have grown, will have been)*. In such uses, *will* and *have* are called **auxiliary verbs.** More auxiliary verbs are examined in Lesson 5.

With the "naming" words (nouns and pronouns) and the "action" words (verbs), you can construct true sentences:

Janice arrived.
He laughed.
Power corrupts.

But to make sentences more varied and complete, you need "describing" words (adjectives and adverbs) and prepositional phrases.

Adjectives

An **adjective** is a word that describes or limits—that is, gives qualities to—a noun. Adjectives are found in three different positions in a sentence:

1. Preceding a noun that is in any of the noun positions within the sentence

   The *small* child left. He is a *small* child. I saw the *small* child. I gave it to the *small* child.

2. Following a describing (linking) verb and modifying the subject

   The child is *small.* Mary looked *unhappy.* We became *upset.*

3. Directly following the noun (less common than the two positions described above)

   He provided the money *necessary* for the trip. The hostess, *calm and serene,* entered the hall.

Certain characteristics of form and function help you to recognize adjectives. There are several suffixes that, when added to other words or roots of other words, form adjectives. Here again, an understanding of the meaning of a suffix can save trips to the dictionary.

For instance, in the hundreds of adjectives ending in *able (ible)*, the suffix means "capable of" or "tending to"; thus *usable* means "capable of being used" and *changeable* means "tending to change."

> able, ible [read*able*, irresist*ible*]; al [internation*al*]; ant, ent [resist*ant*, diverg*ent*]; ar [lun*ar*]; ary [budget*ary*]; ful [meaning*ful*]; ic, ical [cosm*ic*, hyster*ical*]; ish [fool*ish*]; ive [invent*ive*]; less [blame*less*]; ous [glamor*ous*]; y [greas*y*]
>
> (One note of warning: Many other words in English end with these letters, but you can easily see that they are not employing the suffix. Ta*ble*, fer*ment*, arr*ive*, d*ish*, and pon*y*, for instance, are not adjectives.) See Supplement 1 for more information on adjectives.

Adjectives Used in Comparisons. Nearly all adjectives, when they are used in comparisons, can be strengthened or can show degree by changing form or by using *more* and *most*:

> *great* trust, *greater* trust, *greatest* trust
> *sensible* answer, *more sensible* answer, *most sensible* answer

The base form (*great* trust, *sensible* answer) is the **positive degree**. The second form (*greater* trust, *more sensible* answer) is the **comparative degree**: it compares two things. The third form (*greatest* trust, *most sensible* answer) is the **superlative degree** and distinguishes among three or more things. (See Supplement 2.)

Adverbs

Another modifier is the **adverb**, a word that modifies anything except a noun or a pronoun. Most adverbs modify verbs (He returned *soon*). Other adverbs modify adjectives and other adverbs (The *very* old man walked *quite* slowly). Some adverbs modify whole sentences (*Consequently*, we refused the offer). Adverbs tell certain things about the verb, the most common being:

1. **Manner:** John performed *well*. We worked *hard*. The child laughed *happily*. I would *gladly* change places with you.
2. **Time:** I must leave *now*. I'll see you *later*. *Soon* we shall meet *again*.
3. **Frequency:** We *often* go on picnics, *sometimes* at the lake but *usually* in the city park.
4. **Place:** *There* he sat, alone and silent. *Somewhere* we shall find peace and quiet.
5. **Direction:** The police officer turned *away*. I moved *forward* in the bus.
6. **Degree:** I could *barely* hear the speaker. I *absolutely* refuse to believe that story.

This gives you helpful clues for recognizing the most frequently used adverbs, which answer such questions as "How?" (manner or degree), "When?" (time or frequency), and "Where?" (place or direction).

Adverbs of a subclass called **intensifiers** modify adjectives or adverbs but not verbs. For example, a *very* good meal, his *quite* surprising reply, *too* often, *somewhat* reluctantly, and so on.

Many adverbs change form the way adjectives do, to show degree:

> to drive *fast*, to drive *faster*, to drive *fastest*
> to perform *satisfactorily*, to perform *more satisfactorily*, to perform *most satisfactorily*

See Supplement 2 for details on some common irregular intensifiers.

Prepositions

A **preposition** is a word that introduces a phrase and shows the relationship between its object and some other word in the sentence. Notice that many prepositions show a relationship of space or time. Here are some common prepositions; those in the last column are called *group prepositions:*

about	beside	inside	through	according to
above	besides	into	throughout	because of
across	between	like	till	by way of
after	beyond	near	to	in addition to
against	by	of	toward	in front of
around	down	off	under	in place of
at	during	on	unfit	in regard to
before	except	out	up	in spite of
behind	for	outside	upon	instead of
below	from	over	with	on account of
beneath	in	since	without	out of

Every preposition has an object; with its object and any modifiers, the preposition makes a prepositional phrase. You can easily illustrate the function of prepositions by constructing sentences like the following:

After breakfast I walked *to* town *without* my friend. [Objects: *breakfast, town, friend.*]

On account of the rain, I canceled my plans for a game of tennis at the park *with* John. [Objects: *rain, game, tennis, park, John.*]

The trees *outside* the window *of* the kitchen are full *of* blossoms *during* the spring. [Objects: *window, kitchen, blossoms, spring.*]

Supplement 1

There are other classes of words, besides true adjectives, that modify nouns, but if you concentrate on the *functions* of the various kinds of words, you can safely classify as adjectives all words that precede nouns and limit their meaning. Such adjectives include articles, numerals, and possessives (*an* apple, *the* weather, *my three* roommates); modifiers that can be used also as pronouns (*these* people, *some* friends, *all* workers); and nouns that modify other nouns (*basketball* players, *summer* days, *crop* failures).

Many words can be used as adjectives or as pronouns; the position of a word within the sentence determines which part of speech it is.

Several [*adj.*] classmates of mine [*pron.*] read this [*adj.*] report.
Several [*pron.*] of my [*adj.*] classmates read this [*pron.*].

Supplement 2

A few commonly used modifiers form their comparative and superlative degrees irregularly:

good (*adj.*),	better,	best
well (*adv.*),	better,	best
bad (*adj.*),	worse,	worst

Parts of Speech

NAME _____ SCORE _____

Directions: In each space at the left, write one of the following numbers to identify the part of speech of each italicized word:

1. Noun	3. Verb	5. Adverb
2. Pronoun	4. Adjective	6. Preposition

_____ 1. Jim's work *on* the car failed to make *any* improvement in its performance.

_____ 2. My *answer puzzled* Mr. White.

_____ 3. Martha explained *her* solution *to* the first problem.

_____ 4. For his *great* effort in Saturday's game, Craig *truly* deserved the game ball.

_____ 5. Her *loud* screams *woke* all of us.

_____ 6. *Certainly,* we will try *it* again.

_____ 7. My poor performance *in* the game probably caused the *loss.*

_____ 8. *Last* night's loss was a *sharp* disappointment.

_____ 9. The teacher *looked sharply* at the two students in the back of the room.

_____ 10. That *look* silenced *their* laughter immediately.

_____ 11. We liked *her* idea better than *yours.*

_____ 12. His *best* work on that *test* came on the last question.

_____ 13. The chief *ordered* an investigation of *that* man's background.

_____ 14. Her *order* covered the last *five* years.

_____ 15. We made *hardly* any impact in *our* first attempt.

_____ 16. *Before* our first class, *all* of us met for breakfast.

_____ 17. Jim was *happy* to find his lost book *under* the couch.

_____ 18. He smiled *happily* at the *sight* of the book.

_____ 19. I finally *sighted* the hawk at the top of the tree.

_____ 20. *Many* of the workers left *early* today.

_____ 21. *Many* people took the *early* bus.

_____ 22. Her *quiet voice* calmed the frightened children.

_____ 23. The umpire *called* that *pitch* a strike.

_____ 24. His *call* was *obviously* a mistake.

_____ 25. *Clearly,* we should offer the position to *her* as soon as possible.

_____ 26. "My options at this *time* are not *clear* to me," said Mira.

_____ 27. *She* needed a *clear* explanation of her choices.

_____ 28. *Primarily,* he *used* only two sources for that paper.

_____ 29. Jim used two *primary sources* for his paper.

_____ 30. His *use* of *those* sources was not wise.

_____ 31. The candidate made a *wise* choice for a running *mate.*

_____ 32. There is no *better way* to get from here to school.

_____ 33. I can work *more quickly with* that new saw.

_____ 34. Jan's *work* at the factory is quite *tiresome.*

_____ 35. Jan is often *quite tired* after work.

_____ 36. *Outside,* the *snow* piled up quickly.

_____ 37. Alex acquired *his* interest in computers from his mother, a computer *programmer.*

_____ 38. We have an *outside* chance of finding that *lost* dog.

_____ 39. The small boat sailed *beyond* the *horizon.*

_____ 40. Last night's *sail* was *very* pleasant.

Exercise 2   *Parts of Speech*

NAME _____ SCORE _____

Directions: In each space at the left, write one of the following numbers to identify the part of speech of each italicized word:

1. Noun	3. Verb	5. Adverb
2. Pronoun	4. Adjective	6. Preposition

_____ 1. "I would like to buy a new compact disc player *for my* office," said Art.
_____

_____ 2. The *news* from the branch office *is* very exciting.
_____

_____ 3. The two girls in the *back* of the room seemed *genuinely* confused.
_____

_____ 4. *In* fact, confusion *reigned* throughout the classroom.
_____

_____ 5. The *reign* of Alexander the Great *ended* with his death in 323 B.C.
_____

_____ 6. "The *end* of this trip is very near," sighed Jane *thankfully.*
_____

_____ 7. The *selection* process for admission *to* that program works very slowly.
_____

_____ 8. The Cleveland Indians *selected* my brother Allan as their second round draft
_____   *choice.*

_____ 9. *Some* courses *at* this college require lab work along with class work.
_____

_____ 10. *Some* of the students resent the *time* spent in lab.
_____

_____ 11. *Resentment* grew among the town's younger citizens because of the *new*
_____   curfew.

_____ 12. *Her* slow reaction to the officer's command caused *Jill* a great deal of
_____   trouble.

_____ 13. Because of the blizzard, *we* stayed *inside* the house all weekend.
_____

_____ 14. *Inside,* we were *quite* warm and comfortable.
_____

_____ 15. That plan is an exact *copy* of *last* year's plan.
_____

_____ 16. *Many* of the seniors found jobs in *other* states.
_____

_____ 17. *Others* found the search *very* difficult.
_____

_____ 18. "We looked *everywhere* for you," said Mark *to* Rhoda.
_____

_____ 19. *Alice's delight* at the unexpected gift was clear to everyone in the room.
_____

_____ 20. The coach's *criticism* of Jack's performance was not *fair.*
_____

Directions: Each of these words is labeled as a noun, verb, adjective, or adverb. In the spaces following each word, write related words of the part of speech indicated. Do not use adjectives ending in *-ing* or *-ed*.

Example:

wide (adj.) _____*width*_____ (n.) _____*widen*_____ (v.)

1. adjust (v.) _____ (n) _____ (adj.)

2. apology (n.) _____ (adv.) _____ (v.)

3. alertly (adv.) _____ (adj.) _____ (n.)

4. bashful (adj.) _____ (adv.) _____ (n.)

5. brightly (adv.) _____ (adj.) _____ (v.)

6. complete (v.) _____ (adv.) _____ (adj.)

7. construct (v.) _____ (n.) _____ (adv.)

8. deplore (v.) _____ (adj.) _____ (adv.)

9. defiant (adj.) _____ (v.) _____ (n.)

10. foolishly (adv.) _____ (n.) _____ (adj.)

11. gossip (n.) _____ (adj.) _____ (v.)

12. hypnotic (adj.) _____ (adv.) _____ (v.)

13. injure (v.) _____ (adj.) _____ (adv.)

14. luxury (n.) _____ (v.) _____ (adj.)

15. mystery (n.) _____ (adj.) _____ (adv.)

16. openly (adv.) _____ (adj.) _____ (v.)

17. rely (v.) _____ (n.) _____ (adj.)

18. secure (adj.) _____ (n.) _____ (v.)

19. service (n.) _____ (adj.) _____ (v.)

20. wearily (adv.) _____ (adj.) _____ (n.)

Exercise 2A   *Subjects and Verbs*

NAME _____   SCORE _____

Directions: In the first space at the left, copy the word that is the subject of the sentence. In the second space, copy the verb. Many of the verbs consist of more than one word.

S. _____   1. Behind the shoes in the back of his closet, Mel found his lost
V. _____   baseball glove.

S. _____   2. None of the shirts on that rack are my size.
V. _____

S. _____   3. Next year the company will need an entirely new line of women's
V. _____   golf clubs.

S. _____   4. Every kid in my neighborhood believes the story about the
V. _____   haunted house.

S. _____   5. Few of the members of that class made a grade lower than C on
V. _____   that test.

S. _____   6. The hardest part of that run is the last steep hill.
V. _____

S. _____   7. I've never seen a funnier movie.
V. _____

S. _____   8. There are no tests until next week.
V. _____

S. _____   9. Out behind the house lies a huge pile of brush.
V. _____

S. _____   10. Because of the storm, all of the stores on the south side of town
V. _____   closed at noon today.

S. _____   11. On the east side of the creek under the bridge, Alice found the
V. _____   two lost calves.

S. _____   12. The next flight to Buffalo will not depart until tomorrow at
V. _____   9:00 A.M.

S. _____   13. The real prize from last spring's draft was Williams, the new des-
V. _____   ignated hitter.

S. _____   14. A lack of replacement parts will cause a long delay in the repairs
V. _____   on my truck.

S. _____   15. Many of our new employees have come to us from California.
V. _____

S. _____   16. With the closing of the Thruway, traffic has increased on the
V. _____   street in front of our house.

S. _____   17. Yesterday two of my suite mates went home for the weekend.
V. _____

S. _____   18. The people in that car seemed quite confused.
V. _____

S. _____ 19. There's only a tiny margin for error on the narrow fairways of
V. _____ that golf course.

S. _____ 20. The new president, along with her family, will arrive in town next
V. _____ Monday.

S. _____ 21. Ron's pleased with his grade on the last algebra test.
V. _____

S. _____ 22. We took the shortcut to the lake last week.
V. _____

S. _____ 23. Marge's mother has recently taken a new job with an electronics
V. _____ manufacturer.

S. _____ 24. The sight of Power Rangers no longer excites any of the children
V. _____ in the neighborhood.

S. _____ 25. Several of the staff members will no longer work on that report.
V. _____

S. _____ 26. That section of new books is the most interesting in the entire
V. _____ library.

S. _____ 27. Beside the Homecoming Queen stood the former queen along
V. _____ with the other members of this year's court.

S. _____ 28. Under his napkin my little brother had hidden the hated broccoli
V. _____ and peas.

S. _____ 29. My response to your request, along with a discussion of the entire
V. _____ situation, appears in my letter.

S. _____ 30. Students from all the colleges in the state rallied behind our
V. _____ efforts at environmental reform.

S. _____ 31. After the President's speech, several television commentators
V. _____ explained the proposed legislation.

S. _____ 32. Evelyn is the only person in this office with a computer on her
V. _____ desk.

S. _____ 33. In spite of Roy's best efforts in the final lap, our relay team fin-
V. _____ ished last at the state track meet.

S. _____ 34. A little girl with beautiful dimples and long brown hair charmed
V. _____ the group with her song.

S. _____ 35. After two busy signals and one wrong number, I finally reached
V. _____ the registrar's office.

S. _____ 36. Jan Brown, on the platform with the other officers in the class,
V. _____ will deliver a brief speech.

S. _____ 37. Several of the students came late for the exam last Friday.
V. _____

S. _____ 38. Our excitement turned to fear because of the flimsy construction
V. _____ of the footbridge over the river.

S. _____ 39. Ray's afraid his GPA is too low for admission to the law school.
V. _____

S. _____ 40. Harry's efforts on behalf of the poverty-stricken family saved
V. _____ their home from foreclosure.

The sentence, a combination of subject and predicate arranged to make a statement, is a basic unit of written and oral communication. That basic unit, the sentence, actually comes in just five types or patterns, and learning to recognize those five patterns can help you to become a more effective communicator. In this lesson and the following lesson, we will look at these five patterns so that you can learn to use them in your writing.

The nature of the verb is the key to recognizing sentence patterns: Verbs come in two types, intransitive and transitive. The prefix *trans* means across, and the letters *it* come from the Latin word meaning to *go*, so *transit* means to go across. The additional prefix *in* means *not*, so *intransit* means to not go across. (Don't confuse the Latin word with the colloquial *in-transit*, which means in the act of going somewhere.)

Intransitive Verbs

The term **intransitive** means, very simply, that the verb does not "go across" to a complement, or more accurately, does not transfer its action to an object. In the sentence "John spoke softly." the action (the verb) is *spoke* and the actor (the subject) is *John*. The action does not "go across" to a noun that receives that action. The verb is intransitive. Some intransitive verbs do not express an action; they simply connect or link the subject to a noun that renames the subject or an adjective that modifies the subject. In the following sentences there is no action.

> *John* is a *genius.*
> *John* is *brilliant.*

The subject *John* is simply linked to a word that identifies or modifies it.

Transitive Verbs

The term **transitive** means that the action "goes across" to some noun that receives the action. That noun is called the direct object and is the receiver of the action expressed in the verb. So in the sentence "John watched a movie." the action is *watched* and the actor is *John*. The receiver of the action (direct object) is *movie*. The direct object can be found by asking the question "What?" after the subject and verb have been found. "John watched what? John watched a movie."

In our system, Sentence Patterns 1 and 2 use intransitive verbs. Sentence Patterns 3, 4, and 5 use transitive verbs.

Sentence Pattern 1

Sentence Pattern 1 contains an intransitive verb and is the only basic sentence that does not require a word to complete the sense of the action. For example, in the sentence "The child runs," the action of the verb *runs* is complete within itself; it does not transfer to an object. Pattern 1 sentences nearly always contain modifiers that tell how, when, and where the action occurred:

Yesterday the neighborhood children played noisily in the vacant lot.

Notice that the material associated with the verb is all adverbial: "When?" *Yesterday.* "How?" *Noisily.* "Where?" *In the vacant lot.* The important characteristic of a Pattern 1 sentence is that there is no noun answering the question "What?" after the verb. The best way to recognize an intransitive verb is to spot the lack of a noun answering the question "What?" after the verb.

In some Pattern 1 sentences, the purpose of the statement is simply to say that the subject exists. Usually some adverbial material is added to show the place or the time of the existence:

The glasses *are* in the cabinet.
Flash floods often *occur* in the spring.
There *were* several birds around the feeder.

In most Pattern 1 sentences, however, some activity takes place, but no completer is needed because the action is not transferred to anything:

The tree *fell.*
The customer *complained* loudly.
The professor *walked* into the room unexpectedly.

Before you study the remaining sentence patterns, we need to define a term that identifies an important part of sentences in the four remaining patterns. The two parts of any sentence are the subject and the predicate. The central core of the predicate is the verb, but the predicate also often includes words that complete the thought of the sentence. Words that follow the verb and complete the thought of the sentence are called **complements.** Complements can be nouns, pronouns, or adjectives, but all serve the same purpose in the sentence: they complete the idea or sense of the sentence.

Sentence Pattern 2

Pattern 2 includes two closely related kinds of sentences. The purpose of the first type of Pattern 2 sentence is to rename the subject, to say that the subject is the same as something else. In the sample sentence "The child is a genius," the noun *genius* is called a **subjective complement** because it completes the verb and renames the subject. The intransitive verb used in Pattern 2 sentences is called a **linking verb,** and is often a form of *be.*

Einstein was a scientist.

Subject   Verb   Subjective Complement

Note that both words, *Einstein* and *scientist,* refer to the same thing. There is no action; rather, a connection is established between the subject and the verb. (See Supplement 1.)

In the second type of Pattern 2 sentence, the subjective complement is an adjective, a word that describes rather than renames the subject. In the example "The child is clever," the subject is joined by the verb to an adjective, again called a subjective complement. Comparatively few verbs serve the linking function. For convenience, you can think of them in three closely related groups:

1. *Be,* the most commonly used linking verb, and a few others meaning essentially the same thing: *seem, appear, prove, remain, continue,* and a few others.

   John *is* a talented musician.
   The performer *seemed* nervous.
   He *remained* calm.
   His words *proved* meaningless.

2. *Become,* and a few others like it: *turn, grow, work, get, wear,* and a few others.

   Later she *became* an accountant.
   Soon he *grew* tired of the game.
   Billy *turned* red from embarrassment.

3. A few verbs referring to the senses (*look, smell, taste, feel, sound*), which can be followed by adjective subjective complements that describe the condition of the subject.

   The roses *look* beautiful in that vase.
   This milk *tastes* sour.

Ability to recognize this kind of sentence pattern will help you understand a few troublesome usage problems that will be examined in a later lesson—to understand why, for instance, careful writers use "feel bad" rather than "feel badly": *I feel* bad about the election results.

Supplement 1

A note about grammatical terminology is needed here. The noun following a linking verb and renaming the subject is sometimes called a *predicate noun* or a *predicate nominative;* and the adjective following a linking verb and describing the subject is sometimes called a *predicate adjective.*

subjective complement (n.) = predicate noun
predicate nominative
subjective complement (adj.) = predicate adjective

NAME _____   SCORE _____

Directions: Each of the following sentences is a Pattern 2 sentence containing a noun (or pronoun) subjective complement. In the space at the left, copy the subjective complement.

_____ 1. Our first effort in Jim O'Connel's class was a success.

_____ 2. Those two teams have been rivals for many years.

_____ 3. That bike was a good choice for your little brother.

_____ 4. Yours was the only offer I received on that car.

_____ 5. That movie is not a favorite with the critics.

_____ 6. Perhaps Barb's plan is the best way out of this mess.

_____ 7. Magazines are often good sources of information on technical subjects.

_____ 8. Once again, we were not winners in the state tournament.

_____ 9. With careful attention to your work, you can become a better math student.

_____ 10. The construction noise outside the classroom became a source of great annoyance to the teacher.

_____ 11. Marge Banks has been a great addition to our basketball team.

_____ 12. You can become a member of the medical profession only after long years of study.

_____ 13. The name of the person behind that gift to the college will probably remain a secret.

_____ 14. Friday night's performance was Mary's first appearance as a singer.

_____ 15. The instrumental solo is an important part of a jazz musician's work.

_____ 16. The clerk at the hardware store has been a great help in this repair project.

_____ 17. That little town is the birthplace of several famous athletes.

_____ 18. Clearly her efforts on behalf of the smaller children were a great success.

_____ 19. Al's opponent in tomorrow's match will be the winner of today's match.

_____ 20. Through constant practice, my little sister has become a highly skilled softball player.

Directions: Each of the following sentences is a Pattern 2 sentence containing an adjective subjective complement. In the space at the left, copy the subjective complement.

_____ 1. The others soon grew tired of his constant complaints.

_____ 2. In the light of earlier events, her late arrival was predictable.

_____ 3. I was delighted with my grade on that first test.

_____ 4. Jim seemed quite discouraged after this afternoon's game.

_____ 5. That movie did not remain faithful to the story in the book.

_____ 6. The mountains look quite hazy in that photograph.

_____ 7. All the boys grew tired toward the end of the hike.

_____ 8. Dad's disappointed in the return on that stock.

_____ 9. That meadow looks wonderfully peaceful.

_____ 10. Jack's not very open to suggestions from outside experts.

_____ 11. That colt proved totally unmanageable in spite of all that training.

_____ 12. After the rain, the weather turned quite cold.

_____ 13. In spite of weeks of practice, the team was not really ready for opening day.

_____ 14. The entire search for that old man's story proved fruitless.

_____ 15. The reasons for her resignation were never clear to any of us.

_____ 16. The women obviously felt quite elated over their victory in the first race.

_____ 17. In the unbearable summer heat, the syrup turned sour almost immediately.

_____ 18. After midnight, Julie became extremely sleepy.

_____ 19. By noon, the parade route was full of men, women, and children.

_____ 20. Rob felt quite ill long before morning.

NAME _____   SCORE _____

Directions: Circle the subject and underline the verb in each of the following sentences. If the sentence is a Pattern 2 sentence, copy the subjective complement in the space at the left. If the sentence is a Pattern 1 sentence, leave the space blank.

_____   1. About three miles into the hike, Arline grew frustrated with the slow pace of the other people.

_____   2. Outside on the street, the pedestrians shivered in the cold rain.

_____   3. The people outside the theater chattered excitedly about the new movie.

_____   4. The rookie was a victim of the oldest practical joke in the book.

_____   5. Jodie's last experiment in the chemistry lab was extremely difficult.

_____   6. All the ticket takers stood in the hot sun for at least three hours.

_____   7. A short nap always feels good in the late afternoon.

_____   8. One mile from the end of the road, at the end of a steep, narrow trail, stands the first shelter.

_____   9. The formula for the solution to that problem about annuity payouts is very complex.

_____   10. The number of requests for information about financial aid always rises during a recession.

_____   11. Her resignation was the most important result of that shake-up in the office staff.

_____   12. After graduation Mirta moved right down the street to a job with an important law firm.

_____   13. The basketball team always felt inspired by the coach's halftime speeches.

_____   14. After her outburst, Yolanda sat motionless at the table for almost five minutes.

_____   15. Gradually the sounds of the crew members on the boat grew fainter.

_____   16. That was my last attempt at contact with Joel.

_____   17. On a hook in the back of the shop hung a beautiful new jacket.

_____ 18. At the end of the lecture the students drifted slowly out of class.

_____ 19. That's my new car, the one on the right side of that building.

_____ 20. After the long, tiring examination, all the students walked slowly to the Student Center.

_____ 21. The answer to that question about real estate taxes is on page fifteen of your text.

_____ 22. Analysis of the results of that public opinion poll is an extremely complex task.

_____ 23. Analysis of the results of that public opinion poll is extremely difficult.

_____ 24. Tomorrow will be a good time for the start of my diet.

_____ 25. Tomorrow at breakfast my new diet will begin.

_____ 26. That tiny screw from the back of the television fell down the heater grate on the floor.

_____ 27. My grandmother is happy with her new tricycle.

_____ 28. That report was already outdated before its presentation to the executive committee.

_____ 29. The bright blue of Carol's favorite shirt has faded to a rather dull gray.

_____ 30. The new computers for the firm's library arrived yesterday.

_____ 31. The best hope for correction of our problems is a widespread application of common sense.

_____ 32. At the first rumble of thunder, all the children wading in the lake ran to the shore.

_____ 33. We have not enrolled for next semester yet.

_____ 34. There's my coat, the brown one on the last hook.

_____ 35. The defendant seemed very nervous during today's testimony.

_____ 36. A very different picture of that situation emerged from that last discussion.

_____ 37. The two little boys slept peacefully on the back seat of the car.

_____ 38. That book is an authentic copy of the first edition of that famous novel.

_____ 39. Our first objective at this time is the restoration of the oldest part of the library.

_____ 40. My grandmother was appalled by the clothes and the manners of the young people in the crowd.

In Sentence Pattern 2, the verb links the subject to a noun or adjective that completes the idea of the sentence. "Maria is our pitcher." "Maria is brilliant."

Pattern 3 Sentences

In Pattern 3 sentences the verb does not link or connect; instead, the verb identifies an action and transfers that action to a receiver or object of that action. In Pattern 3 sentences the subject–verb combination does not complete a thought unless there is an object to receive the action named in the verb. In the sample sentence "The child hits the ball," it is clear that *The child hits* does not make a complete statement. A complete statement here requires that the child hit *something.*

Direct Objects

The noun that receives the action named by a transitive verb is the **direct object.** In other words, a transitive verb transfers the action to an object. The direct object is always a noun or a noun equivalent, such as a pronoun, and you find it by asking the question "What?" of the transitive verb:

> *I broke my glasses.* What names the activity? *Broke* is the verb. Who broke? *I* is the subject. I broke what? *Glasses.* Thus, *glasses* is the direct object.
>
> *Someone saw us.* What names the activity? *Saw.* Who saw? *Someone* saw. Someone saw what? *Us* is the direct object.

We need to draw a contrast between a Pattern 2 sentence and a Pattern 3 sentence. In a Pattern 2 sentence such as "The child is a genius," the subject is either renamed or modified by the subjective complement. It is clear that in the sentence "Someone saw us," *someone* and *us* are not the same. *Us* is the receiver of the action *saw* and simply can't be taken as the someone who saw. In both Pattern 2 and Pattern 3 sentences, the thought of the sentence is not complete without a complement, but in Pattern 3 sentences the subject acts upon the complement, the direct object; the subject is not the same thing as the complement, as it is in Pattern 2 sentences.

Pattern 4 Sentences

Pattern 4 sentences contain a direct object, as do Pattern 3 sentences. But because Pattern 4 sentences use verbs such as *give* or *show,* the sentence needs a **second** complement to complete the thought of the sentence. After a transitive verb such as *shows, gives,* or *tells,* the direct object (the receiver of the action) answers the question "Who?" or "What?" and the **indirect object** answers a question such as "To whom" or "For whom?" Thus, "She sang a lullaby," is a Pattern 3 sentence, but "She sang the children a lullaby," is a Pattern 4 sentence.

In the sample sentence "The parents give the child a present," you can easily see why the two complements are used. The sentence mentions the thing that is given (*present*, the direct object) and also the person to whom the direct object is given (*child*, the indirect object). Although the indirect object usually names a person, it can name a nonhuman thing, as in "We gave your *application* a careful reading."

Other verbs that are commonly used this way and therefore produce a Pattern 4 structure are *allow, assign, ask, tell, write, send, pay, grant,* and so on. Nearly all sentences using such verbs can make essentially the same statement by using a prepositional phrase, the preposition usually being *to* or *for*. When the prepositional phrase is actually present in the sentence, it is a Pattern 3 sentence.

The postman brought me a letter. [Pattern 4; *me* is an indirect object.]

The postman brought a letter to me. [Pattern 3; *me* is the object of a preposition.]

Mother bought us some candy. [Pattern 4]

Mother bought some taffy for us. [Pattern 3]

Pattern 5 Sentences

Pattern 5 Sentences regularly use verbs such as *consider, call, think, find, make, elect, appoint,* and *name,* and consist of two closely related types of sentences. Each type starts out like a Pattern 3 sentence:

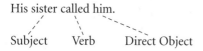

His sister called him.

Subject   Verb   Direct Object

But the nature of the verb *called* allows the use of a second complement answering the question "What?" after *called him*. His sister called him what?

His sister called him a genius.

Thus there are two complements in Pattern 5 sentences. The one closer to the verb is the direct object, and the second one is the **objective complement,** which we can define as a noun that *renames* the direct object or an adjective that *describes* the direct object.

His sister called him a genius.
His sister called him brilliant.

The reference of the two nouns following the verb is a key to the difference between this type of sentence and a Pattern 4 sentence. (In a Pattern 4 sentence the two noun complements refer to different things, but in a Pattern 5 sentence they refer to the same thing.)

Mother made us some fudge. [Pattern 4; *us* and *fudge* refer to different things.]

This experience made John an activist. [Pattern 5; *John* and *activist* are the same thing.]

Because the objective complement renames or describes the direct object, we can use a handy test to help us recognize Pattern 5: the insertion of *to be* between the complements will give us acceptable English wording.

We appointed Jones [to be] our representative.
I thought this action [to be] unnecessary.

Sometimes in Pattern 5 sentences the word *as* is used between the direct object and the objective complement:

We appointed Jones as our representative.

Some adjective objective complements are very important to the meaning of the verb. It is sometimes effective to place these objective complements immediately after the verb and before the direct object:

Usual order: He set the caged animals [D.O.] free [O.C.].
Variation: He set free [O.C.] the caged animals [D.O.].

Supplement 1

With one special kind of verb, there is a problem of distinguishing between a direct object and the object of a preposition. Here are two examples:

Harry jumped off the box.
Harry took off his raincoat.

The first sentence is Pattern 1. *Off* is a preposition, *box* is the object of the preposition, and the prepositional phrase is used as an adverbial modifier, because it tells *where* Harry jumped. The second sentence is Pattern 3. The verb, with its adverbial modifier *off,* is the equivalent of the transitive verb *remove. Raincoat* is the direct object.

There is another way to distinguish between the adverbial use and the prepositional use of such a word as *off* in the preceding examples. When the word is a vital adverbial modifier of the verb, it can be used in either of two positions: following the verb or following the direct object.

Harry took off his raincoat.
Harry took his raincoat off.

But when the word is a preposition, the alternate position is not possible: "Harry jumped the box off" is not an English sentence. Here are some other examples of verbs with adverbial modifiers. Notice that in each case you can easily find a transitive verb synonym for the combination:

Give up [*relinquish*] her rights.
Leave out [*omit*] the second chapter.
Put out [*extinguish*] the fire.
Make over [*alter*] an old dress.
Make up [*invent*] an excuse.

SUMMARY OF VERBS USED IN DIFFERENT SENTENCE PATTERNS

Verbs that serve a linking function and commonly form Pattern 2 sentences:
1. Be, seem, appear, prove, remain, continue.
2. Become, turn, grow, work, get, wear.
3. Look, smell, taste, feel, sound.

Verbs that commonly produce a Pattern 4 sentence structure:
   Allow, assign, ask, tell, write, send, pay, grant.

Verbs that commonly produce a Pattern 5 sentence structure:
   Consider, call, think, find, make, elect, appoint, name.

Complements of Transitive Verbs

NAME _____ SCORE _____

Directions: Each of these sentences is a Pattern 3 sentence. In the space at the left, copy the direct object.

_____ 1. Yesterday Will lost his new textbook somewhere on the campus.

_____ 2. Jane skipped two paragraphs in her history paper.

_____ 3. We used some lumber from that old barn in repairs on the garage.

_____ 4. The coach saw two members of the team in town after curfew.

_____ 5. The eighth graders need a little assistance with their project.

_____ 6. Just for a laugh, Rob loosened the top on the salt shaker at our lunch table.

_____ 7. Three of the people in my algebra class dropped the course last Friday.

_____ 8. Within three hours I had moved all the files from my old office to the new one.

_____ 9. Alicia wasted three hours Friday in the line at the registrar's office.

_____ 10. By the end of October, we will have read almost three hundred pages of material for that course.

_____ 11. The staff members had already prepared one hundred copies of the report before the discovery of the error.

_____ 12. On the first page of the book the writer told a very frightening story.

_____ 13. Bill made the best grade in the class on that last test.

_____ 14. Walt doused the fire in the trash can with water from the kitchen sink.

_____ 15. At dawn Lisa turned on the heater because of the chill in the air.

_____ 16. David furtively slipped a handful of chocolate cookies into the pocket of his jacket.

_____ 17. The movers had boxed up all of the books before nine o'clock.

_____ 18. None of the players in the scavenger hunt had discovered the last clue.

_____ 19. Few of us had any idea of the location of the hidden staircase.

_____ 20. Because of errors in the computer program we did not receive our checks on time this week.

Directions: The following are Pattern 3, 4, or 5 sentences. Identify the italicized complement by writing the abbreviation in the space at the left:

      D.O. [direct object]   I.O. [indirect object]   O.C. [objective complement]

———————— 1. The old man on the corner gave *us* directions to the grocery store.

———————— 2. The woman painted the bedroom wall *lavender.*

———————— 3. We chipped up all those *branches* for mulch.

———————— 4. The grateful parents called the young man a *hero.*

———————— 5. The teacher paid *Marsha* a great compliment.

———————— 6. Tom shows very little *promise* as a chemistry student.

———————— 7. The baby-sitter always shows the little *kids* a video just before bedtime.

———————— 8. My neighbor finally turned off her car *alarm* after fifteen minutes.

———————— 9. The staff members all consider that program very *difficult.*

———————— 10. That work in the heat of the afternoon left *me* exhausted.

———————— 11. Cathy will have paid off that small *loan* from her uncle before the end of the summer.

———————— 12. The library has granted all *students* an amnesty for overdue books.

———————— 13. The club will probably make Myrna its *representative* at the conference.

———————— 14. The squad leader's orders left little *room* for doubt about his toughness.

———————— 15. Tammy's uncle left *her* a small inheritance in his will.

———————— 16. The loss of the conference championship left the *fans* in tears.

———————— 17. Wally left his *books* on the table in the hallway this morning.

———————— 18. After dinner, my father called *us* a taxi for the trip home.

———————— 19. The boss called Rosa *brilliant* after the success of her proposal.

———————— 20. My grandfather told *us* a fascinating story about the early settlers in this valley.

Exercise 4 *Complements*

NAME _____ SCORE _____

Directions: Circle the subject and underline the verb in each of the following sentences. Identify the italicized complement by writing one of the following in the space at the left.

S.C. [subjective complement]   D.O. [direct object]
I.O. [indirect object]   O.C. [objective complement]

_____ 1. The boss read my *memo* very quickly.

_____ 2. The trip to the lake was a wonderful *break* from our studies.

_____ 3. The instructor offered *us* a special review session the day before the exam.

_____ 4. We looked for that silly little *puppy* almost all night.

_____ 5. The clothes in the back closet smelled *musty.*

_____ 6. The research team made Janice the *leader* for this project.

_____ 7. She's *one* of the few good students in that class.

_____ 8. The coach called Alice a real team *player.*

_____ 9. In answer to my question, the teacher told *us* a long, involved story about the 1948 presidential election.

_____ 10. For us New Englanders, the heat in Texas was almost *frightening.*

_____ 11. The work crew mistakenly painted those two dorm rooms bright *red.*

_____ 12. All of us took the same *bus* home from the game.

_____ 13. The coaches at the tournament named *Karen* the Most Valuable Player.

_____ 14. John paid the *dealer* $700 for that set of tires for his truck.

_____ 15. The police questioned *everyone* at the scene about the accident.

_____ 16. The department has not selected anyone as *representative* to that committee.

_____ 17. The boss gave *Ellen* a special award for that money-saving idea.

_____ 18. Carl's mother will be *ecstatic* about his scholarship for next year.

_____ 19. The announcement of the scholarship made Carl's mother very *happy.*

_____ 20. The company treasurer has appointed *Tom* her executive assistant.

Directions: Using appropriate forms of the verb indicated, write twenty original sentences illustrating the following patterns:

Sentences 1–5: Pattern 2   Sentences 6–10: Pattern 3
Sentences 11–15: Pattern 4   Sentences 16–20: Pattern 5

Circle every subjective complement and every direct object; underline with one line every indirect object; underline with two lines every objective complement.

1. be   _____

2. seem   _____

3. become   _____

4. look   _____

5. grow   _____

6. grow   _____

7. throw   _____

8. see   _____

9. choose   _____

10. tell   _____

11. tell   _____

12. allow   _____

13. bring   _____

14. assign   _____

15. make   _____

16. make   _____

17. call   _____

18. color   _____

19. name   _____

20. select   _____

Lesson 5 — *Forms of the Verb; Auxiliary Verbs*

In this lesson you will examine a few more forms and uses of verbs, including some additional auxiliary verbs. With these forms and those that you have already examined, you will be acquainted with nearly all verb forms that the average speaker and writer will ever use.

In Lesson 2 you examined a partial conjugation of three verbs, *earn, grow,* and *be.* You may want to refer to that conjugation (pages 9–10) as we discuss a few more points about changes in verb form.

Remember that third person singular verbs in the present tense end in *s* (or *es*): *earns, teaches, is, has.* Notice that on nouns, the *s(es)* ending shows a plural form, whereas on verbs it shows a singular form.

dogs, noses   (plural nouns)
wags, sniffs   (singular verbs)

The verb *be* is completely irregular. The conjugation shows you that, unlike any other verb in the language, it has three forms (*am, is,* and *are*) in the present tense and two forms (*was* and *were*) in the past tense.

In general, the tenses are used as follows:

Present: Action occurring at the present moment.
    He *earns* a good salary.

Past: Action occurring at a definite time before the present moment.
    Last year he *earned* a good salary.

Future: Action occurring at some time beyond the present moment.
    Next year he *will earn* a good salary.

Present perfect: Action continuing to the present moment.
    So far this year he *has earned* ten thousand dollars.

Past perfect: Action continuing to a fixed moment in the past.
    Before leaving for college, he *had earned* ten thousand dollars.

Future perfect: Action continuing to a fixed moment in the future.
    By next Christmas he *will have earned* ten thousand dollars.

In Lesson 21 you will be reminded of a few usage problems involving the use of tenses.

The conjugation shows you that the two verbs *earn* and *grow* differ in form in all tenses except the present tense and the future tense. *Earn* is a regular verb and *grow* is an irregular verb.

Participles

We customarily make use of three distinctive forms, called the **principal parts** of the verb, to show the difference between regular and irregular verbs. The principal parts are the:

- *Base* or infinitive, the "name" of the verb, used in the present tense with *(e)s* added in the third person singular
- *Past,* the form used in the simple past tense
- *Past participle,* the form used in the three perfect tenses

On the basis of these three forms, we classify verbs as being regular or irregular. In all regular verbs, the past and the past participle are alike, formed simply by the addition of *ed* to the base form (or only *d* if the base word ends in *e*). The irregular verbs are more complicated, because for nearly all of them the past tense and the participle are not spelled alike. Following are the three forms of some irregular verbs, illustrating spelling changes and endings that are found.

Base	Past	Past Participle
be	was, were	been
become	became	become
bite	bit	bitten
break	broke	broken
catch	caught	caught
do	did	done
eat	ate	eaten
put	put	put
ring	rang	rung
run	ran	run
see	saw	seen

You will study more principal parts of verbs and the usage problems associated with them in Lesson 21. For both regular and irregular verbs, adding *ing* to the base form produces the **present participle.** One of its important uses is explained next.

Auxiliary Verbs

In the sample conjugation, you observed the use of *shall/will* and *have* as auxiliary verbs in the future tense and the perfect tenses. Another important auxiliary is *be,* used with the *ing* form (the present participle) of the main verb to produce what is called the **progressive** form. As an example of its use, if someone asks about the assignment in your English class, you would probably not reply, "Right now, we *review* parts of speech." Instead, you would say, "Right now, we *are reviewing* parts of speech," to show that the action is not fixed in an exact moment of time but is a continuing activity. This very useful type of verb occurs in all six tenses:

We are reviewing.
We were reviewing.
We shall be reviewing.

We have been reviewing.
We had been reviewing.
We shall have been reviewing.

Another type of auxiliary verb includes *may, might, must, can, could, would,* and *should.* These words are called **modal auxiliaries,** and they are used the way *will* and *shall* are used:

I *should study* this weekend.
I *should have studied* last weekend.

Variations of Some Modals. Do as an auxiliary verb combines with the base form of a main verb to make a rarely used "emphatic" form (But I *did pay* that bill last month). In Lesson 6 you will examine the much more common use of the *do* auxiliary, in questions and negatives. Here are a few other points to remember about auxiliary verbs:

1. *Have, be,* and *do* are not used exclusively as auxiliaries; they are three of the most commonly used main verbs:

   I *have* a brown pen. [Main verb]
   I *have* lost my brown pen. [Auxiliary]
   He *is* a good speaker. [Main verb]
   He *is* becoming a good speaker. [Auxiliary]
   He *did* a good job for us. [Main verb]
   Yes, I *did embellish* the story somewhat. [Auxiliary]

2. When the verb unit contains auxiliaries, there may be short adverbial modifiers separating parts of the whole verb phrase:

   We *have* occasionally *been* sailing.
   He *has,* of course, *been telling* the truth.

3. In a few set expressions following introductory adverbs, usually adverbs of time, the subject is placed within the verb phrase between an auxiliary and the main verb:

   Only lately *have* I *learned* to drive.
   Rarely *do* we *turn on* the television set.

Variations Using "To". Variations of some modals and "time" auxiliaries make use of *to* in the verb phrase. Here are examples of some that you use and hear regularly:

Mr. Nelson *has to retire* [must retire] early.
You *ought to eat* [should eat] more vegetables.
I *used to be* a secretary.
Jim *was supposed to be here* at ten o'clock.
I *am to depart* for Miami early in the morning.
I *am going to depart* for Miami early in the morning.

Directions: Each of theses sentences contains at least one auxiliary verb. (Some have two; some have three.) Copy the auxiliary verb(s) in the first space at the left. In the second space, write 1, 2, 3, 4, or 5 to identify the sentence pattern.

_____ 1. I have seldom seen such a wide variety of books in one collection.
_____

_____ 2. Ms. Jackson will expect extremely careful work on these math
_____ problems.

_____ 3. Roberta should have shown us that message yesterday afternoon.
_____

_____ 4. More careful attention to detail would have caught that error
_____ long before today.

_____ 5. I must buy a new textbook for my history class.

_____ 6. Michelle's response might have given you a wrong impression.
_____

_____ 7. Jack should have painted his car a lighter color.
_____

_____ 8. A few people could have been working on that part of the pro-
_____ ject already.

_____ 9. That silly dog has brought us several old shoes and some other
_____ junk.

_____ 10. You probably should have worked harder during the early weeks
_____ of the semester.

_____ 11. I have already given the bursar my tuition payment for next term.
_____

_____ 12. By the end of March we will have visited every hospital in the
_____ state.

_____ 13. Janie is still feeling quite weak from that bout with pneumonia.
_____

_____ 14. Her surprising resignation has left us extremely shorthanded this
_____ week.

_____ 15. You should send off that order as soon as possible.
_____

_____ 16. Marcie has never been sure of her choice of major.
_____

_____ 17. With the approach of the storm, the barometer has been falling
_____ steadily for the past three hours.

_____ 18. In fact, the club has appointed Karen as its representative at that
_____ convention.

_____ 19. As late as yesterday we had not heard of those plans for revisions
_____ in that estimate.
_____ 20. The questions on that last section in the chapter could be the
_____ hardest part of the test.
_____ 21. Our return on that investment has been increasing rapidly in
recent months.
_____ 22. There should be a simpler solution to your problem.
_____

_____ 23. The loss of that copy machine has given the entire staff some seri-
_____ ous problems.
_____ 24. By the end of the week that committee will have completed all
the work on that proposal.
_____ 25. In the light of the flashlight, the boy could just barely find his way
_____ up the stairs.
_____ 26. The two boys were holding the sign upright in spite of the strong
_____ wind.
_____ 27. No one has paid them anything for all that extra work last
_____ Saturday.
_____ 28. We've received a fax about that new restaurant every day this
_____ week.
_____ 29. The chair of that committee has been calling Louise because of
_____ her brilliant suggestion last week.
_____ 30. Occasionally you will find an arrowhead out in that field.
_____

_____ 31. Extraordinary interest in that particular concert has made the
_____ supply of tickets very limited.
_____ 32. There should be some response to our request within the next
_____ few days.
_____ 33. By late morning we had already been working on the yard for
_____ several hours.
_____ 34. An itinerary so filled with meetings does not offer the president
_____ any time for paper work.
_____ 35. A change to a newer, faster computer would be extremely helpful
_____ to the staff.
_____ 36. The two of us have already been looking for that missing file for
_____ almost three hours.
_____ 37. I should leave for home after my last class.

_____ 38. At some point we will need a replacement for that defective
_____ switch.
_____ 39. Robin has not found any of the lost files.

_____ 40. Tomorrow we must look carefully at the reports from the sales
_____ departments.

Exercise 5 — *Complements*

NAME _____ SCORE _____

Directions: In the space at the left, write one of the following to identify the italicized word:
    S.C. [subjective complement]   I.O. [indirect object]
    D.O. [direct object]   O.C. [objective complement]

_____ 1. The accounting department has discovered some serious *problems* with that new computer program.

_____ 2. Someone showed *Harry* a new route to the lake.

_____ 3. The huge Thanksgiving turkey made all the children very *happy*.

_____ 4. Cheryl was *delighted* with the new version of our group's term paper.

_____ 5. The coach made Mary the acting *captain* for this next tournament.

_____ 6. No one offered *us* that option at the time.

_____ 7. I backed up all my important *files* before my vacation last week.

_____ 8. The people on the staff were not very *open* to the possibility of early retirement.

_____ 9. Last year Iris played the viola in the school *orchestra*.

_____ 10. The first grade teacher told the *children* a very funny story.

_____ 11. The politicians looked over the *results* of the opinion poll very carefully.

_____ 12. The water ran over the *top* of the dike and down into the streets.

_____ 13. My sister ran over a large *rock* with my car.

_____ 14. In the cold, the little boy's lips turned absolutely *blue*.

_____ 15. Observers called the new building a *model* of modern architecture.

_____ 16. At noon, Miles folded up the *papers* on his desk.

_____ 17. To most of us, the time in the library seemed very *short*.

_____ 18. The teacher should allow *us* more time for work on our research projects.

_____ 19. I need the answer key to these math *problems*.

_____ 20. Many people consider that type of paddle a *necessity* for successful white water canoeing.

_____ 21. The leaders of the fund drive felt *good* about the results of yesterday's work.

_____ 22. At last the teacher remembered the *name* of that former student.

_____ 23. Yesterday Bob brought *some* of his wife's wonderful homemade doughnuts to the office.

_____ 24. The registrar's assistant saved *me* from a fairly serious mistake in my class selection.

_____ 25. The kids saved *me* one chocolate cookie from that last batch.

_____ 26. Marshal has always been one of the most effective *workers* in the club.

_____ 27. The cost of that car repair left Tom *short* of money until the first of the month.

_____ 28. My Aunt Martha has always been a tireless *worker* for the local historical society.

_____ 29. A long, heavy rain would be a welcome *relief* from this terrible drought.

_____ 30. On the map, the old man pointed out a little-known *trail* to the other side of the lake.

_____ 31. Tomorrow the teacher will show a *group* of slides from the Grand Canyon.

_____ 32. Tomorrow the teacher will show the *group* some slides from the Grand Canyon.

_____ 33. Larry has been appointed *secretary* for the committee on campus clean-up.

_____ 34. The group has appointed Larry *secretary* for the committee on campus clean-up.

_____ 35. The man with the rope moved very slowly toward the *horse*.

_____ 36. Eventually, efforts at campaign reform will be *successful*.

_____ 37. After the rain there was a huge *puddle* in the middle of the parking lot.

_____ 38. The noise from my neighbor's car alarm woke *me* at five o'clock this morning.

_____ 39. California is considered a vital *state* in any candidate's run for the nomination.

_____ 40. Fortunately for all of us, the trail heads *downhill* in the last mile.

Any long piece of writing made up exclusively of basic sentences would be too monotonous to read. You should think of the basic sentences not as models for your writing but as elementary units, important because they are the structures from which more effective sentences develop. In this lesson we shall look at two alterations of basic sentence patterns:

Sentences that use passive verbs

Sentences in the form of a question

Lessons 7 through 11 will then show how basic sentences can be combined and certain elements can be reduced to subordinate clauses and phrases to produce varied, well-developed sentences.

Passive Voice

In Lesson 2, you examined a partial conjugation of the verb *earn*. The forms listed there are in the active voice, which means that the subject is the doer of the action. A more complete conjugation would include the passive verb forms. These make use of the auxiliary verb *be* combined with the past participle of the verb, as shown in the following illustration of the third-person singular in the six tenses:

This amount is earned.
This amount was earned.
This amount will be earned.
This amount has been earned.
This amount had been earned.
This amount will have been earned.

The present and past tenses of progressive verbs can also be shifted to the passive voice, giving us forms in which *be* is used in two auxiliary capacities in the same verb form:

These cars *are being sold* at a loss.
These cars *were being sold* at a loss.

Because only transitive verbs have passive forms, the basic patterns that can be altered to passive versions are Patterns 3, 4, and 5. When the idea of a Pattern 3 sentence is expressed with a passive verb, there is no complement in the sentence:

Active Voice: Children play games.

Passive Voice: Games are played [by children].

If the actor is expressed in a sentence using a passive verb, the actor must occur as the object of the preposition *by*. When a Pattern 4 sentence is altered to form a passive con-

45

struction, the indirect object that follows the active verb becomes the subject of the passive verb:

Active Voice: John gave Allen a model plane.

Passive Voice: Allen was given a model plane [by John].

Here the passive verb is followed by a complement, *plane,* which we can continue to call a direct object in spite of the fact that it follows a passive verb.

Notice also how a Pattern 5 sentence can be given a different kind of expression by means of a passive verb, with the direct object becoming the subject:

Active Voice: The parents consider the child a genius.
                  The parents consider the child clever.

Passive Voice: The child is considered a genius [by the parents].
                  The child is considered clever [by the parents].

Here also the passive verb requires a complement (*genius, clever*), which, because it renames or describes the subject, should be called a subjective complement.

The passive voice serves a real purpose in effective communication: it should be used when the *doer* of the action is unknown or is of secondary interest in the statement. In such a situation, the writer, wishing to focus attention on the *receiver* of the action, places that unit in the emphatic subject position. The passive verb form makes this arrangement possible. Thus, instead of some vague expression such as "Somebody should wash these windows," we can say, "These windows *should be washed.*"

Sometimes the passive voice is described as "weak." Admittedly some writers do get into the habit of using the passive form when there is little justification. In most narrative writing, the doer of the action is logically the subject of the verb. "The fullback crossed the goal line" would certainly be preferred to "The goal line was crossed by the fullback," a version that gives the same information but tends to stop any action suggested by the sentence. The passive voice also lends itself to a kind of muddied, heavy-footed writing that produces prose like this:

> "It *is now rumored* that the Secretary of Defense *has been informed* that contingent plans *have been made to. . . .*"

The writer of such a sentence, however, probably finds the passive voice very useful to hide the identity of the person who is spreading the rumor, who has informed the Secretary of Defense, or who has made the plans. This use of the passive voice creates an impersonal, bureaucratic language very popular in many institutions.

You should practice with passive constructions so you can use this important device when it is called for. Equally important, if a criticism of your writing mentions doubtful uses of the passive, you need to be able to recognize passive verbs in order to change them when it is necessary.

Questions

In the sentence types you examined in earlier lessons, you noted the normal positioning of the main sentence parts: the subject first, followed by the verb, followed by the complement, if any. In questions, however, other arrangements are possible. As we study these new structures, we must first recognize the fact that there are two kinds of questions:

Questions answered by "Yes" or "No"
Questions answered by information

Questions Answered by "Yes" or "No"

In the following paired sentences, the first sentence is a statement and the second sentence a related question. These sentences demonstrate how the structure of a "Yes/No" question differs from that of a statement.

If the verb is *be* in the present or past tense, the subject and the *be* form (*am, are, is, was,* or *were*) reverse positions.

With other one-word verbs in the present or past tense, the proper form of the auxiliary *do* is used, followed by the subject and the base form of the main verb.

1. John is happy.   Is John happy?
2. You were there.   Were you there?
3. You see Ms. Locke often.   Do you see Ms. Locke often?
4. You heard the announcement.   Did you hear the announcement?

If the verb already has an auxiliary, the subject follows the auxiliary verb. If there are two or more auxiliaries, the subject follows the first one.

5. You have seen the movie.   Have you seen the movie?
6. They will arrive later.   Will they arrive later?
7. The house is being painted.   Is the house being painted?
8. He should have been told.   Should he have been told?

When the verb is *have* in the present tense, two versions of the question are possible, the subject-verb reversal and the *do* auxiliary. (See Supplement 1.)

9. You have enough money.   Have you enough money?
10. You have enough money.   Do you have enough money?

Questions Answered by Information

Some questions ask for information rather than for a "Yes" or a "No." These questions make use of words called **interrogatives,** words that stand for unknown persons, things, or descriptive qualities. The most commonly used interrogatives are these:

pronouns: *who (whom), which, what*
adjectives: *whose, which, what*
adverbs: *when, where, why, how*

The interrogative pronoun *who,* which stands for an unknown person or persons, has three forms:

1. *Who,* when it is used as a subject or a subjective complement
2. *Whose,* when it is used as a possessive modifier of a noun
3. *Whom,* when it is used as an object

(In a later lesson you will learn that these three forms of *who* have another important use in subordinate clauses. And the choice between *who* and *whom* as a problem of usage is discussed more extensively in Lesson 24.) In questions using these interrogatives, the normal arrangement of the main sentence parts is retained only when the interrogative is the subject or a modifier of the subject. (Here again we shall use paired statements and related questions to demonstrate these structures.)

> *My brother* [S.] paid the bill.
> *Who* [S.] paid the bill?
>
> *Five cars* [S.] were damaged.
> *How* many cars [S.] were damaged?

In all other situations the subject–verb positioning is altered as it is with "Yes/No" questions, and the interrogative word, or the unit containing the interrogative word, stands at the beginning of the sentence to signal that a question, not a statement, is forthcoming:

> I studied *geometry* [D.O.] last night.
> *What* [D.O.] did you study last night?
>
> You saw *Jim* [D.O.] at the party.
> *Whom* [D.O.] did you see at the party?
>
> She is Mother's *cousin* [S.C.].
> *Who* [S.C.] is she?
>
> You gave the note to *Sue* [O.P.].
> *To whom* [O.P.] did you give the note?
>
> We can use Bill's *car* [D.O.].
> *Whose* car [D.O.] can we use?
>
> You spent fifteen *dollars* [D.O.].
> *How* much money [D.O.] did you spend?
>
> *You* [S.] called *Bob* [D.O.] a *thief* [O.C.].
> *Who* [S.] called Bob a thief?
> *Whom* [D.O.] did you call a thief?
> *What* [O.C.] did you call Bob?

When the interrogative unit is the object of a preposition, two versions of the question are often possible:

1. The entire prepositional phrase may stand at the beginning.
2. The interrogative may stand at the beginning with the preposition in its usual position.

> The speaker was referring *to the mayor.*
> *To whom* was the speaker referring?
> *Whom* was the speaker referring to?

(See Supplement 2.)

Supplement 1

The four-part classification of the verb also determines the structuring of sentences that are negative rather than positive. The positioning of the negator *not* (or its contraction *n't*) depends on the presence or absence of an auxiliary verb. Sentences using *be* or *have* must be considered special cases.

1. If the verb is *be* in the present tense or in the past tense, used either as the main verb or as an auxiliary verb, the *not* follows the *be* form:

   I *am not* pleased with the report.
   He *was not* [wasn't] available.
   They *were not* [weren't] invited.

2. With other one-word verbs in the present or past tense, the proper form of the auxiliary *do* is used, followed by the negator and the base form of the main verb:

   I *do not* [don't] expect a reward.
   He *does not* [doesn't] attend regularly.
   We *did not* [didn't] respond.

3. If the verb already has an auxiliary, the negator follows the auxiliary. When there are two or more auxiliaries, the *not* follows the first one:

   We *could not* [couldn't] see very well.
   I *may not* have understood him.
   They *will not* [won't] refund my money.
   This cake *ought not* to have been baked so long.

4. When *have* in the present tense is the main verb, two negative forms are possible:

   I *have not* [haven't] enough time to play.
   I *do not* [don't] have enough time to play.

Supplement 2

At the informal language level another version—"Who was the speaker referring to?"—is often found, despite the traditional demand for the objective case for the object of a preposition. The formal level of both spoken and written English would call for: "*To whom* was the speaker referring?"

NAME _____ SCORE _____

Directions: These sentences are Pattern 3, 4, or 5 sentences. In the first space at the left, write the pattern number. In the second space write the verb form that is used when the italicized word in the sentence is made the subject. An example has been provided.

_____4_____
will be sent
Later I will send *you* a copy of the bulletin.

_____
_____
1. Sol printed that four-color *graph* with his new laser printer.

_____
_____
2. Most people consider *Alice* a natural athlete.

_____
_____
3. Our press secretary will give the *reporters* a new statement at 4:00 P.M.

_____
_____
4. The elections committee counted those *ballots* very carefully.

_____
_____
5. The contestants must solve two more *puzzles* before the end of the program.

_____
_____
6. The sales manager has offered *us* a real bargain on that used car.

_____
_____
7. The group selected *Maria* as its representative to the council.

_____
_____
8. The children should not cut up those new *magazines*.

_____
_____
9. Everyone called *Alex* a genius because of his solution to that problem.

_____
_____
10. Jim's sister sent him some delicious *cookies*.

Directions: The purpose of this exercise is to contrast the structure of a question with the structure of a statement. In the space at the left, copy the word from the question that serves the function of the italicized word in the statement.

—————————— 1. To whom did Jane give that mystery novel?
Jane gave that mystery novel to *Alex.*

—————————— 2. What did Jane give to Alex?
Jane gave that mystery *novel* to Alex.

—————————— 3. Who gave Alex that mystery novel?
Jane gave that mystery novel to Alex.

—————————— 4. What color did Anne paint her dorm room?
Anne painted her dorm room *gray.*

—————————— 5. Who will the new station manager be?
The new station manager will be *Joan Street.*

—————————— 6. Who will be the new station manager?
Joan Street will be the new station manager.

—————————— 7. Whom should I choose as my assistant?
I should choose *Art Moore* as my assistant.

—————————— 8. Whom should I choose as my assistant?
I should choose Art Moore as my *assistant.*

—————————— 9. Whose paper did you read?
I read Jim's *paper.*

—————————— 10. Whose paper is that?
That is Jim's *paper.*

—————————— 11. What are you concerned about in this situation?
I am concerned about the large *crowd* in the building.

—————————— 12. How many people will attend tomorrow's game?
Ten thousand *people* will attend tomorrow's game.

—————————— 13. How many children did you see in the boat?
I saw three *children* in the boat.

—————————— 14. To whom was that message sent?
That message was sent to *Ms. Kent.*

—————————— 15. Who was the winner of yesterday's match?
The winner of yesterday's match was *Alice.*

Alterations of Basic Sentence Patterns:
Passive Verbs; Questions

NAME _____   SCORE _____

Directions: Each of the following sentences uses a passive verb. Underline the verb. Rewrite each sentence using an active form of the verb. (You will have to supply a logical subject of the active verb if the passive verb does not provide one.) If your rewrites are correctly done, your first four sentences will be Pattern 3, your next three will be Pattern 4, and your final three will be Pattern 5.

1. Before lunch all the sandwiches had been eaten by the cafeteria staff.

   _____

2. The pieces of that puzzle must be fitted together very carefully.

   _____

3. That church was founded by the town's settlers in 1795.

   _____

4. That car was designed by two people in a small shop in England.

   _____

5. We should have been given an explanation of those changes before the start of work on the project.

   _____

6. The mayor had not been shown the agenda for the morning's meeting.

   _____

7. Bill was sent a second notice by the college library.

   _____

8. That woman should not have been found guilty by the jury.

   _____

9. That emergency door was left open two nights last week.

   _____

10. Alexis was chosen as our representative at the political convention.

    _____

53

Directions: The italicized word in each of the following questions is a complement or the object of a preposition. In the space at the left, write one of the following to identify the italicized word:

D.O. [direct object] O.C. [objective complement]
S.C. [subjective complement] O.P. [object of preposition]
I.O. [indirect object]

_____ 1. What *present* did you buy for your sister?

_____ 2. Which *secretary* did the courier give the package to?

_____ 3. Why did those boys leave the back door *open*?

_____ 4. *Who* will the new manager be?

_____ 5. Whom should the boss appoint as the new *manager*?

_____ 6. *Whom* should the boss appoint as the new manager?

_____ 7. Which *book* did you check out from the library?

_____ 8. How *small* was that closet?

_____ 9. *What* will the cost of the repairs on your car be?

_____ 10. How much credit do you give the advertising *campaign* for your victory in the election?

_____ 11. What *program* were you listening to a few minutes ago?

_____ 12. To *whom* shall I send this invitation?

_____ 13. How *much* did you tell Albert about the trip?

_____ 14. *Which* of those two problems can you solve?

_____ 15. How many *people* did you see on the trail?

_____ 16. How *difficult* was yesterday's test?

_____ 17. How *short* has the supply of medicine become?

_____ 18. Whom did the team choose as *captain*?

_____ 19. *Whom* did the team choose as captain?

_____ 20. How *sad* were you about the loss of last night's game?

_____ 21. What did Aunt Leslie send *you*?

_____ 22. *What* did Aunt Leslie send you?

_____ 23. To *whom* did you tell your story?

_____ 24. To whom did you tell your *story*?

_____ 25. How *many* of your textbooks have you purchased?

Clauses and Phrases

Lessons, Practice Sheets, and Exercises

Lesson 7 — *Coordination: Compound Sentences*

To begin to study sentences that build on the simple patterns we have already studied, let's examine a student writer's description of a snowstorm. Each sentence is numbered for later reference.

(1) The first really serious snowfall began at dusk and had already spread a treacherous powdering over the roads by the time the homeward-bound crowds reached their peak. (2) As the evening deepened, porch and street lights glowed in tight circles through semisolid air. (3) The snow did not fall in a mass of fat, jovial flakes; it squatted in a writhing mist of tiny particles and seemed less snow than a dense, animated fog. (4) Through the night the wind rose, worrying the trees as a puppy shakes a slipper. (5) It rushed round the corners of buildings and tumbled over roofs, from which it snatched armfuls of snow to scatter in the streets. (6) Save for the occasional grumble of a sanitation truck sullenly pushing its plow, all sound stopped. (7) Even the wind was more felt than heard. (8) Day did not dawn. (9) The world changed from charcoal gray to lead between six and seven, but the change was one from night to lesser night. (10) The snow still whirled. (11) Drifts had altered the neat symmetry of peaked roofs into irregular mountain ranges ending in sheer cliffs four or five feet above the leeward eaves. (12) The downwind side of every solid object cast a snow shadow that tapered away from a sharp hump until it merged into the surrounding flat pallor. (13) Along the street, windshield wipers, odd bits of chrome, startling blanks of black glass, and isolated headlights decorated large white mounds. (14) Men and women shut off their alarm clocks, stretched, yawned, looked out of their windows, paused in a moment of guilt, and went back to bed. (15) Snow had taken the day for its own, and there was no point in arguing with it.

The fifteen sentences of this paragraph are all made up of groups of related words called **clauses.** A clause is a group of words that always contains a subject and a verb in combination. The entire passage is based on short, simple sentences of the patterns studied in the preceding lessons. Recalling the scenes, actions, and responses associated with the event, the author created a series of subject-verb combinations, in other words, *clauses:* the snowfall began, the snowfall had spread a powdering, the homeward-bound crowds reached their peak, the evening deepened, lights glowed, and so on.

The writer's problem was to combine or alter these short statements and put them into their most pleasing and effective form. Presenting all of them as basic sentences would communicate the author's ideas but in a form that, in addition to being monotonous, would not give proper emphasis to the most important ideas. Only two sentences (8 and 10) are retained as one-subject, one-verb basic sentences. Some of the sentences (3, 9, and 15) combine two basic sentences, giving each clause equal force. Two sentences (1 and 5) join more than one verb to the same subject. Sentence 13 joins four subjects to the same verb, and Sentence 14 has two subjects joined to six verbs.

In the next several lessons we shall be examining the word groups—independent clauses, subordinate clauses, and phrases—that are the language tools allowing a writer to apply various strategies to produce effective sentences.

Combining Simple Sentences

A sentence, as you learned in Lesson 1, is a word group containing a subject and a verb. From this definition, and from the one already given for a clause, it would seem that a sentence and a clause are identical. And this is true for one kind of clause, the **independent clause** (also called the *main clause* or *principal clause*). The independent clause can stand by itself as a sentence. Every example sentence and every exercise sentence that you have worked with thus far in this book has been made up of one independent clause. We call a sentence consisting of only one independent clause a **simple** sentence.

Compounding Sentences

One means of combining or altering short, simple sentences is called *compounding,* joining grammatically equal parts so that they function together. We can join two or more subjects, verbs, complements, or modifiers, by using a **coordinating conjunction.** (**Conjunctions** are words that join words, phrases, or clauses; those that join grammatically equal units are called *coordinating.*) The three common coordinating conjunctions for this use are *and, but,* and *or;* other coordinators are *nor, for, and, yet,* and *so.* Thus, we can join two very short sentences and create a longer, more readable sentence.

Dad read the notice. I read the notice.
Dad *and* I read the notice. [Compound subjects]

Marge enjoys golf. Marge enjoys tennis.
She enjoys golf *and* tennis. [Compound direct objects]

I studied very hard. I failed the test.
I studied very hard *but* failed the test. [Compound verbs]

I found the lecture interesting. I found the lecture instructive.
I found the lecture interesting and instructive. [Compound objective complements]

I can see you during your lunch hour. I can see you after five.
I can see you during your lunch hour or after five o'clock. [Compound prepositional phrases]

Compounding is often used with two (sometimes more than two) independent clauses; the result is a common type of sentence called the **compound sentence.** We can create compound sentences in two ways.

The Two Clauses Are Joined by a Coordinating Conjunction. Any of the coordinating conjunctions mentioned already can be used to join two independent clauses. The normal punctuation is a comma before the conjunction:

I had reviewed the material, and I did well on the test.

It is important to distinguish this sentence from a nearly synonymous version using a compound verb:

I had reviewed the material and did well on the test.

In this second version the sentence is not a compound sentence because there is no separate subject for the second verb. It is a simple sentence with a compound verb and should be written without a comma.

The Two Independent Clauses Are Joined by a Semicolon. (See Supplement 1.) Sometimes, in this kind of compound sentence, the two independent clauses stand side by side with no word tying them together:

No one was in sight; I was alone in the huge auditorium.

Adverbial Units

Often the second clause begins with an adverbial unit that serves as a kind of tie between the clauses. This adverbial unit may be:

A simple adverb:
Currently we are renting an apartment; later we hope to buy a house.
These were last year's highlights; now we must look at plans for next year.

A short phrase:
I cannot comment on the whole concert; in fact, I slept through the last part of it.

A conjunctive adverb.
Your arguments were well presented; *however,* we feel that the plan is too expensive.

The most common conjunctive adverbs are *therefore, however, nevertheless, consequently, moreover, otherwise, besides, furthermore,* and *accordingly.* These words, often followed by a comma, should be used cautiously; they usually contribute to a heavy, formal tone. To lessen this effect, writers often place them, set off by commas, within the second clause:

Your arguments were well presented; we feel, *however,* that the plan is too expensive.

Because adverbial units like *later* and *therefore* are not coordinating conjunctions, the use of a comma to join the two clauses is inappropriate. The important thing to remember is that when the independent clauses are joined by a coordinating conjunction, the use of a comma is the custom. When there is no coordinating conjunction, the comma will not suffice; the customary mark is the semicolon. We will study these punctuation rules thoroughly in Lesson 17.

Coordination: Compound Sentences

NAME _____ SCORE _____

Directions: The twenty-five sentences here illustrate three types of sentences:

Type 1. The sentence is a simple sentence with the subject having two verbs joined by a coordinating conjunction. Normal punctuation: none.

We worked all day on the car but could not find the trouble.

Type 2. The sentence is a compound sentence with the two independent clauses joined by a coordinating conjunction: and, but, or, nor, for, yet, or so. Normal punctuation: a comma before the conjunction.

We worked all day on the car, and now it runs well.

Type 3. The sentence is a compound sentence without one of the coordinating conjunctions joining the independent clauses. (The second clause often begins with an adverbial unit.) Normal punctuation: a semicolon.

We worked all day on the car; now it runs well.

In each of the following sentences, the ∧ symbol marks a point of coordination. Indicate whether each sentence is Type 1, 2, or 3 by writing a number in the blank at the left. Then write in the correct punctuation for sentence types 2 and 3 (comma for type 2, semicolon for Type 3). Sentence Type 1 gets no punctuation.

_____ 1. That article was written in 1980 ∧ it is amazingly relevant to our situation today.

_____ 2. The news from the flood area must have been distressing ∧ for the whole town is talking about it.

_____ 3. Jim already owns a dictionary and a thesaurus ∧ but he does not have any other reference books at home.

_____ 4. "We should have left yesterday," said Harold ∧ "today there is a bad storm up north."

_____ 5. The left-hander swung hard at the first pitch ∧ and pulled it foul along the first base line.

_____ 6. Angela will not move to Atlanta after graduation ∧ she has decided to take a job with a local company.

_____ 7. Angela will not move to Atlanta after graduation ∧ for she has decided to take a job with a local company.

_____ 8. Paul worked very hard on that report ∧ yet he didn't get any credit for his efforts.

_____ 9. We might have taken the expressway from downtown ∧ but traffic was very heavy at that time.

_____ 10. Alice hired a tutor for her math course ∧ but hasn't made much improvement in her grade at this time.

_____ 11. Roger has dropped that history course ∧ for some reason he was not interested in that period of time.

_____ 12. Roger has dropped that history course ∧ for he was not interested in that period of time.

_____ 13. You can buy a new textbook on the campus ∧ or find a used copy at the Textbook Warehouse.

_____ 14. "Please help me," said Alfie ∧ "I've lost that new girl's telephone number."

_____ 15. My car had a flat tire ∧ thus I could not come to class.

_____ 16. Mary has looked everywhere ∧ but cannot find her car keys.

_____ 17. Mario studied for two hours every night this week ∧ therefore he felt very confident this morning.

_____ 18. Usually Jim is home much earlier than this ∧ he must be working late tonight.

_____ 19. The plot of that movie is very complicated ∧ we should have paid more attention at the beginning.

_____ 20. The plot of that movie is very complicated ∧ but the killer should have been obvious from the beginning.

_____ 21. Roberta enjoyed that novel ∧ but didn't understand the characters very well.

_____ 22. Aunt Ella genuinely enjoyed her vacation at the dude ranch ∧ so she is thinking about a return visit next year.

_____ 23. Aunt Ella genuinely enjoyed her vacation at the dude ranch ∧ and is thinking about a return visit next year.

_____ 24. Aunt Ella genuinely enjoyed her vacation at the dude ranch ∧ next year, however, she is going to Europe.

_____ 25. The officer neither accepted my excuse ∧ nor offered to reduce my fine.

NAME _____ SCORE _____

Directions: The twenty-five sentences here illustrate three types of sentences:

Type 1. The sentence is a simple sentence with the subject having two verbs joined by a coordinating conjunction. Normal punctuation: none.

    The women worked all day on the report and finally finished it late that night.

Type 2. The sentence is a compound sentence with the two independent clauses joined by a a coordinating conjunction: and, but, or, nor, for, yet, or so. Normal punctuation: a comma before the conjunction.

    The women worked all day on the report, and they finally finished it late that night.

Type 3. The sentence is a compound sentence without one of the coordinating conjunctions joining the independent clauses. (The second clause often begins with an adverbial unit.) Normal punctuation: a semicolon.

    The women worked all day on the report; they finally finished it late that night.

In each of the following sentences ∧ marks a point of coordination. Indicate whether each sentence is Type 1, 2, or 3 by writing a number in the blank at the left. Then insert the correct punctuation, if any is required.

_____ 1. That ill-mannered secretary did not give me an appointment ∧ in addition, she told me not to come back any more.

_____ 2. That ill-mannered secretary did not give me an appointment ∧ and, in addition, she told me not to come back any more.

_____ 3. That ill-mannered secretary did not give me an appointment ∧ but did tell me to come back later.

_____ 4. The paper is due next Monday ∧ if you ask for an extension, however, you may turn it in one day late.

_____ 5. The paper is due next Monday ∧ but you may turn it in one day late if you ask for an extension.

_____ 6. I want to learn to play the saxophone ∧ my uncle played a saxophone in the university band some years ago.

_____ 7. Jim left early yesterday ∧ and came in late this morning.

_____ 8. That politician always takes moderate positions ∧ thus he hopes to offend no one.

61

———— 9. I studied hard for tomorrow's test ∧ for I want to make a good grade on it.

———— 10. Some people needed several hours of work before that test ∧ for a few people, however, it seemed quite easy.

———— 11. June looked everywhere for that lost book ∧ yet Jane found it right there on that bookshelf.

———— 12. June had been looking for that lost book for a week ∧ but had not found it in time for class this morning.

———— 13. Walk carefully on that stretch of the trail ∧ for the rocks and debris make that part of the trail treacherous.

———— 14. Walk carefully on that stretch of trail ∧ for several people it has proved to be very treacherous.

———— 15. "Please explain this problem to me," begged Robert ∧ "I can't seem to understand its basic principles."

———— 16. I talked to several experts about that situation ∧ but they don't agree on a course of action.

———— 17. Either print enough copies of the report for all of us ∧ or ask the secretary to make several copies of the original.

———— 18. Alicia will not work on that project ∧ nor will she help in the personnel office.

———— 19. "I'm leaving early tomorrow morning ∧ I intend to be in Akron before dinner," said Louise.

———— 20. "I'm leaving early tomorrow morning ∧ and will be in Akron before dinner," said Louise.

———— 21. Tom has had the flu for four days ∧ so he will probably not play in tomorrow's golf tournament.

———— 22. That critic neither understood the book's real message ∧ nor appreciated the skill of the writer.

———— 23. Our lawmakers acknowledge the value of that project ∧ but refuse to appropriate funds for it.

———— 24. Frank tried to look up the word in the dictionary ∧ but he didn't know it started with *ph*, not with *f*.

———— 25. The fire has already burned hundreds of acres ∧ this morning the governor mobilized the National Guard.

Directions: Combine the short sentences in each numbered item into one longer sentence.

1. Jim walked to the store.
   Al walked to the store.

   _____

2. Marge saw Mary last night.
   Marge saw Rosie last night.

   _____

3. Tom picked up his books.
   He walked out of the house.

   _____

4. Marcie walked into class.
   She sat down in the back row.

   _____

5. Marcie sat down in the back row.
   The teacher began the lecture.

   _____

6. Marcie looked for Jim.
   Jim was not in the class.

   _____

7. Marcie had studied very hard for the test.
   Therefore she made a very high grade.

   _____

Lesson 8 — *Subordination: Adverb Clauses*

To this point you have had practice with the simple sentence (one independent clause) and the compound sentence (two or more independent clauses). Basic as these sentences are to our thinking and writing, we need to move beyond these structures in order to make our writing flexible and effective. Often we can improve the precision of our statements if we use slightly more complex structures.

"Rain began to fall, and we stopped our ball game" is a perfectly correct sentence. But notice these slightly altered versions:

When rain began to fall, we stopped our ball game.
After rain began to fall, we stopped our ball game.
Because rain began to fall, we stopped our ball game.

These three, in addition to lessening the singsong tone of the compound sentence, are more informative. The first two tell the time at which the game was stopped—and notice that *when* and *after* point out slightly different time frames. The third version gives a different relation between the two statements; it tells not the time of, but the reason for, stopping the game.

If, instead of writing the compound sentence, "Rain was falling, and we continued our ball game," you write "Although rain was falling, we continued our ball game," you have refined your thinking and your expression. Your readers now interpret the sentence exactly as you want them to: They now know that the ball game was continued in spite of the fact that rain was falling.

Subordination

The process by which a statement is reduced to a secondary form to show its relation to the main idea is **subordination.** The grammatical unit that expresses a secondary idea as it affects a main idea is the **subordinate,** or **dependent, clause,** which we define as *a subject-verb combination that cannot stand alone as a sentence.* Instead, a subordinate clause works in a sentence in the same way that a single part of speech—an adverb, an adjective, or a noun works. Instead of a single word—quickly, quick, quickness—a group of words is used in the same way as those single words. A sentence made up of one independent clause and at least one dependent clause is a **complex sentence.**

Adverb Clause

The **adverb clause** works in exactly the same way a one-word adverb works; it provides information, it modifies the verb. The most common types of adverb clauses, in fact, answer direct questions about the action: "When?" (time); "Where?" (place); "Why?" (cause); and "How?" (manner). The role of the adverb clause is shown by the conjunction that introduces the adverb clause. Remember that the conjunction—the structural signal of subordination—is not an isolated word standing between the two clauses. It is part of the subordinate clause. In such a sentence as, "We left the house after the rain stopped," the unit "the rain stopped" could stand alone as an independent clause. But the clause is made dependent by the inclusion of *after,* which makes the clause dependent (subordinate). The dependent clause "after the rain stopped" establishes the time when "we left the house." Thus, the clause works as an adverb of time in the same way that the one-word adverbs work in the following sentences:

> We left the house *early.*
> We left the house *late.*
> We left the house *yesterday.*

Various types of adverb clauses, together with their most common conjunctions, are listed for you next, with examples.

Time (*when, whenever, before, after, since, while, until, as, as soon as*):

> The baby cried *when the telephone rang.*
> The cat ran out *before Lou could shut the door.*
> *After the bell rings,* no one can enter.
> I've known Palmer *since he was in high school.*
> You should not whisper *while Dr. Fuller is lecturing.*
> You may leave *as soon as your replacement arrives.*

Place (*where, wherever*):

> We parted *where the paths separated.*
> I shall meet you *wherever you want me to.*

Cause (or **Reason**) (*because, since, as, in order that*):

> I walk to work every day *because I need the exercise.*
> *Since she could not pay the fine,* she could not drive the car.
> *As you are the senior member,* you should lead the procession.
> They came to America *in order that they might have freedom.*

Purpose (*so that, that*):

> We left early *so that we could catch the last bus.*
> They died *that their nation might live.*

Manner (*as, as if, as though*):

> Stan acted *as if the party was boring him.*
> Please do the work *as you have been instructed.*

Result (*so . . . that, such . . . that*):

> Jerry arrived *so late that he missed the concert.*
> The workmen made *such a racket that I got a headache.*

Condition (*if, unless, provided that, on condition that*). This kind of adverb clause gives a condition under which the main clause is true:

Sit down and chat *if you are not in a hurry.*
He will not give his talk *unless we pay his expenses.*
She will sign the contract *provided that we pay her a bonus.*
If I were you, I would accept the offer.
If you had told me earlier, I could have helped.

Certain kinds of conditional clauses can occur in an alternate arrangement. The *if* is not used; instead, a subject-verb inversion signals the subordination. Sentences like the last two preceding examples sometimes take this form:

Were I you, I would accept the offer.
Had you told me earlier, I could have helped.

Concession (*although, though, even if, even though*). This clause states a fact in spite of which the main idea is true:

Although she is only nine years old, she plays chess.
Our car is dependable *even though it is old.*

Comparison (*than, as*). Two distinctive characteristics of the adverb clause of comparison should be noted:

1. Part or all of the verb, although it is needed grammatically, is usually not expressed; and
2. when an action verb is not expressed in the subordinate clause, the appropriate form of the auxiliary *do* is often used even though the *do* does not occur in the main clause. Examples:

Gold is heavier *than iron* [is].
Your computer is not as new *as mine* [is].
Her theme was better *than any other student's in the class* [was].
Ellen earned more bonus points *than her brother* did.

Elliptical Clause

Ellipsis means *omission,* to *leave something out.* A clause that leaves some parts understood or unexpressed is called an **elliptical clause.** (See Supplement 1.) You should be aware of elliptical clauses because they can lend variety to your writing. In the following examples, brackets enclose the parts of the clauses that may be unexpressed. Note that all the types of adverb phrases (time, place, cause, purpose, manner, result, condition, concession, and comparison) may be elliptical.

While [I was] *walking home,* I met Mr. Jones.
When [he is] *in Cleveland,* he stays with us.
Call your office *as soon as* [it is] *possible.*
Adjustments will be made *whenever* [they are] *necessary.*
Mary, *although* [she is] *a talented girl,* is quite lazy.
If [you are] *delayed,* call my secretary.
Your ticket, *unless* [it is] *stamped,* is invalid.

Adverb clauses may modify adjectives and adverbs. In this type of clause, the conjunction *that* is sometimes unexpressed.

> We are sorry *that you must leave early.* [Modifies the adjective *sorry*]
> I am sure *(that) he meant no harm.* [Modifies the adjective *sure*]
> The car is running better *than it did last week.* [Modifies the adverb *better*]

A Note on Sentence Variety

Although some adverb clauses—those of comparison, for instance—have a fixed position within the sentence, many adverb clauses may be placed before, inside, or following the main clause. You should practice various arrangements to relieve the monotony that comes from reliance on too many "main-subject-plus-main-verb" sentences:

> *When they deal with the unknown,* Greek myths are usually somber.
> Greek myths, *when they deal with the unknown,* are usually somber.
> Greek myths are usually somber *when they deal with the unknown.*

Notice in the third example above, no comma is used. Usually a comma is not needed when the adverbial clause is the final element of the sentence, as the third example below also illustrates.

> *Although he did not have authority from Congress,* President Theodore Roosevelt ordered construction of the Panama Canal.
>
> President Theodore Roosevelt, *although he did not have authority from Congress,* ordered construction of the Panama Canal.
>
> President Theodore Roosevelt ordered construction of the Panama Canal *although he did not have authority from Congress.*

Supplement 1

Occasionally an elliptical adverb clause of comparison must be recast because the exact meaning is unclear when parts of the clause are unexpressed. Here are two sentences that are ambiguous in the shortened forms of the clauses:

> Mr. Alton will pay you more *than Stan.*
>
> **Probable Meaning:** Mr. Alton will pay you more than [he will pay] Stan.
> **Possible Meaning:** Mr. Alton will pay you more than Stan [will pay you].

> Parents dislike homework as much *as their offspring.*
>
> **Probable Meaning:** Parents dislike homework as much as their offspring [dislike homework].
> **Possible Meaning:** Parents dislike homework as much as [they dislike] their offspring.

SUMMARY OF ADVERB CLAUSES

1. Function: to modify a verb, an adjective, or an adverb.
2. Position: fixed for some types (She sold more tickets *than I did*); others may be at the beginning, in the interior, or at the end of main clause.
3. Subordinators: conjunctions, most of which show adverbial relationships such as time (*when, since, while*), cause (*because, as*), and so on.
4. Special structures:
    a. A clause modifying an adjective subjective complement and subordinated by *that* is sometimes unexpressed:

    I'm sure *(that) you are wrong.*

    b. Elliptical clauses:

    Mary is older than I (am).
    If (you are) unable to attend, call me.
    While (she was) preparing lunch, Mary cut her finger.

Adverb Clauses

NAME _____ SCORE _____

Directions: Identify each of the italicized clauses by writing a label in the space at the left. You may abbreviate your label if you want.

Time	Purpose	Condition	Modification of an
Place	Manner	Concession	adjective or adverb
Cause	Result	Comparison	

_____ 1. Anna went to work *after she left the chemistry lab.*

_____ 2. *Although he was very tired,* Bill finished the work on that carpentry project.

_____ 3. *When you have a chance,* please call and order a pizza for us.

_____ 4. We are all quite hungry *because we missed lunch today.*

_____ 5. We have not heard from Jose *since he left for vacation.*

_____ 6. "I'm very happy *that you are taking biology,*" said Mother.

_____ 7. *"If, and only if, I make an A on this paper,"* said Roxanne, "I can pass this course."

_____ 8. Only one member of the team collected more money *than Alex.*

_____ 9. *Before you leave for class this morning,* you should write those two checks.

_____ 10. Please take your beeper with you *so that we can reach you in an emergency.*

_____ 11. That one tomato plant is taller *than all the others.*

_____ 12. *If we had not taken that wrong turn,* we would have been here fifteen minutes ago.

_____ 13. The test was so long *that Charlie could not finish it.*

_____ 14. The men left for lunch a little early *so that they could avoid the long line in the cafeteria.*

_____ 15. At Mark's arrival, Martha looked *as though she had seen a ghost.*

_____ 16. *As we turned into the driveway,* a hard rain began to fall.

_____ 17. *As we could not finish the project that afternoon,* we decided to return the next day.

_____ 18. *As soon as he gets up in the morning,* Oscar drinks a Coke.

_____ 19. I'm not certain *that Julie will be at work tomorrow.*

_____ 20. Follow those instructions exactly *as I gave them to you.*

_____ 21. Park your car *wherever you find an open space.*

_____ 22. *Since I could not find a space,* I left the car in the driveway.

_____ 23. *Since Tom arrived with his three children,* we have had little peace and quiet at our house.

_____ 24. Strangely enough, Howard acted *as if he did not want to take a day off.*

_____ 25. We need to work rapidly *so that we can finish this paper by the due date.*

_____ 26. That sweater, *although slightly faded,* still looks good.

_____ 27. My old, slow computer works better *than Janice's fancy new one.*

_____ 28. Maria was delighted *that she was able to schedule her vacation during the Olympics.*

_____ 29. Lisa was so tired *that she almost fell asleep at the wheel of her car.*

_____ 30. *If I were you,* I would practice my swimming before I took that canoe trip.

_____ 31. *Unless you buy a faster computer,* you cannot run that new program.

_____ 32. *If you see Atkins this afternoon,* ask him for directions to his house.

_____ 33. *Where the road forks,* take the left fork.

_____ 34. *If we don't have that report finished,* we should postpone the meeting.

_____ 35. *Because Carla was late,* she didn't finish the exam.

_____ 36. He looked *as if he hadn't slept for days.*

_____ 37. Andrew is convinced *that the downsizing will cost us our jobs.*

_____ 38. *If you don't have a fishing license,* you may be forced to pay a fine.

_____ 39. *Whenever you come to a stopping place,* let's go to lunch.

_____ 40. *Although you can't see them,* the air all around you is filled with dust mites.

NAME _____ SCORE _____

Directions: Each sentence contains one adverb clause. Underline each adverb clause. To identify the adverb clause, write a label in the space at the left.

Time	Purpose	Condition	Modification of an
Place	Manner	Concession	adjective or adverb
Cause	Result	Comparison	

_____ 1. When you see Madelyn, give her the message about the meeting.

_____ 2. Although the snow had melted, it was still very cold outside.

_____ 3. I found that last assignment much more difficult than any we had written earlier.

_____ 4. Late papers, if you have not arranged for an extension, will not be accepted without a penalty.

_____ 5. My little dog barked as if she had seen a burglar.

_____ 6. My mother was delighted that we had been able to find the lost book.

_____ 7. Because the little kids were very tired, we left the park and went to the yogurt store for a snack.

_____ 8. How can we find Janice's office if we have lost the address?

_____ 9. Please send me the check as soon as possible so that I can pay my tuition.

_____ 10. You need to use patching plaster wherever you find a crack in that wall.

_____ 11. If we had taken the earlier flight, we would have arrived home well ahead of the storm.

_____ 12. Unfortunately, Julia talks so fast that I cannot understand her.

_____ 13. Marcia is sure that we can make the drive in less than four hours.

_____ 14. The map to the cabin, although quite old and faded, was still readable.

_____ 15. My old running shoes feel better on my feet than these expensive new ones.

_____ 16. In the emergency, the pilot dumped almost all the fuel so that the plane could reach the landing strip.

_____ 17. The horse shied as though it had seen a snake.

_____ 18. Since I bought a chain saw, cutting firewood has been a very easy task.

_____ 19. Since she has moved out of town, Cindy cannot use her health club membership.

_____ 20. Bring me the book as soon as possible.

_____ 21. Jim is certain that he can pass the physical fitness test.

_____ 22. Unless we can find a replacement for Kate, we won't have a full team for the softball game tonight.

_____ 23. Even though Alicia had trained hard for two months, she still wasn't able to finish the marathon.

_____ 24. The office manager was glad that he was able to hire two highly skilled temporary workers.

_____ 25. Please do not come to the window until you have filled out the form.

_____ 26. Please type that letter exactly as I wrote it.

_____ 27. The girls came to the campus early so that they could get moved into their rooms without any problems.

_____ 28. The weather has been so cold that we haven't been out of the house for three days.

_____ 29. The two men probably would have bought tickets if they had known about tonight's game.

_____ 30. My fourteen-year-old cousin is more skilled with a computer than I.

_____ 31. Just as we approached the ticket booth, the attendant slammed the window shut.

_____ 32. My father wants to take his vacation in a place where there are no telephones.

_____ 33. I'll be able to leave as soon as I finish printing my report.

_____ 34. Even though Maggie was a good math student in high school, she has had difficulty with this calculus course.

_____ 35. If you want to come with us, you'll need to get ready now.

_____ 36. Jill solved that problem more quickly than anyone else in the class.

_____ 37. Alex was sorry that he did not get to hear the lecture on early rock music.

_____ 38. The little girl cried as if she had lost her best friend.

_____ 39. Because he can't find the receipt, Mike can't return that textbook for a refund.

_____ 40. I thought your paper was better than mine.

Directions: Rewrite the sentence or sentences in each numbered item as a single complex sentence; use the subordinating conjunction that properly establishes the relationship between the two sentences. You may need to delete some words.

1. Alice launched the boat carefully.
   She sailed slowly out through the harbor.

   _____

2. Jim had not packed a lunch that morning.
   He went to the cafeteria to buy a sandwich.

   _____

3. Marcie walked into class.
   She sat down in the back row.

   _____

4. Marcie sat down in the back row.
   The teacher began to lecture.

   _____

5. Marcie had studied very hard for the test.
   Therefore she made a very high grade on the test.

   _____

6. You need to find your ticket.
   If you do not, you will not be admitted to the game.

   _____

7. We raced home from work.
   We wanted to watch the news at 6:00 P.M.

   _____

8. Jim already owns a dictionary and a thesaurus.
   He does not have any other reference books at home.

   _____

Lesson 9 Subordination: Adjective Clauses

Just as a single-word adjective—blue—modifies a noun—sky—clauses that begin with who, whom, which, or that (**adjective or relative clauses**) can modify a noun or a pronoun. These clauses give information about the noun in the same way that the one-word adjectives do. Both one-word adjectives and adjective clauses can be seen as basic sentences that have been worked into a main clause.

I looked into the sky. The sky was blue.
I looked into the blue sky.

I looked into the sky. The sky was filled with towering cumulous clouds.
I looked into the sky, which was filled with towering cumulous clouds.

In Item 1 the sentence, "The sky was blue," becomes the one-word adjective *blue* and modifies the noun *sky*. In Item 2 the sentence, "The sky was filled with towering cumulous clouds," cannot become a one-word adjective; therefore, the sentence becomes an adjective or relative clause opened by the word *which*. But the clause **modifies** the word *sky* in the sense that it provides us with information about the sky.

Position of the Adjective

The normal position of an adjective clause is immediately following the noun or the pronoun that it modifies. The following paired units illustrate this process. Every "A" unit has two simple sentences; the second repeats a noun from the first sentence. The "B" sentence shows how the second idea has been reduced to a subordinate clause and has become part of the first sentence:

A. This is a well-built truck. *The truck* will save you money.
B. This is a well-built truck *that* will save you money.
   [The clause modifies *truck*. *That*, the relative pronoun, is the subject in the adjective clause.

A. Alice has a new boyfriend. *The new boyfriend* [or *He*] sings in a rock group.
B. Alice has a new boyfriend *who* sings in a rock group.
   [*Who* is the subject in the clause that modifies *boyfriend*.]

A. Here is the book. I borrowed *the book* [or *it*] yesterday.
B. Here is the book *that* I borrowed yesterday.
   [*That* is the direct object in the adjective clause.]

A. The firm hired Chet Brown. The boss had known *Chet Brown* [or *him*] in Omaha.
B. The firm hired Chet Brown, *whom* the boss had known in Omaha.
   [*Whom* is the direct object in the adjective clause.]

A. May I introduce Dick Hart? I went to college *with Dick Hart* [or *him*].
B. May I introduce Dick Hart, with *whom* I went to college?
  [The clause modifies *Dick Hart*. Notice that the preposition *with* stands at the beginning of the clause with its object *whom*. At the informal level of language usage, the preposition in this structure is sometimes found at the end of the clause. See also Supplement 2 of Lesson 6 on page 50.]

A. She is a young artist. I admire the young *artist's* [or *her*] work.
B. She is a young artist *whose* work I admire.
  [*Work* is in this position because, although it is the direct object of *admire*, it cannot be separated from its modifier, the relative adjective *whose*, which must be placed at the beginning of the adjective clause.]

Relative Pronouns

Nearly all of the adjective clauses you read, write, or speak use *that, which, who, whom,* or *whose* to tie the adjective clause to the noun it modifies. These words, in spite of the fact that they join one clause to a word in another clause, are not conjunctions. They are pronouns that have a connective or relating function; thus they are called **relatives.** Relatives function *within* the adjective clause as subjects, direct objects, or objects of prepositions.

It is helpful to think of an adjective clause as a simple sentence that is incorporated within another sentence. This combining is possible when the second clause repeats, directly, a noun in the first clause. The relative word, by substituting for the repeated noun, refers ("relates") the clause directly to the word being modified. Notice that the relative, because it is the word signaling the subordination, always begins the adjective clause.

We also use the adverbs *when* and *where* as relatives. *When* and *where* introduce adjective clauses in combinations meaning "time when" and "place where." The following examples show that the subordinator is really the equivalent of an adverbial prepositional phrase. (The "B" sentences are complex sentences combining the material of the two "A" sentences.)

A. Beth and I recalled the time. We considered ourselves rebels *at that time*.
B. Beth and I recalled the time *when* we considered ourselves rebels.

A. This is the spot. The explorers came ashore at this spot.
B. This is the spot *where* the explorers came ashore.

These clauses are logically considered adjective clauses because they immediately follow nouns that require identification, and the clauses give the identifying material. If you remember the "time-when" and "place-where" combinations, you will not confuse this type of adjective clause with other subordinate clauses that may use the same subordinators.

Note: In certain adjective clauses the relative word is often unexpressed; the meaning is instantly clear without it: the food *(that) we eat*, the house *(that) he lived in*, the man *(whom) you saw*, the time *(when) you fell down*, and so on.

Restrictive and Nonrestrictive Adjective Clauses

Depending on their role in a sentence, relative or adjective clauses are called restrictive or nonrestrictive. A restrictive clause provides identification of the noun it modifies. A nonrestrictive clause provides information that is not essential for identification. Thus, in the sentence "The man who owns that car just walked up," the man is identified by the clause *who owns that car.* But in the sentence "John Williams, who owns that car, just walked up," the clause *who owns that car* does not identify John Williams (he is identified by his name); the clause tells us something **additional,** it adds information about John Williams.

Restrictive Clauses

The restrictive adjective clause is not set off by commas because it is essential to the identification of the word being modified.

> The grade *that I received on my report* pleased me.
> Anyone *who saw the accident* should call the police.

You can see that without the modifying clauses ("that I received on my test"; "who saw the accident") the nouns are not identified. What grade and what anyone are we talking about? But when we add the modifiers, we identify the *particular* grade and *the particular* anyone. In other words, this kind of clause restricts the meaning of a general noun to one specific member of its class.

Nonrestrictive Adjective Clause

The nonrestrictive adjective clause, which does require commas, supplies additional or incidental information about the word that it modifies, *but the information is not needed for identifying purposes.* Don't, however, get into the habit of thinking that a nonrestrictive clause is unimportant; unless it has some importance to the meaning of the sentence, it has no right to be in the sentence.

If the noun being modified does not require identification, the modifier following it is nonrestrictive and requires commas. It follows, then, that nonrestrictive modifiers are found following proper nouns *(Mount Everest, Philadelphia, Mr. Frank Smith;* nouns already identified (the oldest *boy* in her class, her only *grandchild);* and one-of-a-kind nouns (Alice's *mother,* the *provost* of the college, the *writer* of the editorial).

Examples

The following examples contrast restrictive and nonrestrictive adjective clauses. (See Supplement 1.)

> I visited an old friend *who is retiring soon.* [Restrictive]
> I visited my oldest and closest friend, *who is retiring soon.* [Nonrestrictive]
>
> The man *whose car had been wrecked* asked us for a ride. [Restrictive]
> Mr. Ash, *whose car had been wrecked,* asked us for a ride. [Nonrestrictive]
>
> A small stream *that flows through the property* supplies an occasional trout. [Restrictive]
> Caldwell Creek, *which flows through the property,* supplies an occasional trout. [Nonrestrictive]
>
> She wants to retire to a place *where freezing weather is unknown.* [Restrictive]
> She wants to retire to Panama City, *where freezing weather is unknown.* [Nonrestrictive]

Supplement 1

A few distinctions in the use of *who, which,* and *that* in adjective clauses are generally observed. *Which* refers only to things; *who* refers to people; and *that* refers to things or people. *That* is used only in restrictive clauses; in other words, a "that" adjective clause is not set off by commas. Because *which* is the relative pronoun that must be used in a non-restrictive clause modifying a thing, there is a convention that *which* should not introduce a restrictive adjective clause. This convention is generally, but by no means always, observed. People tend to use *which* in their writing when *that* would be better.

SUMMARY OF ADJECTIVE CLAUSES

1. Function: to modify a noun or a pronoun.
2. Position: follows the noun or pronoun that it modifies.
3. Subordinators:
   a. relative pronouns (*who, whom, which, that*), which function within the adjective clause as subjects, direct objects, or objects of prepositions
   b. relative adjectives (*whose, which*)
   c. relative adverbs (*when, where*)
4. Special problem: Adjective clauses that are vital to the identification of the nouns being modified are restrictive and do not require commas. Clauses not necessary for identification are nonrestrictive and are set off by commas.

Adjective Clauses

NAME _____ SCORE _____

Directions: Each italicized unit is an adjective clause. In the space at the left, copy the word the clause modifies. Be prepared to explain in class why some of the clauses (nonrestrictive) are set off by commas and some (restrictive) are not.

_____ 1. In my home town there is only one restaurant *that is open all night.*

_____ 2. We ate at the Pentagon Restaurant, *which is open all night.*

_____ 3. We last saw Otis in 1989, *when we played in the regional baseball finals.*

_____ 4. The time *when a typewriter was a satisfactory tool for writing* has long since passed.

_____ 5. Jill Wright, *who works in the registrar's office,* showed me the schedule for next term.

_____ 6. There is the woman *who showed me the schedule for next term.*

_____ 7. Those passengers *who hold seats in rows 16 through 31* may board the plane at this time.

_____ 8. Tom Wilson, *whose seat is in row 30,* may board the plane at this time.

_____ 9. All the classes *that meet at 8 A.M.* were cancelled this morning because of the torrential rains.

_____ 10. The Chinese Literature class, *which meets at noon today,* will have a guest lecturer.

_____ 11. Yesterday at the library, I talked to a girl *who was a student in my elementary school.*

_____ 12. Every person *who had been assigned to jury duty* was present and on time this morning.

_____ 13. Anyone *who found that novel interesting* will probably not enjoy the movie.

_____ 14. The car *I'm driving now* does not get good gas mileage.

_____ 15. My car, *which I bought for $750,* does not get good gas mileage.

Directions: Each sentence contains one adjective clause. Underline the adjective clause and copy the word it modifies in the space at the left.

_____ 1. The articles that I need for my research paper are available on the Internet.

_____ 2. One article, which is titled "Why the Wind Blows," is especially useful.

_____ 3. The boys who have applied for the part-time jobs are out in the hallway.

_____ 4. I met James Rogers, who is applying for one of the jobs.

_____ 5. You need to call all the people to whom we sent invitations.

_____ 6. I was extremely busy at the moment when you called me.

_____ 7. Mr. Johnson asked the name of the person whose book I borrowed.

_____ 8. Alice talked to Paul Rollins, whose softball glove is missing.

_____ 9. The writer of that letter, whose spelling is truly atrocious, is actually a very intelligent person.

_____ 10. Jamie cannot be in town on the day when we need to see her.

_____ 11. The detective walked slowly to the place where the body was found.

_____ 12. I don't think I know the person who wrote the memo about the new account.

_____ 13. Jim Shavers, who works down the street at the hardware store, went to high school with my brother.

_____ 14. I probably shouldn't expect much, however, from a car that was so inexpensive.

_____ 15. The elementary school students who live near me are unhappy with their school's physical education program.

Exercise 9   *Adjective Clauses*

NAME _____   SCORE _____

Directions: Each of these sentences contains an adjective clause. None of the clauses are set off with commas. Put parentheses around each adjective clause and set off the nonrestrictive clauses with commas. In the first space at the left, write the word the clause modifies. In the second space, write *R* (restrictive) or *N* (nonrestrictive). (Note: In some sentences an adverb clause that is part of the adjective clause should be included in the parentheses.

_____   1. That little pamphlet told us nothing we needed to know about
_____   the proposed law.

_____   2. Janice needs a computer that will run a desktop publishing
_____   program.

_____   3. Janice ought to buy an Intermezzo 2000-16 which has sixteen
_____   megabytes of RAM.

_____   4. Yesterday in her attic, my aunt found a baseball card that was
_____   autographed by Joe Dimaggio.

_____   5. Joe Dimaggio who was a very famous baseball player played for
_____   the New York Yankees.

_____   6. We're still waiting to hear from all those to whom we sent
_____   invitations.

_____   7. The college sent a letter to all the students whose parking permits
_____   have expired.

_____   8. Alice and Jim are searching the places where Jim might have lost
_____   his keys.

_____   9. That song takes me back to the time when we were in junior high
_____   school.

_____   10. I got a call yesterday from Alex Ortega whom I met when I toured
_____   Venezuela last summer.

_____   11. Alex is visiting his Aunt Marta who is a museum curator in
_____   Chicago.

_____   12. Could you possibly identify the woman to whom you gave the
_____   book when you were in the library?

_____   13. Tomorrow we will try to find that spot in the lake where we
_____   caught those two big fish.

_____ 14. Tomorrow we will fish near Deer Island where we caught those
_____   two big fish last week.

_____ 15. We have hired a guide who knows the lake well.
_____

_____ 16. We have hired Joe Robertson who knows the lake well.
_____

_____ 17. Arline wants to move to a little town where she can find some
_____   peace and quiet.

_____ 18. Roberta recommended Aliceville which is a small town in the
_____   mountains.

_____ 19. Do you know all the students who made an A on the last test?

_____ 20. I know Joe Preston who makes an A on every test.
_____

_____ 21. We all need to study the history of the company for which we are
_____   writing that proposal.

_____ 22. Jack can't remember the name of the book he read for our next
_____   report.

_____ 23. Do you know the name of the man whom the company hired last
_____   week?

_____ 24. That man is Paul Hartford who joined the company last week.
_____

_____ 25. Please tell me the name of one author whose work you admire.
_____

_____ 26. I have always admired the work of Ernest Hemingway who wrote
_____   *The Old Man and the Sea.*

_____ 27. The dog you found in our backyard probably belongs to our
_____   neighbors the Randolphs.

_____ 28. The place where Tom's family usually spends vacations is near
_____   Townsend, Tennessee.

_____ 29. Townsend reminds them of an earlier time when life was much
_____   less hectic.

_____ 30. In the registrar's office, the person to whom you should give your
_____   application is Wanda Smith.

Directions: The two sentences in each item can be combined into one sentence by resolving the second sentence into an adjective clause. Be sure to punctuate the adjective clauses correctly.

1. That car is beautifully maintained. It once belonged to my father.

   _____

2. I am returning the book. I borrowed it yesterday.

   _____

3. Yesterday I met Alice Martin. She joined the firm last week.

   _____

4. Hemingway is an American novelist. I admire his work.

   _____

5. I believe that is the very spot. Jose fell off the dock at this spot.

   _____

6. That song recalled a time. Life was a little more carefree at that time.

   _____

7. There is the man. I gave my receipt to him.

   _____

8. I'd like you to meet James Roberts. I worked very closely with him on that last project.

   _____

9. The man asked us for help. His car has a flat tire.

   _____

10. A small pond makes a fine swimming hole. It is about 100 yards from the house.

   _____

Lesson 10 *Subordination: Noun Clauses*

An adverbial clause such as *after the rain stopped* can work in the same way a single-word adverb *yesterday* works to set the time of the main verb. The adjective clause *whom I knew well* can work in the same way a single-word adjective *tall* works to modify our understanding of a noun *woman*. **A noun clause works in a similar way to do the work of a regular noun.**

A **noun clause** is a group of words containing a subject-verb combination and a subordinating word. A noun clause can perform the same function as a regular noun: a noun clause can be a subject, direct object, subjective complement, object of a preposition, or appositive. You can understand the uses of the noun clause if you think of it as a clause equivalent to a "something" or a "someone" in one of these noun slots:

Subject (S)
The *girl* opened the window. [single-word noun as S.]
Whoever came in first opened the window. [noun clause as S.]
His *story* is very convincing. [noun as S.]
What he told us is very convincing. [noun clause as S.]

Subjective Complement (S.C.)
This is his *story.* [single-word as S.C.]
This is *what he told us.* [noun clause as S.C.]

Direct Object (D.O.)
Mr. Allen announced *something.* [single-word D.O.]
Mr. Allen announced *his resignation.* [noun clause D.O.]
Mr. Allen announced *that he would resign.* [noun clause D.O.]
Can you tell me your *time* of arrival? [single-word D.O.]
Can you tell me *when you will arrive?* [noun clause D.O.]

Object of a Preposition (O.P.)
Give the package to the *man.* [single-word O.P.]
Give the package to *whoever opens the door.* [noun clause O.P.]

Most of the noun clauses that you read and write will be used as subjects, direct objects (the most common use), subjective complements, or objects of prepositions. Two other rather special uses should be noted, the *delayed* noun clause and the *appositive* noun clause.

Delayed Noun Clause

One common use of a noun clause is as a delayed subject. The signal for this construction is the word standing in the subject position, with the meaningful subject being a noun clause following the verb:

It is unfortunate *that you were delayed.*

Although the clause follows the verb, it is the real subject and therefore is a noun clause. The meaning of the sentence is "That you were delayed is unfortunate." The delayed noun clause also can be the object of a preposition:

> Give the package to *someone.*
> Give the package to *the janitor.*

A related noun clause use puts it in the direct object slot with a noun clause following an objective complement. This use, which is encountered less frequently than the delayed subject, gives us a clause that we can call a delayed direct object:

> We think it unlikely that Jones will be reelected.

Appositive Noun Clause

To understand the other special noun clause, you must know what an appositive is. The **appositive** is a noun unit inserted into a sentence to *rename* another noun that usually immediately precedes the appositive. A simple example occurs in the following sentence:

> Senator Jones, a dedicated environmentalist, objected.

Because any noun unit can be used as an appositive, noun clauses sometimes function in this position. Some noun clause appositives are separated from the first noun by at least a comma, sometimes by a heavier mark:

> There still remains one mystery: *how the thief knew your name.* [The noun clause renames the preceding noun, *mystery.*]

A rather special type of noun appositive clause, subordinated by *that* and following such nouns as *fact, belief, hope, statement, news,* and *argument,* is usually not set off by any mark of punctuation:

> You cannot deny the fact *that you lied under oath.*
> Your statement *that the boss is stupid* was undiplomatic.

(See Supplement 1.)

Subordinating Words

The subordinating words that serve to introduce noun clauses are conjunctions (*that, if, whether*); pronouns (*who, whom, what, which, whoever, whatever, whichever*); adjectives (*whose, which, what*); and adverbs (*when, where, why, how*). Remember that the subordinating word is part of the clause and always stands at or near the beginning of the clause. Remember also that in noun clauses used as direct objects, the conjunction *that* is often unexpressed because the meaning is usually clear without it.

> I know *that you will be happy here.*
> [Noun clause subordinated by the conjunction *that.*]

Jill now wonders *if her answer was the correct one.*
[Noun clause subordinated by the conjunction *if.*]

All of us hope *you'll return soon.*
[Noun clause subordinated by the understood conjunction *that.*]

I do not know *who he is.*
[Noun clause subordinated by the pronoun *who* used as the S.C. within the clause.]

I know *what I would do with the extra money.*
[Noun clause subordinated by the pronoun *what* used as the D.O. within the clause.]

Tell me *whom Mary is feuding with now.*
[Noun clause subordinated by the pronoun *whom* used as the O.P. *with.*]

You must decide *which car you will use today.*
[Noun clause subordinated by the adjective *which* modifying the direct object *car.*]

Why Morton left school still puzzles his friends.
[Noun clause subordinated by the adverb *why.*]

(See Supplement 2.)

Supplement 1

Because an appositive is a renamer, it represents a reduced form of a Pattern 2 sentence in which a subject and a noun subjective complement are joined by a form of *be.* The writer of the sentence "Senator Jones, a dedicated environmentalist, objected" could have written in two simple sentences, the second one repeating a noun used in the first:

Senator Jones objected.
Senator Jones [or *He*] is a dedicated environmentalist.

The adjective clause offers the writer one device for compressing this information into one sentence:

Senator Jones, who is a dedicated environmentalist, objected.

The appositive represents a further compression:

Senator Jones, a dedicated environmentalist, objected.

If you think of the appositive as a renamer of the preceding noun (the two nouns could be joined by a form of *be*), you have a handy test to help you recognize any noun appositive use:

There still remains one mystery: *how the thief knew your name.*
[Test: The mystery *is* how the thief knew your name.]

You can't deny the fact *that she has real talent.*
[Test: The fact *is* that she has real talent.]

Your contention *that the witness lied* has some merit.
[Test: The contention *is* that the witness lied.]

If you remember a few points about the form, the function, and the positioning of adjective clauses and noun clauses, you should have little difficulty in distinguishing between them. Although certain kinds of noun clauses in apposition may, at first glance, look like adjective clauses, a few simple tests clearly show the difference:

> The news *that you brought us* is welcome. [Adjective clause]
> The news *that Bob has recovered* is welcome. [Noun clause]

If you remember that an adjective clause is a *describer* and that an appositive noun clause is a *renamer,* you can see that in the first sentence the clause describes—in fact, identifies—the noun *news,* but it does not actually tell us what the news is. In the second sentence the clause does more: It tells us what the news is. Remember the *be* test. "The news is *that you brought us...*" does not make sense, but "The news is *that Bob has recovered...*" does; therefore the second clause is a noun clause in apposition.

Which / That Test

Another test that can be applied to these two types of sentences is based on the fact that in adjective clauses, but not in noun clauses, *which* can be substituted for *that.* "The news *which* you brought us ..." is acceptable English; the clause, in this case, is an adjective clause. But because we can't say "The news *which* Bob has recovered ..." this time the clause is a noun clause; it cannot be an adjective clause.

Supplement 2

You have probably already noticed that the pronouns, adjectives, and adverbs that subordinate noun clauses are essentially the same words that are used in questions (Lesson 6). The two uses are alike in the important respect that they always stand at the beginning of the clause. The two uses differ in that, as interrogatives, the words bring about the subject-verb inversion, whereas in noun clauses the subject-verb positioning is the normal one:

> *Whom* will the mayor appoint?
> [This sentence is a direct question; it calls for an answer. *Whom* is the D.O. of the main verb.]

> *I wonder whom* the mayor will appoint.
> [This sentence is a statement, not a direct question. Notice that a question mark is not required. *Whom* is the D.O. within the noun clause.]

SUMMARY OF NOUN CLAUSES

1. Function: to work as a noun within the main clause.
2. Positions: subject (or delayed subject), renaming subjective complement, direct object (or delayed direct object), object of preposition, or appositive.
3. Subordinators:
    a. conjunctions (*that, if, whether*)
    b. pronouns (*who, whom, which, what,* and . . . *ever* forms, standing for unknown persons or things)
    c. adjectives (*whose, which, what*)
    d. adverbs (*when, where, why, how*)
4. Special problem: Some noun appositive clauses closely resemble adjective clauses. But they differ in that, in addition to *describing* the noun, the appositive clause *renames* the noun:

    The remark *that Jim made* (adjective clause) was unwise.
    The remark *that Mr. Smith cannot be trusted* (noun appositive clause) was unwise.

NAME _____ SCORE _____

Directions: Identify the use of each italicized noun clause by writing one of the following abbreviations in the space at the left.

S.	[subject or delayed subject]	S.C.	[subjective complement]
D.O.	[direct object or delayed direct object]	O.P	[object of preposition]
		Ap.	[appositive]

_____ 1. And that is *why I was late for work yesterday.*

_____ 2. And that is the reason *why I was late for work yesterday.*

_____ 3. In *what I read* I did not find any instructions for correcting that problem.

_____ 4. We don't know *whether Jim is coming or not.*

_____ 5. I wish *someone would help me study for this math test.*

_____ 6. *When we will arrive* is open to question because of the bad weather.

_____ 7. Was that exactly *what she said in answer to your question?*

_____ 8. There seems to be no explanation for *what she said.*

_____ 9. *That weather forecasting is not an exact science* became apparent during that winter storm.

_____ 10. Her idea *that we ought to leave early Monday* did not get a warm reception from the group.

_____ 11. I don't have a full grasp of the implications of *what the senator proposes in his legislation.*

_____ 12. "That statement is not *what I wrote down in the meeting,*" said Alice.

_____ 13. The club president hasn't explained *how we should accomplish that task.*

_____ 14. *How we should accomplish that task* was not explained by the club president.

_____ 15. How can we best respond to *what that letter alleges?*

_____ 16. It is thought by some people *that he was actually fired from his job.*

_____ 17. My first problem was *that I had lost my textbook.*

_____ 18. In her class, you must know *when you should speak up and when you should be quiet.*

_____ 19. My grandmother thought it odd *that I was not interested in a job with her company.*

_____ 20. The idea *that Jane is lazy* is simply untrue.

Directions: Each of the following sentences contains a noun clause. Put parentheses around each noun clause and identify its use by writing one of the following in the space at the left.

S.	[subject or delayed subject]	S.C.	[subjective complement]
D.O.	[direct object or delayed direct object]	O.P	[object of preposition]
		Ap.	[appositive]

Note: In the following sentences the noun clause is within another subordinate clause: 2, 4, 9, 13, 15. In the following sentences the noun clause contains another subordinate clause: 3, 7, 10, 14, 18, 19, 20.

_____ 1. It seems unlikely that we will arrive before noon tomorrow.

_____ 2. I need to speak to whoever was in class for that lecture last week.

_____ 3. We hope that all the people who attended the dinner will make contributions to the homeless shelter.

_____ 4. Because Jan has read whatever was assigned, she can help us with the report.

_____ 5. The fact that Miriam had been training for six months certainly helped her in that 10K race.

_____ 6. Whoever worked out that solution certainly has my undying gratitude.

_____ 7. Does the coach think Jim is a better foul shooter than I am?

_____ 8. For that information, look under whatever headings seem likely to deal with the subject.

_____ 9. We should visit Aunt Hattie, who can tell us when the first settlers came to this valley.

_____ 10. Val thinks she needs one of those new, fast computers everyone is buying.

_____ 11. Will whoever hid my jacket from me please bring it back?

_____ 12. The faint hope that we would arrive with no more problems died when the plane's engine sputtered.

_____ 13. The group wasted ten minutes while Pam and Joe decided how they should divide the check.

_____ 14. It seems likely that everyone else will arrive before we do.

_____ 15. Unless Will believes that there will be a test, he skips class on Mondays.

_____ 16. The senator's position is that this bill will hurt the farmers in her district.

_____ 17. Most experts believe, however, that very few people are in favor of any tax increase.

_____ 18. From the instructor's remarks, we can infer that there will be a test when we return from spring break.

_____ 19. That there will be a test when we return from spring break was implied by the instructor's remarks.

_____ 20. The instructor implied that there will be a test when we return from spring break.

NAME _____ SCORE _____

Directions: Each of the following sentences contains one noun clause. Put parentheses around each noun clause and identify its use by writing one of the following in the space at the left.

S.	[subject or delayed subject]	S.C.	[subjective complement]
D.O.	[direct object or delayed direct object]	O.P	[object of preposition]
		Ap.	[appositive]

_____ 1. Jim's statement that he intended to leave at 5:00 A.M. did not surprise anyone.

_____ 2. No one is ever surprised by what they hear from Jim.

_____ 3. The reason Marge gave for buying a used car was that she did not have the money for a new car.

_____ 4. It has become quite obvious that we cannot expect much help on this project from Al.

_____ 5. How the puppy escaped from the yard is a complete mystery to me.

_____ 6. The entire staff believes that the company has been in financial difficulty for some time.

_____ 7. If you don't see what you need on the shelf, just ask a sales clerk for help.

_____ 8. If what's on the shelf is not what you need, just ask a sales clerk for help.

_____ 9. What we heard in that meeting is not to be mentioned outside that room.

_____ 10. Jane was excited when she heard that we have a three-day weekend next week.

_____ 11. "I'd like to talk to whoever answers the phone at the ad agency," said Mr. Lance.

_____ 12. The fact that we can't go any further on this project became clear very early this morning.

_____ 13. Does it matter if I turn in my assignment one day late?

_____ 14. Some of us thought that Scott should have done better on that exam.

_____ 15. "The idea that anyone could possibly have liked that movie just astonishes me," said Lucy.

_____ 16. Unfortunately, we simply don't know when Ms. Albury will return from Boston.

_____ 17. It is likely that we can study in the library on Saturday afternoon.

_____ 18. Mrs. Roberts thought it unusual that Harry had not called before lunch.

_____ 19. The results of the poll showed that most students prefer morning classes to afternoon classes.

_____ 20. Jack's impression was that most of the people in the theater enjoyed that movie very much.

Directions: Combine the following pairs of sentences into a single sentence by joining the second sentence to the first as a noun clause.

1. Ellen promised (something).
   She would return my raincoat tomorrow.

   _____

2. (Something) is not clear from Barbara's letter.
   Whether or not she will return to school next semester.

   _____

3. Please give that envelope to (someone).
   Whoever answers the door.

   _____

4. Does Joe know (something)?
   When is the next game scheduled?

   _____

5. The news surprised everyone on the staff.
   (The news is that) Jim is leaving the company at the end of the month.

   _____

6. The news came as a surprise to everyone on the staff.
   (The news is that) Jim is leaving the company at the end of the month.

   _____

7. The manager believes (something).
   The team should trade for a left-handed pitcher.

   _____

8. Janice does not know (something).
   Who will her replacement be?

   _____

9. (Something) was very good luck.
   We had a spare key hidden on the car.

   _____

10. (Someone) should be ashamed.
    Whoever repeated that story.

    _____

NAME _____   SCORE _____

Directions: The italicized material in each sentence is a subordinate clause. In the first space at the left, write Adv., Adj., or N. to identify the clause.

_____ 1. The men left the office so rapidly *that they forgot their copies of the report.*

_____ 2. I can't believe *that Lauren refused to take a day off.*

_____ 3. The woman *who is taking Walt's place* has been with the company for five years.

_____ 4. *What I read in the paper yesterday* is certainly good news.

_____ 5. You will probably be warm enough *if you wear your down vest.*

_____ 6. If you wear your down vest, I think *you will be warm enough.*

_____ 7. Mary Jo tries to write down everything *the teacher says in class.*

_____ 8. Mary Jo tries to write down *whatever the teacher says in class.*

_____ 9. Art, who is a very good student, writes down only *what seems to be important.*

_____ 10. That movie confuses many of its viewers *because it has a very complicated plot.*

_____ 11. If their attention wanders for even a moment, the viewers lose track of *what is happening on the screen.*

_____ 12. The person *who wrote that article* is a very persuasive writer.

_____ 13. *Whoever wrote that article* is a very persuasive writer.

_____ 14. The points in Alex's argument became less clear *as I became more drowsy.*

_____ 15. Few people in the class agreed with Jorge's notion *that a test just before the holiday was a good idea.*

_____ 16. Everyone in the arena laughed heartily at *what they saw at the end of the half-time show.*

_____ 17. Rob used the last book *he found in the library* as the principal source for his research paper.

_____ 18. No one in the department seems to know *who will teach that course next semester.*

_____ 19. The name of the person *who will teach that course next semester* has not been announced by the department.

_____ 20. *Because the wording of that sentence was confusing,* I had to rewrite it completely.

Directions: In each pair of sentences, use the first word group as the main clause and add the second word group to the first by making it an adjective clause, an adverb clause, or a noun clause. Rewrite enough of the two word groups to make the new sentence clear and identify the subordinate clause you create by writing one of the following in the space at the left:

Adj.   (Adjective Clause)   Adv.   (Adverb Clause)   N.   (Noun Clause)

————— 1. The person has retired.
   That person wrote those humorous columns for the paper.

_____

————— 2. We might need to lower the rent on the apartment.
   It has been vacant for several months.

_____

————— 3. The fact was not known to the people making the decision.
   One hundred people would lose their jobs because of the change.

_____

————— 4. We decided to move the picnic inside the gymnasium.
   Heavy rains began to fall.

_____

————— 5. No one on the campus knows (a fact).
   Classes will be cancelled next Tuesday for a special conference.

_____

————— 6. Do you know the man?
   The man owns that beautiful convertible.

_____

————— 7. It is important.
   We get started on that report as soon as possible.

_____

————— 8. The fact should not stop us.
   James is not here for the first meeting.

_____

————— 9. I need to talk to (someone).
   Anyone who might have information about that subject.

_____

————— 10. You need to follow those directions (in a certain way).
   Exactly as I gave them to you.

_____

Directions: In place of the "someone" or "something" in the first sentence put a noun clause formed from the idea of the second sentence or phrase. The suggested subordinating word is provided in parentheses.

Example: *Someone* should turn on the heat. (Whoever)
           The unknown person who gets to the cabin first.
           Whoever gets to the cabin first should turn on the heat.

1. I'd like to talk to *someone*. (whoever)
   The unknown person who knows how to run this program.

   _____

2. *Something* will be delivered to your desk today. (whatever)
   The unknown things you need to finish your report.

   _____

3. Please tell me *something*. (when)
   When your flight arrives.

   _____

4. Jim thought *something*. (that)
   We might be late for the meeting.

   _____

5. We think *something* is unlikely. (that)
   We will finish early tonight.

   _____

6. There is still one puzzling thing about *something*. (how)
   How did the man get your unlisted telephone number?

   _____

7. We cannot explain *something*. (how)
   How did the man get your unlisted telephone number?

   _____

8. I know *something*. (that)
   You will meet some very interesting people at the meeting.

   _____

9. We all hope *something*. (that)
   You will help us with that project.

   _____

10. I know *something*. (what)
    The thing I want to do after work today.

    _____

Lesson 11   *Subordination: Gerund and Infinitive Phrases*

A phrase is a group of related words that does *not* contain a subject and a verb in combination. Like the subordinate clause, the phrase is used in the sentence as a single part of speech. Many of the sentences that you have studied so far have used examples of the **prepositional phrase,** which consists of a preposition (see Lesson 2), a noun or a pronoun used as its object, and any modifiers of the object. Most prepositional phrases are used as adjectives or adverbs:

> Most of my friends live in the East.
> [The first phrase is used as an adjective to modify the pronoun *most;* the second is used as an adverb to modify the verb *live.*]

Much less commonly, a prepositional phrase is used as a noun:

> *Before lunch* is the best time for the meeting.
> [The phrase is the subject of the verb *is.*]

> She waved to us from *inside the phone booth.*
> [The phrase is the object of the preposition *from.*]

Another very important kind of phrase makes use of a verbal. A **verbal** is a word formed from a verb but used as a different part of speech. There are three kinds of verbals: the gerund, the participle, and the infinitive.

Gerunds

A **gerund** is a noun formed by using the -ing form of the verb either on the simple form (*studying*) or on an auxiliary (*having studied, being studied, having been studied*). As was suggested about noun clauses, you might think of the gerund phrase as the equivalent of a "something" that appears in any place in a sentence where a noun might appear: subject, direct object, renaming subjective complement, object of preposition, or (rarely) appositive.

> *Studying* demands most of my time. [Subject]
> I usually enjoy *studying.* [Direct object]
> My main activity is *studying.* [Renaming subjective complement]
> You won't pass the course without *studying.* [Object of preposition]
> Might I suggest to you another activity: *studying*? [Appositive]

These single-word gerund uses are uncomplicated. "He enjoys *studying*" and "He enjoys football" are alike in their structure; the only difference is that in one the direct object is a word formed from a verb and in the other it is a regular noun. Because they are formed from verbs, are "verbal nouns," gerunds can be followed by a direct object or a subjective complement. The following examples will help to clarify this important point.

101

He enjoys *walking in the snow.*
[The gerund has no complement. Compare "He walks in the snow."]

She enjoys building model airplanes.
[*Airplanes* is the direct object of the gerund *building.* Compare "She builds model airplanes."]

He enjoys *being helpful.* He enjoyed *being elected treasurer.*
[*Helpful* is the subjective complement of the gerund *being; treasurer* is the subjective complement of the passive gerund *being elected.* Compare "He is helpful." and "He was elected treasurer."]

She enjoyed *telling us the good news.*
[*Us* is the indirect object and *news* is the direct object of the gerund *telling.* Compare "She told us the good news."]

He enjoyed *making our vacation pleasant.*
[*Vacation* is the direct object and *pleasant* the objective complement of *vacation.* Compare "He made our vacation pleasant."]

Infinitives

An **infinitive** is a verbal consisting of the simple stem of the verb, generally preceded by *to* (*to* is called the sign of the infinitive). The infinitive uses auxiliaries to show tense and voice: *to study, to have studied, to be studying, to have been studying, to be studied, to have been studied.* An **infinitive phrase** consists of an infinitive plus its modifiers and/or complements. Infinitive units are used as nouns, as adjectives, and as adverbs:

To attend the party without an invitation would be tactless.
[The infinitive phrase is used as the subject of the sentence. Within the phrase, *party* is the direct object.]

It would be tactless *to attend the party without an invitation.*
[In this pattern the infinitive phrase is called a delayed subject; hence it serves a noun use. The signal word is *it;* although *it* stands in subject position, the infinitive phrase is the meaningful subject. Sometimes the *it* is in the direct object slot with the delayed infinitive phrase following an objective complement: I would consider it tactless *to attend the party without an invitation.* Compare a similar noun clause use in Lesson 10.]

I wanted *to give Charles another chance.*
[The infinitive phrase is the direct object of *wanted.* Within the phrase, *Charles* is the indirect object and *chance* the direct object of the infinitive. Compare "I gave Charles another chance."]

My plan is *to become an active precinct worker.*
[The infinitive phrase is used as a noun; it is a subjective complement that renames the subject plan. Within the phrase, *worker* is the subjective complement of the infinitive. Compare "I became an active precinct worker."]

The test *to be taken next Friday* is an important one.
[The infinitive phrase is used as an adjective modifying *test.*]

I am happy *to meet you.*
[The infinitive phrase is used as an adverb modifying the adjective *happy.*]

To be sure of a good seat, you should arrive early.
[The infinitive phrase is used as an adverb modifying *should arrive.*]

Infinitive phrases sometimes include their own subjects. (Notice that a pronoun used as the subject of an infinitive is in the objective case.)

> We wanted her to resign.
> We know him to be a good referee.

In a rather common sentence type, the subject of an infinitive is preceded by *for,* which in this case is considered part of the phrase.

> For us to leave now would be impolite.
> It's silly for you to feel neglected.

The infinitive without the *to* may form a phrase that is used as the direct object of such verbs as *let, help, make, see, hear,* and *watch*:

> The teacher let *us leave early.*
> Martha watched *her son score the winning touchdown.*

The infinitive without *to* is also sometimes used as the object of a preposition, such as *except, but,* or *besides*:

> He could do nothing except *resign gracefully.*

SUMMARY OF GERUND PHRASES; INFINITIVE PHRASES

Gerund Phrases

1. Forms: studying, having studied, being studied, having been studied.
2. Function: used as a noun within the larger unit.
3. Positions: subject, renaming subjective complement, direct object, object of preposition, and (rarely) appositive.

Infinitive Phrases

1. Forms: to study, to have studied, to be studying, to have been studying, to be studied, to have been studied. Some infinitive phrases have subjects (We wanted her to run for office).
2. Function: may be used as adjective (Here are the letters *to be mailed today*), as adverb (I am happy *to meet you*), or as noun (*To leave* now would be unwise).
3. Positions: subject (or delayed subject), direct object (or delayed direct object), renaming subjective complement, and (rarely) object of preposition.
4. Special structures:
   a. "For" sometimes introduces a phrase that has a subject.

   For you to criticize his work would be presumptuous.

   b. A phrase with a subject but without the marker "to" is often used as a direct object following one of these verbs: *let, help, make, see, hear, watch*:

   Mother let us mix the cookie dough.
   Ms. Jones heard the man threaten the cashier.

Supplement 1

In Lesson 6 you learned that in a direct question, an interrogative unit stands at the beginning of the sentence. Notice how this positioning can affect the internal makeup of a gerund phrase or an infinitive phrase:

How many natives did the missionaries succeed in *converting*?
[*Converting* is the gerund form of a transitive verb and therefore requires a direct object, in this case *natives*.]

Which car did you finally decide *to buy*?
[*Car* is the direct object of the infinitive *to buy*.]

NAME _____ SCORE _____

Directions: In the space at the left, copy one of the following codes to identify the use of the italicized gerund phrase:

S.	[Subject]	S.C.	[Subjective complement]
D.O.	[Direct object]	O.P.	[Object of preposition]

_____ 1. Tim does not enjoy *running the copier.*

_____ 2. You can make the work go faster by *recruiting someone as a helper.*

_____ 3. The last part of our workout was *running wind sprints.*

_____ 4. Last year Senator Bradford briefly considered *running for president.*

_____ 5. In *writing that paper,* you will find a computer quite useful.

_____ 6. *Climbing Mount Rainier* is John's lifelong dream.

_____ 7. "How could anyone get tired from *doing that little bit of work?*" asked Mary Lou with a smirk.

_____ 8. *Making coffee* is not part of the secretary's job description.

_____ 9. After I moved to town, my first concern was *finding a job.*

_____ 10. *Finding a job which fit my schedule* was a difficult task.

_____ 11. I did not especially enjoy *looking for a job.*

_____ 12. I finally found a job by *asking friends for help.*

_____ 13. My grandmother always enjoyed *telling scary stories to us kids.*

_____ 14. *Balancing my check book* has always been a serious problem for me.

_____ 15. Without *saying a word,* the entire group left the room.

_____ 16. "I don't like *swimming in the lake,*" said Marcy; "the water is too cold."

_____ 17. Most of the senators are in favor of *voting on that bill before the next recess.*

_____ 18. Janie's favorite sport is *teasing her little brother.*

_____ 19. Politicians discover important issues by *polling members of their voting districts.*

_____ 20. *Collecting stamps* was always one my grandfather's hobbies.

Directions: In the space at the left, write one of the following abbreviations to identify the use of the italicized infinitive phrase within the sentence:

N. [noun (subject, delayed subject, direct object, subjective complement, object of preposition)]	Adj. [adjective] Adv. [adverb]

———— 1. *To find the source of the creek,* you must walk upstream a great distance.

———— 2. Sofia did not make much of an effort *to find sources for her paper.*

———— 3. "Please help me *climb that tree,*" said little Alfie.

———— 4. When the lights went out, we couldn't do anything except *dismiss the class.*

———— 5. The college needs a way *to simplify the registration process.*

———— 6. It would be better *to start over from the beginning.*

———— 7. Mr. Carter should let *us turn in that paper tomorrow.*

———— 8. We should go to early registration *to get the best selection of classes.*

———— 9. Can you teach me *to read a spreadsheet?*

———— 10. When the wagon train got lost, the leader was trying *to find a new route through the mountains.*

———— 11. I did not hear *Tom make that statement.*

———— 12. You would be wise *to choose another subject for your paper.*

———— 13. The plan was *to follow Jim downtown to the movie.*

———— 14. I was certainly happy *to find that lost library book.*

———— 15. The route *to be taken on this morning's hike* is extremely difficult.

———— 16. *To have selected the other route* would have made things easier for all of us.

———— 17. We want *Alice to give us advice about that new course.*

———— 18. Tad watched *his little brother hit a home run in that game.*

———— 19. That new computer program has done nothing but *fail since we installed it.*

———— 20. The only thing left for the defeated army was *to beat a hasty retreat.*

Exercise 11   *Gerund Phrases; Infinitive Phrases*

NAME _____   SCORE _____

Directions: Each sentence contains one gerund phrase. Underline the gerund phrase. In the space at the left, write one of the following codes to show the use of the gerund phrase:

S.	Subject	D.O.	Direct object
S.C.	Subjective complement	O.P.	Object of preposition

_____ 1. You can review basic programming techniques by watching this new video.

_____ 2. Aunt Julia says that she will never forget watching the Rose Bowl Parade when she was a child.

_____ 3. I did not enjoy getting treatments for that cut on my foot.

_____ 4. The most difficult part of my research was finding an author who wrote clearly about the politics of that era.

_____ 5. Finding my way through that maze of conflicting statements was the most difficult part of my research.

_____ 6. Mr. Wilson says, "The only way out of that problem is electing a new mayor."

_____ 7. Should we try reviewing those options again before we make a decision?

_____ 8. Alicia's favorite summer activity involved working on a ranch out west.

_____ 9. Alicia's favorite summer activity was working on a ranch out west.

_____ 10. Working on a ranch out west was Alicia's favorite summer activity.

_____ 11. Eric thinks we could reduce our expenses by buying used textbooks.

_____ 12. Learning the multiplication tables was very difficult for me when I was young.

_____ 13. The city commission's most unpopular decision in recent months is charging a fee for admission to the city parks.

_____ 14. Our best hope for success on that project lies in finding a new leader for that work group.

_____ 15. We soon saw that following the directions to the camp would be very difficult.

_____ 16. Al does not enjoy working at a computer for more than fifteen minutes.

_____ 17. Working at a computer for an extended period of time is not Al's favorite activity.

_____ 18. Unfortunately, a large part of Al's income comes from working at a computer.

_____ 19. Replacing the tires on my car now rather than later seems like a good idea.

_____ 20. Joan found that little Italian restaurant by searching a computerized list of restaurants.

107

Directions: Each sentence contains one infinitive phrase (some with subjects). Underline each infinitive phrase. In the space at the left, write N. [noun], Adj. [adjective], or Adv. [adverb] to show the use of the infinitive phrase.

————— 1. The security guard ordered James to leave the property.

————— 2. To correct that mistake in the program took about a week's work.

————— 3. "Our objective in this class is to master the basics of first aid," said the instructor.

————— 4. "I am extremely happy to be with you this morning," said the politician with a smile.

————— 5. No one at the office knows any way to solve that particular problem.

————— 6. There's about two hours of work to do on that project before we finish it.

————— 7. Tommy said, "I think that I'm fast enough to finish ahead of Roy in tomorrow's race."

————— 8. Apparently, the college will not allow Alex to enroll in that course without taking a qualifying test.

————— 9. The new fitness standards make it more difficult for everyone to qualify for that trip down the river.

————— 10. Do you think that the teacher will let us leave a few minutes early tomorrow?

————— 11. It was relatively easy to find the house once we reached Centerville.

————— 12. Can the librarian help me to find a few more sources for my report?

————— 13. Yes, I saw Mario hit that home run in yesterday's game.

————— 14. Mr. Allison wants you to lead the group in that discussion.

————— 15. The car to be tested today is in the parking lot.

————— 16. If you give me a few minutes, I will be happy to help you with that problem.

————— 17. To borrow a book from that other library, fill out one of those request forms available at the librarian's desk.

————— 18. The security guard watched her walk out of the store with the stolen belts.

————— 19. After he slipped on the ice, Rob could do nothing except sit and laugh at himself.

————— 20. Our attempt to sneak into that game without tickets failed miserably when the police spotted us.

Directions: Combine the two sentences in a each item into a single sentence by resolving one sentence into a gerund phrase or an infinitive phrase to replace the italicized words in the other sentence.

1. At work Joe runs the copier.
   He does not enjoy *that job.*

   _____

2. Marlene wants to climb Mt. Rainier.
   This is her lifelong dream.

   _____

3. When I moved to town, I needed to find a job.
   Doing this was my first concern.

   _____

4. When I was in elementary school, I learned the multiplication tables.
   Doing this was difficult for me.

   _____

5. Jim did not say a word.
   Without *doing something,* Jim left the room.

   _____

6. The only possibility for the losing team was *something.*
   It would compete again next year.

   _____

7. If you give me a few minutes, I will be happy *to do something.*
   I will help you with that problem.

   _____

8. So that you can borrow a book from that other library.
   To do something, fill out one of those forms available at the librarian's desk.

   _____

9. Finding the house was easy.
   It was easy *to do something* once we reached Centerville.

   _____

10. Mastering the basics of first aid is our objective in this class.
    To do something is our objective in this class.

    _____

The participle is an adjective formed from a verb by adding *-ing* or *-ed* to the simple form of the verb. By itself, a participle works exactly as any one-word adjective works:

The injured bird clung to the *swaying* branch.
[The past participle *injured* modifies the noun *bird;* the present participle *swaying* modifies the noun *branch.*]

Participial Phrase

A **participial phrase** consists of a participle plus its modifiers and/or complements. As with the gerund phrase and the infinitive phrase, the kind of complement(s), if any, is determined by the kind of verb from which the participle is derived:

Handing me the receipt, the manager thanked me.
[The participial phrase modifies the noun *manager.* Within the phrase, *me* is an indirect object and *receipt* is a direct object.]

The taxi driver, *being a war veteran,* signed the petition.
[The participial phrase modifies the noun *taxi driver.* Within the phrase, *veteran* is a subjective complement.]

Calling the bomb threat a hoax, the authorities did nothing.
[The participial phrase modifies the noun *authorities.* Within the phrase, *threat* is a direct object and *hoax* is an objective complement.]

The similarity between an adjective clause and a participial phrase is obvious:

A man grabbed the microphone. The man [*or* He] was wearing a black mask.
[Two independent clauses.]

A man *who was wearing a black mask* grabbed the microphone.
[Adjective clause. *Mask is* a direct object of the verb.]

A man *wearing a black mask* grabbed the microphone.
[Participial phrase. *Mask* is a direct object of the participle.]

Jo's parents left the concert early. They found the music uncomfortably loud.
[Two independent clauses.]

Jo's parents, *who found the music uncomfortably loud,* left the concert early.
[Adjective clause. *Music* is a direct object and *loud* an objective complement of the verb.]

Jo's parents, *finding the music uncomfortably loud,* left the concert early.
[Participial phrase. *Music* is a direct object and *loud* an objective complement of the participle.]

These two examples point out another similarity: Like the adjective clause, the participial phrase can be either restrictive or nonrestrictive. The phrase in the first example identifies

111

the man; it is restrictive and is not set off by commas. The phrase in the second example is not needed to identify parents; it requires commas because it is nonrestrictive.

Like adjective clauses, participial phrases must be very close to the noun they modify. Adjective clauses must follow the noun they modify. Restrictive (identifying) participial phrases normally follow the noun they modify, as in the sentence, "A man wearing a black mask . . .". But the nonrestrictive participial phrase, unlike the nonrestrictive adjective clause it closely resembles, can move into another position in the sentence. Observe the positions of the participial phrase in the following sentences:

Steve, having passed the test with flying colors, decided to celebrate.
Having passed the test with flying colors, Steve decided to celebrate.

Occasionally, the participial phrase can be moved to the end of the clause:

Steve decided to celebrate, having passed the test with flying colors.
[In moving the phrase to this position, you must take care that no other nouns come between the noun and its modifier to confuse the reader.]

Because a participle is an adjective formed from a verb and thus suggests an action, the participial phrase can be used to relieve the monotony of a series of short, independent clauses:

Pam wanted desperately to hear the rock concert, but she was temporarily short of funds, and she knew that her cousin Alice had an extra ticket, and so she decided to call her. [Four independent clauses]

Wanting desperately to hear the rock concert but being temporarily short of funds, Pam decided to call her cousin Alice, knowing that she had an extra ticket. [One independent clause and three participial phrases]

Jensen stood at home plate. He waggled his bat. He eyed the pitcher coldly. He took a mighty swing at the first pitch. He hit the ball out of the park. [Five independent clauses]

Standing at home plate, waggling his bat and eyeing the pitcher coldly, Jensen took a mighty swing at the first pitch, hitting the ball out of the park. [One independent clause and four participial phrases]

Absolute Phrase

The **absolute phrase** is a special kind of phrase, different from the standard participial phrase in both form and function. Within the absolute phrase, the participle follows a noun or a pronoun that is part of the phrase. The phrase adds to the meaning of the whole sentence, but it does not directly modify any noun or pronoun in the sentence. The absolute phrase is a versatile structure capable of many variations and widely used in modern prose writing to point out subtle relationships underlying the ideas within a sentence:

All things being equal, Mary should easily win the race.

The storm having passed, the ball game resumed.

The police recovered eight of the paintings, *three of them badly damaged.*

The mob reached the palace gates, *the leader (being) a burly, red-haired sailor.*
[Occasionally an absolute phrase having a noun plus a complement appears with the participle unexpressed.]

A special kind of phrase using *with* to introduce one of these absolute phrases can add subtle modifying and narrative coloring to a sentence:

> With the band playing and the crowd applauding furiously, Jim Kinman was obviously uncomfortable as he stood on the stage.

> They held the funeral on the second day, with the town coming to look at Miss Emily beneath a mass of bought flowers, with the crayon face of her father musing profoundly above the bier. . . . (W. Faulkner)

> But we can't possibly have a garden party with a dead man just outside the front gate. (K. Mansfield)

> The face was a curious mixture of sensibility, *with some elements very hard and others very pretty*—perhaps it was in the mouth. (K. A. Porter)

Notice that the *with* in this construction is quite unlike *with* in its common prepositional use:

> The acquitted woman left the courtroom *with her* lawyer.

> The acquitted woman left the courtroom *with her head held high.*

SUMMARY OF PARTICIPIAL PHRASES; ABSOLUTE PHRASES

Participial Phrases

1. Forms: *studying, studied, having studied, being studied, having been studied, having been studying.*
2. Function: to modify a noun or pronoun. Those that *identify* the noun or pronoun are restrictive and require no punctuation; others are nonrestrictive and are set off by commas.
3. Position: If restrictive, the phrase always follows the word it modifies. Nonrestrictive phrases may stand after the noun, at the beginning of the sentence, and occasionally at the end of the sentence.

Absolute Phrases

1. Form: a noun or pronoun followed by a participle.

   The crops having failed, Grandfather sold the farm.

2. Function: does not modify a word or fill a noun "slot."
3. Position: at the beginning, in the interior, or at the end of the larger unit; it is always set off by commas.
4. Special structures:
   a. The phrase sometimes begins with the word *with*.

   With its supply of ammunition exhausted, the garrison surrendered.

   b. The participle *being* is sometimes unexpressed.

   Its chairman [being] a retired military person, the committee is well disciplined.

NAME _____   SCORE _____

Directions: The italicized unit in each sentence is either a participial phrase or an absolute phrase. If the unit is a participial phrase, copy in the space at the left the noun or pronoun the phrase modifies. If the phrase is an absolute phrase, leave the space blank.

_____ 1. *The term having ended,* Julie began to look for a summer job.

_____ 2. Mike, *knowing the roads very well,* was able to give me very clear instructions to the construction site.

_____ 3. *Parked in the outdoor lot,* all the cars were damaged by the hailstorm.

_____ 4. Payments *made after the closing date* will appear on next month's statement.

_____ 5. "We can't possibly have a good time *with the baby crying so much,"* whined Jane plaintively.

_____ 6. *Having slept a little late,* Jan was forced to rush to her first class.

_____ 7. *Her alarm clock having gone off a little late,* Jan was forced to rush to her first class.

_____ 8. *With their enthusiasm newly rekindled,* the political volunteers worked hard to get out the vote for their candidate.

_____ 9. *With their gloves oiled and their spiked shoes shined,* thirty women reported for the first day of softball practice.

_____ 10. "Anyone *arriving late for the first meeting* will be fined," said the coach.

_____ 11. *The repairs on her car completed,* Rita paid the bill and drove happily away.

_____ 12. Yesterday Mark sat for hours in the library, *working diligently on his research paper.*

_____ 13. *With his research paper progressing nicely,* Mark decided to go out for a sandwich.

_____ 14. "Funds *deposited after 2:00 P.M.* will be credited to your account on the next business day," says the bank's statement.

115

_____ 15. Mr. Miller, *trying desperately to locate a rental car,* spent almost an hour on the telephone.

_____ 16. *With the polls closing in about an hour,* the results of the election should begin to trickle in about two hours from now.

_____ 17. *Having spent an hour arguing unsuccessfully with the service manager,* Jennifer left the shop in a huff.

_____ 18. All appears lost for our baseball team, *its only hope a rookie pitcher with a high ERA.*

_____ 19. The police want a list of all the numbers *called from our phone in the last 24 hours.*

_____ 20. *Winnie having toured Europe several times,* we asked for her advice on our upcoming trip.

_____ 21. Arnie, *desperately needing a good grade on the next test,* spent the entire weekend hard at work on his notes.

_____ 22. The man *standing just inside the door* is the person who reports on the stock market for the local paper.

_____ 23. *With the wind rapidly dying,* the sailors plotted the shortest course for home.

_____ 24. I found my lost textbook *hidden under a pile of dirty clothes in the corner of my room.*

_____ 25. *Having traveled extensively in Europe last year,* Winnie proved to be a valuable source of information about our trip.

_____ 26. *My paper successfully completed,* I slept contentedly until eleven o'clock Saturday morning.

_____ 27. *With the clouds building rapidly in the west,* we decided to move the buffet inside before the rains began.

_____ 28. *Warily watching the dark clouds in the west,* Barbara suggested that we should move the buffet inside.

_____ 29. *All the others having arrived much earlier,* we finally reached the hotel well after midnight.

_____ 30. *Arriving quite early in the evening,* the rest of our party was settled at the hotel by the time we arrived.

Exercise 12   *Participial Phrases; Absolute Phrases*

NAME _____   SCORE _____

Directions: Each of the following sentences contains one participial phrase or one absolute phrase. Underline these phrases. If the phrase is a participial phrase, copy in the space at the left the noun or pronoun the phrase modifies. If the phrase is an absolute phrase, leave the space blank.

_____ 1. With my paper due tomorrow, I began to work very hard shortly after dinner.

_____ 2. Having just finished her workout, Sandra went to the refrigerator for a cold drink.

_____ 3. Everyone holding a reserved seat ticket must be admitted before the gates close.

_____ 4. Out of the corner of her eye, Jan saw a car coming into the intersection.

_____ 5. Coming into the intersection, Jan saw a car out of the corner of her eye.

_____ 6. That jacket is very old, its sleeves all tattered and torn.

_____ 7. Rising quickly to their feet, the people in the audience gave the speaker a round of applause.

_____ 8. Jim, his clothes soaked from the heavy rain, walked slowly into the room.

_____ 9. Anyone needing a ride to the next meeting should go to the lobby immediately.

_____ 10. Having fallen seriously behind our schedule, we decided to work overtime for a few nights.

_____ 11. With the snow building up rapidly on the highway, the boys decided to stay overnight at the hotel.

_____ 12. Feeling hopelessly lost, Roberta sat down under a tree to rest and check her map.

_____ 13. The friends sat on the dock laughing and joking as the sun set over the water.

_____ 14. We were finally ready to leave for the day, the last of the data having been entered in the computer.

117

_____ 15. Feeling elated because exam week had finally ended, we left for home as soon as we had packed the car.

_____ 16. At 6:15 P.M. we locked the office door, all the work for the day finally completed.

_____ 17. Working line by line through my checkbook, I finally found the error that produced the overdraft.

_____ 18. The young woman, juggling a briefcase, a pager, and a cellular phone, struggled into her car and drove away.

_____ 19. The young woman, her hands filled with a briefcase, a pager, and a cellular phone, struggled into her car.

_____ 20. Charlie's uncle wandered around for years, always searching for a quiet place to live.

_____ 21. Anyone thinking of a career in accounting will want to meet Mr. Ackerman.

_____ 22. The Senate having passed the bill, it was sent to the President for his signature.

_____ 23. With repairs to the sidewalk completed, we were able to leave the building by the main entrance.

_____ 24. Waiting impatiently for the last student to finish, the teacher sat at the front desk and filed her nails.

_____ 25. The policeman quickly wrote the parking ticket, ignoring the man who was waving at him from down the street.

_____ 26. Several people approached the desk, two of them exceptionally angry about something.

_____ 27. The group, with three members limping badly, walked slowly into camp.

_____ 28. Suffering from bruises and blisters, the three boys walked slowly into camp.

_____ 29. All the team members ran onto the field, excited by the surprising victory.

_____ 30. The old car sat forlornly in the garage, its windows broken and its body covered with dents.

Exercise 12A

Verbal Phrases; Complements in Phrases

NAME _____ SCORE _____

Directions: In the first space at the left, write one of the following letters to identify the italicized phrase:

        G   [gerund phrase]   I   [infinitive phrase]
        P   [participial phrase]   A   [absolute phrase]

In the second space, write one of the following abbreviations to identify the complement printed in boldfaced type within the phrase:

        S.C.   [subjective complement]   I.O.   [indirect object]
        D.O.   [direct object]   O.C.   [objective complement]

_____ 1. My mother considered *painting the house dark* **green.**

_____
_____ 2. *Having won the* **lottery** *last month,* my Uncle Joseph moved to the French Riviera.

_____
_____ 3. The plumber worked desperately *to stop the* **leak,** but, in spite of all her efforts, she could only slow it a little bit.

_____
_____ 4. Jim and Manny, *finding no* **jobs** *available in town,* went to work on a farm ten miles out in the country.

_____
_____ 5. *To make up the* **course** *she failed in the fall term,* Esther was forced to enroll for the summer term.

_____
_____ 6. People who know Mr. Rollins well have often accused him of *being too* **generous** *to his family.*

_____
_____ 7. We are grateful to Joyce for *tutoring* **us** *when we fell behind in that history course.*

_____
_____ 8. *With three members* **unwilling** *to meet on such short notice,* the chair rescheduled the meeting for next Thursday.

_____
_____ 9. *Having told* **us** *about his low grade in a psychology course,* Art spoke eagerly of his desire to become an engineer.

_____
_____ 10. You could easily find that information by *searching the* **Internet** *for a few minutes.*

_____
_____ 11. We were forced to look for another route, *the road to Circle City having sustained severe* **damage** *during the flood.*

———— 12. *With all the fans standing **silent,*** Johnson trotted onto the field to attempt a
————   field goal.

———— 13. Wilma, *being the most **experienced*** with that particular program, is often
————   called on to solve problems for the other operators.

———— 14. Our baseball team rarely seems *to generate that little bit of extra **effort** which
————   produces victory.*

———— 15. *Finding that last **source*** simplified my work on that paper.
————

———— 16. *Having lost the **light,*** the photographers put up their cameras and left for
————   home.

———— 17. *The chess match having been declared a **draw,*** the players agreed to play again
————   the next day.

———— 18. How did we manage *to waste so much **time*** while we were in the library
————   yesterday?

———— 19. Despite her hard work, Mrs. Martin succeeded only in *making the class more
————   **confused** about debits and credits.*

———— 20. Did you actually see *Alex give **Jane** that message?*
————

Directions: Combine the two sentences in each item into a single sentence by converting the second sentence into a participial phrase or an absolute phrase.

1. Mr. Jackson recognized the song immediately.
   He knows the score of that musical by heart.

   _____

2. Joe stood silently on the path.
   His lecture notes were blowing merrily across the lawn.

   _____

3. The soldier stood rigidly at attention.
   His eyes were fixed firmly on the flag.

   _____

4. James worked very hard on the lawn today.
   He raked up all the leaves and left them in huge piles.

   _____

5. Alice searched everywhere for her lost watch.
   She looked in every drawer and under all the furniture.

   _____

6. For a few minutes I watched a man.
   He walked slowly down the road toward the house.

   _____

7. Some of the men stood up.
   They gathered their papers and left the room.

   _____

8. The entire team left on the bus yesterday.
   Some members were sleeping and others were studying for exams.

   _____

9. The project is finished.
   We all left the office.

   _____

10. Martin ran down the street.
    He called out the name of his lost dog.

    _____

Sentence Building

Lessons, Practice Sheets, and Exercises

Lesson 13   *Completeness*

To be complete, a sentence must have two vital qualities:

1. It must contain a subject and a verb.

2. It must be able to stand alone as an independent unit.

A group of words without both a subject and a verb cannot be a complete sentence. A group of words containing both a subject and a verb (a clause) but opening with a subordinating conjunction cannot be a complete sentence. The subordinating conjunction makes the clause dependent instead of independent.

Sentence Fragments

Even if a group of words is punctuated like a sentence, it is not a complete sentence unless it contains a subject and a verb, and it can stand alone, independent of other clauses. A word group without these two qualities is an incomplete sentence, or **sentence fragment.** The mistake of punctuation that creates a sentence fragment is called a **period fault.** You should learn to avoid using fragments in your writing. Sentence fragments almost always fit one of the following patterns:

1. A subordinate clause standing as a sentence. (But remember that *and, but, for, or,* and *nor* do not subordinate. A clause introduced by one of these words may stand as a sentence.)

   Fragments: The clerk finally let us see the contract. *Although she clearly hated to reveal its contents.*
   Bob tried to start the old lawn mower. *Which never seemed to work properly for him.*

2. A verbal phrase punctuated as a sentence:

   Fragments: The delegates agreed on a compromise wage scale. *Realizing that the strike could not go on indefinitely.*
   Nell had ordered her tickets a month ago. *To be sure of getting good seats.*

123

3. A noun followed by a phrase or a subordinate clause but lacking a main verb:

> Fragments: The committee should include Ms. Jones. *A tireless worker with many constructive ideas.*
>
> The mayor asked Bentley to take the job. *Bentley being the only available person with field experience.*
>
> The coach thinks our prospects are good. *A chance, perhaps, to win back the conference championship.*
>
> Junior will require a special kind of tutor. *Someone who will realize how sensitive the child really is.*

Usually a close reading of anything you have written will reveal sentence fragments so that you can correct them. You can improve your skill at identifying fragments by using the following strategy: When you check what you have written, read the sentences in a paragraph in reverse order. Start with your last sentence and work back to your first. This process, by breaking the tie between a fragment and the sentence that it depends on, makes any grammatically incomplete sentence stand out.

Correcting Sentence Fragments

When you have discovered a fragment in your writing, any one of several possible corrections is easy to make.

- You can attach the fragment to the preceding sentence by doing away with the fragment's capital letter and supplying the right punctuation.
- You can change the fragment to a subordinate clause and attach it to the appropriate main clause by means of the right connective.
- You can change the fragment to an independent clause by supplying a subject or a verb or both. Consider the following corrected sentences.

> The clerk finally let us see the contract, *although she clearly hated to reveal its contents.*
>
> Bob tried to start the old lawn mower, *which never seemed to work properly for him.*
>
> The delegates agreed on a compromise wage scale *because they realized that the strike could not go on indefinitely.*
>
> *To be sure of getting good seats,* Nell had ordered her tickets a month ago.
>
> The committee should include Ms. Jones, *a tireless worker with many constructive ideas.*
>
> The mayor asked Bentley to take the job, *Bentley being the only available person with field experience.*
>
> The coach thinks our prospects are good; *we have a chance, perhaps, to win back the league championship.*
>
> Junior will require a special kind of tutor. *He or she must be someone who will realize how sensitive the child really is.*

A few types of word groups, although lacking a complete subject-verb combination, are not objectionable fragments. They are accepted as legitimate language patterns. These are:

1. **Commands,** in which the subject *you* is understood:

   Please be seated. Put your name on a slip of paper. Pass the papers to the left aisle.

2. **Exclamations:**

   What excitement! Only two minutes to go! Good Heavens, not a fumble? How terrible!

3. **Bits of dialogue:**

   "New car?" she asked. "Had it long?"
   "Picked it up last week," he replied.

4. **Occasional transitions between units of thought:**

   On with the story.
   And now to conclude.

You have very likely observed in your reading that experienced writers sometimes use sentence fragments, especially in narrative and descriptive writing. But they are skilled workers who know how to use fragments to achieve particular stylistic effects. You should first master the fundamental forms of the sentence. Once you have learned to write clear, correct sentences without faltering, there will be plenty of time for experimenting.

NAME _____ SCORE _____

Directions: Study these word groups for completeness. In the space at the left, write S if the word group is a grammatically complete sentence. Write F if the word group is a fragment.

_____ 1. But they did come, and we were very glad to see them.

_____ 2. A worker who never fails to give her very best to the job at hand.

_____ 3. A good idea, perhaps, but an idea that might confuse some people.

_____ 4. Use a socket wrench to loosen that bolt.

_____ 5. Because we weren't actually trying to confuse you.

_____ 6. But he didn't realize the importance of that one little fact.

_____ 7. Hand over that water pistol right now, my young friend.

_____ 8. Although the desserts looked extremely appetizing because they had been provided by a well-known catering company.

_____ 9. Running down the hallway came a man with a desperate look on his face.

_____ 10. Wow! What a brilliant save!

_____ 11. Riding a bike down that steep mountain path, an idea filled with potential danger.

_____ 12. Riding a bike down that steep mountain path tantalized all of us that entire summer.

_____ 13. To ride a bike down that steep mountain path, a thought that challenged each one of us all summer long.

_____ 14. Traveling, owning a boat, running her own company—those were the goals that motivated Maryanne when she was in college.

_____ 15. Try to put this block under the corner of the chest when I lift it with this bar.

_____ 16. A person whose entire life had been devoted to becoming a concert pianist.

———— 17. But an inexperienced worker should never have attempted that project.

———— 18. A virus seeming to move unmolested through all my computer files.

———— 19. Surely those skills will be useful later on in your career.

———— 20. That's not a very good idea.

———— 21. Oh, my, do I ever need a nap.

———— 22. Coming over that last hill, the bike left the ground in a jump so high that my heart went into my throat.

———— 23. Coming over that last hill gave me a thrill I won't soon forget.

———— 24. Coming over that hill, a thrill I won't soon forget.

———— 25. Definitely the only person in this office who might be able to solve that problem.

———— 26. Neither of whom was willing to offer any advice.

———— 27. Neither of them was willing to offer any advice.

———— 28. Only a few players work hard enough to satisfy the new coach.

———— 29. Only a few players who work hard enough to satisfy the new coach.

———— 30. Only a few players who work hard enough to satisfy the new coach will return from last year's team.

NAME _____ SCORE _____

Directions: Correct the following sentence fragments by changing punctuation, adding either a subject or a verb, or providing a main clause for the fragment.

1. A worker who never fails to give her very best to the job at hand.

   _____

2. A good idea, perhaps, but an idea that might confuse some people.

   _____

3. Because we weren't actually trying to confuse you.

   _____

4. Although the desserts looked extremely appetizing because they had been provided by a well-known catering company.

   _____

5. Riding a bike down that steep mountain path, an idea filled with potential danger.

   _____

6. To ride a bike down that steep mountain path, a thought that challenged each one of us all summer long.

   _____

7. A person whose entire life had been devoted to becoming a concert pianist.

   _____

8. A virus seeming to move unmolested through all my computer files.

   _____

9. Coming over that hill, a thrill I won't soon forget.

   _____

10. Definitely the only person in this office who might be able to solve that problem.

    _____

11. Neither of whom was willing to offer any advice.

_____

12. Only a few players who work hard enough to satisfy the new coach.

_____

13. The ideal job, all inside work with no heavy lifting.

_____

14. A job that offered great challenges but little financial reward.

_____

15. With only the hard working, dedicated students still in the class.

_____

16. Unless we can find someone to take Jim's place immediately.

_____

17. Only a person with a strong sense of dedication, a person who is willing to work hard and make sacrifices.

_____

18. Jackson being the only candidate in the race who seems even remotely qualified for the office.

_____

19. Standing in the middle of the cornfield, a scarecrow dressed in what was left of an old tuxedo.

_____

20. If we had only taken that computer in for repairs before it failed completely.

_____

Exercise 13A

Completeness

NAME _____ SCORE _____

Directions: Each numbered unit consists of a sentence followed by a fragment. In the space provided, rewrite enough of the material to show how you would correct the error, by either attaching the fragment, properly punctuated, to the sentence, or by recasting the fragment so that it becomes a complete sentence.

1. Electing a president was a difficult task. Finally causing a serious split in the organization.

   _____

2. Jane left early for the weekend. Thinking that she could not make any more progress on her paper.

   _____

3. "I need to buy a new car. A car that will start every morning even when the weather is very cold," said Al.

   _____

4. We need to do something decisive here. Probably either to hire a consultant for help or to cancel the project entirely.

   _____

5. A student who is rarely on time for class and only occasionally prepared. Kim is having difficulty earning passing grades.

   _____

6. To get a head start on the crowd going to the game. Tom and Joe left the dorm early and parked their car near the stadium.

   _____

7. We have a new family living next to us now. The family having recently moved here from Portland.

   _____

8. I looked for sources for my paper in several major libraries. By using the Internet and two new search engines.

   _____

9. My older brother just bought a car that can reach 110 MPH. The speed limit on nearby highways having been raised to 70 MPH.

   _____

10. The college president declared next Tuesday a holiday. The college volleyball team having won the conference championship recently.

   _____

11. The fraternity brothers want to open a pizza-delivery service on campus. A business venture opposed by the college administration.

   _____

12. No one in my class passed the last test. The test being very long and quite confusing.

   _____

13. The city's mayor is opposed to the new stadium. The stadium being a part of the college's expansion program.

   _____

14. Jan's car failed to pass inspection yesterday. The emissions-control system having been disabled by the previous owner.

   _____

15. With no short books available from the library. Tim was forced to read a very long book for his book report.

   _____

16. The two workers had dug up half our front yard before noon. Trying to find the sewer pipe clean-out.

   _____

17. A woman who has a great reputation as a surgeon. Mayra's aunt went to speak at the local high school's Career Day.

   _____

18. A strange sight greeted us when we opened the door to the house. Five strangers stretched out asleep on the living room floor.

   _____

19. Aunt Lillian recently returned to college to finish her degree. The kind of person my family calls a late-bloomer.

   _____

20. Because she wanted desperately to go to the Blues Festival. Wanda accepted a date with a boy she did not actually like.

   _____

Lesson 14 *Misplaced Modifiers; Dangling Modifiers*

Proper arrangement of the parts of your sentence will help make your meaning clear. Ordinarily the main parts—the subjects, the verbs, the complements—cause no problems. Modifying words and phrases and subordinate clauses can cause problems if they are not located carefully. Here we shall consider five possible trouble spots in the placing of modifiers.

1. Although we sometimes use a rather loose placement for some common adverbs, such as *only, nearly, almost,* and *hardly,* we can write precise sentences only when such adverbs are placed close to the words they modify:

Loose:	This will *only* take five minutes.
	Jill *nearly* saw ninety movies last year.
Better:	This will take *only* five minutes.
	Jill saw *nearly* ninety movies last year.

2. Words and phrases that attach themselves to the wrong word can confuse the reader:

Loose:	I wish every person in this class could know the man I'm going to talk about *personally.*
Better:	I wish every person in this class could know *personally* the man I'm going to talk about.
Loose:	It was reported that the Italian premier had died *on the eight o'clock newscast.*
Better:	*On the eight o'clock newscast,* it was reported that the Italian premier had died.
Loose:	The police department will be notified of all reported obscene phone calls *by the telephone company.*
Better:	The police department will be notified *by the telephone company* of all reported obscene phone calls.

3. The **squinting modifier** is one that is placed between two units, either of which it could modify:

Loose:	Students who can already type *normally* are put into an advanced class.
Better:	Students who can already type are *normally* put into an advanced class.
Loose:	He said *after the dinner* some color slides would be shown.
Better:	He said some color slides would be shown *after the dinner.*

4. The **split infinitive** results from the placing of an adverbial modifier between the *to* and the root verb of an infinitive. Although greatly overemphasized by some as an error, the split infinitive, particularly with a modifier consisting of more than one word, is usually avoided by careful writers:

Loose:	Dad likes to *once in a while* plan and cook a dinner.
Better:	*Once in a while,* Dad likes to plan and cook a dinner.

5. The **correlatives** *both . . . and, not only . . . but also, either . . . or,* and *neither . . . nor* are used in pairs and should be placed immediately before the parallel units that they connect:

Loose: We sent invitations *both* to Webster and Jenkins.
Better: *We sent invitations to both Webster and Jenkins.*
           [*The parallel words are Webster and Jenkins.*]

Loose: This woman *not only* can get along with young people *but also* with their parents.
Better: This woman can get along *not only* with young people *but also* with their parents

Loose: You must *either* promise me that you will come *or* send a substitute.
Better: You must promise me that you will *either come or* send a substitute.

Dangling Modifiers

Any modifying phrase that does not attach itself clearly to the word it is supposed to modify can create a confusing sentence. Participial phrases are especially apt to float free in a sentence in a way that does not form a clear relationship between the word and the modifying phrase.

> Stepping into the boat, my camera fell into the water.

This sentence contains a phrase and a main clause, but the phrase does not actually modify any word in the main clause. The sentence is made up of two short sentences:

> I stepped into the boat.
> My camera fell into the water.

We can make the two sentences a compound sentence:

> I stepped into the boat, and my camera fell into the water.

Or make the first clause an introductory adverbial element:

> As I stepped into the boat, my camera fell into the water.

But we can't convert the first sentence into a participial phrase because the only noun the phrase could modify is camera, and the camera did not step into the boat. The sentence, if read literally, becomes nonsense. It contains a dangling modifier, a dangling participial phrase. We could rework the sentence by changing the subject of the second clause in a way that allows the participial phrase to modify the new subject:

> Stepping into the boat, I dropped my camera into the water.

Because the person who dropped the camera and the person stepping into the boat are the same, *I*, the sentence is now correct.

Gerund Phrases and Infinitive Phrases

Gerund phrases and infinitive phrases can also cause problems when they are randomly inserted into sentences:

> After studying all morning, a nap was Mary's only goal for the afternoon.

The intended meaning of the sentence is clear, but the literal meaning is that the nap studied all morning; the phrase attaches itself to the first available noun, in this case, a noun that produces a nonsense statement.

> To qualify for that job, good typing skills are a necessity.

Again, the intended meaning is clear, but the literal meaning is nonsense: good typing skills are not qualifying for that job; a person with good typing skills is qualifying for that job.

Correcting Danglers

The easiest way to correct a dangler is to supply the word that the phrase should modify and to place the phrase next to that word. Another way is to change the dangling phrase to a subordinate clause with a subject and verb expressed.

1. The most common type of dangler is the participial phrase beginning a sentence:

Dangler:	*Stepping into the boat,* my camera dropped into the water.
	[Was the camera stepping into the boat? Of course not. The trouble here is that the word that the phrase should modify is not expressed in the sentence.]
Dangler:	*Burned to a cinder,* I could not eat the toast.
	[The sentence sounds as if I were burned to a cinder. The word that the dangler should modify is *toast*, but this word is too far from the phrase immediately associated with it.]
Better:	Stepping into the boat, I dropped my camera into the water.
	As I was stepping into the boat, my camera dropped into the water.
	Burned to a cinder, the toast could not be eaten.
	I could not eat the toast because it was burned to a cinder.

2. Another type of dangler is the gerund that follows a preposition. The phrase that contains the verbal must have a word to refer to, and that word must be close enough to the phrase so that the reader does not associate the phrase with the wrong word:

Dangler:	Before *making a final decision,* other cars should be driven.
	[Are the other cars making a final decision? That is not what is meant, and yet that is what the sentence states.]
	On graduating from high school, my father let me work in his office.
	[The sentence says that your father let you work in his office when **he**, not you, graduated from high school.]
	Since *breaking my leg,* my neighbors have helped with my farm chores.
	[A logical sentence only if the neighbors broke your leg.]

Better: Before making a final decision, drive other cars.
Before you make a final decision, you should drive other cars.

On graduating from high school, I was given a chance to work in my father's office.
After I had graduated from high school, my father let me work in his office.

Since breaking my leg, I have been helped with my farm chores by my neighbors.
My neighbors have helped with my farm chores since I broke my leg.

3. One type of introductory elliptical clause (see Lesson 8) that must be used carefully is a "time" clause, usually introduced by *when* or *while*. The clause becomes a dangler if the understood subject of the adverb clause is different from the subject of the main clause. The reader wrongly assumes that both clauses have the same subject, and the result can be a ridiculous meaning that the writer never intended:

Dangler: *When ten years old,* my father sold the farm and moved to Dallas.
While weeding my vegetable garden, a garter snake startled me.

Better: When ten years old, I moved to Dallas after my father sold the farm.
When I was ten years old, my father sold the farm and we moved to Dallas.

While weeding my vegetable garden, I was startled by a garter snake.
While I was weeding my vegetable garden, a garter snake startled me.

4. You may occasionally have trouble with an introductory infinitive phrase. If the infinitive names a specific action, be sure that the word that the phrase attaches to names the logical doer of that action.

Dangler: *To enter the contest,* a box top must be sent with your slogan.

Better: To enter the contest, you must send a box top with your slogan.
If you want to enter the contest, a box top must be sent with your slogan.
When you enter the contest, send a box top with your slogan.

NAME _____ SCORE _____

Directions: From each of the following pairs of sentences select the one that is more precise and write its letter in the space. Be prepared to explain your choice.

_____ 1. A. I discovered that I had nearly two hours to wait for my plane.
　　　　　　 B. I discovered that I nearly had two hours to wait for my plane.

_____ 2. A. Mr. Roberts both said that he would send the package and call to verify its safe arrival.
　　　　　　 B. Mr. Roberts said that he would both send the package and call to verify its safe arrival.

_____ 3. A. Jack lost almost twenty pounds on that special diet.
　　　　　　 B. Jack almost lost twenty pounds on that special diet.

_____ 4. A. When their parents were out of town, the twins spent every day sleeping late and playing video games.
　　　　　　 B. The twins spent every day sleeping late when their parents were out of town and playing video games.

_____ 5. A. Yesterday's hike not only was long but also very rugged.
　　　　　　 B. Yesterday's hike was not only long but also very rugged.

_____ 6. A. The librarian said either that I must return the book or renew it for another week.
　　　　　　 B. The librarian said that I must either return the book or renew it for another week.

_____ 7. A. For weeks Jane had been reading every new romance novel.
　　　　　　 B. Jane had been reading every new romance novel for weeks.

_____ 8. A. Just sitting around and doing nothing is more tiring than working often.
　　　　　　 B. Just sitting around and doing nothing is often more tiring than working.

_____ 9. A. May had been sitting for only a moment when the bell rang.
　　　　　　 B. May had only been sitting for a moment when the bell rang.

_____ 10. A. All the people in the room were not interested in the report from the finance office.
　　　　　　 B. Not all the people in the room were interested in the report from the finance office.

Directions: In the space at the left, write either **A** or **B** to indicate the logical place for the modifier written in the parentheses at the beginning of the sentence.

———— 1. (either) When you pass the school building, you may **A** turn **B** left or right; turn right.

———— 2. (very early) "When I was a kid," said my grandmother, "I had to **A** get up **B** and walk to school."

———— 3. (with a big hug) Whenever I see him, my uncle always **A** greets me **B**.

———— 4. (almost) That hailstorm **A** killed **B** all Mom's petunias.

———— 5. (in the dust) Those fast runners **A** left the rest of us **B** almost immediately.

———— 6. (not only) We **A** have an exam **B** on Monday but also on Tuesday.

———— 7. (only) Although he had **A** been gone **B** three days, he returned to work today.

———— 8. (rapidly) Students who can't read **A** are **B** placed in a speed-reading course.

———— 9. (nearly) Yesterday Robert **A** read **B** 250 pages in that novel.

———— 10. (running down the street) **A** Martha hurried into a doorway to get out of the rain **B**.

———— 11. (on the evening news) Last night it was reported **A** that several people were delayed by the flash flood **B**.

———— 12. (hardly) "At my last class reunion, I **A** saw **B** anyone whose face I could remember," said Dad.

———— 13. (easily) I thought I would be able to **A** finish my report **B** by six o'clock tonight.

———— 14. (individually) The boss **A** talked to each member of that committee **B**.

———— 15. (both) First, the teacher gave instructions **A** about **B** essay and the multiple-choice parts of the test.

Exercise 14　　*Misplaced Modifiers*

NAME _____　　SCORE _____

Directions: In each of the following sentences there is a poorly positioned word or phrase. Rewrite each sentence to position the word or phrase more precisely.

1. Jack said, "It seems I have to always study very late on the night before a big test."
   _____
   _____

2. Only students who work can rapidly solve all these difficult problems within the time limit.
   _____
   _____

3. After the argument with Bobby, Maria almost bought him two pounds of chocolate candy.
   _____
   _____

4. "I want to talk to everyone who saw that movie in the morning," said the instructor.
   _____
   _____

5. Mark said, "I need to both sew a button on that blue shirt and to iron it before I can wear it to work."
   _____
   _____

6. If you can complete that preliminary test, you can probably successfully do the work in the advanced class.
   _____
   _____

7. I read that the president has left for Paris for a conference in the newspaper.
   _____
   _____

8. Since Alice's car failed to start regularly last semester, she often rode to class with Marcia.
   _____
   _____

9. Karen only saw two students whom she knows when she went through registration.
   _____
   _____

10. Linda told us shortly after lunch that we would be leaving for the field trip.
    _____
    _____

Directions: In the space at the left, write A or B to indicate the logical place for the modifier written in the parentheses at the beginning of the sentence.

_____ 1. (almost) Trying to get in shape, I've **A** gone to **B** every gym in town," said Tony.

_____ 2. (neither) That idea **A** has **B** careful development nor any support from the people working in that area.

_____ 3. (only) Marilyn is on a very limited diet; she **A** eats **B** fruits and a few vegetables.

_____ 4. (surely) We **A** need to **B** be more careful next time.

_____ 5. (with the mechanic) Nora needs to talk at length **A** before she goes to work **B**.

_____ 6. (at nine o'clock) Pedro has an appointment with his advisor **A** to talk about dropping that course **B**.

_____ 7. (personally) **A**, I don't think you will enjoy watching that movie about the bull fights **B**.

_____ 8. (both) We need to **A** show that report to **B** Jim and his boss before we go any further.

_____ 9. (not only) The limousine that picked us up at the airport **A** had **B** a stereo but also a small television in the back seat.

_____ 10. (carefully and slowly) My grandmother likes to **A** work through the crossword puzzle **B** every morning after breakfast.

_____ 11. (either) I think you should **A** ask **B** Mark or Albert to tutor you before that exam.

_____ 12. (clearly) "I **A** saw the thief **B** take the bracelet from the counter," said Penny.

_____ 13. (clearly) **A** Anyone who can speak **B** can read the announcements over the PA system.

_____ 14. (regularly) Those who smoke **A** are **B** asked to sit in the balcony at the theater.

_____ 15. (someday) **A** Jim wants to **B** visit Alaska and watch the Iditirod, a famous dog-sled race.

NAME _____ SCORE _____

Directions: One sentence in each pair contains a dangling modifier. In the space at the left, write the letter that identifies the correct sentence.

_____ 1. A. While cooking supper, the kitten sat on the floor and ate the scraps.
          B. While I was cooking supper, the kitten sat on the floor and ate the scraps.

_____ 2. A. Diving to the bottom of the pond, I found the sunglasses Matt lost yesterday lying in the mud.
          B. Diving to the bottom of the pond, the sunglasses Matt lost yesterday were lying in the mud.

_____ 3. A. Following those clear directions, there should be no problems in installing that program.
          B. Following those clear instructions, you should have no problems in installing that program.

_____ 4. A. Before choosing a college, visits to several campuses would be very helpful.
          B. Before choosing a college, you might find it helpful to visit several campuses.

_____ 5. A. While I was attending that class, my father helped me with the readings.
          B. While attending that class, my father helped me with the readings.

_____ 6. A. To fix that problem, the cover of the connection box must be removed first.
          B. To fix that problem, you must first remove the cover of the connection box.

_____ 7. A. Covered with dirt, Gina found her jacket in the driveway.
          B. Gina found her jacket, covered with dirt, in the driveway.

_____ 8. A. After leaving the house, I was caught in the rain about halfway down the block.
          B. After leaving the house, the rain caught me about halfway down the block.

_____ 9. A. Hiding under the blanket, I found the puppy with my new boat shoe in his mouth.
          B. I found the puppy hiding under the blanket with my new boat shoe in his mouth.

141

_____ 10. A. Having worked for two hours in the library, Callie found no usable sources for her paper.

      B. Having worked for two hours in the library, no usable sources for her paper were found by Callie.

_____ 11. A. While Will was walking down the road, a bolt of lightning hit a tree just ahead of him.

      B. While walking down the road, a bolt of lightning struck a tree just ahead of Will.

_____ 12. A. To register for a computer programming course, *Introduction to Data Processing* must be taken as a prerequisite.

      B. To register for a computer programming course, you must take *Introduction to Data Processing* as a prerequisite.

_____ 13. A. Before leaving for the summer, your apartment must be inspected by the manager.

      B. Before you leave for the summer, your apartment must be inspected by the manager.

_____ 14. A. Trying to find that new Italian restaurant, a puzzling series of one-way streets confused us.

      B. Trying to find that new Italian restaurant, we were confused by a puzzling series of one-way streets.

_____ 15. A. Waiting hungrily beneath the table, Diane gave the dog the scraps left from dinner.

      B. Diane gave the scraps left from dinner to the dog waiting hungrily beneath the table.

_____ 16. A. Watching the weather reports very carefully, we determined that tomorrow will probably not be a good day for sailing.

      B. Watching the weather reports very carefully, tomorrow will probably not be a good day for sailing.

_____ 17. A. While reading the evening news, the reporter made two silly grammatical errors.

      B. While reading the evening news, two silly grammatical errors were made by the reporter.

_____ 18. A. To protect that fragile vase, pack it carefully in shredded newspaper.

      B. To protect that fragile vase, shredded newspaper should be carefully packed around it.

_____ 19. A. Since moving to Arizona, I have found the weather far too hot for my taste.

      B. Since moving to Arizona, the weather has been far too hot for my taste.

_____ 20. A. After looking everywhere in the house, my wallet appeared in the glove compartment of my pickup.

      B. After looking everywhere in the house, I found my wallet in the glove compartment of my pickup.

Dangling Modifiers

Directions: Rewrite each of the following sentences twice:
    a. Change the dangling modifier to a complete clause with a subject and verb.
    b. Retain the phrase but begin the main clause with a word it can logically modify.

1. Looking everywhere in the library, the books I needed were not on the shelves.

    a. _____

    b. _____

2. Before buying that computer, its speed of operation should be carefully checked.

    a. _____

    b. _____

3. To make a long-distance call from this office, a calling-card number must be used.

    a. _____

    b. _____

4. While going to the movies last night, someone stole all Marv's chocolate chip cookies from his dorm room.

    a. _____

    b. _____

5. Looking down from the tall building, the extreme height made Ann a little dizzy.

    a. _____

    b. _____

6. Hurrying to catch the taxi, the folder with the report in it fell into a mud puddle.

    a. _____

    b. _____

7. To find that telephone number, long-distance information is your best source.

    a. _____

    b. _____

8. Before filing that report, every line must be checked for errors in arithmetic.

   a. _____

   b. _____

9. Playing hard in spite of the pain in her ankle, Jodie's valiant efforts inspired the rest of the players.

   a. _____

   b. _____

10. While walking along the edge of the pool, Hal's foot slipped and he fell headlong into the water.

   a. _____

   b. _____

Lesson 15 *Subordination*

Beginning writers sometimes string together too many short sentences, or they tie clauses together with conjunctions—and, but, or—that fail to establish precise relations between the clauses.

Poor: Sally usually attends each concert. She missed this one. She went to the airport to meet her cousin Ellen. Ellen was arriving from Atlanta.

I rode around town for three days, but I couldn't find a place to stay, and then I located this apartment, and so I am comfortable.

If you use the methods of creating and combining sentences that we have studied, you will make your writing more precise, more economical, and more meaningful:

Improved: Although Sally usually attends each concert, she missed this one because she went to the airport to meet her cousin Ellen, who was arriving from Atlanta.

After riding around town unsuccessfully for three days without finding a place to stay, I finally located this apartment, where I am comfortable.

Get in the habit of trying out the various methods of subordinating material. Notice in the following sentences how an idea can be expressed in a variety of ways:

Two Sentences:	The small car was inexpensive to drive. It had only four cylinders.
Compound Verb:	The small car had only four cylinders and was inexpensive to drive.
Compound Sentence:	The small car was inexpensive to drive, for it had only four cylinders.
Adverbial Clause:	Because the small car had only four cylinders, it was inexpensive to drive.
Adjective Clause:	The small car, which had only four cylinders, was inexpensive to drive.
Participial Phrase:	The small car, having only four cylinders, was inexpensive to drive.
	Having only four cylinders, the small car was inexpensive to drive.
	The small car was inexpensive to drive, having only four cylinders.
Absolute Phrase:	The small car having only four cylinders, it was inexpensive to drive.
Prepositional Phrase:	The small car with only four cylinders was inexpensive to drive.
Appositive:	The small car, a four-cylinder model, was inexpensive to drive.
Adjective Modifier:	The small four-cylinder car was inexpensive to drive.

Note that the use of subordination produces more than a pleasing surface texture in writing. It also makes a crucial contribution to meaning by eliminating uncertainty about what is most important in a message.

The management and union representatives announced an agreement. A strike had been threatened but was averted. The employees of Grantex Company reported for work today. They were relieved.

In that string of simple sentences there is no way of knowing which fact is most significant: The agreement? The avoidance of a strike? The workers' reporting for work? Their relief? Rewritten with proper subordination, the news reveals the writer's sense of significance:

> The relieved employees of Grantex Company reported for work today after the management and union representatives announced an agreement that averted a threatened strike.

The only independent clause in the sentence concerns the workers' return to work. That is the important message. A writer more interested in strikes and their effect on the general economy might report the event thus:

> The threatened strike was averted at Grantex Company when the management and union representatives announced an agreement, after which the relieved employees reported for work today.

A Note on Sentence Variety

Preceding lessons have demonstrated how subordinate clauses and phrases, by compressing material, help the writer avoid tiresome strings of independent clauses. You have also seen that certain subordinate units—adverbial clauses and participial phrases in particular—can be put in several places within the sentence, thus helping to prevent monotony in your sentences.

Another unit useful for achieving compression and variety is the appositive. (See Lesson 10.) As noun renamers, appositives closely resemble—they might be called the final reduction of—Pattern 2 clause and phrase modifiers of nouns:

> Ted could explain the trick to us. Ted [or He] is an amateur magician. [Two independent clauses]
>
> *Ted, who is an amateur magician,* could explain the trick to us. [Adjective clause]
>
> *Ted, being an amateur magician,* could explain the trick to us. [Participial phrase]
>
> Ted, *an amateur magician,* could explain the trick to us. [Appositive]

Although the usual position of appositives is immediately following the nouns they rename, many of them, like many nonrestrictive participial phrases, can precede the main noun (in which case we call them *pre-positional appositives*); sometimes they are effectively placed at the end of the clause:

> Lawyer Somers, *a master of wit and guile,* cajoles and browbeats in the courtroom.
>
> *A master of wit and guile,* Lawyer Somers cajoles and browbeats in the courtroom.
>
> Lawyer Somers cajoles and browbeats in the courtroom, *a master of wit and guile.*

As a final example of language tools for renaming and modifying nouns, study this tightly constructed sentence:

> One of the five largest towns in Roman England, home of King Arthur's legendary Round Table, seat of Alfred the Great, whose statue looks down its main street, early capital of England, and

victim of Cromwell's destructive forces, Winchester is an enchanting cathedral city in which layer after layer of history is visibly present.

Elisabeth Lambert Ortiz "Exploring Winchester,"
Gourmet, March 1978, p. 21

This sentence is made up of one independent clause, which includes an adjective clause, and five pre-positional appositives, the third of which contains an adjective clause. The statements underlying this sentence might be charted as follows:

Winchester is an enchanting cathedral city.
In [this city] which layer after layer of history is visibly present.
Winchester was one of the five largest towns in Roman England.
Winchester was the home of King Arthur's legendary Round Table.
Winchester was the seat of Alfred *the* Great.
[Alfred the Great's] whose statue looks down its main street.
Winchester was the early capital of England.
Winchester was the victim of Cromwell's destructive forces.

We see here that eight statements—enough to make up a paragraph of clear but unrelieved simple sentences—have been shortened into one complex sentence. The layering of appositives and adjective clauses produces compression, sentence variety, and proper emphasis.

NAME _____ SCORE _____

Directions: In each sentence you will find a subordinate unit in italics. In the space at the left of each sentence, write one of the following numbers to identify the italicized subordinate unit:

     1. Adverb clause   4. Gerund phrase   7. Infinitive phrase
     2. Adjective clause   5. Absolute phrase
     3. Participial phrase   6. Appositive

_____ 1. *To pass that test,* you will need to study chapters six and seven in the text.

_____ 2. Jim left class early *because he has an appointment with the coach.*

_____ 3. Alice has a brand new nephew, *whom she is going to visit this weekend.*

_____ 4. *The date for beginning the trip having been set,* we began to make hotel reservations.

_____ 5. *Having set the date for the beginning of the tour,* we began to make hotel reservations.

_____ 6. *By leaving the game a few minutes early,* we were able to miss the traffic jam outside the stadium.

_____ 7. *Unless you "bubble" in your student number,* your test cannot be scored by the machine.

_____ 8. Jane Albury, *the new treasurer,* will take over the club's accounts today.

_____ 9. *If I can't meet you for lunch tomorrow,* I will call you before eleven o'clock.

_____ 10. I last saw that silly dog *running across the yard with my newspaper in his mouth.*

_____ 11. *With the election clearly lost,* the unhappy politician made her concession speech early in the evening.

_____ 12. It would be quite tactless *to leave the concert hall before the end of the last number.*

_____ 13. The company needs to hire someone *who can straighten out that mess in the shipping department.*

_____ 14. *Reading that ancient philosopher's essay* is the hardest work I've done this term.

_____ 15. The Board of Trustees has asked Jim Redmond *to lead the next fundraising drive.*

Directions: Change the italicized sentence to the structure indicated in the parentheses and write the two sentences as one sentence.

1. *My entire family is coming to visit this weekend.* I am not planning to give any kind of party. (adverbial clause)

———————————————————————————————————

———————————————————————————————————

2. *My entire family is coming to visit this weekend.* I am planning to give a huge party. (adverbial clause)

———————————————————————————————————

———————————————————————————————————

3. *I wanted to watch an old movie on TV.* I stayed home last night. (participial phrase)

———————————————————————————————————

———————————————————————————————————

4. You can consult Hugh Johnson about your tennis elbow. *He is our athletic trainer.* (appositive)

———————————————————————————————————

———————————————————————————————————

5. You can consult Hugh Johnson about your tennis elbow. *He is our athletic trainer.* (adjective clause)

———————————————————————————————————

———————————————————————————————————

6. *Install air conditioning in your office.* It will increase your efficiency. (gerund phrase)

———————————————————————————————————

———————————————————————————————————

7. Install air conditioning in your office. *It will increase your efficiency.* (infinitive phrase)

———————————————————————————————————

———————————————————————————————————

8. *Jim washed his car.* He drove to the game. (preposition *after* plus gerund phrase)

———————————————————————————————————

———————————————————————————————————

9. *The last flight has been canceled.* Everyone in this room needs a new reservation. (absolute phrase)

———————————————————————————————————

———————————————————————————————————

10. *The last flight has been canceled.* Everyone in this room needs a new reservation. (adverbial clause)

———————————————————————————————————

———————————————————————————————————

NAME _____ SCORE _____

Directions: Rewrite each sentence by removing the coordinating conjunction and changing the italicized section to the construction indicated in the parenthesis.

1. *The last flight has been canceled,* and we need to find another flight to Cleveland. (adverbial clause)

   _____

   _____

2. *The last guest has finally left,* so we turned out the lights and went home. (absolute phrase)

   _____

   _____

3. *The last person has left the room,* yet I can't bring myself to leave such a wonderful party. (adverbial clause)

   _____

   _____

4. Yesterday I met Janice McGivens, and *she is our new group leader.* (adjective clause)

   _____

   _____

5. *Jack was exhausted from studying for finals,* and he stayed home all weekend. (participial phrase)

   _____

   _____

6. Everyone stayed home all weekend, *for they wanted to study for final exams.* (infinitive phrase)

   _____

   _____

7. My sister has just bought a new bicycle, and *it has those special knobby tires for riding in sand and mud.* (adjective clause)

   _____

   _____

8. *Finish this job early,* and you can leave early for the weekend. (adverbial clause)

   _____

   _____

9. *The last delegate has finally arrived,* and we can begin the serious discussions. (absolute phrase)

_____

_____

10. *Change the oil every three thousand miles,* and you will prevent problems later in the life of the car. (gerund phrase)

_____

_____

11. Change the oil every three thousand miles, and *you will prevent problems later in the life of the car.* (infinitive phrase)

_____

_____

12. *Jim saw the trout on the edge of the stream,* and he immediately cast the fly in front of the fish. (participial phrase)

_____

_____

13. *Jim saw the trout on the edge of the stream,* and he immediately cast the fly in front of the fish. (adverbial clause)

_____

_____

14. *The alarm bells rang in the firehouse,* and the firefighters jumped on the truck as it roared into the street. (preposition *with* plus an absolute phrase)

_____

_____

15. Order those brake pads for me, and I will pick them up in a few days. (adverbial clause)

_____

_____

16. I've never learned to enjoy her music, for her voice sounds very unpleasant to me. (adverbial clause)

_____

_____

Lesson 16 *Parallel Structure; Comparisons*

We need to examine two more situations in writing where logic requires us to make very careful selections of structure and position.

Parallel Structure

When two or more parts of a sentence are similar in function, they should normally be expressed in the same grammatical construction; in other words, they should be made parallel. The principle of parallelism implies that, in a series, nouns should be balanced with nouns, adjectives with adjectives, prepositional phrases with prepositional phrases, clauses with clauses, and so forth. The following sentence owes much of its clarity and effectiveness to the careful parallel arrangement: Two adjective clauses are joined with *and*, two adverbs with *but*, and three noun direct objects with *and*.

> Anyone who studies world affairs *and* who remembers our last three wars will realize sadly *but* inevitably, that another conflict will endanger the economic strength of our nation, the complacency of our political institutions, *and* the moral fiber of our people.

Two types of errors, the false series and the *and who* construction, both work to destroy parallelism by using a coordinate conjunction to join grammatical units that are not alike.

The False or Shifted Series

Weak: Most people play golf for exercise, pleasure, and so they can meet others.
        [The *and* ties an adverb clause to two nouns.]
Better: Most people play golf for exercise, for pleasure, and for social contacts.

Weak: Our new teacher was young, tall, slender, and with red hair.
        [The *and* suggests that it will be followed by a fourth adjective, not a prepositional phrase.]
Better: Our new teacher was young, tall, slender, and red-haired.

Weak: Mr. Little's speech was tiresome, inaccurate, and should have been omitted.
Better: Mr. Little's speech was tiresome, inaccurate, and unnecessary.

The *And Who* or *And Which* Construction

Weak: Their son is an athlete with great talent *and who* will soon be well known.
Better: Their son is an athlete who has great talent and who will soon be well known.
        Their son is a greatly talented athlete who will soon be well known.
        [Here the unbalanced modification is avoided.]

Weak: I am taking Physics 388, a difficult course *and which* demands much time.
Better: I am taking Physics 388, which is a difficult course and demands much time.
        I am taking Physics 388, which is difficult and demands much time.

153

Comparisons

When you write sentences that make comparisons or contrasts, you need to observe certain forms if your writing is to be clear and precise.

1. Be sure that you compare only those things that are capable of being compared:

Faulty:	The storage capacity of this computer is much greater than our old one. [What is wrong with this sentence is that two unlike things, the storage *capacity* and the computer are being compared.]
Improved:	The storage capacity of this computer is much greater than *the capacity of* our old one.
	The storage capacity of this computer is much greater than *that of* our old one.
Faulty:	The influence of the political leader is more ephemeral than the artist. [Here *influence,* an abstract quality, is being compared to a person, the artist.
Improved:	The influence of the political leader is more ephemeral than *the influence of* the artist.
	The influence of the political leader is more ephemeral than *that of* the artist.
	The political leader's influence is more ephemeral than *the artist's.*

2. When you are using the comparative form of an adjective in a comparison, use *any other* when it is necessary to exclude the subject of the comparison from the group:

Faulty:	Wilson, the first-string center, is heavier than any man on the team. [In this version the writer is comparing Wilson to the members of a group that *includes* Wilson.]
Improved:	Wilson, the first-string center, is heavier than *any other* man on the team.

3. When your sentence contains a double comparison, you should include all the words necessary to make the idiom complete:

Faulty:	He is now as tall *as,* if not taller *than,* his mother.
Improved:	He is now as tall as his mother, if not taller.
Faulty:	She is one of the best *runners,* if not the best *runner,* in the club.
Improved:	She is one of the best runners in **the** club, if not the best.

See Supplement 1 for more details on sentences used to compare and contrast.

Supplement 1

In addition to requiring the structural units already mentioned, comparison-contrast sentences place a few constraints on *the form* of the adjective or adverb. When your comparison is limited to two things, use the comparative degree. Use the superlative for more than two things.

Both Jane and Laura sing well, but Jane has the *better* voice.

Which takes more time, your studies or your job?

January is the *worst* month of the year.

You learned in Lesson 2 that there are two ways of forming the comparative and superlative degrees. In general, *er* and *est* are used with short words, and *more* and *most* with longer words.

> When I was *younger,* I was *more apprehensive* about thunder and lightning.
>
> This encyclopedia is the *newest* and the *most comprehensive.*
>
> Maria works *faster* than I and also *more accurately.*

Remember that in present-day standard English we don't combine *er* or *est* with *more* or *most* in the same word. We don't say, for example, *more pleasanter, most loveliest,* or *more faster.*

NAME _____ SCORE _____

Directions: In the space at the left of each pair of sentences, copy the letter identifying the sentence that is logically structured.

_____ 1. A. The letter was long, detailed, and threatening to the staff.
               B. The letter was long, detailed, and threatened the staff.

_____ 2. A. Jane is a person of wide experience and who has great ability to learn on the job.
               B. Jane is a person of wide experience who has great ability to learn on the job.

_____ 3. A. The ideal politician is interested in solving the city's problems and not to try to keep herself in office.
               B. The ideal politician is interested in solving the city's problems and not in trying to keep herself in office.

_____ 4. A. Far away we saw a runner struggling to cross the river and falling as he climbed the bank.
               B. Far away we saw a runner struggling to cross the river, and he fell as he climbed the bank.

_____ 5. A. The table top is smoothly sanded, carefully finished, and with very few blemishes.
               B. The table top is smoothly sanded and carefully finished, and it has very few blemishes.

_____ 6. A. We decided to go away for the weekend rather than staying home.
               B. We decided to go away for the weekend rather than stay home.

_____ 7. A. That teacher is pleasant, humorous, but who demands a great deal of work.
               B. That teacher is pleasant and humorous, but she demands a great deal of work.

_____ 8. A. Look at my brother, staring at his notes and pretends to study.
               B. Look at my brother, staring at his notes and pretending to study.

_____ 9. A. Martin Jones is a broker who has a terrific nose for new stocks and a great sense of timing for purchases.
               B. Martin Jones is a broker whose nose for new stocks is terrific and has a great sense of timing for purchases.

_____ 10. A. My baseball will improve if I practice hard and study the game carefully.
               B. My baseball will improve if I practice hard and studying the game carefully.

Directions: From each of the following pairs of sentences, select the one that states the comparison correctly.

_____ 1. A. Police and fire protection here in Elmwood is not much different from other small towns.
 B. Police and fire protection here in Elmwood is not much different from the protection in other small towns.

_____ 2. A. Jan's new four-cylinder coupe gets better mileage than any car she tested.
 B. Jan's new four-cylinder coupe gets better mileage than any other car she tested.

_____ 3. A. Is Alice the younger of your two sisters?
 B. Is Alice the youngest of your two sisters?

_____ 4. A. Rick, a star student at a small school, found the competition at the new school harder to manage than his sister Ann.
 B. Rick, a star student at a small school, found the competition at the new school harder to manage than did his sister Ann.

_____ 5. A. Karen's short story is more interesting than the other students.
 B. Karen's short story is more interesting than the other students' stories.

_____ 6. A. Racquel has a better serve than any member of her team.
 B. Racquel has a better serve than any other member of her team.

_____ 7. A. That car is as fast, if not faster, than any other car on the track.
 B. That car is as fast as, if not faster than, any other car on the track.

_____ 8. A. Mike is proud because his tractor is more powerful than Harold.
 B. Mike is proud because his tractor is more powerful than Harold's tractor.

_____ 9. A. The mountains of the eastern United States are far older than the mountains of the western United States.
 B. The mountains of the eastern United States are far older than the western United States.

_____ 10. A. It seems odd that the opinion of one person should be more important than the opinion of an entire committee.
 B. It seems odd that the opinion of one person should be more important than an entire committee.

NAME _____ SCORE _____

Directions: Rewrite each sentence to correct the faulty parallelism.

1. That new clerk is more of a hindrance than helpful.

   _____

   _____

2. Jack wants to buy an inexpensive car but which will impress his friends.

   _____

   _____

3. James Drake is a man whose charisma is great and has great organizational ability.

   _____

   _____

4. I go to the beach for the sunshine, the sound of the waves, and so I can feel free of the pressure of work.

   _____

   _____

5. Alice is studying metal sculpture, a difficult art and which requires considerable physical strength.

   _____

   _____

6. My new notebook computer is lightweight, compact, and has a fast operating speed.

   _____

   _____

7. That lecture was dated, boring, and actually should not have been given.

   _____

   _____

8. Julio is a talented artist and who should win art department scholarship.

   _____

   _____

9. Those three men go scuba diving for the thrills and to see the beauty of the reefs.

   _____

   _____

10. That particular drill improved my play at the net, and my stamina increased also.

    _____

    _____

159

Directions: Rewrite each sentence to correct the faulty comparison.

1. The weather here is often too hot, but I like the weather here better than Tucson.

   _____

   _____

2. Jenny is one of the most cheerful, if not the most cheerful girl, I know.

   _____

   _____

3. That local garage has better mechanics than any garage in this area.

   _____

   _____

4. Of the twins, Alexis is the most skilled in gymnastics.

   _____

   _____

5. Wanda loves her cat just as much as her mother.

   _____

   _____

6. We hope our new apartment will be more quieter and peaceful than the last place we lived.

   _____

   _____

7. Mary's reaction to that vaccination was as bad, if not worse than, any I've ever seen.

   _____

   _____

8. Using a computer to balance your checkbook is not any more easier or accurate than using a calculator.

   _____

   _____

9. I did not know that the work in college would be so much harder than high school.

   _____

   _____

10. Marcia, an executive secretary, says that her work is more important than the executives.

    _____

    _____

Punctuation

Lessons, Practice Sheets, and Exercises

Lesson 17   *Commas to Separate*

Commas are used to separate certain parts of the sentence so that written communication will be clear and direct. Commas to separate are used in the following situations.

1. Use commas before <u>and</u>, <u>but</u>, <u>for</u>, <u>or</u>, <u>nor</u>, and <u>yet</u> when they join the clauses of a compound sentence.

> I placed the typed sheet on his desk, and he picked it up and read it slowly. His face turned red, but he did not say a word. I knew he was angry, for he rose and stomped out of the room. [Note that no comma is used before the conjunction in a compound predicate.]

At this point you might reread Lesson 7. There you will find a detailed explanation, with examples, of this rule. Remember that a semicolon rather than a comma is usually required in a compound sentence when no coordinating conjunction is present.

2. Use commas between the items of a series. A series is composed of three or more words, phrases, or clauses of equal grammatical rank. A series usually takes the form of *a, b,* and *c*; sometimes it may be *a, b,* or *c.* In journalistic writing the comma is omitted before *and* or *or*; in more formal writing it is generally not omitted. The beginning writer will do well to follow formal practice:

> The land looked brown, parched, lifeless, and ominous. [Four adjectives]
> Volunteers included high schoolers, office workers, housewives, and retirees. [Four nouns]
> The dog charged through the door, down the steps, and into the garage. [Three phrases]
> He understands what he must do, when he must do it, and why it must be done.
> [Three subordinate clauses]
> Larry fetched the water, Mort built the fire, and I opened the cans. [Independent clauses]

Notice the last example. Three or more short independent clauses arranged in the form of a series may be separated by commas. But long clauses—independent clauses especially, but sometimes dependent clauses also—are better separated by semicolons, particularly if there is other punctuation within the clauses. The following sentences illustrate the punc-

161

tuation between and within the long clauses. Although you would probably hesitate to attempt such sentences, you will encounter them in your reading. The following two examples both involve three lengthy independent clauses in series, with internal punctuation.

> The first week of the tour called for long hops and little free time; the second week, with longer rest periods in Amsterdam and Antwerp, was less exhausting; but the third week, which took us to four countries in seven days, left us numb and bewildered.

> These dark days will be worth all they have cost if they show us that happiness is not a matter of money; if they force upon us the joy of achievement, the thrill of creative effort; if they teach us that our true destiny is to serve, to the best of our ability, our fellow citizens.

3. Use commas between coordinate adjectives preceding a noun. A comma separating two adjectives signifies that the two adjectives are equal in their modifying force. A comma is not used when the modifier closer to the noun has more importance as an identifier of the noun. Thus we use a comma with "a difficult, unfair examination" but not with "a difficult midterm examination." Another explanation is that in the first example *difficult* and *unfair* modify *examination* with equal force, whereas in the second example *difficult* really modifies the unit *midterm examination*. The problem here is to determine when adjectives are coordinate, that is, equal in modifying force. Two tests may prove helpful.

- If the insertion of *and* between the modifiers produces a reading that still makes sense, the adjectives are equal and a comma should be used. "A difficult *and* unfair examination" would sound correct to most native speakers of English, but "a difficult *and* midterm examination" would not.
- If the adjectives sound natural in reversed position, they are equal and should be separated by a comma. Thus we could say "an unfair, difficult examination" but not "a midterm difficult examination" without meaning something quite different from a difficult midterm examination.

When you use a noun preceded by more than two adjectives, you should test the adjectives by pairs, the first with the second, the second with the third, and so on. It may help you to know that we usually do not use commas before adjectives denoting size or age. And you must remember that we never use a comma between the last adjective and the noun. Observe how use of the above-mentioned tests determines punctuation like the following:

a tall, dark, and handsome gentleman	a tall, dark, handsome gentleman
the dark, cold, drafty classroom	a neat, courteous little boy
a heavy, soiled leather ball	her funny little upturned nose
a mean old local gossip	

4. Use commas after most introductory modifiers, especially if they are long and not obviously restrictive. In this situation modern usage varies considerably. You must depend on your own good sense and judgment. The following explanations will provide a general guide.

- Put commas after introductory adverbial clauses except those that are short or in no need of special emphasis. No hard-and-fast rule governs this situation. The inexperienced writer would probably do well to use commas after all introductory adverbial clauses except very short clauses denoting time:

Unless the flood water recedes soon, we're in trouble.

If we can prove that the signature was forged, we will win the case.

Before sophomores will be admitted to courses numbered 300 or above, they must have official permission.

Before I answer you I want to ask another question.

When he arrived he seemed distraught.

- Put commas after introductory verbal-phrase modifiers:

  Having climbed the steep trail up Cougar Mountain, Bob decided to take some pictures. To get the best view of the valley, he walked to the edge of the cliff. After opening his rucksack, he searched for his new telephoto lens.

- Put a comma after an introductory absolute element, such as a phrase, an adverb modifying the whole sentence, a mild exclamation, and *yes* and *no*.

  In fact, there was no way to keep the front door closed.
  Certainly, I'll be glad to help you.
  Well, what are we to do now?
  No, we are not in danger.

- Ordinarily, do not put a comma after a prepositional phrase that precedes a main clause unless the phrase is long or unless a comma is needed to add special emphasis or to prevent a misreading:

  After a heavy dinner we usually went for a short walk.
  In early summer many birds nested there.
  In spite of the very heavy wind and the pelting hailstones, the third race was completed.
  Never at a loss for words, he answered with a joke.
  After school, teachers were expected to find time for grading papers and preparing lessons.

5. *Use commas between any two words that might be mistakenly read together:*

   Before, he had been industrious and sober. [Not *before he had been.*]
   Once inside, the dog scampered all over the furniture. [Not *inside the dog.*]
   While we were eating, the table collapsed. [Not *eating the table.*]
   After we had washed, Mother prepared breakfast. [Not *washed Mother.*]
   Ever since, he has been afraid of deep water. [Not *ever since he has been.*]
   Shortly after ten, thirty new recruits appeared. [Not *shortly after ten thirty.*]

NAME _____   SCORE _____

Directions: Each of the following sentences has two commas missing. Add the commas where they are necessary. Then in the spaces at the left, write the numbers of the rules that apply to the commas you have added.

1. Before a coordinating conjunction in a compound sentence
2. In a series
3. Between coordinate adjectives
4. After an introductory modifier
5. To prevent misreading

_____ 1. June has taken the required courses in history psychology, and math but she
_____   must also take a course in biology.

_____ 2. Because Jim found two new sources for that long difficult report his work is
_____   going more quickly now.

_____ 3. The handsome well-dressed television anchor looked once more at his
_____   script, cleared his throat and began to read.

_____ 4. Working to catch up with the rest of the runners Marta ran hard up the long
_____   winding hill.

_____ 5. Racquel ordered the art work, the titles and the slides but she still needs to
_____   write the script for her new sales presentation.

_____ 6. The children in that class can play on the swings this afternoon or they can
_____   play a noisy colorful video game.

_____ 7. After the dog wandered away the boys looked in the barn the pasture and the
_____   corn fields.

_____ 8. After waking up the girls wandered over to the restaurant for a leisurely delicious breakfast.

_____ 9. Kate had once ridden with a police officer on patrol; after that training to
_____   become an officer became an immediate compelling goal.

_____ 10. Arriving early for the meeting Audrey sat down in the back for a short
_____   refreshing nap.

_____ 11. Carla tried valiantly to start the car but she had to call her sleepy reluctant
_____   brother for help.

———— 12. Because the women want to study computer graphics they must also take
————   math, computer programming and an art course.

———— 13. I've tried for three years to grow big juicy tomatoes but the bugs have killed
————   the plants every year.

———— 14. Overwhelmed by the number of choices Arthur decided to buy only the sim-
————   plest least expensive tape player he could find.

———— 15. The girls already have the tables, chairs and umbrellas but they will have to
————   find help to set them up on the patio.

———— 16. After they had walked about three miles in the cold driving rain Roger and
————   Mike were glad to catch a ride with an old farmer.

———— 17. Marge closed the book, stood up slowly and walked directly from the quiet
————   dimly lit library to the cafeteria.

———— 18. After the men finished mopping the floors were squeaky clean and they
————   shone brightly in the sunlight coming in the windows.

———— 19. Elaine called Mary, Robert and Helen but they were all studying and could
————   not go water skiing with her.

———— 20. After I answered the first nineteen questions I was unable to understand the
————   last most difficult question.

Exercise 17 — *Commas to Separate*

NAME _____ SCORE _____

Directions: Each of the following sentences has two commas missing. Add the commas where they are necessary. Then in the space at the left, write the numbers of the rules that apply to the commas you have added.

1. Before a coordinating conjunction in a compound sentence
2. In a series
3. Between coordinate adjectives
4. After an introductory modifier
5. To prevent misreading

_____ 1. Because there was a big sale the entire mall was filled with eager pushy
_____   people.

_____ 2. After the car stopped the man walked away with some books, a lunch box
_____   and an umbrella in his arms.

_____ 3. Searching eagerly for the fish we waded downstream in the cold rushing
_____   waters of the creek.

_____ 4. The quiet unassuming man walked to the head of the table but few of the
_____   people present paid any attention to him.

_____ 5. After the air conditioning failed, we packed up our books, stood up and
_____   walked quickly from the hot steamy classroom.

_____ 6. The track was empty early in the morning but at eight thirty people came
_____   out of the gym and began to walk around.

_____ 7. Moving quickly down the aisle of the store Monica picked up junk food soft
_____   drinks, and a variety of cheeses for the party.

_____ 8. After Mike left the three women finished their lab assignment but they did
_____   not type up the results as the instructor had asked.

_____ 9. If we can hire someone from the temporary agency we can avoid the tedious
_____   tiring work of taking inventory.

_____ 10. As the men began to lift the box broke open and the entire collection of nuts,
_____   bolts and washers fell out onto the floor.

Directions: Under each rule, write two sentences of your own composition to illustrate the punctuation to be used. Bring your work to class for discussion. The purpose of this exercise is to help you recognize punctuation situations in your own writing.

1. Comma used before a coordinating conjunction in a compound sentence.

   a.

   b.

2. Commas used in a series (one series of single words and one series of phrases).

   a.

   b.

3. Comma used after an introductory modifier (one adverbial clause and one verbal phrase).

   a.

   b.

4. Comma used between coordinate adjectives.

   a.

   b.

5. Comma used to prevent misreading.

   a.

   b.

NAME _____ SCORE _____

Directions: The following sentences contain numbered spots where punctuation might be needed. In the correspondingly numbered spaces at the left, write C if a comma is needed, S if a semicolon is needed, or 0 if no punctuation is needed.

1. _____ (1) After he fried the eggs, cooked the bacon¹ and brewed the coffee²

2. _____ Jimmy called the others for breakfast.

3. _____ (2) The telephone call from the office manager came at 7:00 A.M.³ she

4. _____ offered me the job⁴ and I accepted immediately.

5. _____ (3) Watching a hawk soaring in the sky⁵ should remind you⁶ that such

6. _____ birds are among nature's truly great fliers.

7. _____ (4) The sad young boy⁷ had found a saw, a hammer and nails⁸ and a few

8. _____ wood chisels in his grandfather's toolbox.

9. _____ (5) Unless the weather changes⁹ we won't go to the island¹⁰ the trip across

10. _____ the lake is too dangerous in high winds.

11. _____ (6) The long-winded¹¹ boring speaker droned on and on¹² the people in the

12. _____ audience either dozed or doodled on their note pads.

13. _____ (7) After dinner¹³ we moved into the den and watched a fascinating¹⁴

14. _____ quiz show on television.

15. _____ (8) When you can¹⁵ go out to the shed and bring in¹⁶ a few more logs for

16. _____ the fire.

17. _____ (9) The raw whipping wind continued for hours¹⁷ but the driving rain¹⁸

18. _____ stopped after a few minutes.

19. _____ (10) Working well past midnight¹⁹ Jennifer wrote the last part of her

20. _____ paper²⁰ and printed two copies of the entire assignment.

21. _____ (11) Once inside²¹ the house seems less dark and dreary²² the rooms are

22. _____ cheerfully lit by burning candles.

23. _____ (12) The small fuzzy dog scampered around the room and jumped up
24. _____   on the children, putting muddy paw prints on their clothes.

25. _____ (13) After we had driven only a few miles we knew that the car had
26. _____   serious problems and was probably unsafe.

27. _____ (14) Having walked around the track three times, Marge and Jim sat
28. _____   down on a nearby park bench to rest.

29. _____ (15) Although the view of the valley was beautiful some children chased
30. _____   a squirrel others simply sat quietly on the ground.

31. _____ (16) Football is a fast exciting sport but baseball allows time for thought
32. _____   between pitches.

33. _____ (17) Marilyn is a tall slender girl she is, I think, almost six feet
34. _____   tall.

35. _____ (18) After leaving the newspaper in the driveway the carrier moved on
36. _____   down the street to the other houses.

37. _____ (19) "I think," said Max, "that this is a good location for our tent
38. _____   it's dry and sunny and it's well off the trail.

39. _____ (20) After leaving the two men walked slowly down the driveway;
40. _____   they were thinking about the long difficult task that lay ahead of
               them.

Lesson 18   *Commas to Enclose*

Commas are used to set off words, phrases, or clauses that break into the normal word order of a sentence. Notice that these interrupters are *set off* by commas. This means that although interrupters that begin or end a sentence have only one comma, any such unit that comes in the interior of the sentence has *two* commas, one before it and one after it.

The most common types of interrupters are discussed below.

1. Use commas with nonrestrictive adjective clauses and phrases. To understand this comma use, you should now reread pages 78–79 of Lesson 9 for an explanation of the difference between restrictive and nonrestrictive adjective clauses.

Other modifiers of nouns—participial phrases especially and, less frequently, prepositional phrases—must be set off by commas when they are nonrestrictive, that is, when they are not necessary for the *identification* of the noun modified. (The same distinction applies also to a few appositives, as noted in the next item of this lesson.)

Examine these additional examples contrasting restrictive and nonrestrictive modifiers of nouns. Notice in the last pair of sentences how the writer, by using or not using commas with the adjective clause, gives important information to the reader:

The speech *that the coach made at the awards banquet* was one of her best.
[Restrictive adjective clause]

The coach's awards banquet speech, *which was one of her best,* should be printed.
[Nonrestrictive adjective clause]

Anyone *holding a winning ticket* should come to the desk. [Restrictive participial phrase]

Jan's mother, *holding a winning ticket,* went to the desk. [Nonrestrictive participial phrase]

A woman *at the far end of the head table* summoned a waiter. [Restrictive prepositional phrase]

Professor Angela Cheney, *at the far end of the head table,* summoned a waiter.
[Nonrestrictive prepositional phrase]

My brother-in-law *who lives in Akron* is a chemist.
[The writer has more than one brother-in-law. The restrictive clause is needed to distinguish this brother-in-law from other brothers-in-law.]

My brother-in-law, *who lives in Akron,* is a chemist.
[Identification is not explicit, so the writer is telling us that he has only one brother-in-law.]

2. Use commas with most appositives. As you learned in Lesson 10, the most common type of appositive immediately follows the noun or pronoun that it renames:

One comedian, *the one with the lisp,* was booed.
The major, *a veteran of three wars,* accepted the award.
Mr. Tate, *our head counselor,* will speak.
Our head counselor, *Mr. Tate,* will speak.

171

Appositives like these are called *loose* or *nonrestrictive* appositives and are set off. But an appositive may sometimes function the same way that a restrictive adjective clause functions; that is, it may identify a preceding noun that, without the appositive, could refer to any member of a class. An appositive of this sort is not set off:

> my brother Jack, the poet Keats, the apostle Paul, the preposition *to*, Henry IV

3. Use commas with absolute phrases. An absolute phrase, which consists of a noun or a pronoun plus a verbal (see p. 112, Lesson 12), modifies the sentence as a whole, not any special part of it:

> *Today being a holiday,* I plan to loaf and relax.
> *Her replacement having arrived early,* Bea had time to shop.
> He sat there in silence, *his left cheek twitching as usual.*
> He stood in the doorway, *his wet cloak dripping water on the rug,* and waited for some sign of recognition.

4. Use commas with parenthetical expressions. These are words, phrases, or clauses that break into the sentence to explain, to emphasize, to qualify, or to point the direction of the thought:

> The text, *moreover,* had not been carefully proofread.
> You will find, *for example,* that the format is not attractive.
> The meal, *to tell the truth,* was quite unappetizing.
> His appearance, *I must admit,* would startle anyone.

5. Use commas with words used in direct address.

> "Remember, *Jimmy,* that we like your work," he said.
> "*Henry,*" said the teacher, "you must remain after school."
> "I believe, *sir,* that you have been misinformed," she replied.
> "And now, *dear friends and neighbors,* let us eat," announced Father Jamison.

6. Use commas with expressions designating the speaker in direct quotations.

> "With your permission," *he replied,* "there's nothing I'd rather do."
> "That must do," *he said,* "until we think of something better."

Other marks may be used instead of the comma if the sentence justifies their use:

> "How shall I tell him?" *asked Mary timidly.* [Question mark after question]
> "Silence!" *he shouted.* "Get to work at once!" [Exclamation point]
> "Two of the buildings are firetraps," *replied the comptroller;* "moreover, the library needs a new roof." [Semicolon required to avoid a comma fault between independent clauses]

7. Use commas with negative insertions used for emphasis, units out of their position, and "tag" questions (short interrogative clauses combined with statements).

Our plane was an old propeller model, *not the 747 we had expected.*
Tired and footsore, the hikers finally reached camp.
The hikers finally reached camp, *tired and footsore.*
[*Or*] The tired and footsore hikers finally reached camp.
Her answer was a good one, *don't you think?*
You remember, *don't you,* Dr. Wade's eloquent eulogy?

8. Use commas with degrees, titles, and the like when they follow names.

Helen Lyle, *Ph.D.,* gave the opening address.
The new ambassador is Peter Jones, *Esq.*

9. Use commas in dates and addresses.

On July 14, *1904,* in a cottage at 316 High Street, *Mayville, Iowa,* they were wed.
[Note, however, that journalistic practice usually omits the comma *after* the year and the state.]

When a year follows a month, rather than a day of the month, it is usually not set off. And a comma is not needed before a zip-code number.

As of March 1985 his address was 1675 East Union Street, Seattle, Washington 98122.

NAME _____ SCORE _____

Directions: Insert commas where they are necessary in the following sentences. Then, before each sentence, write one of the following numbers to indicate the rule that governs the punctuation of the sentence. Some of the sentences may be correct as they are.

1. A nonrestrictive clause or phrase   4. A parenthetical element
2. An appositive   5. The speaker in dialogue
3. A noun in direct address   6. An absolute phrase

_____ 1. "Now then Sam tell me when you will finish hanging the wallpaper," said Mary.

_____ 2. The dogs by this time almost starved swallowed their food in less than a minute.

_____ 3. The managers worried about the production quotas began to push the workers to greater efforts.

_____ 4. I was alone all day Saturday my roommate having gone off for the day.

_____ 5. "I wonder" said Josie "where the repair crew for our cable television is."

_____ 6. People who read widely get the most benefit from a college education.

_____ 7. Last year I visited New Jersey where the Statue of Liberty is actually located.

_____ 8. Michelle who is usually very understanding became quite angry when she saw the damaged painting.

_____ 9. The hikers departed yesterday their backpacks heavy with food and supplies.

_____ 10. Tom's next class analytic geometry meets in Newton Hall.

_____ 11. I got that little item from Maggie who has a real nose for gossip.

_____ 12. Alfred the youngest member of the chess team is also the quickest learner of them all.

_____ 13. Ronnie needing only a few additional points to make an A hired a high-priced tutor before the exam.

_____ 14. Show the other children Mark what you brought back from your uncle's farm.

_____ 15. Joe his motivation to study Spanish having almost vanished sold the taped instructional course to his sister.

_____ 16. Rolando easily our most talented programmer could not work the bugs out of the new accounting program.

_____ 17. "I need someone to clarify the president's remarks for me" said Barbara.

_____ 18. The mercury having climbed into the high nineties we all stayed in the air-conditioned library until it closed.

_____ 19. That angry memo it seems to me should never have been written.

_____ 20. The fire occurred in Mason County which has no fire department at all.

175

Directions: Each of the following sentences contains either an adjective clause or a participial phrase in italics. Insert commas where they are needed. In the space at the left of each sentence write:

R if the clause or phrase is restrictive
N if the clause or phrase is nonrestrictive

_____ 1. Anyone *waiting in the outer office* should return tomorrow morning at nine o'clock.

_____ 2. The book *that I checked out this morning* contained little information on my research topic.

_____ 3. Marie wants to buy a car just like Jim Thompson's *which is an extremely fast convertible.*

_____ 4. Jamie will take that math course next fall *when she will be taking only two other courses.*

_____ 5. Williams *trying to find an alarm system for his car* has been to four auto parts stores this week.

_____ 6. The students *who have not taken Dr. Singer's course* have missed a very interesting experience.

_____ 7. Mike Lofton *who took Dr. Singer's course last term* found it extremely enlightening.

_____ 8. The famous author's first book *which did not sell when it was first published* is being released again in paperback.

_____ 9. The book *that made him really famous* was his third novel.

_____ 10. Amanda's sister Tammy *who works for a publishing company* is leaving that company to join a public relations firm.

_____ 11. A friend *who works for a brokerage firm* told Amanda that the publishing company may go bankrupt soon.

_____ 12. Arthur wants to go to a school *where he can study taxidermy.*

_____ 13. The artifacts *dug up on Mr. Atkins farm* will be displayed in the local historical museum.

_____ 14. The artifacts from Mr. Atkins farm *which were discovered by the local archeological society* were the first found in this area.

_____ 15. All students *needing a new ID card* should report to the registrar's office sometime this week.

_____ 16. Alice Wilson *needing an ID card for admission to Saturday's game* was the first student to report.

_____ 17. We must be very careful about setting fires in any area *where there has been very little rain.*

_____ 18. Residents of the Wayne Valley *where there has been little or no rain* must be careful about setting fires.

_____ 19. That shirt *still one of my favorites* is badly faded from the sun.

_____ 20. Any player *scoring a goal in the first three games* will receive a free T-shirt from a local sporting goods store.

NAME _____ SCORE _____

Directions: Recognizing typical punctuation situations in your own writing is a very important skill. In the spaces provided, write two sentences to illustrate each of the rules indicated. Be sure to include all necessary punctuation.

1. Two sentences with nonrestrictive adjective clauses.
   a.

   b.

2. Two sentences with nonrestrictive participial phrases.
   a.

   b.

3. Two sentences with appositives.
   a.

   b.

4. Two sentences with nouns used in direct address.
   a.

   b.

5. Two sentences with parenthetical elements.
   a.

   b.

6. Two sentences with absolute phrases.
   a.

   b.

Directions: Each of the following sentences contains one adjective clause or one participial phrase. Underline the phrase or clause. Insert commas where they are needed. In the space at the left of each sentence write:

R if the clause or phrase is restrictive
N if the clause or phrase is nonrestrictive

_____ 1. How tall is that tree standing beside the school?

_____ 2. Jimmy Thomas who played baseball here three years ago has been called up by a major league club.

_____ 3. My father needs someone who will mow his yard twice a month.

_____ 4. The maple is one of the trees that lose their leaves every fall.

_____ 5. I got a phone call yesterday from my sister Sally who calls about once a week to check up on me.

_____ 6. The little kid standing in the last row of that class is my nephew Tim.

_____ 7. Manny poking his head around the corner of the house saw the thief just as he left the yard.

_____ 8. Our new accountant is Ralph Marks who just moved to town.

_____ 9. We need an accountant who has a good understanding of tax law.

_____ 10. A couple of men standing on the street corner helped Bertha push her car off the street.

_____ 11. This morning I met two students that had just entered school yesterday.

_____ 12. This morning I met Ron Jansen who just entered school yesterday.

_____ 13. Lois Larkin owns a shop that sells cross-country ski equipment.

_____ 14. Lois Larkin owns *The Snow Shop* which sells cross-country ski equipment.

_____ 15. A woman wearing a blue suit and a bright red tie just walked into my office.

_____ 16. Joan Williams wearing a blue suit and a bright tie just walked into my office.

_____ 17. That old truck dented and dusty will have to last through one more winter.

_____ 18. My roommate only goes to movies that are odd, old comedies.

_____ 19. The sailing club needs volunteers who know how to repair fiberglass.

_____ 20. Rich Houston who is an expert with fiberglass just joined the sailing club.

NAME _____ SCORE _____

Directions: The following sentences contain fifty numbered spots, some with punctuation and some with no punctuation. In the correspondingly numbered spaces at the left, write C if the punctuation is correct or W if the punctuation is incorrect.

1. _____   (1) Mark had some bad luck yesterday; he lost his glasses, got a
2. _____   parking ticket and missed an algebra test.
3. _____   (2) After running Harry often goes to the gym and lifts weights for an
4. _____   hour.
5. _____   (3) We took, I'm sure a longer route, but we were able to avoid that
6. _____   monstrous traffic jam on Highway 60.
7. _____   (4) The test was long difficult, and a little tricky but Jim passed it quite
8. _____   easily.
9. _____   (5) The new computers will arrive this Monday, everyone therefore,
10. _____   will need to work late on Tuesday and Wednesday.
11. _____   (6) Angie Thompson a recent graduate of the state university, has
12. _____   accepted a job as our new systems analyst.
13. _____ (7) As the storm clouds gathered the band members moved their instru-
14. _____   ments inside, and set up on the stage.
15. _____   (8) The trip that we planned for next weekend has been canceled,
16. _____   the hotels in that area are all booked up.
17. _____   (9) The only way to the waterfall is to drive to the park, walk up the
18. _____   hill and climb that steep rocky path to the top.
19. _____ (10) The old church once very shabby, has been completely restored by
20. _____   a company that wants to open a restaurant.
21. _____ (11) That woman is Georgie Butler the new company president, her first
22. _____   name is really Georgina.

23. _____ (12) My brothers graduated from high school on June 12, 1989, they en-
24. _____   listed in the Navy the next day.

25. _____ (13) When that hard rain started several sensitive car alarms went off
26. _____   in the parking lot.

27. _____ (14) Richard Abbott, who is well known in Texas as a horseman
28. _____   recently bought a ranch in northern Idaho.

29. _____ (15) Did it ever occur to you, that we should have studied before we went
30. _____   to take the exam?

31. _____ (16) The unhappy, frowning teacher looked straight at me and said;
32. _____   "Please answer question number two for us, Robin."

33. _____ (17) Looking quickly at the books on the shelf, Carla selected one and
34. _____   walked to the desk looking at the index as she walked.

35. _____ (18) When she returned the book lay on the table, she had not, as she
36. _____   thought, left it at work.

37. _____ (19) Although Edwin is an attorney who has little experience in actual
38. _____   trials he has a good chance to win this case.

39. _____ (20) Onto our work table the boss dropped a huge box containing the
40. _____   advertising fliers and a large number of envelopes.

41. _____ (21) For most people in the office politics at the local level is a sub-
42. _____   ject they never think about.

43. _____ (22) The tallest building in town, the City Trust Building has been
44. _____   sold; the new owners plan to demolish it next year.

45. _____ (23) Madge's favorite type of book is a thick, romance novel; she reads
46. _____   two or three of those novels a month.

47. _____ (24) The class having ended the new teacher closed her notes and
48. _____   walked wearily back to her office.

49. _____ (25) Andrea doesn't understand why her brothers enjoy baseball, she
50. _____   much prefers to talk about politics.

Lesson 19 *Tricky Punctuation Marks*

This lesson covers a number of tricky punctuation marks.

Apostrophe

The apostrophe (') has three uses:

1. To form the possessive case of nouns and indefinite pronouns.
2. To mark the omitted material in contractions.
3. To form certain plurals, such as those of letters and abbreviations.

Forming Possessives

Any noun, whether singular or plural, that does not end in *s* forms its possessive by adding an apostrophe and *s:*

> a boy's hat, the horse's tail, Carol's car, men's shoes, children's toys

Plural nouns that end in *s* form possessives by adding an apostrophe after the *s:*

> boys' hats, horses' tails, the Smiths' home, ladies' dresses

In singular nouns ending in *s* or *z,* an apostrophe following the *s* or *z* is the usual way to form the possessive:

> the countess' castle, Frances' reply, Archimedes' law, Mr. Gomez' report

However, modern-day usage is divided. Some dictionaries and style manuals sanction the *'s* spelling also if the possessive form can be easily pronounced with an extra syllable and if the following word does not begin with an *s:*

> the boss' [*or* boss's] answer, Mr. Jones' [*or* Jones's] house, the witness' [*or* witness's] testimony [*but*] the witness' story

The indefinite pronouns, but not the personal pronouns, form the possessive with the aid of the apostrophe:

> somebody's sweater, anyone's opinion, anybody's game [But note the possessive forms of these pronouns: his, hers, its, theirs, ours, yours, whose.]

Omitted Material

The apostrophe is used to stand for the omitted material in contractions:

> doesn't [does not], won't [will not], she's [she is, she has], o'clock [of the clock], rock 'n' roll [rock and roll]

181

You must learn to distinguish carefully between the following pairs of contractions and possessives:

it's [it is, it has]	its	who's [who is, who has]	whose
there's [there is, there has]	theirs	you're [you are]	your
they're [they are]	their		

Unusual Plurals

In the past the apostrophe was quite regularly used to form the plural of numbers, letters, symbols, words treated as words (too many *and's*), and so forth.

the three R's, mind your p's and q's, several OK's, studying for M.A.'s and Ph.D.'s

In such matters usage today is noticeably divided. The trend, however, is well stated in *Webster's Dictionary of English Usage* (1989): "The use of -*'s* to form the plurals of numerals, abbreviations and symbols is not now as common as pluralization with simple -*s*; 1970s, CPUs, &s are more likely to be found than their apostrophized counterparts" (p. 109). Fortunately, the situation arises so rarely in the writing of the average college student that the matter should cause little concern. But many beginning writers need to be reminded regularly of an important related fact: An apostrophe is never used in forming the plural of either a common or a proper noun.

There are two Kathys in the class. Two grandmas attended.

Colon

The colon (:) is a formal mark announcing a list, an explanation, or a quotation to follow.

My fellow Americans: My speech tonight will examine . . .
All hikers must bring the following: a flashlight, a small ax, and a waterproof tarpaulin.

Note that after a colon it is permissible to have an initial capital letter, as in the first example above. This is properly done when the text following the colon is a complete sentence. **Note: Do not use a colon to separate a verb from its complement or a preposition from its object.**

Faulty: All hikers must bring: a flashlight, a small ax, and a waterproof tarpaulin.
Faulty: The things a hiker must bring are: a flashlight, a small ax, and a waterproof tarpaulin.
Faulty: The hiker's equipment should consist of: a flashlight, a small ax, and a waterproof tarpaulin.

Dash

The dash (—) is used to show an abrupt change in thought in the sentence. It must be used sparingly and never as a substitute for other marks.

Superior students—notice that I said *superior*—will not have to take the test.
New surroundings, new friends, a challenging new job—all these helped Eugene overcome his grief.

Hyphen

The hyphen (-) is used to divide a word at the end of a line and to join words to form various types of compounds. Divide a word only between syllables. With words having a prefix or a suffix, divide the word after the prefix and before the suffix. Avoid dividing a word so that a single letter ends or begins a line. (Consult your dictionary for problems of syllabic division.)

mathe-matics [not] mathem-atics
inter-collegiate [not] intercol-legiate
govern-ess [not] gov-erness
enough [not] e-nough
many [not] man-y

Use hyphens to join the parts of compound modifiers preceding nouns.

Observe his well-kept lawn. His lawn is well kept.
We deplore your devil-may-care attitude.

This use of a hyphen sometimes determines an exact meaning:

a roll of twenty-dollar bills; a roll of twenty dollar bills
all-American boys; all American boys

Use hyphens with compound numbers from twenty-one to ninety-nine and with fractions:

Twenty-two people claimed the one-third share of the reward money but received only one-eighth.

Use hyphens, particularly with prefixes and suffixes, to avoid awkward combinations of letters or to distinguish between two meanings of a word:

anti-intellectual
pre-Aztec
her doll-like face
re-cover a couch [not recover the money]

Quotation Marks

Quotation marks (" ") are used to enclose quoted material and words used in some special way. Use double quotation marks (" ") to enclose the exact words of a quoted speech. Quotation marks always come in pairs. The marks show the beginning and the end of a speech, whether it is part of a sentence, one sentence, or several sentences. If a speech is interrupted by material showing who said it, quotation marks set off the quoted material from the explanatory material. Use quotation marks where the directly quoted material begins and where it ends or is interrupted. Indirect quotations are *not* set off by quotation marks:

"I admit," said Ralph, "that I was mistaken."
[Note that the explanatory material is set off from the direct quotation.]

Peg answered, "I didn't attend. I wasn't in town." [More than one sentence.]
Peg answered that she hadn't attended because she hadn't been in town.
[This is an indirect quotation. Words not directly quoted do not need quotation marks.]

Use double quotation marks to set off the subdivisions of books, names of songs, and titles of units of less than book length, such as short stories, short poems, essays, and articles:

The second chapter of *Moby Dick* is entitled "The Carpet-Bag."

Nanki-Poo sings "A Wandering Minstrel I" early in Act I of *The Mikado.*

Our anthology includes "Threes," a poem from Sandburg's *Smoke and Steel.*

The first article I read for my research paper was John Lear's "How Hurricanes Are Born" in the *Saturday Review.*

In printed material, titles of books, magazines, long poems, newspapers, motion pictures, and radio and television series are set in italic type. Other special uses of italics are for foreign words and phrases and for names of ships, planes, and spacecraft. In handwritten or typewritten papers, underlining (<u>typescript like this</u>) is the equivalent of italics in printed material *(type like this).* Word-processors can produce effects such as **bold** and *italic,* which gives students a capability previously not available except through typesetting.

Double Quotation Marks. Use double quotation marks to set off slang words used in serious writing. Quotation marks are also sometimes used to set off words when they are referred to as words:

The witness had only recently been released from the "slammer."
Words like "seize" and "siege" are often misspelled.

Usage is divided on these uses of quotation marks. In printed material the two words in the second example would almost certainly appear in italics. Student writers of handwritten or typed material should underline such words or set them off by quotation marks, the first method being the more common practice.

Quotation Marks with Other Punctuation. Follow this usage in the placing of quotation marks in relation to other marks:

1. Commas and periods always inside quotes
2. Semicolons and colons always outside quotes
3. Question marks and exclamation points inside if they belong to the quoted part, outside if they do not

"Come in," said my uncle, "and take off your coats." [Comma and period]

Mr. Lowe said, "I heartily endorse this candidate"; unfortunately most of the audience thought he said *hardly* instead of *heartily.* [Semicolon outside]

"Heavens!" he exclaimed. "Is this the best you can do?" [Exclamation point and question mark]

Mother asked, "Where were you last night?" [No double punctuation]

Did she say, "I came home early"?
[Question mark belongs to the whole sentence, not to the quoted part]

Did Mother ask, "Where were you last night?"
[Note that there is only one question mark after a double question like this]

Single Quotation Marks. Use single quotation marks to enclose a speech within a speech:

"I wonder what he meant," said Betty, "when he said, 'There are wheels within wheels.' "

You may not write many sentences like this one, but just the same, you should note that when you have quotes within quotes, the period comes inside both single and double quotes.

NAME _____ SCORE _____

Directions: In the spaces at the left, write C if the punctuation is correct or W if it is incorrect. Within the incorrect sentences, correct the faulty punctuation by adding, removing, or changing marks.

_____ 1. "Tomorrow we'll be going over to Jim's to help set up the newsletter," said Marsha.

_____ 2. 'My paper failed—too short, I think,' said Alex.

_____ 3. "I came to work early," said Yolanda, "but I forgot that the building is closed until seven o'clock."

_____ 4. That's too bad—its always difficult to get to a seven o'clock class on time.

_____ 5. My register drawer doesn't have twenty five dollar bills in it, does yours?

_____ 6. We bought several new pieces of equipment; a computer, a scanner, and two specialized printers.

_____ 7. Our new manager doesn't like anyones ideas but your's and Jim's.

_____ 8. That message is yours; Alice's are in that other stack.

_____ 9. Thats a great story—you read the book, didn't you?

_____ 10. "Who's jacket is that one on the table?" asked Mike. "Is yours in the closet?"

_____ 11. Nobody's in the office that early in the morning: only the guards are here at that time.

_____ 12. "Did Bob say, 'I'll be through in a minute?' " asked Wanda.

_____ 13. A neighbors dog barked all night outside my window: I wish that I could find which neighbor owns it.

_____ 14. You'll need seven hundred dollars to pay for the repair on that old car of your's.

_____ 15. Seven hundred dollar bills is too much cash to be carrying around.

Directions: Sentences 1–5 are indirect quotations. In the space provided, rewrite each sentence as a direct quotation. Sentences 6–10 are direct quotations. Rewrite each as an indirect quotation. You will have to alter some verb forms and some pronoun forms as well as the punctuation.

1. The programmer told us that the new program is very complicated.

2. Marge said that she needs to take a few days off next week.

3. Benny said that he had signed up for the course in bowling so that he can improve his game.

4. One person in the audience announced that the singer would be back at this same auditorium next month.

5. Does our contract with the maintenance firm say that we must pay for parts after the first six months?

6. The president's assistant said, "We will need to examine that policy more closely in the light of yesterday's events."

7. My neighbor said, "I need to hire someone to paint my house."

8. The little boy responded, "I lost all my marbles when the bag broke in the middle of the street."

9. Mrs. Williams asked, "When will the repairs on my chair be completed?"

10. Did I hear the television meterologist say, "There will be snow flurries in the higher elevations tonight?"

Exercise 19   *Tricky Punctuation Marks*

NAME _____   SCORE _____

Directions: In the spaces at the left, write C if the punctuation is correct or W if it is incorrect. Within the incorrect sentences, correct the faulty punctuation by adding, removing, or changing marks.

_____ 1. "I didn't find anyone at the house," said Mark; I think they all left about three o'clock."

_____ 2. My brother-in-law—he has an engineering degree—left his job to go back to graduate school," said Jack.

_____ 3. Marias new car—it's the one parked out front has a very interesting anti-theft system.

_____ 4. "I haven't seen anyone else's project," said Monica, "but mine is about ten pages long."

_____ 5. "We need to get the car ready," said Walt; "lets go out to the garage—but wait, John has the car right now."

_____ 6. On her twenty first birthday Gina's parents gave her twenty one hundred dollar bills to help her buy a new car.

_____ 7. Everyone knows that the secret to success in sports is: practice, practice, and more practice.

_____ 8. It's not generally understood that our teams performance on the obstacle course is very ordinary.

_____ 9. When someone's project proposal sounds impossible, Mark always says, "We can do it; all it takes is money—lots of money."

_____ 10. The mornings work was lost when a brief power failure erased all the data entered that morning.

_____ 11. "Who's going to find out whose car that is parked by the curb?" asked Rolando.

_____ 12. Where's your jacket? Mines at home and I need to borrow your's," said Connie.

_____ 13. We need to load the truck with: lumber, two size's of nails, and three rolls of roofing paper.

_____ 14. Patrick Henry said to the Continental Congress: Give me liberty, or give me death.

_____ 15. The new manager—he just arrived yesterday—has a great deal of experience in personnel evaluation.

189

Directions: Sentences 1–5 are indirect quotations. In the space provided, rewrite each sentence as a direct quotation. Sentences 6–10 are direct quotations. Rewrite each as an indirect quotation. You will have to alter some verb forms and some pronoun forms as well as the punctuation.

1. Laurie said that she had already met with the committee and was ready to begin work.

2. The speaker responded that she intended to cover that topic in the afternoon session.

3. John's niece reminded him that he agreed to tutor her in math before the next test.

4. Five minutes after the trip began, four-year old Sammy began to ask when we would get there.

5. Did you hear the proctor say that time would be up on the test in five minutes?

6. The mechanic said, "I need to check the electrical system first."

7. As the meeting began, Melanie said, "I'm ready to move for adjournment."

8. Tom said, "I'll be home about 7:30 P.M. tonight."

9. The worried students asked, "Can we write another paper for extra credit?"

10. Has anyone ever told you, "You should study every day rather than only the night before a test?"

Lesson 20 — *End Marks; Summary of Punctuation Rules*

This lesson discusses end marks and summarizes all the punctuation rules presented in this book.

Period

The **period** is used after a complete declarative sentence and after ordinary abbreviations. Its use as end punctuation after sentences needs no examples. Its use after abbreviations is a little more complicated.

Personal Titles

A few abbreviations are proper in the ordinary sort of writing, such as *Mr., Mrs., Ms., Messrs., Mmes.,* and *Dr.,* before names; *Jr., Sr., Esq., D.D., Ph.D.,* and so forth, after names. Miss does not require a period. *Ms.,* used instead of *Miss* or *Mrs.* when marital state is not indicated, is usually considered an abbreviation and uses a period, although some modern dictionaries have entries for it either with or without a period.

Latin-Based Terms

The following, correct in footnotes, bibliographies, and tabulations, should be written out in ordinary writing: *e.g. (for example), etc. (and so forth), i.e. (that is), p., pp. (page, pages),* and *vol. (volume).* A.D., B.C., A.M., and P.M. (usually set in small caps in printed material) are used only with figures and where necessary for clearness.

Addresses

The following are acceptable in addresses but should be spelled out in ordinary writing: *St. (Street), Ave. (Avenue), Blvd. (Boulevard), Dr. (Drive), Rd. (Road), Co. (Company),* and *Inc. (Incorporated).* Conventionally, periods have been used with abbreviations of the states *(Mass., Minn., Tex., W. Va.).* However, the two-letter capitalized symbols authorized by the U.S. Postal Service *(MA, MN, TX, WV)* do not require periods.

Poor:	Last Mon. P.M. I met my two older bros., who live in N.Y. Chas. works for a mfg. co. there. Thos. attends NYU, preparing himself for a gov't. job. He's coming home for Xmas.
Right:	Last Monday afternoon I met my two older brothers, who live in New York. Charles works for a manufacturing company there. Thomas attends New York University, preparing himself for a government job. He's coming home for Christmas.

Acronyms and Measurements

In modern usage, the "alphabet" name forms, or acronyms, of various governmental or intergovernmental agencies, social or professional organizations, and units of measurement used in scientific contexts are usually not followed by periods: *ACLU, CARE, CBS,*

CEEB, CIA, ICBM, NCAA, NATO, SEC, UNESCO, Btu, mpg, mph, rpm. New acronyms and abbreviated forms spring into existence nowadays with regularity. The following examples contain some that have gained common acceptance fairly recently: *AIDS* (acquired immune deficiency syndrome), *CAT scan* (computerized axial tomography), *CATV* (community antenna television), *CD* (certificate of deposit), *CEO* (chief executive officer), *COLA* (cost-of-living adjustment), *CPR* (cardiopulmonary resuscitation), *DWI* (driving while intoxicated), *IRA* (individual retirement account), *MIA* (missing in action), *MRI* (magnetic resonance imaging), *OPEC* (Organization of Petroleum-Exporting Countries), *PC* (personal computer), *STOL* (short takeoff and landing), *VCR* (videocassette recorder). Refer to your dictionary when in doubt about the meaning of an abbreviated form or the possibility of using periods. Be prepared to find apparent inconsistencies and divided usage.

Question Mark

The **question mark** is used after a direct question, which is an utterance that calls for an answer. (See Lesson 6.) But we do not use a question mark after an indirect question, which is a *statement* giving the substance of a question but not the words that would be used in a direct question.

Direct: Who goes there? Is that you? When do we eat? How much do I owe you? "Who goes there?" he demanded. [In dialogue]

Indirect: She asked me how old I was. I wondered why she would ask such a question. [Note that periods are used. These are statements, not direct questions.]

Exclamation Point

The **exclamation point** is used sparingly in modern writing and should be reserved for statements of strong feeling. Mild exclamations, such as *oh, goodness, well, yes,* and *no,* are followed by commas, not exclamation points. Be sure to place the exclamation mark after the exclamation itself.

"Help! I'm slipping!" he shouted. [Note the period after *shouted.*]
"Stop that!" she screamed. [Do not put the exclamation point after *screamed.*]
"Well, it was exciting, wasn't it?" "Oh, I had a pleasant time."

SUMMARY OF PUNCTUATION RULES

Punctuation is not complex, nor are the rules many and involved; they can be learned quickly. In this review we shall simplify them still more by listing only the important ones that you use constantly in your everyday writing. You can see how few of them there actually are. Colons, dashes, parentheses, hyphens, and even question marks and exclamation points do have other uses for special occasions or effects; but these occasional applications rarely cause problems for most writers.

The important thing for you to do now is to study these really indispensable rules until you are perfectly at home with them. And then, of course, if all of this is to do you any good, you must use your knowledge in everything you write, whether it is "for English," or in a letter to a friend, or in a notebook for a course in biology.

Commas to Separate: Five Rules

1. Coordinate clauses
2. Items in a series
3. Coordinate adjectives
4. Introductory modifiers
5. Words that may be misread together

Colon: Two Rules

1. If the text following a colon is a complete sentence, use an initial capital letter.
2. Do not use a colon to separate a verb from its complement or a preposition from its object.

Apostrophe: Two Rules

1. With possessives
2. With contractions

Period: Two Rules

1. After declarative sentences
2. After most abbreviations

Commas to Enclose: Eight Rules

1. Nonrestrictive clauses and phrases
2. Appositives
3. Absolute phrases
4. Parenthetical expressions
5. Words in direct address
6. The speaker in dialogue
7. Negative insertions
8. Dates, addresses, degrees, and titles

Semicolon: One Rule

1. In compound sentences without conjunction

Quotation Marks: Three Rules

1. About direct quotations
2. About titles
3. About words used in some special way

Question Mark: One Rule

1. After direct questions

NAME _____   SCORE _____

Directions: The following sentences contain fifty numbered spaces between words or beneath words. (The number is beneath the word when the problem involves the use of an apostrophe in that word.) In the correspondingly numbered spaces at the left, write C if the punctuation is correct or W if it is incorrect.

1. _____   (1) Jim's successes in sales are caused by: his outgoing personality,
                                                        1

2. _____   his work habits, and a network of friends.
                              2

3. _____   (2) Mr. Allan, who teaches physics, said, "Fifteen quotations on one page
                                              3   4

4. _____   is simply too many."

5. _____   (3) "Did anyone," asked Miss. Jacobs, "read the editorial in this morn-
                                        5

6. _____   ing's paper titled 'No Landfill in our County'?"
                                                          6

7. _____   (4) I know I can learn to be a touch-typist, I have an excellent typing
                                                    7   8

8. _____   tutorial in my computer.

9. _____   (5) Our program calls for three sessions a week, if that is too many,
                                                        9   10

10. _____   we can make adjustments.

11. _____   (6) Whenever we go to the farm; we get a wonderful quiet break from
                                            11   12

12. _____   the hectic pace of the city.

13. _____   (7) I shot two rolls of film yesterday, the best picture is one of that
                                              13

14. _____   old boat of our's.
                          14

15. _____   (8) We had a long conversation with our contractor last night, as she
                                                                    15

16. _____   left, she said, "Its been good to do business with you."
                              16

17. _____   (9) "When will your report be completed?" asked Mrs. Roberts, who
                                              17   18

18. _____   had been waiting for it for three days.

19. _____ (10) All her dreams, all that work, all that time—all seemed worth-
                                            19   20

20. _____   while on that graduation night.

21. _____ (11) The smiling cheerful students left the room after they finished
                          21

22. _____   the difficult final exam.
                              22

195

23. _____ (12) The smiling teacher walked slowly into the room, then she made
23

24. _____ a long, difficult assignment for the next class.
24

25. _____ (13) After the trumpet players came two guitar players and a man car-
25
26

26. _____ rying a saxophone.

27. _____ (14) My neighbor's house is bright pink, the only soft color is in the
27

28. _____ trees, standing in the front yard.
28

29. _____ (15) Many young lawyers now have an unusual goal; writing a novel
29
30

30. _____ that will make them wealthy.

31. _____ (16) Although the pollsters called several hundred people among my
31

32. _____ friends, no one has been contacted.
32

33. _____ (17) "This book was on my desk," said Marilyn, "but it's not mine;
33

34. _____ I'll ask Helen if its hers."
34

35. _____ (18) I wonder why I can't find a typist who works quickly, makes few
35

36. _____ mistakes, and does not charge a high rate?
36

37. _____ (19) If properly maintained cars can last for several years, with only
37
38

38. _____ minor repairs.

39. _____ (20) Alex has been trying to learn about politics; last week, he visited
39
40

40. _____ the local headquarters of the Democratic Party.

41. _____ (21) The school children poured out of the building; it was three
41

42. _____ o'clock and school was over for the day.
42

43. _____ (22) "I wonder," mused Wanda, "why most people's sense of humor of-
43

44. _____ ten exercises itself at the expense of others?"
44

45. _____ (23) Several of our friends have gone on vacation; they have gone to the
45

46. _____ beach, to the mountains and to the lakes region.
46

47. _____ (24) And then we saw friends, the most beautiful awe-inspiring sunset
47
48

48. _____ that I can remember.

49. _____ (25) Running down the dusty road we saw two deer and several wild tur-
49
50

50. _____ keys hiding in the woods.

NAME _____ SCORE _____

Directions: Draw a circle around each error in punctuation. If the punctuation is incorrect, write a W in the space before the sentence. If the punctuation is correct, write C in the space.

_____ 1. " 'Blues Highlights,' our new show here on 99.9 FM, offers the best of the blues at 8:00 P.M. every Friday," said Mr. Andrews.

_____ 2. Both NASA and NOAA use satellites in their operations.

_____ 3. Is James' office address 8000 Riverbend Road, Atlanta, GA 30577.

_____ 4. "Watch out!" shouted Ron; there's an angry bull in that pasture."

_____ 5. Mrs. Johanssen and Ms. Robinson have declined our invitation to a 1:00 P.M. luncheon meeting on Friday, haven't they?

_____ 6. The N.C.A.A. has issued a new ruling, hasn't it, on eligibility?

_____ 7. "It was President Truman who said, 'If you can't stand the heat, stay out of the kitchen,' " said Professor Tyler.

_____ 8. We have to hurry," snapped John; the plane arrives at 1:00 P.M. sharp."

_____ 9. The note card says that the article is in vol. III, no. 2, p.p. 232 of *National Geographic.*

_____ 10. After you finish the M.S. degree, will you work for a Ph.D.

_____ 11. Many of the new cars, e.g., the Ford Explorer, can be ordered with anti-lock brakes.

_____ 12. Ms. Haskins is the new sales manager at Holbrook Fixtures, Inc.

_____ 13. "Did she say, 'I can't find my notes for the history test,'?" asked Mrs. Reynolds.

_____ 14. Please ask him why we do not yet have the report?

_____ 15. Wrenches, pliers, several screwdrivers, etc were scattered over the mechanic's work table.

_____ 16. Ryan Phillips, D.D.S, is the new dentist here in Southport.

_____ 17. Is the expression "stutter-step" a new term in football jargon?

_____ 18. "Grab my hand! I'm slipping off the dock," screamed Mary!

_____ 19. My V.C.R. doesn't play the tapes from my camcorder without an adapter.

_____ 20. COLAs will probably be dropped from the company's contract with A.F. of L.-CIO, which is up for renewal on March 18, 1999.

Directions: In the following sentences, correct every error in punctuation. Then, in the column of figures at the left, circle every number that represents an error in that sentence. Use these numbers:

1. Comma omitted
2. Apostrophe omitted or misused
3. Comma misused for semicolon
4. Semicolon misused for comma

1 2 3 4   (1) At one o'clock today my family left for Salt Lake City, they will stay in a friends condo while they are there.

1 2 3 4   (2) Since we left the stadium we have seen Marge, Joe and Tom.

1 2 3 4   (3) Mario saw several interesting sights in Canada, he saw, for instance a bighorn sheep on the side of a mountain.

1 2 3 4   (4) Walking across the valley we got caught in a storm, the rain, the thunder and the lightning made the hike a terrifying experience.

1 2 3 4   (5) Although Ann followed James directions very carefully; the car still misfired after she changed the plugs.

1 2 3 4   (6) "Were going to see a great movie tonight," said Tina, "it's story comes from a novel by one of my former English teachers."

1 2 3 4   (7) That route you know, was planned by the automobile club, the bad roads we encountered should not be on the club's list.

1 2 3 4   (8) All the people in the office looked admiringly at the results of Claudia's research, she had spent weeks' assembling statistics, photographs and interviews.

1 2 3 4   (9) On Saturday, April 19, 1993, the three students set out for Springfield, Illinois, another, older Springfield is in Massachusetts.

1 2 3 4 (10) After the three women left the office; they drove down to a small rustic restaurant located in a forest beside a river.

NAME _____   SCORE _____

Directions: The following sentences contain fifty numbered spots between words or beneath words. (The number is beneath the word when the problem involves the use of an apostrophe in that word.) In the correspondingly numbered spots at the left, write C if the punctuation is correct or W if it is incorrect.

1. _____   (1) Since it was Wednesday afternoon; all the shops in the little country
2. _____   town were closed except: the drugstore, the grocer, and one gas station.
3. _____   (2) When Joe left for school, he had a few day's pay coming, there-
4. _____   fore the manager will mail it to him tomorrow.
5. _____   (3) "I had the map before I got in the car, but I couldn't find it later
6. _____   on," said Martin, the absent-minded member of our group.
7. _____   (4) The graduation presents Jim's rich uncle sent him must have been
8. _____   a joke: a box of pencils, two note pads and a small eraser.
9. _____   (5) The price of that car—as you had suggested—being far too high;
10. _____   Jordan decided to look at another dealer for a new car.
11. _____ (6) Scooping up all the marbles and putting them in the box the kid
12. _____   said, "When you play for keeps; you can lose them all."
13. _____ (7) When Pop Olson found the two puppies, he guessed they might be
14. _____   your's or Jane Van de Meer's.
15. _____ (8) A good fisherman must have certain qualities; a love for early ris-
16. _____   ing, a fondness for being wet, and an inability to feel the cold until
17. _____   long after it has arrived.
18. _____ (9) James Dowling, who manages the track team said, "We can't seem to
19. _____   find shoes big enough for old George, size 14EEE is pretty rare."
20. _____ (10) Richard left this morning for Oregon, in fact, he took all his
21. _____   possessions with him and said he'd never be back.
22. _____ (11) "We all finished work about 4:00 o'clock," reported Sarah, "then we
               played trash-can basketball until time to leave."

199

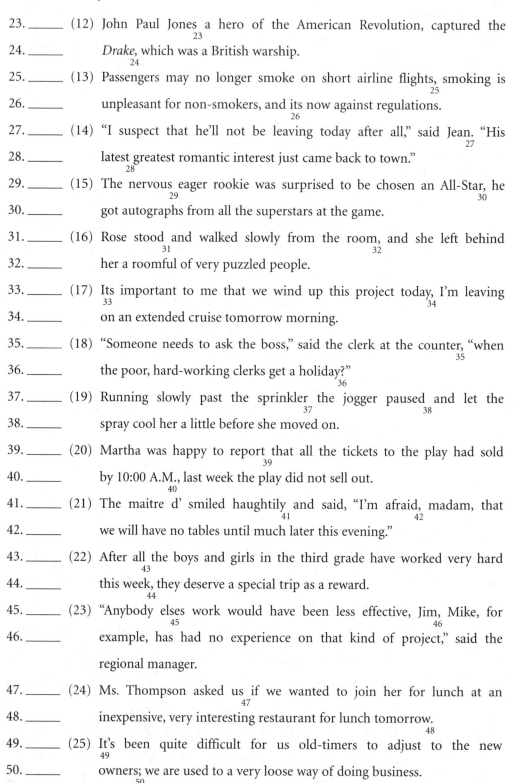

23. _____ (12) John Paul Jones a hero of the American Revolution, captured the
24. _____ *Drake,* which was a British warship.

25. _____ (13) Passengers may no longer smoke on short airline flights, smoking is
26. _____ unpleasant for non-smokers, and its now against regulations.

27. _____ (14) "I suspect that he'll not be leaving today after all," said Jean. "His
28. _____ latest greatest romantic interest just came back to town."

29. _____ (15) The nervous eager rookie was surprised to be chosen an All-Star, he
30. _____ got autographs from all the superstars at the game.

31. _____ (16) Rose stood and walked slowly from the room, and she left behind
32. _____ her a roomful of very puzzled people.

33. _____ (17) Its important to me that we wind up this project today, I'm leaving
34. _____ on an extended cruise tomorrow morning.

35. _____ (18) "Someone needs to ask the boss," said the clerk at the counter, "when
36. _____ the poor, hard-working clerks get a holiday?"

37. _____ (19) Running slowly past the sprinkler the jogger paused and let the
38. _____ spray cool her a little before she moved on.

39. _____ (20) Martha was happy to report that all the tickets to the play had sold
40. _____ by 10:00 A.M., last week the play did not sell out.

41. _____ (21) The maitre d' smiled haughtily and said, "I'm afraid, madam, that
42. _____ we will have no tables until much later this evening."

43. _____ (22) After all the boys and girls in the third grade have worked very hard
44. _____ this week, they deserve a special trip as a reward.

45. _____ (23) "Anybody elses work would have been less effective, Jim, Mike, for
46. _____ example, has had no experience on that kind of project," said the
regional manager.

47. _____ (24) Ms. Thompson asked us if we wanted to join her for lunch at an
48. _____ inexpensive, very interesting restaurant for lunch tomorrow.

49. _____ (25) It's been quite difficult for us old-timers to adjust to the new
50. _____ owners; we are used to a very loose way of doing business.

5 Usage

Lessons, Practice Sheets, and Exercises

Lesson 21 Using Verbs Correctly: Principal Parts; Tense

In Lesson 2 you learned that verbs are either regular or irregular and that the principal parts of the two classes are formed in different ways. We shall now examine certain trouble spots where incorrect forms sometimes appear because of confusion in the use of the principal parts. (See Supplement 1.)

To gain assurance in your use of verbs, you must remember how the past tense and the past participle are used. The **past tense** is always a single-word verb; it is never used with an auxiliary:

I *ate* my lunch. [Not I *have ate* my lunch.]

The **past participle** is *never* a single-word verb; it is used with the auxiliary *have* (to form the perfect tenses) or the auxiliary *be* (to form the passive voice):

I *have done* the work. The work *was done*. [Not I *done* the work.]

The past participle is used as a single word when it is a modifier of a noun: the *broken* toy, the *worried* parents, some *known* criminals.

Four groups of verbs that often cause confusion are illustrated in this lesson, each group containing verbs that have similar trouble spots. The basic solution for the problem in each group is to master the principal parts of the verbs; they are the ones that account for most of the verb form errors found in writing. The principal parts are listed in the customary order: base form, past tense, and past participle.

Past Tense versus Past Participle

In one common type of error, the problem in the form of the verb results from a confusion of the past tense and the past participle (P.P.):

	Verb	Past tense	P.P.
Later they *became* [not *become*] more friendly.	become	became	become
They *began* [not *begun*] to laugh at us.	begin	began	begun

201

He had never *broken* [not *broke*] the law.	break	broke	broken
I should have *chosen* [not *chose*] a larger car.	choose	chose	chosen
Yesterday the child *came* [not *come*] home.	come	came	come
I *did* [not *done*] what she told me to do.	do	did	done
He *drank* [not *drunk*] some water.	drink	drank	drunk
I had *driven* [not *drove*] all day.	drive	drove	driven
The lamp had *fallen* [not *fell*] over.	fall	fell	fallen
The bird has *flown* [not *flew*] away.	fly	flew	flown
Small puddles have *frozen* [not *froze*] on the sidewalks.	freeze	froze	frozen
Dad has *given* [not *gave*] me a car.	give	gave	given
Theresa has *gone* [not *went*] to school.	go	went	gone
I've never *ridden* [not *rode*] a horse.	ride	rode	ridden
We ran out when the fire alarm *rang* [not *rung*].	ring	rang	rung
Lenny has *run* [not *ran*] in two marathons.	run	ran	run
I *saw* [not *seen*] your nephew yesterday.	see	saw	seen
It must have *sunk* [not *sank*] in deep water.	sink	sank	sunk
She should have *spoken* [not *spoke*] louder.	speak	spoke	spoken
The car had been *stolen* [not *stole*].	steal	stole	stolen
The witness was *sworn* [not *swore*] in.	swear	swore	sworn
John has *swum* [not *swam*] across the lake.	swim	swam	swum
Someone had *torn* [not *tore*] the dollar bill.	tear	tore	torn
You should have *worn* [not *wore*] a hat.	wear	wore	worn
I have already *written* [not *wrote*] my essay.	write	wrote	written

Regular versus Irregular

Another type of error results from a confusion of regular and irregular verb forms:

	Verb	*Past tense*	*P.P.*
The wind *blew* [not *blowed*] steadily all day.	blow	blew	blown
John *brought* [not *bringed*] Mary some flowers.	bring	brought	brought
This house was *built* [not *builded*] in 1795.	build	built	built
Barbara *caught* [not *catched*] two trout.	catch	caught	caught
Slowly they *crept* [not *creeped*] up the stairs.	creep	crept	crept
He *dealt* [not *dealed*] me a good hand.	deal	dealt	dealt
The men quickly *dug* [not *digged*] a pit.	dig	dug	dug
She *drew* [not *drawed*] a caricature of me.	draw	drew	drawn
All the men *grew* [not *growed*] long beards.	grow	grew	grown
Ben *hung* [not *hanged*] his cap on the hook.	hang	hung	hung
I *knew* [not *knowed*] him at college.	know	knew	known
I have never *lent* [not *lended*] him money.	lend	lent	lent
We *sought* [not *seeked*] shelter from the rain.	seek	sought	sought
The sun *shone* [not *shined*] all day yesterday.	shine	shone	shone
The prince *slew* [not *slayed*] the fierce dragon.	slay	slew	slain
I soon *spent* [not *spended*] the money.	spend	spent	spent
Ms. Andrews *taught* [not *teached*] us algebra.	teach	taught	taught
Lou *threw* [not *throwed*] the receipt away.	throw	threw	thrown
The old man *wept* [not *weeped*] piteously.	weep	wept	wept

Obsolete or Dialectal Forms

A third type of error results from the use of an obsolete or dialectal form of the verb, a form not considered standard now:

I *am* [not *be*] working regularly. I *have been* [not *been*] working regularly.	be*	was, were	been
The child *burst* [not *busted*] out crying.	burst	burst	burst
I've *bought* [not *boughten*] a car.	buy	bought	bought
I *climbed* [not *clumb*] a tree for a better view.	climb	climbed	climbed
The women *clung* [not *clang*] to the raft.	cling	clung	clung
The dog *dragged* [not *drug*] the old shoe home.	drag	dragged	dragged
The boy was nearly *drowned* [not *drownded*].	drown	drowned	drowned
At the picnic I *ate* [not *et*] too many hot dogs.	eat	ate	eaten
Betty *flung* [not *flang*] the stick away.	fling	flung	flung
You *paid* [not *payed*] too much for it.	pay	paid	paid
It had been *shaken* [not *shooken*] to pieces.	shake	shook	shaken
He had never *skinned* [not *skun*] a cat.	skin	skinned	skinned
A bee *stung* [not *stang*] me as I stood there.	sting	stung	stung
The girl *swung* [not *swang*] at the ball.	swing	swung	swung
I wonder who could have *taken* [not *tooken*] it.	take	took	taken

Confusing Verb Forms

A fourth type of verb error results from a confusion of forms of certain verbs that look or sound almost alike but are actually quite different in meaning, such as *lie, lay; sit, set;* and *rise, raise.* Note that three of these troublesome verbs—*lay, set,* and *raise*—in their ordinary uses take an object. The other three—*lie, sit, rise*—do not take an object.

Please *lay* your books [D.O.] on the table. Mary *laid* several logs [D.O.] on the fire. The men have *laid* some boards [D.O.] over the puddle.	lay	laid	laid
Our cat often *lies* [not *lays*] on the couch. Yesterday our cat *lay* [not *laid*] on the couch. Our cat has *lain* [not *laid*] on the couch all morning.	lie	lay	lain
She *sets* the plate [D.O.] in front of me. An hour ago Tom *set* out some food [D.O.] for the birds. I had *set* the camera [D.O.] at a full second.	set	set	set
I usually *sit* in that chair. Yesterday he *sat* in my chair. I have *sat* at my desk all morning.	sit	sat	sat
At her command they *raise* the flag [D.O.]. The boy quickly *raised* his hand [D.O.]. He had *raised* the price [D.O.] of his old car.	raise	raised	raised

*As you learned in Lesson 2, the irregular verb *be* has three forms (*am, are, is*) in the present tense, and two forms (*was, were*) in the past tense.

He *rises* when we enter the room.

Everyone *rose* as the speaker entered the room.

The water has *risen* a foot since midnight.

rise   rose   risen

Exceptions

The rules and illustrations given here will serve as a guide in most situations. They show the importance of knowing the principal parts of these verbs. Note, however, that there are a few exceptions, such as the intransitive uses of *set:*

A *setting* [not *sitting*] hen *sets.* [That is, *broods;* of course, a hen, like a rooster or any other appropriate entity, may be said to *sit* when that is what is meant.]

The sun *sets* in the west.

Cement or a dye *sets.*

A jacket *sets (fits)* well.

With a few verbs, special meanings demand different principal parts. For example, the past tense and the past participle of *shine,* when the verb is used as a transitive verb, are *shined:*

This morning I *shined* [not *shone*] my shoes.

The verb *hang* with the meaning "to execute by suspending by the neck until dead" uses *hanged,* not *hung,* for the past tense and the past participle. When in doubt, always refer to your dictionary.

Sequence of Tenses

In Lesson 2 you studied a partial conjugation showing the forms of three sample verbs as they occur in six tenses. And in Lesson 5 you were told the basic uses of the six tenses. Although most student writers usually have little difficulty in establishing and maintaining logical time relationships in their sentences, we should note a few situations that sometimes cause confusion.

Subordinate Clauses

The tense in a subordinate clause is normally the same as that in the main clause unless a different time for the subordinate statement is clearly indicated.

We suspect that Jim *cheats* on his tax return.

We suspect that Jim *cheated* on his tax return last year.

We suspect that Jim *will cheat* on his tax return next year.

We suspect that Jim *has* often *cheated* on his tax returns.

We suspect that Jim *had cheated* on his tax return before he finally was arrested.

Universally True Statements

The present tense is used for a statement that is universally true.

The dietitian reminded us that whipped cream *is* (not *was*) fattening.

I wonder who first discovered that oysters *are* (not *were*) edible.

Careful Narrative Writing

In narrative writing a shift from past tense to present tense, a device sometimes used effectively by skilled writers, should be used cautiously.

> The library *was* silent except for an occasional whisper, when suddenly a side door *opened* [not *opens*] and a disheveled young man *dashed* [not *dashes*] in and *started* [not *starts*] yelling "Man the lifeboats!" After the librarians *had managed* to restore order . . .

Present Perfect Tense

The perfect form of an infinitive should not be used when the controlling verb is in the present perfect tense.

Correct: I would like to have seen that performance.
Correct: I would have liked to see that performance.
Incorrect: I would have liked to have seen that performance.

Supplement 1

Mention should be made here of another slight change in verb form that is possible. The partial conjugation given in Lesson 2 showed only the **indicative mood** (or **mode**), the forms that are used in nearly all statements and questions that you read or write. A second mood, the **imperative,** causes no complications; it is merely the base form of the verb when used to give a command or a request, with the subject *you* generally not expressed:

> *Be* here by noon.
> Please *come* to my office.

Subjunctive

A third mood, the **subjunctive,** is sometimes shown by a change in the form of the verb. In this change *be* is used instead of *am, is,* or *are; were* is used instead of *was;* and, rarely, a third-person singular verb is used without the *s,* for instance, "he *leave*" instead of "he *leaves.*"

Were versus Was. There is really only one situation in modern English in which the subjunctive form *were* is regularly used instead of *was,* and that is in an if clause making a statement that is clearly and unmistakably contrary to fact. The most obvious example is the everyday expression "If I *were* you, I'd . . . ." Remember the "If-I-*were*-you" set pattern to remind you of other "contrary-to-fact" clauses in which the subjunctive *were* would be expected in serious writing and speaking:

> If I *were* able to fly . . . *Were* I president of this country . . . If she *were* thirty years younger . . .

Divided usage prevails in a few other remnants of earlier subjunctive uses, especially in formal writing, for example, in "wish" clauses (reflecting also a contrary-to-fact situation):

> On frigid days like this, I wish I *were* in Tahiti.

The subjunctive is also found in certain set patterns of resolutions and demands:

> I move that Mr. Shaw *be* appointed.
> The chairman demanded that the reporter *leave* the room.
> It is imperative that you *be* here by ten o'clock.

In many of these and similar sentence situations in which older English insisted on subjunctive forms, modern speakers and writers often choose either an indicative form or one of the modal auxiliaries, such as *should, may,* or *might.*

Using Verbs Correctly: Principal Parts; Tense

NAME _____ SCORE _____

Directions: In the space at the left, write the correct form of the verb shown within parentheses. Do not use any *-ing* forms.

_____
_____ 1. As soon as she (see) the smoke, Laura (run) into the house and called the fire department.

_____
_____ 2. The child who had (fall) from the boat paddled to the end of the dock and (cling) to a rung of the ladder.

_____
_____ 3. When Velma (begin) to back her car out of the driveway, a speeding truck (come) very close to hitting her.

_____
_____ 4. Yesterday at noon some of us (swim) out to the sand bar in the bay, where we (lie) sunning ourselves most of the afternoon.

_____
_____ 5. As we (sit) in the car watching the flooded stream, we noticed that the water had (rise) nearly a foot since the night before.

_____
_____ 6. Because of my awkwardness in the saddle, anyone would have (know) that I had never before (ride) a horse.

_____
_____ 7. "After you have (shake) the snow from your coats," said the innkeeper, "come in and warm your (freeze) hands and feet."

_____
_____ 8. Tommy (throw) away the bunch of seaweed that he had patiently (drag) up from the beach.

_____
_____ 9. The four men, completely (wore) out from the long search, eagerly (drink) the hot coffee and started to write their report.

_____
_____ 10. As she (lie) there in the infirmary, Stella bemoaned the fact that she had (eat) so many of the so-called mushrooms.

_____
_____ 11. Yesterday afternoon our neighbor Betsy (bring) over her Uncle Frank, who had just (fly) in from Boston.

_____
_____ 12. We could have (go) downtown to see the parade, but instead we (choose) to stay home and watch it on television.

_____ 13. Shortly after lunch yesterday one of the children (come) running
_____ to the infirmary and said that she had been (sting) by a bee.

_____ 14. "You (do) a wise thing when you reported to the police that the
_____ lock on the door had been (break)," said the officer.

_____ 15. Jenkins was accused of having (buy) materials that had been
_____ (steal) from a nearby Army base.

_____ 16. Ms. Swenson (become) leery of her business partner when she
_____ saw that he had (spend) expense money on frivolous items.

_____ 17. The morning broadcast reported that last week a ferry boat in
_____ China had (sink) and that hundreds were feared (drown).

_____ 18. On her kitchen wall Mrs. Denham has (hang) nearly all of the
_____ pictures that her granddaughter has (draw) in kindergarten.

_____ 19. Before I had (speak) a dozen words, the man interrupted by say-
_____ ing, "Sorry, lady, but I've already (give) at the office."

_____ 20. The first three witnesses had already (swear) that they had never
_____ (lend) any money to the accused embezzler.

Directions: Each sentence contains two italicized verb units. If the principal part or tense of the verb is the form proper in serious writing, write C in the corresponding space at the left. If the verb is incorrect, write the correct form in the space.

_____ 1. Ginny was upset when she *tore* the dress because she had *wore* it
_____   only three times.

_____ 2. The foreman told me that I should have *set* the timber firmly in
_____   concrete instead of *laying* it on the ground.

_____ 3. When Egbert *seen* the questions on the midterm examination, he
_____   *become* even more confused.

_____ 4. If I *was* you, I wouldn't *lie* near the open window on a cold, damp
_____   night like tonight.

_____ 5. The puppy was half-*froze*, but it lapped up the warm milk as if it
_____   hadn't *eaten* in days.

_____ 6. We now realize that it would have been wiser to *have admitted*
_____   that it was you who *stoled* the camera.

_____ 7. Cecil has *bought* new pipes for his summer cabin because the
_____   original ones *burst* during the winter freeze.

_____ 8. After the guide had *swum* across the river, the water *raised* and
_____   flooded our old campsite.

_____ 9. Last night the wind *blowed* a tree down that blocked the highway,
_____   and this morning a crew *dragged* it to one side.

_____ 10. Some child had *throwed* an old beach ball into the patch of tall
_____   weeds that had *grown* in the vacant lot.

_____ 11. In a few short weeks the leaves will have *fallen* and the birds will
_____   have *flew* south for the winter.

_____ 12. Denny *begun* to feel uneasy as soon as he had *rung* the doorbell
_____   of the dilapidated old house.

_____ 13. Had I *knew* that you needed the car today, I would have *rode* the
_____   bus to work.

_____ 14. Professor Lee *lay* aside his notes and concluded his speech by say-
_____   ing, "Unfortunately, this early scholar was later *hung* for horse
    stealing."

_____ 15. "I was *laying* down for a nap when you called," said Norma. "You
_____   should have *wrote* a note and left it in the mailbox."

_____ 16. The final bell must have *rung,* for the children have all *risen* and
_____   are waiting to be dismissed.

_____ 17. Ms. Canwell *done* the wise thing when she laughed heartily at the
_____   caricature of her that some student had *drawed* on the chalk-
     board.

_____ 18. Shortly after class ended, Jeremy *come* back to the classroom and
_____   told Ms. Saylor that someone had *taken* his jacket.

_____ 19. Jenny *climbed* out of the pool and said, "All of you were laughing,
_____   and I came close to *drowning.*"

_____ 20. Betsy Leavitt has been *setting* next to me all term in my algebra
_____   class, but I have *spoke* to her only a few times.

Exercise 21 — Using Verbs Correctly: Principal Parts; Tense

NAME _____ SCORE _____

Directions: In the space at the left, write the correct form of the verb shown within parentheses. Do not use *-ing* forms.

_____
_____
1. In the middle of the seventh inning, the crowd (rise) to its feet and (sing) "Take Me Out to the Ballgame."

_____
_____
2. "Marcia has (be) a friend for years, and I have often (lend) my car to her," said Mr. Johnson.

_____
_____
3. My roses have just (begin) to grow again; I could not have (choose) better weather for their growth.

_____
_____
4. We (see) Tom's new car yesterday and wondered how much he had (pay) for it.

_____
_____
5. Yesterday the wind (blow) briskly, and we (swim) in the waves for quite some time.

_____
_____
6. After the sailors had (shine) all the brass, they (lie) around on the deck resting.

_____
_____
7. Real estate prices have (rise) quite rapidly this year; I should have (buy) that acreage months ago.

_____
_____
8. Last Tuesday Jan (fly) to Seattle; she had never (fly) anywhere in a plane before.

_____
_____
9. The farmer has (sink) a 300-foot well in his pasture because the drought had (dry) up the springs.

_____
_____
10. Sam walked into the office, (set) his briefcase on the desk, and (say), "I've done a good day's work today."

_____
_____
11. After the bailiff had (swear) in the witness, the prosecutor (begin) to ask questions.

_____
_____
12. "That was the hardest exam I've ever (take)," said Marv. "I (write) two blue books full of material."

211

_____ 13. The young girl (run) to the bank, (dive) into the river, and raced
_____   to the island.

_____ 14. Just after my cat had (lie) down in the driveway, a car (drive) in
_____   and frightened him away.

_____ 15. Yesterday's violent wind has (shake) loose several awnings and
_____   has (bend) several small trees into knots.

_____ 16. He's never (wear) that coat before because he (tear) a button off
_____   the cuff when he first hung it in the closet.

_____ 17. When he (see) the golfer's pants, my brother (burst) into laugh-
_____   ter at the strange colors.

_____ 18. Sobbing softly, the girl slowly (climb) the ladder and (cling) fear-
_____   fully to the top rung.

_____ 19. By the time we had (drag) the logs from the field, the sun had
_____   (fall) below the horizon and we were exhausted.

_____ 20. The newspaper carrier has (fling) my paper onto the roof again;
_____   I wish he (be) a little less dedicated.

Directions: Each sentence has two italicized verb units. If the principal part or tense of the verb is the form proper in serious writing, write C in the corresponding space at the left. If the verb is incorrect, write the correct form in the space.

_____ 1. The reporter sighed and said, "I've *wrote* two long stories since I
_____ *seen* the world outside this building."

_____ 2. "I hope you have all *ate* a good breakfast and you weren't just *lay-*
_____ *ing* in bed," said the scoutmaster.

_____ 3. The two boys *creeped* out on the dock and would have *doven* into
_____ the water except the guard stopped them.

_____ 4. Janet falls onto the couch, kicks off her shoes, and *said,* "These
_____ shoes have *hurted* my feet all day long."

_____ 5. John has *payed* for his tuition and his books, but he has not *dug*
_____ up the money for his meal ticket.

_____ 6. I've *lain* my class work aside for a day because my car *thrown* a
_____ rod and I need to get it to a shop.

_____ 7. Perhaps I could have *understanded* your answer better if I had
_____ *known* you misunderstood my question.

_____ 8. I *read* in my encyclopedia that the moon *was* about 240,000 miles
_____ from Earth.

_____ 9. When George *come* back from his vacation he found that a tree
_____ had *fell* on the roof of his garage.

_____ 10. Although we could have *shaken* a few pears from the tree, my sis-
_____ ter *clumb* halfway to the top for the best fruit.

_____ 11. I've *drove* all those stakes on that line, and I've *worn* blisters on
_____ both hands with this sledge hammer.

_____ 12. Most students would have *chose* to *have written* a take-home test
_____ rather than an in-class test.

_____ 13. The work *was* so easy I almost felt that I *had stolen* the money in
_____ my paycheck.

_____ 14. When they first *become* available, people across the country
_____ *buyed* millions of those gadgets.

_____ 15. The soldiers all *shone* their shoes until the tips *shined* like stars.
_____

_____ 16. My family first *set* foot in this county 100 years ago, and we *been*
_____ living here ever since.

_____ 17. The earliest we have ever *swum* in the river was the first of May,
_____ but this year warm weather *come* earlier.

_____ 18. My father has *flown* so often recently that he wishes someone
_____ would *have given* him a train ticket.

_____ 19. When the seller *raised* the price of the car, I should have *rose* from
_____ my chair and cancelled the deal.

_____ 20. That book has *lain* on the table for three days, but no one can tell
_____ me who *laid* it there originally.

Observe that in the present tense, the third-person singular *(He, She, It)* verb form differs from the third-person plural *(They)* verb form.

I earn   We earn
You earn   You earn
He, She, It earns   They earn

This change we call a change in number: **Singular number** means that only one thing is talked about; **plural number** means that more than one thing is talked about. Notice how verbs and nouns differ in this respect: The *s* ending on nouns is a plural marker, but on verbs it designates the singular form.

The following examples show how the number of the subject (one, or more than one) affects the form of the verb. The verbs *have, do,* and *be* are important because they have auxiliary uses as well as main-verb uses. *Be* is an exceptional verb; it changes form in the past tense as well as in the present tense.

Singular   *Plural*

She *walks* slowly.   They *walk* slowly.
Mother *seems* pleased.   My parents *seem* pleased.
Mary *has* a new dress.   All of the girls *have* new dresses.
He *has traveled* widely.   They *have traveled* widely.
She *does* her work easily.   They *do* their work easily.
Does he *have* enough time?   *Do* they *have* enough time?
He *is* a friend of mine.   They *are* friends of mine.
My brother *is coming* home.   My brothers *are coming* home.
His camera *was taken* from him.   Their cameras *were taken* from them.

Verb Agrees in Number

The relation of verb form to subject follows an important principle of usage: **The verb always agrees in number with its subject.** Although the principle is simple, some of the situations in which it applies are not. You will avoid some common writing errors if you keep in mind the following seven extensions of the principle. The first is probably the most necessary.

*1. **The number of the verb is not affected by material that comes between the verb and the subject.*** Determine the *real* subject of the verb; watch out for intervening words that might mislead you. Remember that the number of the verb is not altered when other nouns are attached to the subject by means of prepositions such as *in addition to, together with, as well as, with, along with.* Remember also that indefinite pronoun subjects like *either, neither, each, one, everyone, no one, somebody* take singular verbs:

215

Immediate *settlement* of these problems *is* [not *are*] vital. [The subject is *settlement. Problems,* being here the object of the preposition *of,* cannot also be a subject.]

The *cost* of replacing the asbestos shingles with cedar shakes *was* [not *were*] considerable.

Tact, as well as patience, *is* [not *are*] required.

Mr. Sheldon, together with several other division heads, *has* [not *have*] left.

Each of the plans *has* [not *have*] its good points.

Is [not *Are*] *either* of the contestants ready?

None may take either a singular or a plural verb, depending on whether the writer wishes to emphasize "not one" or "no members" of the group. (See Supplement 1.)

None of us *is* [or *are*] perfect.

2. A verb agrees with its subject even when the subject follows the verb. Be especially careful to find the real subject in sentences starting with *there* or *here:*

On the wall *hangs* a *portrait* of his father. [*Portrait hangs.*]
On the wall *hang portraits* of his parents. [*Portraits hang.*]
He handed us a piece of paper on which *was scribbled* a *warning.* [*Warning was scribbled.*]
There *was* barely enough *time* remaining.
There *were* only ten *minutes* remaining.
There *seems* to be one *problem* remaining.
There *seem* to be a few *problems* remaining.
Here *is* a free *ticket* to the game.
Here *are* some free *tickets* to the game.

3. Compound subjects joined by and *take a plural verb:*

A little *boy* and his *dog were* playing in the yard.
On the platform *were* a *table* and four *chairs.*

But the verb should be singular if the subjects joined by *and* are thought of as a single thing, or if the subjects are considered separately, as when they are modified by *every* or *each:*

Plain *vinegar* and *oil is* all the dressing my salad needs. [One thing]
Every *man* and every *woman is* asked to help. [Considered separately]

4. Singular subjects joined by or *or* nor *take singular verbs:*

Either a *check* or a money *order is* required.
Neither the *manager* nor his *assistant has* arrived yet.
Was Mr. *Phelps* or his *son* put on the committee?

In some sentences of this pattern, especially in questions like the last example, a plural verb is sometimes used, both in casual conversation and in writing. In serious and formal writing, the singular verb is considered appropriate. If the subjects joined by *or* or *nor* differ in number, the verb agrees with the subject nearer to it:

Neither the *mother* nor the two *boys were* able to identify him.
Either the *players* or the *coach is* responsible for the defeat.

5. *Plural nouns of amount, distance, and so on, when they are used as singular units of measurement, take singular verbs:*

A hundred *dollars was* once paid for a single tulip bulb.
Thirty *miles seems* like a long walk to me.
Seven *years* in prison *was* the penalty that he had to pay.

6. *A collective noun is considered singular when the group is regarded as a unit; it is plural when the individuals of the group are referred to.* Similarly, words like *number, all, rest, part, some, more, most, half* are singular or plural, depending on the meaning intended. A word of this type is often accompanied by a modifier or referred to by a pronoun, either of which gives a clue to the number intended. When the word *number* is a subject, it is considered singular if it is preceded by *the* and plural if it is preceded by *a:*

The *audience is* very enthusiastic tonight.
The *audience are* returning to their seats. [Notice pronoun *their.*]
The *band is* playing a rousing march.
Now the *band are* putting away their instruments. [Again note *their.*]
Most of the book *is* blatant propaganda.
Most of her novels *are* now out of print.
The *rest* of the fortune *was* soon gone.
The *rest* of his debts *were* left unpaid.
The *number* of bank failures *is* increasing.
A *number* of these bank failures *are* being investigated.

7. *When the subject is a relative pronoun, the antecedent of the pronoun determines the number (and person) of the verb:*

He told a joke *that was* pointless. [*Joke was*]
He told several jokes *that were* pointless. [*Jokes were*]
I paid the expenses of the trip, *which were* minimal. [*Expenses were*]
Jack is one of those boys *who enjoy* fierce competition. [*Boys enjoy*]

The last example, sometimes called the "one of those . . . who" sentence, is particularly troublesome. Generally we find a plural verb used. If we recast the sentence to read "Of those boys who enjoy fierce competition, Jack is one," it becomes clear that the logical antecedent of *who* is the plural noun *boys.* However, usage is divided. And notice that a singular verb must be used when the pattern is altered slightly:

Jack is the only *one* of my friends *who enjoys* fierce competition.

Because a relative pronoun subject nearly always has an antecedent that is third-person singular or third-person plural, we are accustomed to pronoun–verb combinations like these:

A boy *who is . . .*
Boys *who are . . .*
A woman *who knows . . .*
Women *who know . . .*

But in those occasional sentences in which a relative pronoun subject has an antecedent that is in the first or second person, meticulously correct usage calls for subject–verb combinations like the following:

I, *who am* in charge here, should pay the bill. [*I . . . am.*]
They should ask me, *who know* all the answers. [*I . . . know.*]

You, *who are* in charge here, should pay the bill. [*You . . . are.*]
They should ask you, *who know* all the answers. [*You . . . know.*]

Supplement 1

One particular error of subject–verb agreement warrants special attention. The third-person singular present tense form of the verb *do* is *does*. The plural form is *do*. The misuse of the negative contraction *don't* (instead of *doesn't*) with a third-person singular subject is quite often encountered in spoken English. Many people, justly or unjustly, look on the "it-don't" misuse as an important marker of grossly substandard English. Such forms as the following should be avoided in all spoken and written English:

Faulty: My father *don't* like broccoli.
Faulty: It really *don't* matter.
Faulty: Jack Johnson *don't* live here now.
Faulty: One of her teachers *don't* like her.
Faulty: This fudge tastes good, *don't* it?
Faulty: The fact that the bill is overdue *don't* bother him.

SUMMARY OF CORRECT VERB USE

1. The principal parts of a verb are the present, the past, and the past participle. Avoid confusing principal parts of irregular verbs (*run, ran, run; eat, ate, eaten; fly, flew, flown*) with those of regular verbs (*study, studied, studied*). Be especially careful with the often confused principal parts of *lie* and *lay, sit* and *set*.
2. Singular verbs are used with singular subjects; plural verbs are used with plural subjects.
   a. Nouns intervening between the subject and the verb do not determine the number of the verb. (Resistance to the actions of these government agencies *is* [not *are*] growing.)
   b. Singular subjects joined by *and* normally take plural verbs. Singular subjects joined by *or* or *nor* normally take singular verbs.
   c. Some nouns and pronouns (collective nouns, and words like *number, all, half,* etc.) are singular in some meanings, plural in others.

NAME _____ SCORE _____

Directions: These sentences are examples of structures that often lead to errors in subject–verb agreement. In the space at the left, copy the correct verb in parentheses. In each sentence the subject of the verb is printed in bold type.

_____ 1. The pugnacious **acrobat** with his two assistants (was, were) taken into custody by the police.

_____ 2. "There (is, are) only a few **people** in this whole town who should be allowed to vote," said the irate colonel.

_____ 3. The many **activities** of daily living in a rural community (leaves, leave) little time for a child to be spoiled by the parents.

_____ 4. International law is useless unless **understanding** and a **feeling** of brotherhood (exists, exist) among nations.

_____ 5. Statistics show that only **one** out of five medical school seniors (plans, plan) to go into primary care practice.

_____ 6. The first **thing** that impresses visitors as they walk down the main hall (is, are) the spectacular colors of the walls and ceiling.

_____ 7. The velocity of the wind was so great that **portions** of the steel landing mat (was, were) lifted from the runway strip.

_____ 8. The assistant **manager** or **one** of the clerks (is, are) always on duty until 6 P.M.

_____ 9. There (has, have) always been **people** who seem to go out of their way to annoy their neighbors.

_____ 10. The **first** of the semifinal games (is, are) scheduled for Wednesday afternoon.

_____ 11. Jill soon realized that neither her **father** nor her **mother** (was, were) really listening to her arguments.

_____ 12. Not one **dollar** of these huge debts (was, were) ever repaid.

_____ 13. In the tiny room (was, were) a small **table** and four rather flimsy **chairs.**

_____ 14. I own two alarm clocks, **neither** of which (keeps, keep) very good time.

_____ 15. "(Has, Have) every **one** of these plans been approved by the regents?" asked Professor Goodfellow.

219

Directions: If you find an error in subject–verb agreement, underline the incorrect verb and write the correct form in the space at the left. Circle the subject of every verb you change. Some of the sentences may be correct.

————————————— 1. There was, as we all expected, many rumors about the replacement of our unsuccessful basketball coach.

————————————— 2. From fifty kilograms of polished rice a yield of nearly two hundred milligrams of the vitamin were obtained.

————————————— 3. "Why don't the university underwrite at least part of the cost of this experimental program?" asked one member of the audience.

————————————— 4. The success of these five experiments promises eventual control of the disease.

————————————— 5. "We know there's problems here; we're trying to correct them," said one hospital administrator.

————————————— 6. "I'm afraid that one of these bolts don't fit on the front wheel," said the mechanic's helper.

————————————— 7. Crescent Beach is one of the few picnic spots in the state that offer overnight camping privileges.

————————————— 8. At the present time neither of these two schools are turning out enough qualified veterinarians.

————————————— 9. The income from investments in mining and lumbering enterprises pay for the upkeep of the church.

————————————— 10. One out of every twenty persons brought up in these depressing surroundings have trouble eventually with the law.

————————————— 11. The two school buildings appear to be quite new, but a glimpse of the worn steps in the stairways tell a different story.

————————————— 12. The fact that the bill is now fourteen months overdue don't seem to trouble Jess very much.

————————————— 13. Has either of these teams been defeated yet this season?

————————————— 14. Ms. Horton, the adviser, doesn't seem to realize that neither Laura nor Jim are able to devote much time to the school newspaper.

————————————— 15. Posted on the bulletin board the next morning were a list of those seniors who had been put on probation.

NAME _____   SCORE _____

Directions: If you find an error in subject–verb agreement, underline the incorrect verb and write the correct form in the space at the left. Circle the subject of every verb you correct. Some of the sentences may be correct.

_____ 1. Many people were shocked to learn that not one of the arrested rioters were kept in jail for more than twenty hours.

_____ 2. Has either of your parents ever been active in PTA affairs?

_____ 3. Displayed on the mantel was a floral cover of a calendar and several pictures of the Jones's grandchildren.

_____ 4. One of the features of the sports car that Jeff admired most were the pop-up headlights.

_____ 5. "In view of these advantages, don't it seem silly to ban the use of this pesticide?" asked the senator from Clay County.

_____ 6. Each of the four pillars, measuring 2 feet high and about three feet in diameter, were hand-fluted.

_____ 7. Our mayor's enthusiasm for raw oysters, pop art, opera, duck hunting, and oceanography (to name a few) are awesome.

_____ 8. This hodgepodge of business and occupational taxes, licensings, household taxes, and garbage-collection charges is not only regressive but expensive to collect.

_____ 9. Her older son's basketball playing, not only as a freshman player but as a red-shirt, have been putting him through college.

_____ 10. Provision for individual differences provide work for the bright student and for the slower student.

_____ 11. I must admit that hearing classical music in concerts and through discs and tapes has resulted in a changed attitude.

_____ 12. "And so far as the preparation of teachers for these special students are concerned, progress is being made," said the speaker.

_____ 13. Remember that initialing the changes in a will does not necessarily make the changes legal.

_____ 14. The steady stream of new products designed to make life more pleasant present some problems to parents of large families.

_____ 15. Almost immediately the processes of natural selection in the environment begins.

_____ 16. All too often the potentialities of the library in the actual work of the literature class is overlooked.

_____ 17. Also included are a personalized atlas and travel guide, an insurance policy, special travel kits, and two exceptional bonus gifts.

_____ 18. Advantages of the use of a programmed text exists in three areas.

_____ 19. Our company is one of those corporations that are aware of the importance of a contented labor force.

_____ 20. Following the ceremony a sit-down dinner for more than two hundred guests were served at Byron's Country Kitchen.

_____ 21. At Alpine Lake during the summer season, the head lifeguard or one of her assistants are on duty during all daylight hours.

_____ 22. Included last year at our huge family picnic was a sack race, a three-legged race, and a pie-eating contest.

_____ 23. The lack of recognition for the long hours put in by these devoted volunteers are to be deplored.

_____ 24. "It's too bad, isn't it," said Professor Lynch, "that a knowledge of past wars and catastrophes have so little effect on our thinking?"

_____ 25. Mack and I usually do our studying at home; we've found that there's too many distractions at the crowded library.

_____ 26. A number of my friends have already signed the petition.

_____ 27. Two thousand dollars does seem an unreasonably high fine for such a trivial offense.

_____ 28. A copy of the mortgage, together with a record of payments over the past six years, were found in a kitchen drawer.

_____ 29. The fact that these bills are overdue by several months don't seem to worry Edith very much.

_____ 30. Neither the muggy weather nor the noise from the crew working in the street is making my headache any better.

A pronoun is a word that substitutes for a noun or another pronoun. The word for which a pronoun stands is called its **antecedent:**

> I called *Harry,* but *he* didn't answer. [*He* substitutes for *Harry. Harry* is the antecedent of *he.*]
>
> My *cap and scarf* were where I had left *them.* [The antecedent of *them* is the plural unit *cap and scarf.*]
>
> *I* will wash *my* car tomorrow.
>
> *One* of my friends is painting *his* house.
>
> *Three* of my friends are painting *their* houses.

To use pronouns effectively and without confusing your reader, you must follow two basic principles:

1. Establish a clear, easily identified relationship between a pronoun and its antecedent.
2. Make the pronoun and its antecedent agree in person, number, and gender.

Let us examine these requirements more fully.

Role of Antecedents

Personal pronouns should have definite antecedents and should be placed as near their antecedents as possible. Your readers should know exactly what a pronoun stands for. They should not be made to look through several sentences for its antecedent, nor should they be asked to manufacture an antecedent for it. When you discover in your writing a pronoun with no clear and unmistakable antecedent, your revision, as many of the following examples demonstrate, will often require rewriting to remove the faulty pronoun from your sentence.

Faulty: A strange car followed us closely, and *he* kept blinking his lights at us.
Improved: A strange car followed us closely, and the driver kept blinking his lights at us.

Faulty: Although Jenny was a real sports fan, her brother never became interested in *them.*
Improved: Although Jenny really liked sports, her brother never became interested in them.

Faulty: Mike is an excellent typist, although he never took a course in *it.*
Improved: Mike is an excellent typist, although he never took a course in typing.

The indefinite *you* or *they* is quite common in speech and in chatty, informal writing, but one should avoid using either in serious writing:

Faulty: In Alaska *they* catch huge king crabs.
Improved: In Alaska huge king crabs are caught. [Often the best way to correct an indefinite *they* or *you* sentence is to use a passive verb.]

223

Faulty: Before the reform measures were passed, *you* had few rights.
Improved: Before the reform measures were passed, people had few rights.
Before the reform measures were passed, one had few rights.

Faulty: At the employment office *they* gave me an application form.
Improved: A clerk at the employment office gave me an application form.
At the employment office I was given an application form.

A pronoun should not appear to refer equally well to either of two antecedents:

Faulty: Frank told Bill that *he* needed a haircut. [Which one needed a haircut?]
Improved: "You need a haircut," said Frank to Bill. [In sentences of this type, the direct quotation is sometimes the only possible correction.]

Avoid "It Says"

The "it says" introduction to statements, although common in informal language, is objectionable in serious writing. (See Supplement 1.)

Faulty: *It* says in the directions that the powder will dissolve in hot water.
Improved: The directions say that the powder will dissolve in hot water.

Faulty: *It* said on the morning news program that a bad storm is coming.
Improved: According to the morning news program, a bad storm is coming.

Avoid Unclear References

Avoid vague or ambiguous reference of relative and demonstrative pronouns.

Faulty: Only twenty people attended the lecture, *which* was due to poor publicity.
Improved: Because of poor publicity, only twenty people attended the lecture.

Faulty: Good writers usually have large vocabularies, and *this* is why I get poor grades on my themes.
Improved: I get poor grades on my papers because my vocabulary is inadequate; good writers usually have large vocabularies.

Special Cases: Which, This, That

A special situation relates to the antecedent of the pronouns *which, this,* and *that.* In a sentence such as "The children giggled, *which* annoyed the teacher" or "The children giggled, and *this* annoyed the teacher," the thing that annoyed the teacher is not the *children* but "the giggling of the children" or "the fact that the children giggled." This kind of reference to a preceding idea rather than to an expressed noun is unobjectionable provided that the meaning is instantly and unmistakably clear. But you should avoid sentences like the following. In the first one readers would be hard pressed to discover exactly what the *which* means, and in the second they must decide whether the antecedent is the preceding idea or the noun immediately preceding the *which:*

Faulty: Hathaway's application was rejected because he spells poorly, *which* is very important in an application letter.
Improved: Hathaway's application was rejected because he spells poorly; correct spelling is very important in an application letter.

Faulty: The defense attorney did not object to the judge's concluding remark, *which* surprised me.

Improved: I was surprised that the defense attorney did not object to the judge's concluding remark.

Pronoun Agreement

Pronouns should agree with their antecedents in person, number, and gender. The following chart classifies for you the three forms of each personal pronoun on the basis of person, number, and gender:

	Singular	*Plural*
1st person	[the person speaking] *I, my, me*	[the persons speaking] *we, our, us*
2nd person	[the person spoken to] *you, your, you*	[the persons spoken to] *you, your, you*
3rd person	[the person or thing spoken of] *he, his, him* *she, her, her* *it, its, it*	[the persons or things spoken of] *they, their, them*

A singular antecedent is referred to by a singular pronoun; a plural antecedent is referred to by a plural pronoun.

> Dad says that *he* is sure that *his* new friend will visit *him* soon.
> Dad and Mother say that *they* are sure that *their* new friend will visit *them* soon.

This principle of logical pronoun agreement is not as simple as these two examples might suggest. Recent language practices have given rise to two situations for which "rules" that apply in every instance cannot possibly be made. Student writers must, first of all, be aware of certain changing ideas about pronoun usage; then they must prepare themselves to make decisions among the choices available.

Indefinite Pronouns

The first of these two troublesome situations relates to some of the indefinite pronouns: *one, everyone, someone, no one, anyone, anybody, everybody, somebody, nobody, each, either,* and *neither.* These words have generally been felt to be singular; hence pronouns referring to them have customarily been singular and, unless the antecedent specifies otherwise, masculine. Singular pronouns have also been used in formal writing and speaking to refer to noun antecedents modified by singular qualifiers such as *each* and *every.* The four following examples illustrate the traditional, formal practice:

> Everybody has *his* faults and *his* virtues.
> Each of the sons is doing what *he* thinks is best.
> England expects every man to do *his* duty.
> No one succeeds in this firm if Dobbins doesn't like *him.*

The principal difficulty with this usage is that these indefinites, although regarded by strict grammarians as singular in form, carry with them a group or plural sense, with the result that people are often unsure whether pronouns referring to them should be singular or plural. Despite traditional pronouncements, every day we hear sentences of the "Everyone-will-do-*their*-best" type. Beginning writers, however, would do well to follow the established practice until they feel relatively secure about recognizing the occasional sentence in which a singular pronoun referring to an indefinite produces a strained or unnatural effect even though it does agree in form with its antecedent.

Gender Issues

Closely related to this troublesome matter of pronoun agreement is a second problem, this one dealing with gender. The problem is this: What reference words should be used to refer to such a word as *student*? Obviously there are female students and there are male students. With plural nouns there is no problem; *they, their,* and *them* refer to both masculine and feminine. For singular nouns the language provides *she, hers, her* and *he, his, him,* but there is not a pronoun to refer to third-person singular words that contain both male and female members.

Here again, as with the reference to third-person singular indefinites, the traditional practice has been to use masculine singular pronouns. Eighty or so years ago Henry James wrote the following sentence: "We must grant the artist his subject, his idea, his *donné;* our criticism is applied only to what he makes of it." In James's day that sentence was undoubtedly looked upon as unexceptionable; the pronouns followed what was then standard practice. But attitudes have changed. In the 1990s, if that sentence got past the eyes of an editor and appeared on the printed page, its implication that artists are exclusively male would make the sentence unacceptably discriminatory to many readers.

Reliance on the *he or she* pronoun forms is an increasingly popular solution to some of these worrisome problems of pronoun reference. The *he or she* forms agree in number with the third-person singular indefinites. And the use of these forms obviates any possible charge of gender preference. However, excessive use of *he or she, his or her,* and *him or her* is undesirable. (Notice the cumbersome result, for instance, if a *he or she* form is substituted for all four of the third-person singular masculine pronouns in the Henry James sentence.)

Here is a very important point for you to remember: When you are worried about a third-person singular masculine pronoun you have written, either because its reference to an indefinite antecedent sounds not quite right to you or because it shows an undesirable gender preference, you can remove the awkwardness, in nearly every instance that arises, by changing the antecedent to a **plural** noun, to which you then refer by using *they, their,* and *them.*

By way of summary, study these four versions of a sentence as they relate to the two problems just discussed:

Every member of the graduating class, if *he* wishes, may have *his* diploma mailed to *him* after August 15. [This usage reflects traditional practice that is still quite widely followed. The objection to it is that the reference words are exclusively masculine.]

Every member of the graduating class, if *he or she* wishes, may have *his or her* diploma mailed to *him or her* after August 15. [The singular reference is satisfactory, but the avoidance of masculine reference has resulted in clumsy wordiness.]

Every member of the graduating class, if *they* wish, may have *their* diplomas mailed to *them* after August 15. [This version, particularly if used in spoken English, would probably not offend many people, but the lack of proper number agreement between the pronouns and the antecedent would rule out its appearance in edited material.]

Members of the graduating class, if *they* wish, may have *their* diplomas mailed to *them* after August 15. [In this version the pronouns are logical and correct in both number and gender.]

A few other matters of pronoun reference, mercifully quite uncomplicated, should be called to your attention. If a pronoun refers to a compound unit or to a noun that may be either singular or plural, the pronoun agrees in number with the antecedent. (See Lesson 22.)

Wilson and his wife arrived in *their* new car.
Neither Jill nor Martha has finished *her* term paper.
The rest of the lecture had somehow lost *its* point.
The rest of the workers will receive *their* money soon.
The eight-o'clock class has *its* test tomorrow.
The ten-o'clock class finished writing *their* themes.

Beware of "You"

An antecedent in the third person should not be referred to by *you*. This misuse develops when writers, forgetting that they have established the third person in the sentence, shift the structure and begin to talk directly to the reader:

Faulty: In a large university a *freshman* can feel lost if *you* have grown up in a small town.
Improved: In a large university a freshman can feel lost if *he or she* has grown up in a small town.

Faulty: If a *person* really wants to become an expert golfer, *you* must practice everyday.
Improved: If a person really wants to become an expert golfer, *she or he* must practice every day.

Supplement 1

At this point you should be reminded that *it* without an antecedent has some uses that are completely acceptable in both formal and informal English. One of these is in the delayed subject or object pattern. (See Lesson 10.) Another is its use as a kind of filler word in expressions having to do with weather, time, distance, and so forth.

It is fortunate that you had a spare tire.
I find *it* difficult to believe Ted's story.
It is cold today; *it* snowed last night.
It is twelve o'clock; *it* is almost time for lunch.
How far is *it* to Phoenix?

NAME _____ SCORE _____

Directions: One sentence in each of the following pairs is correct, and the other contains at least one reference word that is poorly used. In the space at the left, write the letter that identifies the correct sentence. In the other sentence, circle the pronoun or pronouns that have vague or incorrect reference.

_____ 1. A. Anyone interested in forming a campus chess club should leave their name with Ms. Quinn in Room 227.
  B. Anyone interested in forming a campus chess club should leave his or her name with Ms. Quinn in Room 227.

_____ 2. A. "In my day," said Grandmother, "a girl was considered practically unmarriageable if she couldn't make soap."
  B. "In my day," said Grandmother, "a girl was considered practically unmarriageable if they couldn't make soap."

_____ 3. A. Sue and I finally got into the hiring hall, and then we were told that one had to have an apprentice's card before he or she would be hired.
  B. Sue and I finally got into the hiring hall, and then they told us that you had to have an apprentice's card before you would be hired.

_____ 4. A. The current budget makes one thing clear: the state government is spending more than they are collecting in taxes.
  B. The current budget makes one thing clear: the state government is spending more than it is collecting in taxes.

_____ 5. A. "Any time you change a person's driving habits," said Chief Anthony, "it's always a challenge for them."
  B. "Changing people's driving habits," said Chief Anthony, "is always a challenge for them."

_____ 6. A. Professor Lawson lectured us about the proposed Sanborn Bill, aimed at tax evasion, a bill that he thinks is sorely needed.
  B. Professor Lawson lectured us about the proposed Sanborn Bill, aimed at tax evasion, which he thinks is sorely needed.

_____ 7. A. Dad told the errand boy that he had made a silly mistake.
  B. Dad told the errand boy, "I have made a silly mistake."

_____ 8. A. At the warehouse we found a suitable and inexpensive used piano although it would be two weeks before it could be delivered to us.
  B. At the warehouse we found a suitable and inexpensive used piano although they said it would be two weeks before they could deliver it to us.

_____ 9. A. In one of the pamphlets I used in my research, it gives a chart showing the increase in the costs of state government.
  B. One of the pamphlets I used in my research gives a chart showing the increase in the costs of state government.

229

_____ 10. A. Anyone can become a reasonably good speller if he or she really wants to improve.
   B. Anyone can become a reasonably good speller if you really want to improve.

_____ 11. A. The Puritans, who considered the theater immoral, wanted all theaters closed or, even better, burned to the ground.
   B. The Puritans, who considered the theater immoral, wanted them all closed or, even better, burned to the ground.

_____ 12. A. The Acme Doughnut Company has had such a profitable year that they will expand their facilities next year.
   B. The Acme Doughnut Company has had such a profitable year that it will expand its facilities next year.

_____ 13. A. It said on the morning broadcast that they had another earthquake yesterday in Iran.
   B. The morning broadcast reported that there was another earthquake yesterday in Iran.

_____ 14. A. Lambert is complaining bitterly because neither he nor his son has as yet received their income-tax refund.
   B. Lambert is complaining bitterly because neither he nor his son has as yet received his income-tax refund.

_____ 15. A. The fact that Celia spoke no Spanish and the traffic officer spoke no English made the altercation even more complicated.
   B. Celia spoke no Spanish, and the traffic officer spoke no English, which made the altercation even more complicated.

_____ 16. A. The oldest daughter is a talented musician, but no other member of the large family shows much interest in music.
   B. The oldest daughter is a talented musician, but no other member of the large family shows much interest in it.

_____ 17. A. Whoever sent Jenny the anonymous letter revealed one thing about themself: they have a highly developed sense of humor.
   B. Whoever sent Jenny the anonymous letter revealed one thing: he or she has a highly developed sense of humor.

_____ 18. A. Another car was coming down Corliss Avenue, but the driver saw the oil spill in time to avoid it.
   B. Another car was coming down Corliss Avenue, but he saw the oil spill in time to avoid it.

_____ 19. A. In this industry, when they established assembly-line procedures, it put many people out of work.
   B. In this industry, the establishment of assembly-line procedures put many people out of work.

_____ 20. A. Any reasonably careful thief could break into this warehouse without running much risk to himself.
   B. Any reasonably careful thief could break into this warehouse without running much risk to themself.

Exercise 23   *Using Pronouns Correctly: Reference; Agreement*

NAME _____   SCORE _____

Directions: In the space at the left, copy the correct pronoun or pronoun–verb combination given in parentheses. Circle the antecedent of the pronoun.

_____ 1. Each of the six partners had been active in campus politics in (his, their) younger days.

_____ 2. Whoever sent you that Christmas card should have put (his or her, their) name on it.

_____ 3. In this supermarket even the most inexperienced shopper will have no trouble finding what (he or she wants, they want).

_____ 4. The board members are being criticized for voting generous bonuses for (theirselves, themself, themselves).

_____ 5. For the past fifteen years the class of 1971 of the College of Pharmacy has held (its, it's, their) annual reunion at Gull Lake.

_____ 6. Each of the club members marched solemnly to the platform and deposited (her, their) ballot.

_____ 7. I prefer a light car, chiefly because it is cheaper to operate and maintain (one, them).

_____ 8. Despite the stable price controls, our factory workers demanded an increase in wages and received (it, them).

_____ 9. Each of the amateur contestants chose a seat on the stage and waited nervously for (his or her, their) turn to perform.

_____ 10. In those troubled days the Navy attracted many high school graduates into (its, it's, their) officer's training program.

_____ 11. Anyone undertaking a vigorous mountain-climbing vacation should first visit (his or her, their) doctor for a checkup.

_____ 12. If a new subscriber is dissatisfied with the magazine, (you, he or she, they) can return the copy and get a refund.

_____ 13. The newly organized photography club will hold (its, it's, their) next meeting on Tuesday afternoon.

_____ 14. Not one of the dozens of people surveyed admitted that (he or she, they) had read the voters' pamphlet from cover to cover.

_____ 15. The company, we know, has had a few lean years, but (its, it's, their) prospects for next year are bright.

231

Directions: Each sentence contains at least one reference word that is poorly used. In the space at the left, copy the pronoun or pronouns that have vague or incorrect reference. In the space below each sentence, rewrite enough of the sentence to make the meaning clear.

————————————— 1. Before the end of the sophomore year one should confer with a guidance officer to be sure that your program is fulfilling your needs.

————————————— 2. I hate to see two houses being built on one lot, because this would be like living in a cracker box.

————————————— 3. Mother thought that every girl should master horsemanship, but fortunately it was discovered that I was allergic to them.

————————————— 4. The team captain must be a good sport who will take the blame for his own mistakes instead of passing them on to the next fellow.

————————————— 5. The counselor suggested that a private tutor could help me with my problem, but on my meager salary I can't afford that.

————————————— 6. It says in the advertisement that whoever wants a brochure can get one if you send in a self-addressed envelope.

————————————— 7. A second robbery of the Carlton residence occurred over the weekend, and this time they took some valuable paintings.

————————————— 8. I was told to be careful when I drive through Tipton, because they give you a ticket if you drive over thirty miles an hour.

————————————— 9. "I'm sure," said the director, "that every woman who signed up for our exercise course will say that they got their money's worth."

————————————— 10. If anyone phones for me while I am at lunch, have them leave their number and I'll return it later.

In Lesson 23 a chart classifies the forms of the personal pronouns on the basis of person, number, and gender. For each pronoun the three forms that are listed—first-person singular, *I, my, me;* third-person plural, *they, their, them;* and so on—illustrate the three case forms. *I* and *they* are nominative, *my* and *their* are possessive, and *me* and *them* are objective, for example.

The way you use these pronouns in everyday language, in sentences such as "Two of *my* books have disappeared; *they* cost *me* twenty dollars, and *I* must find *them*," shows you that the case form you choose depends on how the word is used within the sentence. In this lesson we shall examine some spots where the wrong choice of pronoun form is possible.

The only words in modern English that retain distinctions between nominative and objective case forms are a few pronouns. These two forms are identical in nouns, and the correct use of the distinctive form, the possessive, requires essentially only a knowledge of how the apostrophe is used. (See Lesson 19.)

Here are the pronouns arranged according to their case forms. The first eight are the personal pronouns; notice that the only distinctive form of *you* and *it* is the possessive. The last three pronouns, which we shall examine separately from the personal pronouns, are used only in questions and in subordinate clauses.

Nominative	*Possessive*	*Objective*
I	my, mine	me
you	your, yours	you
he	his, his	him
she	her, hers	her
it	its, its	it
we	our, ours	us
you	your, yours	you
they	their, theirs	them
which	———	which
who	whose	whom
whoever	whosever	whomever

Possessive Case

The **possessive case** is used to show possession. Three possible trouble spots should be noted.

Modifiers and Nominals

The preceding chart shows two possessive forms for the personal pronouns. The first form for each pronoun is used as a *modifier* of a noun. The second form is used as a nominal;

in other words, it fills a noun slot, such as the subject, the complement, or the object of a preposition:

> This is *your* seat; *mine* is in the next row.
> Jane preferred *my* cookies; some of *hers* were burned.
> *Their* product is good, but the public prefers *ours*.

Indefinite Pronouns

The indefinite pronouns use an apostrophe to form the possessive case: *everybody's* duty, *one's* lifetime, *everyone's* hopes, someone *else's* car. But the personal pronouns do not:

> These seats are *ours* [not *our's*]. *Yours* [not *Your's*] are in the next row.

Learn to distinguish carefully between the following possessives and contractions that are pronounced alike; *its* (possessive), *it's* (it is, it has); *theirs* (possessive), *there's* (there is, there has); *their* (possessive), *they're* (they are); *whose* (possessive), *who's* (who is, who has); *your* (possessive), *you're* (you are):

> *It's* obvious that the car has outworn *its* usefulness.
> *There's* new evidence that *they're* changing *their* tactics.

Possessive Pronouns with Gerunds

Formal usage prefers the possessive form of pronouns (occasionally of nouns also) preceding gerunds in constructions like the following:

> He was unhappy about *my* [not *me*] voting for the bill.
> Her report led to *our* [not *us*] buying additional stock.
> Chad boasted about his *son's* [not *son*] having won the scholarship.

Nominative and Objective Cases

The rules governing the uses of the other two cases are very simple. A pronoun is in the **nominative case** when it is used:

- As a subject: *They* suspected that *he* was lying.
- As a subjective complement: This is *she* speaking.
- As an appositive of a nominative noun: *We* editors help young writers.

A pronoun is in the **objective case** when it is used:

- As an object of a verb or verbal: Ted told *her* the news. We enjoyed meeting *them*.
- As an object of a preposition: Everyone except *me* had left the room.
- As the subject of an infinitive: The police officer ordered *me* to halt.
- As an appositive of an objective noun: Three of *us* truck drivers stopped to help.

We need not examine in detail every one of these applications. As people become more adept at using the English language, they learn that such usages as "*Them* arrived late" and

"I spoke to *she*" do not conform to the system of the language. Instead, we should examine the trouble spots where confusion may arise.

Common Trouble Spots

When you use the personal pronouns, exercise care in the following situations.

Pronoun Part of Compound Unit

When the pronoun follows *and* (sometimes *or*) as part of a compound unit, determine its use in the sentence and choose the appropriate case form. The temptation here is usually to use the nominative, although the last example in the following list shows a trouble spot where the objective case is sometimes misused. Test these troublesome constructions by using the pronoun by itself, and you will probably discover which form is the correct one:

> The man gave Sue and *me* some candy. [Not Sue and *I*. Both words are indirect objects. Apply the test. Notice how strange "The man gave . . . *I* some candy" sounds.]

> Send your check to either my lawyer or *me*. [Not "to . . . *I*."]

> Have you seen Bob or *her* lately? [Direct objects require the objective case.]

> Just between you and *me*, the lecture was a bore. [Never say "between you and *I*." Both pronouns are objects of the preposition *between*. If this set phrase is a problem for you, find the correct form by reversing the pronouns: You would never say "between I and you."]

> Ms. Estes took *him* and *me* to school.
> [Not *he* and *I* or *him* and *I*. Both pronouns are direct objects.]

> Will my sister and *I* be invited? [Not *me*. The subject is *sister* and *I*.]

Comparisons after As and Than

In comparisons after *as* and *than*, when the pronoun is the subject of an understood verb, use the nominative form:

> He is taller than *I* [*am*]. I am older than *he* [*is*].
> Can you talk as fast as *she* [*can talk*]? No one knew more about art than *he* [*did*].

Sentences like these nearly always call for nominative case subjects. Occasionally the meaning of a sentence may demand an objective pronoun. Both of the following sentences are correct; notice the difference in meaning:

> You trust Mr. Alton more than *I*. [meaning ". . . more than I (trust Mr. Alton")]
> You trust Mr. Alton more than *me*. [meaning ". . . more than (you trust) me."]

"It is" Expressions

Ordinarily, use the nominative form for the subjective complement. The specific problem here concerns such expressions as *It's me* or *It is I*, *It was they* or *It was them*. Many people say *It's me*, but they would hesitate to say *It was her*, *It was him*, or *It was them*, instead of

It was she, It was he, or *It was they.* However, this is a problem that does not arise often in the writing of students. The following are examples of correct formal usage:

It is *I.*
It could have been *he.*
Was it *she?*
Was it *they* who called?

"We" versus "Us" and "I" versus "Me"

See that the appositive is in the same case as the word that it refers to. Notice particularly the first three examples that follow. This usage employing *we* and *us* as an appositive modifier preceding a noun is a real trouble spot:

We boys were hired. [The unit *We boys* is the subject and requires the nominative.]
Two of *us* boys were hired. [The object of a preposition requires the objective case.]
Mr. Elder hired *us* boys. [Not *we boys* for a direct object.]
Two boys—you and *I*—will be hired. [In apposition with the subject.]
Mr. Elder will hire two boys—you and *me.* [In apposition with the object.]

Problems with Who and Whom

The only other pronouns in standard modern English that have distinctive nominative, possessive, and objective forms are *who/whose/whom* and *whoever/whosever/whomever.* (See Supplement 1.) The rules that apply to the personal pronouns apply to these words as well: In the subject position *who/whoever* should be used; in the direct object position *whom/whomever* should be used; and so forth. (These pronouns, it should be noted, are never used as appositives.)

The special problem in the application of the case rules to these words comes from their special use as interrogatives and as subordinating words. As you learned in Lessons 6, 9, and 10, these words, because they serve as signal words, always stand at the beginning of their clauses. To locate the grammatical function of the pronoun within its clause, you must examine the clause to determine the normal subject–verb–complement positioning.

Direct Object or Object of a Preposition

In formal usage, *whom* is required when it is a direct object or the object of a preposition, even though it stands ahead of its subject and verb:

Whom did Mr. Long hire?
[If you are troubled by this sort of construction, try substituting a personal pronoun and placing it after the verb, where it normally comes: "Did Mr. Long hire *him*?" You would never say "Did Mr. Long hire *he*?" The transitive verb *hire* requires a direct object pronoun in the objective case.]
He is a boy *whom* everyone can like. [*Whom* is the object of *can like.*]
Wilson was the man *whom* everybody trusted. [Everybody trusted *whom.*]
She is the girl *whom* Mother wants me to marry. [Object of the verbal *to marry.*]
Whom was she speaking to just then? [To *whom* was she speaking?]

Beginning a Subordinate Clause

When *who(m)* or *who(m)ever* begins a subordinate clause that follows a verb or a preposition, the use of the pronoun *within its own clause* determines its case form:

> We do not know *who* broke the window.
> [*Who* is the subject of *broke*, not the direct object of *do know*.]

> No one knows *who* the intruder was.
> [*Who* is the subjective complement in the noun clause.]

> We do not know *whom* the police have arrested.
> [The objective form *whom* is used because it is the direct object of *have arrested*. The direct object of *do know* is the whole noun clause.]

> I will sell the car to *whoever* offers the best price.
> [The whole clause, *whoever offers the best price*, is the object of the preposition *to*. A subject of a verb must be in the nominative case.]

After a Parenthetical Insertion

When the pronoun subject is followed by a parenthetical insertion like *do you think, I suspect, everyone believes*, or *we know*, the nominative case form must be used:

> *Who* do you think *has* the best chance of winning?
> [*Who* is the subject of *has*. The *do you think* is a parenthetical insertion.]

> Jenkins is the one *who* I suspect *will make* the best impression.
> [Determine the verb that goes with the pronoun. If you are puzzled by this type of sentence, try reading it this way: "Jenkins is the one *who will make* the best impression—I suspect."]

But if the pronoun is not the subject of the verb, the objective form should be used:

> He is an achiever *whom* I suspect you will eventually envy.
> [*Whom* is the direct object of *will envy*.]

Supplement 1

The chart on page 233 shows that the pronoun *which* has no possessive case form, a situation that brings about a minor problem of word choice. As you learned when you studied the adjective clause, *who(m)* normally refers to persons, and *which* to things. But *whose* may be used in an adjective clause as the possessive form of *which* to refer to a nonhuman antecedent:

> It is a disease *whose* long-term effects are minor.

If *whose* is not used in such a sentence, the "of-which" form must be used, producing a perfectly correct but cumbersome sentence:

> It is a disease the long-term effects *of which* are minor.

SUMMARY OF CORRECT PRONOUN USE

1. A pronoun should have a clearly identified antecedent, with which it agrees in person, number, and gender.
2. Be aware of the special problem of pronoun reference to third-person singular antecedents that include both masculine and feminine members—pronouns like *everybody* and *someone* and nouns like *person, student, employee,* and so on. NOTE: Using a plural rather than a singular antecedent is one obvious way of avoiding this problem.
3. Use nominative forms of pronouns used as subjects, subjective complements, and appositives that rename nominative nouns. Use objective forms of pronouns used as objects of verbs or prepositions, subjects of infinitives, and appositives that rename objective nouns.
4. Be aware of a particular pronoun problem when a personal pronoun is tied to a noun or another pronoun by *and* or *or:*

   Mickey and I [not *Mickey and me*] were sent to the principal's office.
   Mr. Case sent *Mickey and me* [not *Mickey and I*] to the principal's office.
   And so, neighbors, please vote for *Ms. Stone and me* [not *Ms. Stone and I*].

5. Remember that the case of *who* is determined by its use in its own clause. It may be a direct object that precedes the subject [*Whom* has your wife invited?] or a subject immediately following a verb or a preposition [We wonder *who* will win. Our dog is friendly with *whoever* pets it.]

NAME _____ SCORE _____

Directions: Each italicized pronoun in these sentences is correctly used. In the space at the left, write one of the following numbers to identify the use of the pronoun:

1. Subject
2. Subjective complement
3. Appositive modifier of nominative noun
4. Direct or indirect object
5. Object of preposition
6. Appositive modifier of objective noun

_____ 1. No one had told *us* ushers that the doors would be opened at noon.

_____ 2. "You may invite *whomever* you want," Mrs. Ellis told her son.

_____ 3. "You may invite *whoever* you think would enjoy the show," Mrs. Ellis told her son.

_____ 4. Would you ask for another appointment, if you were *I?*

_____ 5. "We often argue," Amos said, "but there has never been a serious disagreement between you and *me.*"

_____ 6. President Willis appointed as a search committee Ms. Willard, Dean Thorpe, and *me.*

_____ 7. Those appointed to constitute a search committee were Ms. Willard, Dean Thorpe, and *I.*

_____ 8. "No one worked harder on the campaign than my wife and *I,*" he boasted.

_____ 9. "And I bet that *we* kids will be blamed for the delay," said Bob.

_____ 10. Three of *us* older girls acted as guides.

_____ 11. *Who* did you say would be driving the bus?

_____ 12. Spike will arm wrestle with *whoever* challenges him.

_____ 13. "Sophisticated people like you and *me* would, of course, know better," said Will with a slight smirk.

_____ 14. The owner of the store offered Tracy and *me* part-time jobs.

_____ 15. The only people *whom* Jenny knew in the neighborhood were Mr. and Mrs. Stanton.

_____ 16. I could not remember *who* our first landlady had been.

_____ 17. *Who* did you say made this delicious cake?

_____ 18. People as tall as *I* have trouble sleeping on these old army cots.

_____ 19. Arnie obviously wanted to ride in the same car with Wilma and *me.*

_____ 20. The President has not yet announced *whom* he will appoint to the post.

239

Directions: In the space at the left, copy the correct pronoun from within the parentheses.

_____ 1. No one except (we, us) members is allowed to use the club's tennis courts.

_____ 2. The farmer said that he would give the kittens to (whoever, whomever) would take good care of them.

_____ 3. Can you think of anyone who deserves the honor more than (she, her)?

_____ 4. (Who, Whom) do you suppose the editor was referring to in his speech at the Rotary Club meeting?

_____ 5. That teacher seems to be prejudiced against older students like Morton and (I, me).

_____ 6. Marge waged a good campaign; I predict that the winner will be (she, her).

_____ 7. "I believe this umbrella is (yours, your's), Mr. Wilson," said the janitor.

_____ 8. For (we, us) freshmen the highlight of the class picnic was our tug-of-war victory over the juniors.

_____ 9. Did anyone comment about (us, our) leaving the concert early?

_____ 10. The police are questioning a transient (who, whom) they believe might have turned in the false alarm.

_____ 11. The thief, (whoever, whomever) he was, certainly knew his way around the huge warehouse.

_____ 12. If I were (she, her), I think I'd experiment with a new hair style.

_____ 13. "The only ones here who are supposed to sign for registered mail are the office manager and (I, me)," said Ms. Janes.

_____ 14. I've never known anyone as forgetful as (he, him).

_____ 15. Every Christmas Grandmother Simmons gave my sister and (I, me) a new pearl for our necklaces.

_____ 16. I think that (we, us) four seniors are the only eligible ones left.

_____ 17. The child still refuses to tell anyone (who, whom) he had talked to on the playfield.

_____ 18. Someone (elses, else's) wet topcoat had been placed on top of mine.

_____ 19. The landlord looked at (we, us) six children and shook his head.

_____ 20. The hired man tried to show my brother and (I, me) how to milk a cow.

Exercise 24   *Using Pronouns Correctly: Case*

NAME _____   SCORE _____

Directions: If you find an incorrectly used pronoun, underline it and write the correct form in the space at the left. If a sentence is correct, leave the space blank.

_____ 1. The boss told Francis and me to deliver the package and leave it with whoever was on duty at the loading dock.

_____ 2. Whom do you think has the advantage in tonight's final game?

_____ 3. "I must admit that the birthday party was planned without me suspecting anything," said Dad.

_____ 4. "I don't know whose responsible for this blunder, but it surely isn't you or I," Sue answered angrily.

_____ 5. "Shouldn't us older, more experienced campers be asked to keep order during mealtimes?" asked Treadwell.

_____ 6. He's the kind of person who, I suspect, would do business with whomever has money to spend.

_____ 7. You really don't believe, do you, that people in these countries are allowed to vote for whomever they want?

_____ 8. "In those days," said Al's uncle, "most of we college boys worried about our being drafted into the Army."

_____ 9. I am writing to you concerning Betty Carter, who, I understand, is being considered for a state scholarship.

_____ 10. The new puppy is only four months old, but from the size of her paws, in a year she'll be as big as me.

_____ 11. Maria refused to tell any of us girls whom her escort to the Coronation Ball will be.

_____ 12. The man who's car was parked next to ours signaled for us to leave ahead of him.

_____ 13. I'm glad that Mr. and Mrs. Gates invited my wife and me to ride with them because our car is much smaller than their's.

_____ 14. Some of us girls are wondering whom Wilma Mae will choose as her maid of honor.

_____ 15. Who do you think will become the boss's new assistant?

_____ 16. Who do you think the boss will appoint to be his new assistant?

_____ 17. Just between you and me, is there anyone in this organization whom we can trust completely?

_____ 18. At the reunion Maribeth talked with ex-classmates whom she hadn't seen since high-school days.

241

_____ 19. We kids hate Uncle Bart. It was he, we think, who convinced Dad that the old farm would be a good vacation spot for my sister and I.

_____ 20. An impudent young man whom Maria had just met asked her, "Are those fabulous eyelashes really your's?"

_____ 21. No one knows who made the original mistake, but the chief suspects are we part-time programmers.

_____ 22. Who do you think sent these comic valentines to my roommate and me?

_____ 23. "Our garage survived last week's storm although a few of it's shingles were torn off," said Al's neighbor.

_____ 24. Jan says that this tote bag isn't hers. Whose do you suppose it might be?

_____ 25. Three sophomores—Carlson, Underwood, and I—were put on the committee.

_____ 26. The committee included three sophomores—Carlson, Underwood, and I.

_____ 27. "We maintain that the responsibility is someone elses, not ours," replied Dr. Shaw.

_____ 28. Ms. Trask, who is, I admit, more even-tempered than me, offered to act as a go-between.

_____ 29. Whom can you recommend to teach my older brother and me how to make trout lures?

_____ 30. The champion has a difficult shot remaining; there are two palm trees between he and the eighteenth green.

_____ 31. The Jacobsons report that they're going to sell their mountain cabin because its upkeep has become too burdensome for them.

_____ 32. "The people whom these budget cuts will affect most directly are us pensioners," said Mr. Smedley.

_____ 33. The sergeant warned the crowd that he would arrest whoever tried to enter the building.

_____ 34. Whom do you think will be the pitcher in the opening game?

_____ 35. Whom do you think the manager will choose to be the pitcher in the opening game?

_____ 36. People like you and I are too impatient to play good bridge, with all its rules and bidding conventions.

_____ 37. No one knows, of course, who the next governor will be, but the possibility of its being a woman is very strong.

_____ 38. The manager told us waiters to send to the head table whoever held a gold admission ticket.

_____ 39. The policeman finally agreed with Mother and me that the accident was really nobodys fault.

_____ 40. The only strikers whom the boss would talk to were Coulter and me.

NAME _____ SCORE _____

Directions: Whenever you find an incorrectly used pronoun, copy it in the space at the left. Then in the space below the sentence, rewrite enough of the material to show how you would make the sentence clear and correct. No sentence contains more than two poorly used pronouns; some sentences may be correct.

_____ 1. The person who had parked their car next to our's had left the
_____   lights on.

_____ 2. I was told that whoever wants to borrow books from our lending
_____   library must make a five-dollar deposit before they are given a
                    card.

_____ 3. Anyone whom the trustees appoint to chair the committee must
_____   reconcile themself to a long and thankless chore.

_____ 4. The cool relationship between the office manager and I began
_____   when she objected to me being given an office larger than hers.

_____ 5. It said in the *Morning Post* that anyone who's property was
_____   flooded could apply for a government loan.

_____ 6. Handing the notebook to the librarian, Ellen said, "This must be
_____   someone else's; mine has a picture of Elvis on it's cover."

_____ 7. The camp director told Alf and me that every fellow was respon-
_____   sible for making their own bed in the morning.

_____ 8. An ordinary citizen can understand how the legislature operates
_____   only if you spend some time at the capitol observing them in
                    action.

_____ 9. Every one of us committee members promised not to reveal who
_____   our nominee for governor would be.

_____ 10. Apparently every member of the class except LaVerne and I had
_____   filled out their schedule for next semester.

_____ 11. The shop foreman confided to my partner and me that it was he
_____   who had vetoed the suggested pay raise.

_____ 12. In those olden days in Scotland and Ireland, they could keep you
_____ in prison for long terms if you owed a small debt.

_____ 13. The budget rarely balances, and every politician has their own
_____ idea about how this can be accomplished.

_____ 14. If it wasn't he who warned the police, who do you think it could
_____ have been?

_____ 15. Mr. Washburne told Eddie that he would have to address every
_____ one of the three hundred envelopes.

_____ 16. I finally got to the head of the line, and then they told me that
_____ you must have an adviser's signature on the schedule.

_____ 17. In the advertisement it says that with this kit any fisherman can
_____ make their own trout lures.

_____ 18. We must do what we think is best; after all, it's nobody's business
_____ except your's and mine.

_____ 19. Our father was a very good photographer, and he was bitterly dis-
_____ appointed that neither my sister nor I showed any interest in it.

_____ 20. "All of us trainees are happy about you being appointed our
_____ supervisor," Jerry Blake told Mrs. Inman.

_____ 21. Reverend Watkins began his talk to us Sunday-school youngsters
_____ by saying, "It's often been said that virtue is its own reward."

_____ 22. Luke told Vinny that he really should get a haircut before the
_____ party.

_____ 23. In this class every pre-engineering student must write an essay
_____ and tell why they want to become one.

_____ 24. Although Jean Hoskins has less experience than I, the boss asked
_____ her, not me, to plan the new advertising campaign.

_____ 25. Julia's young brother says he wants to become an airline pilot
_____ because it gives you a chance to see the world.

Lesson 25 *Using Modifiers and Prepositions Correctly*

In Lesson 2 you learned that an adjective is a word that describes or limits a noun or a pronoun. An adverb modifies a verb, an adjective, or another adverb. Many adverbs end in *ly*, such as *happily, beautifully,* and *extremely.* (But some adjectives—*lovely, likely, deadly, neighborly,* and *homely,* for instance—also end in *ly.*). Some adverbs do not end in *ly,* and these happen to be among the most frequently used words in speech and writing: *after, always, before, far, forever, here, not, now, often, quite, rather, soon, then, there, too, very.* Some words can be used either as adjectives or as adverbs, as the following examples show:

Adverbs	*Adjectives*
He came *close.*	That was a *close* call.
She talks too *fast.*	She's a *fast* thinker.
Hit it *hard.*	That was a *hard* blow.
She usually arrives *late.*	She arrived at a *late* hour.
He went *straight* to bed.	I can't draw a *straight* line.

Some adverbs have two forms, one without and one with the *ly: cheap, cheaply; close, closely; deep, deeply; hard, hardly; high, highly; late, lately; loud, loudly; quick, quickly; right, rightly; slow, slowly.* In some of these pairs the words are interchangeable; in most they are not. The idiomatic use of adverbs is a rather complex matter; no rules can be made that govern every situation. We can, however, make a few generalizations that reflect present-day practice.

1. The shorter form of a few of these—*late, hard,* and *near,* for example—fills most adverbial functions because the corresponding *ly* forms have acquired special meanings:

We must not stay *late.*	I have not seen him *lately* [recently].
I studied *hard* last night.	I *hardly* [scarcely] know him.
Winter is drawing *near.*	I *nearly* [almost] missed the last flight.

2. The *ly* form tends toward the formal, with the short form lending itself to more casual, informal speech and writing:

It fell *close* to the target.	You must watch him *closely.*
They ate *high* off the hog.	She was *highly* respected.
Drive *slow*!	Please drive more *slowly.*
Must you sing so *loud*?	He *loudly* denied the charges.
We searched far and *wide.*	She is *widely* known as an artist.

3. Because the short form seems more direct and forceful, it is often used in imperative sentences:

Hold *firm* to this railing.
"Come *quick,*" yelled the officer.

245

4. The short form is often the one used when combined with an adjective to make a compound modifier preceding a noun:

a *wide*-ranging species	The species ranges *widely.*
a *slow*-moving truck	The truck moved *slowly.*

Typical Adverb/Adjective Trouble Spots

For the sake of simplifying the problem of the right use of adverbs and adjectives, we may say that there are three main trouble spots.

Misusing an Adjective for an Adverb

A word is an adverb if it modifies a verb, an adjective, or another adverb. The words that usually cause trouble here are *good, bad, well; sure, surely; real, really; most, almost; awful, awfully;* and *some, somewhat:*

Chip played *well* [not *good*] in the last game. [Modifies the verb *played.*]
This paint adheres *well* [not *good*] to concrete. [Modifies the verb *adheres.*]
Almost [not *Most*] every student has a job. [Modifies the adjective *every.*]
Today my shoulder is *really* [or *very*—not *real*] sore. [Modifies the adjective *sore.*]
He was driving *really* [or *very*—not *real*] fast. [Modifies the adverb *fast.*]
This rain has been falling *steadily* [not *steady*] for a week.
The champion should win his first match *easily* [not *easy*].
You'll improve if you practice *regularly* [not *regular*].
She wants that prize very *badly* [not *bad*].

Misusing Adverbs for Adjectives as Subjective Complements

The most common verb to take the subjective complement is *be;* fortunately mistakes with this verb are nearly impossible. A few other verbs—like *seem, become, appear, prove, grow, go, turn, stay,* and *remain,* when they are used in a sense very close to that of *be*—take subjective complements. This complement must be an adjective, not an adverb.

The house *seems empty.* [House *is* empty.]
Their plans *became apparent.* [Plans *were* apparent.]
The work *proved* very *hard.* [Work *was* hard.]

The adjective subjective complement is also used with another group of verbs, the so-called verbs of the senses. These are *feel, look, smell, sound,* and *taste:*

You shouldn't feel *bad* about this. [Not *badly.*]
His cough sounds *bad* this morning. [Not *badly.*]
At first our prospects looked *bad.* [Not *badly.*]
Doesn't the air smell *sweet* today? [Not *sweetly.*]

Problems with "Feel." The verb *feel* is involved in two special problems. In the first place, it is often used with both *good* and *well.* These two words have different meanings; one is not a substitute for the other. When used with the verb *feel, well* is an adjective meaning "in good health." The adjective *good*, when used with *feel*, means "filled with a sense of vigor and excitement." Of course, both *well* and *good* have other meanings when used with other verbs. In the second place, the expression "I feel badly" has been used so widely, especially in spoken English, that it can hardly be considered an error in usage. Many careful writers, however, prefer the adjective here, with the result that "feel bad" is usually found in written English.

Misusing a Comparative or a Superlative Form of a Modifier

Most adverbs are compared in the same way as adjectives. (For a discussion of the comparison of adjectives, see Lesson 2.) Some common adverbs cannot be compared, such as *here, now, then, when,* and *before.* As you learned in Lesson 16, we use the comparative degree *(taller, better, more intelligent, more rapidly)* in a comparison limited to two things. We use the superlative degree *(tallest, best, most intelligent, most rapidly)* for more than two things.

Two other problems, both of minor importance, are involved in comparisons. First, we do not combine the two forms *(more + er, most + est)* in forming the comparative and superlative degrees:

Later the landlord became *friendlier* [not *more friendlier*].
Please drive *slower* [not *more slower*].
Please drive *more slowly* [not *more slower*].

Second, some purists object to the comparison of the so-called absolute qualities, such as *unique* ("being the only one"), *perfect, round, exact,* and so forth. They argue that, instead of such uses as *most perfect, straighter, more unique,* the intended meaning is *most nearly perfect, more nearly straight, more nearly unique.* General usage, however, has pretty well established both forms.

Problems with Prepositions

Three reminders should be made about the use of prepositions. One problem is the selection of the exact preposition for the meaning intended.

Idioms Using Prepositions

Many words, especially verbs and adjectives, give their full meaning only when modified by a prepositional phrase. In most cases the meaning of the preposition dictates a logical idiom: to sit *on* a couch, to walk *with* a friend, to lean *against* a fence, and so on. For some more abstract concepts, however, the acceptable preposition may seem to have been selected arbitrarily. Here are a few examples of different meanings of different prepositions:

agree *to* a proposal, *with* a person, *on* a price, *in* principle
argue *about* a matter, *with* a person, *for* or *against* a proposition
compare *to* to show likenesses, *with* to show differences [sometimes similarities]
correspond *to* a thing, *with* a person
differ *from* an unlike thing, *with* a person
live *at* an address, *in* a house or city, *on* a street, *with* other people

Note: Any good modern dictionary will provide information about and examples of the correct usage of prepositions.

Unnecessary Prepositions

Although at colloquial levels of language we sometimes find unnecessary prepositions used, examples like the following are improved in serious contexts if written without the words in brackets:

> I met [up with] your uncle yesterday.
> We keep our dog inside [of] the house.
> Our cat, however, sleeps outside [of] the house.
> The package fell off [of] the speeding truck.
> The garage is [in] back of the cottage. [or *behind* the cottage]

Avoid especially the needless preposition at the end of a sentence or the repeated preposition in adjective clauses and in direct or indirect questions:

> Where is your older brother *at*?
>
> He is one of the few people *to* whom I usually feel superior *to*.
> To what do you attribute your luck at poker *to*?
> [Use one *to* or the other, but not both.]

Repeated Prepositions in Compound Units

When two words of a compound unit require the same preposition to be idiomatically correct, the preposition need not be stated with the first unit:

Correct: We were both *repelled* and *fascinated by* the snake charmer's act.

But when the two units require different prepositions, both must be expressed:

Incomplete: The child shows an *interest* and a *talent for* music. [interest . . . *for* (?)]
Correct: The child shows an *interest in* and a *talent for* music.

Incomplete: I am sure that Ms. Lewis would both *contribute* and *gain from* a summer workshop.
Correct: I am sure that Ms. Lewis would both *contribute to* and *gain from* a summer workshop.

NAME _____   SCORE _____

Directions: In the first space at the left, write the word or words that the italicized word modifies. In the second space write Adj. if the italicized word is an adjective or Adv. if it is an adverb.

_____   1. You will find that the prices at the resort will not be *low*.
_____

_____   2. The plane flew *low* to avoid the storm.
_____

_____   3. We are *acutely* aware of the seriousness of the situation.
_____

_____   4. The situation is serious but hardly *acute*.
_____

_____   5. Jones is looking for a *better* job.
_____

_____   6. You will see things *better* after you clean your glasses.
_____

_____   7. You will feel *better* after a short rest.
_____

_____   8. Why not drive *slower* and enjoy the scenery?
_____

_____   9. Repairing this damage will be a *slow* process.
_____

_____   10. "Step *outside* and repeat that remark," said the angry cowboy.
_____

_____   11. The Tigers have an *outside* chance of winning the pennant.
_____

_____   12. His face looked flushed and feverish; I suspect that he did not feel *well*.
_____

_____   13. Do a good job for Mrs. Williams and she will reward you *well*.
_____

_____ 14. Stewart is trying *hard* to pay all of his brother's debts.
_____

_____ 15. The second problem on the test was, I thought, a particularly
_____   *hard* one.

_____ 16. The streets look *clean* after the rainstorm.
_____

_____ 17. *Most* voters object to an increase in the sales tax.
_____

_____ 18. Your cousin was *most* helpful in our emergency.
_____

_____ 19. Shelley usually takes an *early* train into the city on Tuesdays.
_____

_____ 20. *Early* in the fourth quarter Mills kicked a field goal.
_____

Directions: In the space at the left, copy the correct form given in parentheses.

_____ 1. You will be paid well if you wash Mr. Penrose's car (good, well).

_____ 2. All of us feel (bad, badly) about losing our excellent basketball coach.

_____ 3. Toward the end of the semester I could write my themes much (faster, more faster).

_____ 4. You'll have to step very (careful, carefully) over these slippery rocks.

_____ 5. Which one of the twins has the (best, better) disposition?

_____ 6. I'm sure that Andy will work (real, very) hard for you.

_____ 7. Fresh fruits and vegetables can be obtained quite (reasonable, reasonably) at these roadside stands.

_____ 8. The decorator said that pale blue draperies would look (good, well) in the freshly painted nursery.

_____ 9. The teacher told me that I did (good, well) on my English test.

_____ 10. Grandma looked (sad, sadly) as the three boys climbed aboard the bus.

_____ 11. Grandma looked (sad, sadly) at the three boys as they climbed aboard the bus.

_____ 12. (Most, Almost) all of Bill's associates have cellular phones in their cars.

_____ 13. Of these two applicants, which has had the (more, most) field experience?

_____ 14. The bruise on Terry's arm looks ugly, but he says that it doesn't hurt (bad, badly).

_____ 15. Job-hunters are advised to dress (conservative, conservatively) when they are being interviewed.

_____ 16. The children are (sure, surely) excited about this first snowfall of the season.

——————————— 17. The condition of the golf course has improved (considerable, considerably) since the last time I was here.

——————————— 18. In most track events, on the other hand, each participant works (independent, independently) of others.

——————————— 19. "Tamp the ground (good, well) so that the young plants won't blow over," the gardener advised us.

——————————— 20. I had to admit that Willard hadn't done too (bad, badly) in his first driving lesson.

NAME _____   SCORE _____

Directions: Study these sentences for misused adjectives, adverbs, or prepositions. If you find a misused modifier, underline it and write a correct form in the space at the left. If you find a superfluous preposition, circle it and write *omit* in the space at the left. If you find a spot that requires a preposition, write the preposition in the space at the left and use a caret (^) to show where it should be inserted in the sentence. Some of the sentences are correct as they stand; in these cases leave the spaces blank.

_____ 1. I recently heard that Mattie, the oldest of Mrs. Telford's two daughters, is practicing medicine in Alaska.

_____ 2. The local mills are running good and are cutting and shipping timber at top capacity.

_____ 3. Old-timers estimate that damage from last week's storm is equal, if not more than, that of the storm of 1967.

_____ 4. "At first things were awful chaotic in our office," he replied, "but lately the operation is moving ahead quite smoothly."

_____ 5. The witness indignantly replied that he had neither knowledge of nor interest in the projected investment scheme.

_____ 6. If you were I, I'm sure you would feel bad about paying a sizable fine for overtime parking.

_____ 7. These freshly picked oranges surely taste more sweeter than the ones we buy at the local market.

_____ 8. "The pace in our office is rapid-fire," the Congressman testified; "the campaign is moving ahead fast and furious."

_____ 9. Miss Wayland's accompanist was noticeably upset because the only piano available needed tuning bad.

_____ 10. Alice's mother surely looks differently now that she wears tinted contacts instead of those old glasses with thick lenses.

_____ 11. The hailstorm developed so sudden that Dad wasn't able to put covers on all of the lawn furniture.

_____ 12. "Daytime soap opera is a vice to which I have recently become addicted to," Betty confessed.

_____ 13. "All of us are sure proud of you for performing so creditably in the contest," the superintendent told Eddie.

_____ 14. "I'm having trouble with my long iron shots," Val said to the interviewer, "but I must admit that I have been putting real good."

_____ 15. For the first week the weather was damp and foggy, but toward the end of the month it improved some.

_____ 16. "And to whom," asked Mr. Betts, "should I address my next letter of protest to?"

_____ 17. "Several years ago Uncle Clint had an apartment in St. Louis, but I don't know where he's living at now," my cousin told me.

_____ 18. Dolphins are threatened by an epidemic similar to or even worse than the one that killed thousands of North Sea seals.

_____ 19. Delbert was extremely lucky to get a job with a campus orchestra that paid good.

_____ 20. "Your lawn would look better if this old mower I have to use were more sharper," Sven complained to Mrs. Sandstrom.

_____ 21. Most all of my friends seem happy about the recently revised dormitory regulations.

_____ 22. The author's understanding of and sympathy for human beings of all races is persuasive and affecting.

_____ 23. The old hometown had grown considerable, and many things looked strange to me.

_____ 24. Whatever this concoction is, it smells sweet, tastes good, and even looks delicious.

_____ 25. You do look rested and healthy after your long illness, but do you feel well enough to go back to work?

In many of the entries in the following list, the other forms suggested are those usually preferred in standard formal English—the English appropriate to your term papers, theses, term reports, examination papers in all your courses, and most of the serious papers written for your English classes. Many of the words or expressions in brackets, marked *not,* are appropriate enough in informal conversation and in some informal papers.

Some of the entries are labeled *colloquial,* a term you should not think of as referring to slang, to forms used only in certain localities, or to "bad" English. The term applies to usages that are appropriate to informal and casual *spoken* English rather than to formal written English. However, the expressions marked *substandard* should be avoided at all times.

A, an. Use *a* when the word immediately following it is sounded as a consonant; use *an* when the next sound is a vowel sound: *a, e, i, o,* or *u* (*a* friend, *an* enemy). Remember that it is the consonantal or vowel *sound,* not the actual letter, that determines the choice of the correct form of the indefinite article: *a* sharp curve, *an* S-curve; *a* eulogy, *an* empty house; *a* hospital, *an* honest person; *a* united people, *an* uneven contest.

Ad. Clipped forms of many words are used informally, such as *ad* (*advertisement*), *doc* (*doctor*), *exam* (*examination*), *gent* (*gentleman*), *gym* (*gymnasium*), *lab* (*laboratory*), *math* (*mathematics*), and *prof* (*professor*). Formal usage prefers the long forms.

Aggravate. In standard formal English the word means "make more severe," "make worse." Colloquially it means "annoy," "irritate," "exasperate."

Walking on your sprained ankle will aggravate the hurt. [*Informal:* All criticism aggravates him.]

Ain't. Substandard for *am not, are not, is not, have not.*

Am I not [not *Ain't I*] a good citizen?

The command hasn't [not *hain't* or *ain't*] been given yet.

They are not [not *ain't*] going either.

All the farther, all the faster, and the like. Generally regarded as colloquial equivalents of *as far as, as fast as,* and the like.

This is as far as [not *all the farther*] I care to go.

That was as fast as [not *all the faster*] he could run.

A lot of. See *Lots of.*

Alright. This spelling, like *allright* or *allright,* although often used in advertising, is generally regarded as very informal usage. The preferred form is *all right.* In strictly formal usage, *satisfactory* or *very well* is preferred to *all right.*

Very well [not *Alright*], you may ride in our car.

The members agreed that the allocation of funds was satisfactory [not *all right*].

Among, between. *Among* is used with three or more persons or things, as in "Galileo was among the most talented people of his age," or "The estate was divided among his three sons." *Between* usually refers to two things, as in "between you and me," "between two points," "between dawn and sunset."

Amount, number. Use *number,* not *amount,* in reference to units that can actually be counted:

the *amount* of indebtedness, the *number* of debts.

And etc. Because *etc. (et cetera)* means "and so forth," *and etc.* would mean "and and so forth." You should not use *etc.* to replace some exact, specific word, but if you do use it, be sure not to spell it *ect.* And remember that *etc.* requires a period after it.

Anywheres. Colloquial for *anywhere.* Similar colloquial forms are *anyways* for *anyway* or *anyhow, everywheres* for *everywhere, nowheres* for *nowhere, somewheres* for *somewhere.*

I looked for my books everywhere.
They must be hidden somewhere.

As, like. See *Like.*

As to whether. *Whether* is usually enough.

Awful, awfully. Like *aggravate,* these words have two distinct uses. In formal contexts, they mean "awe-inspiring" or "terrifying." Often in conversation and sometimes in writing of a serious nature, *awful* and *awfully* are mild intensifiers, meaning "very."

Because. See *Reason is because.*

Because of. See *Due to.*

Being that, being as how. Substandard for *because, as,* or *since.*

Beside, besides. These two prepositions are clearly distinguished by their meanings. *Beside* means "at the side of" and *besides* means "in addition to."

Lucy sits beside me in class.
Did anyone besides you see the accident?

Between. See *Among.*

But what, but that. Colloquial for *that.*

Both sides had no doubt that [not *but what*] their cause was just.

Can, may. *Can* suggests ability to do something. *May* is the preferred form when permission is involved.

Little Junior can already count to ten.
May [not *Can*] I borrow your pencil?

Can't hardly, couldn't hardly, can't scarcely, couldn't scarcely. Substandard for *can hardly, could hardly, can scarcely, could scarcely.* These are sometimes referred to as double negatives.

I can hardly [not *can't hardly*] believe that story.

We could scarcely [not *couldn't scarcely*] hear the foghorn.

Caused by. See *Due to.*

Complected. Dialectal or colloquial for *complexioned.*

Being light-complexioned [not *light-complected*], Sue must avoid prolonged exposure to sunlight.

Contact. Used as a verb meaning "to get in touch with," this word, probably because of its association with sales-promotion writing, annoys enough people to warrant caution in its use in serious writing.

Continual, continuous. A fine distinction in meaning can be made if you remember that *continual* means "repeated regularly and frequently" and that *continuous* means "occurring without interruption," "unbroken."

Could(n't) care less. This worn-out set phrase indicating total indifference is a colloquialism. A continuing marvel of language behavior is the large number of people who insist on saying "I could care less" when they obviously mean the opposite.

Could of, would of, might of, ought to of, and so on. Substandard for *could have, would have,* and so on.

Couple. Colloquial in the sense of *a few, several.*

The senator desired to have a few [not *a couple*] changes made in the bill.

A couple of is standard English.

Criteria. The singular noun is *criterion;* the plural is *criteria* or *criterions.* Such combinations as *"a criteria," "one criteria"* and *"these criterias"* are incorrect.

Data. Originally the plural form of the rarely used Latin singular *datum, data* has taken on a collective meaning so that it is often treated as a singular noun. "This data has been published" and "These data have been published" are both correct, the latter being the use customarily found in scientific or technical writing.

Different from, different than. *Different from* is generally correct. Many people object to *different than,* but others use it, especially when a clause follows, as in "Life in the Marines was different than he had expected it to be."

Their customs are different from [not *different than*] ours.

Life in the Marines was different from what he had expected it to be.

Different to, a form sometimes used by British speakers and writers, is rarely used in the United States.

Disinterested, uninterested. Many users of precise English deplore the tendency to treat these words as loose synonyms, keeping a helpful distinction between *disinterested* ("impartial," "free from bias or self-interest") and *uninterested* ("lacking in interest," "unconcerned"). Thus we would hope that a referee would be disinterested but not uninterested.

Due to, caused by, because of, owing to. *Due to* and *caused by* are used correctly after the verb *to be:*

His illness was caused by a virus.

The flood was due to the heavy spring rains.

Many people object to the use of *due to* and *caused by* adverbially at the beginning of a sentence, as in "Due to the heavy rains, the streams flooded," and "Caused by the storm, the roads were damaged." It is better to use *because of* in similar situations. *Due to* is also used correctly as an adjective modifier immediately following a noun:

Accidents due to excessive speed are increasing in number.

Note in the examples what variations are possible:

The streams flooded because of the heavy rains.

The flooding of the streams was due to the heavy rains.

The floods were caused by the rapid melting of the snow.

Emigrate, immigrate. To *emigrate* is to *leave* one region to settle in another; to *immigrate* is to *enter* a region from another one.

Enthuse. Colloquial or substandard (depending on the degree of a person's aversion to this word) for *be enthusiastic, show enthusiasm.*

The director was enthusiastic [not *enthused*] about her new program.

Everywheres. See *Anywheres.*

Farther, further. Careful writers observe a distinction between these two words, reserving *farther* for distances that can actually be measured.

Tony can hit a golf ball farther than I can.

We must pursue this matter further.

Fewer, less. *Fewer* refers to numbers, *less* to quantity, extent, or degree.

Fewer [not *Less*] students are taking courses in literature this year.

Food costs less, but we have less money to spend.

Figure. Colloquial for *consider, think, believe, suppose.*

He must have thought [not *figured*] that nobody would see him enter the bank.

Fine. Colloquial, very widely used, for *well, very well.*

The boys played well [not *just fine*].

Graffiti. The singular form is *graffito.* In serious writing *graffiti* takes a plural verb. Avoid combinations such as "a graf-fiti," "this graffiti," etc.

Had(n't) ought. *Ought* does not take an auxiliary.

> You ought [not *had ought*] to apply for a scholarship.

> You ought not [not *hadn't ought*] to miss the lecture.

Hardly. See *Can't hardly.*

Healthy, healthful. *Healthy* means "having health," and *healthful* means "giving health." Thus a person or an animal is healthy; a climate, a food, or an activity is healthful.

Immigrate. See *Emigrate.*

Imply, infer. Despite the increasing tendency to use these words more or less interchangeably, it is good to preserve the distinction: *Imply* means "to say something indirectly," "to hint or suggest," and *infer* means "to draw a conclusion," "to deduce." Thus you *imply* something in what you say and *infer* something from what you hear.

Incredible, incredulous. An unbelievable *thing* is incredible; a disbelieving *person* is incredulous.

In regards to. The correct forms are *in regard to* or *as regards.*

Inside of. *Inside* or *within* is preferred in formal writing.

> We stayed inside [not *inside of*] the barn during the storm.

> The plane should arrive within [not *inside of*] an hour.

Invite. Slang for *invitation.*

> They will be sent an invitation [not *invite*] to join us in a peace conference.

Irregardless. Substandard or humorous for *regardless.*

> The planes bombed the area regardless [not *irregardless*] of consequences.

Is when, is where. The *is-when, is-where* pattern in definitions is clumsy and should be avoided. Write, for example,

"An embolism is an obstruction, such as a blood clot, in the bloodstream," instead of "An embolism is where an obstruction forms in the bloodstream."

Kind, sort. These words are singular and therefore should be modified by singular modifiers. Do not write *these kind, these sort, those kind, those sort.*

> Those kinds [not *those kind*] of videos sell very well.

> Who could believe that sort [not *those sort*] of arguments?

Kinda, sorta, kind of a, sort of a. Undesirable forms.

Kind of, sort of. Colloquial for *somewhat, in some degree, almost, rather.*

> They felt somewhat [not *sort of*] depressed.

Learn, teach. *Learn* means "to acquire knowledge"; *teach* means "to give or impart knowledge."

> Ms. Brown taught [not *learned*] me Spanish.

Leave. Not to be used for *let.*

> Let [not *Leave*] me carry your books for you.

Less. See *Fewer.*

Let. See *Leave.*

Let's us. The *us* is superfluous, because *let's* means "let us."

Like, as, as if. The use of *like* as a conjunction (in other words, to introduce a clause) is colloquial. It should be avoided in serious writing.

> As [not *Like*] you were told earlier, there is a small entry fee.

> She acts as if [not *like*] she distrusts us.

> Do as [not *like*] I tell you.

Line. Often vague and redundant, as in "What do you read *in the line of books*?" "Don't you enjoy fishing and other sports *along that line*?" It is better to say, more directly,

> What kind of books do you read?

> Don't you enjoy fishing and sports like that?

Lots of, a lot of. Colloquial in the sense of *many, much.*

Many [not *Lots of*] families vacation here every summer.

The storms caused us much [not *lots of*] trouble that spring.

All of us owe you much [not *a lot* or *alot*].

Mad. Colloquially *mad* is often used to mean "angry." In formal English, it means "insane."

Marge was angry [not *mad*] because I was late.

May. See *Can.*

Media. A plural noun, currently in vogue to refer to all mass communicative agencies. The singular is *medium.* Careful writers and speakers avoid the use of *media* as a singular noun, as in "Television is an influential media." Even more objectionable is the use of *medias* as a plural.

Might of. See *Could of.*

Most. This word is the superlative form of *much* and *many (much, more, most; many, more, most).* Its use as a clipped form of *almost* is colloquial.

Almost [not *Most*] all of my friends work during the summer.

Nauseated, nauseous. Despite the increasingly wide use of these words as synonyms, there are still speakers and writers of precise English who insist that *nauseated* should be used to mean "suffering from or experiencing nausea" and that *nauseous* should be used only to mean "causing nausea."

Nohow. This emphatic negative is substandard.

Not all that. A basically meaningless substitute for *not very* or *not really*; it can easily become a habit.

The movie was not very [not *not all that*] amusing.

Nowheres. See *Anywheres.*

Number. See *Amount.*

Of. See *Could of.*

Off of. Dialectal or colloquial for *off.*

She asked me to get off [not *off of*] my high horse.

OK. This form calls attention to itself in serious writing. It is appropriate only to business communications and casual speech or writing. Modern dictionaries offer several permissible forms: *OK, O.K.,* and *okay* for the singular noun; *OKs, O.K.s,* and *okays* for the plural noun; and *OK'd, OK'ing, O.K.'d, O.K.'ing, okayed,* and *okaying* for verb forms.

Ought. See *Had(n't) ought.*

Ought to of. See *Could of.*

Owing to. See *Due to.*

Party. Colloquial in the sense of *man, woman, person.*

Dr. Tartar, a man [not *party*] is waiting for you in your office.

Plenty. Colloquial for *very, extremely, fully. Plenty* is a noun, not an adjective or an adverb.

Filmore's defensive work in the second half was very [not *plenty*] effective.

Plenty of is standard English.

Quote, unquote. Although these words may be needed in the oral presentation of quoted material, they have no use in written material, in which quotation marks or indentation sets off the quoted material from the text proper.

Real, really. The use of *real,* which is an adjective, to modify another adjective or an adverb is colloquial. In formal contexts *really* or *very* should be used.

We had a really [not *real*] enjoyable visit.

The motorcycle rounded the corner very [not *real*] fast.

Reason is because, reason is due to, reason is on account of. In serious writing, a *reason is* clause is usually completed with *that*, not with *because, due to,* or *on account of.*

> The reason they surrendered is that [not *because*] they were starving.

> The reason for my low grades is that I have poor eyesight [not *is on account of my poor eyesight*].

Same. The use of *same* as a pronoun, often found in legal or business writing, is inappropriate in most other types of writing.

> I received your report and look forward to reading it [not *the same*].

Scarcely. See *Can't hardly.*

So, such. These words, when used as exclamatory intensifiers, are not appropriate in a formal context. Sentences like the following belong in informal talk: "I am *so* tired," "She is *so* pretty," or "They are having *such* a good time."

Some. Colloquial for *somewhat, a little.*

> The situation at the border is said to be somewhat [not *some*] improved today.

Somewheres. See *Anywheres.*

Sort. See *Kind.*

Such. See *So.*

Suppose to. See *Use to.*

Sure. *Sure* is correctly used as an adjective:

> We are not sure about her plans.
> He made several sure investments.

Sure is colloquial when used as an adverbial substitute for *surely, extremely, certainly, indeed, very, very much.*

> The examination was surely [not *sure*] difficult.

> The lawyer's plea certainly [not *sure*] impressed the jury.

Sure and. See *Try and.*

Suspicion. *Suspicion* is a noun; it is not to be used as a verb in place of *suspect.*

> No one suspected [not *suspicioned*] the victim's widow.

Swell. Not to be used as a general term of approval meaning *good, excellent, attractive, desirable,* and so on.

Teach. See *Learn.*

That there, this here, those there, these here. Substandard for *that, this, those, these.*

Them. Substandard when used as an adjective.

> How can you eat those [not *them*] parsnips?

Try and, sure and. *Try to, sure to* are the preferred forms in serious writing.

> We shall try to [not *try and*] make your visit a pleasant one.

> Be sure to [not *sure and*] arrive on time.

Type. Colloquial when used as a modifier of a noun. Use *type of* or *kind of.*

> I usually don't enjoy that type of [not *type*] movie.

Uninterested. See *Disinterested.*

Use to, suppose to. Although these incorrect forms are difficult to detect in spoken English, remember that the correct written forms are *used to, supposed to.*

Want in, want off, want out. Colloquial and dialectical forms for *want to come in, want to get off, want to go out.* Inappropriate in serious writing.

Ways. Colloquial for *way,* in such expressions as

> It is just a short distance [not *ways*] up the canyon.

> We do not have a long way [not *ways*] to go.

What. Substandard when used for *who, which,* or *that* as a relative pronoun in an adjective clause.

> His raucous laugh is the thing that [not *what*] annoys me most.

When, where clauses. See *Is when.*

Where . . . at. The *at* is unnecessary. Undesirable in both speech and writing.

> Where [not *Where at*] will you be at noon?
>
> Where is your car? [Not *Where is your car at?*]

-wise. The legitimate function of this suffix to form adverbs like *clockwise* does not carry with it the license to concoct such jargon as "Entertainmentwise this town is a dud" or "This investment is very attractive long-term-capital-gainswise."

Without. Not to be used as a conjunction instead of *unless*.

> He won't lend me his car unless [not *without*] I fill the gas tank.

Worst way. Not acceptable for *greatly, very much, exceedingly,* and similar words.

> Della wanted very much [not *the worst way*] to become a vocalist with a rock group.

Would of. See *Could of.*

NAME _____ SCORE _____

Directions: In the space at the left, write the word or phrase given in parentheses that you consider the more appropriate form to use in serious writing.

_____ 1. (Almost, Most) all of the parents think that the operetta is (kind
_____   of, rather) ambitious for us high-schoolers to attempt.

_____ 2. During her visit to Charleston, Laura received many (invitations,
_____   invites) to dances, card parties, boating trips, (and etc., etc.).

_____ 3. No one will (suspect, suspicion) you if you act (as if, like) you
_____   have never seen me before.

_____ 4. (Where, Where at) will I be able to buy tires for (this, this here)
_____   thirty-year-old Ford that I just bought?

_____ 5. Marge (could have, could of) bought a new motorbike, but she
_____   decided that a used one was (good, plenty good) enough for her.

_____ 6. I studied (awful, very) hard this month, but my grades are no
_____   (different from, different than) my usual grades.

_____ 7. Almost (anywhere, anywheres) along the bank of this stream will
_____   do (alright, very well) for our picnic spot.

_____ 8. Lars was determined to (emigrate, immigrate) from Sweden to
_____   America (irregardless, regardless) of his father's misgivings.

_____ 9. Miss Marks, (can, may) I borrow (that, that there) magazine
_____   when you have finished with it?

_____ 10. I'm really (not all that, not very) interested in associating with
_____   (those kind, those kinds) of people.

_____ 11. I (believe, figure) that after this tutoring I'll make (fewer, less)
_____   spelling errors in my themes.

_____ 12. (Because of, Due to) the small turnout, the club members were
_____   (sure, very) disappointed with this year's rummage sale.

_____ 13. At first the strenuous exercises made me (real, very) exhausted,
_____   but now they (ain't, aren't) so tiring.

_____ 14. (Because, Being as how) I was low on funds, I was not at all
_____   (enthused, enthusiastic) about buying three extra tickets.

_____ 15. One reason Miss Lewis won the election was (because, that) (a
_____   lot of, many) voters were disgusted with the "old guard."

_____ 16. This is (all the farther, as far as) the bus goes; we still have quite
_____   a (way, ways) to walk to the cabin.

_____ 17. "I don't feel well; I guess I (shouldn't have, shouldn't of) eaten so
_____   many of (them, those) hot dogs at the carnival," said Ned.

_____ 18. While we watched, a (couple, couple of) young swimmers
_____   jumped (off, off of) the bridge into the river.

_____ 19. Don't you think that we (had ought to, should) (leave, let) our
_____   younger brothers go to the movie with us?

_____ 20. To me, Bill's answer (implied, inferred) that his firm (can hardly,
_____   can't hardly) meet its expenses this month.

Directions: Each sentence contains two italicized words or expressions. If you think that the word or expression is inappropriate in serious writing, write an acceptable form in the space at the left. If an expression is correct, write C in the space.

_____ 1. Sherwood *hadn't ought to* drive over thirty miles an hour in *that*
_____   *there* old jalopy of his.

_____ 2. The school nurse reports that this month there have been *less*
_____   absences *due to* illness than there were last month.

_____ 3. *Lots of* students tell me that they are making *real* progress in Miss
_____   Lang's reading clinic.

_____ 4. Please open the front door; the dog acts *like* he *wants out.*
_____

_____ 5. The chairperson of the committee is becoming *sort of* uneasy
_____   because arrangements for the dance are *nowheres* near complete.

_____ 6. It was *sure* generous of Caldwell to divide the reward money
_____   equally *among* his four co-workers.

_____ 7. The *party* who left a briefcase overnight in the restaurant will be
_____   *plenty* glad to have it returned.

_____ 8. *Almost all* of the noisy youngsters had got *off of* the bus by the
_____   time we reached Albany.

_____ 9. Every one of the amateur actors performed *alright,* and the audi-
_____   ence seemed *enthused* about the play.

_____ 10. The *gent* who called you on the telephone left *this here* message
_____   for you.

_____ 11. Some people *suspicion* that there *might of* been some collusion
_____   before the voting took place.

_____ 12. Just *between* the two of us, I have no doubt *but what* Frank is not
_____   telling us the whole story.

_____ 13. *Irregardless* of our original plan, this is *all the farther* I intend to
_____   hike.

_____ 14. "We were *suppose to* transcribe *these data* onto fresh disks,
_____   weren't we?" asked Jenny.

_____ 15. "I *can hardly* imagine anything worse than attending one of *them*
_____   concerts that you go to regularly," said Timmy.

_____ 16. Jane worked *awful* hard to make her poster *different from* the
_____ usual student effort.

_____ 17. The neighbors complain about the constant barking of a *couple*
_____ large dogs Mr. Singer keeps locked *inside of* a small shed.

_____ 18. *In regards to* your request, Mr. Watts, I'll *try and* have the mater-
_____ ial in the mail for you tomorrow.

_____ 19. When I was young, I *use to* think I couldn't bear to live *anywheres*
_____ except on a farm.

_____ 20. To me it seems *incredible* that no other freshmen *besides* you and
_____ me were chosen to be on the team.

Exercise 26   *Appropriate Use*

NAME _____ SCORE _____

Directions: In the space at the left, write the word or phrase given in parentheses that you consider the more appropriate form to use in serious writing.

_____
_____
1. After Andy gave his report, the teacher asked him (where, where at) he had found all of (them, those) interesting facts about nematodes.

_____
_____
2. (Because of, Due to) Stella's interest in world affairs, her reading has been quite (different from, different than) that of most freshmen.

_____
_____
3. Some (awfully, very) important international conferences have been held in Geneva, and there will surely be (a lot, many) more in the future.

_____
_____
4. Little Mark is (light-complected, light-complexioned), and his mother won't allow him on the beach (unless, without) he carries an umbrella.

_____
_____
5. If we follow these very strict (criteria, criterias), I predict that we will have to process (fewer, less) job applications.

_____
_____
6. The reason the college holds (these kind, these kinds) of social affairs is (because, that) new students need to meet other students.

_____
_____
7. (Let's, Let's us) find some completely (disinterested, uninterested) third person to settle this disagreement.

_____
_____
8. "I have no doubt (but what, that) protests will come in (in regard to, in regards to) the noise from the rock concert," said the chief of police.

_____
_____
9. "I'm (suppose to, supposed to) talk to some (party, person) in this office about my laboratory fees," George told the receptionist.

_____
_____
10. Carl's tennis game has improved (some, somewhat), I'll admit, but he has a long (way, ways) to go before he will be really competitive.

————————— 11. That roofer (could have, could of) injured himself badly when he
————————— fell (off, off of) the roof of the porch.

————————— 12. (Because, Being as how) Luke is quite shy, he hasn't met (lots of,
————————— many) other students.

————————— 13. "(Can, May) I use your binoculars for a (couple, couple of) min-
————————— utes?" Ellen asked Mr. Lessing.

————————— 14. My question obviously (aggravated, annoyed) Professor Lee, and
————————— he acted (as if, like) he hadn't heard me correctly.

————————— 15. (Irregardless, Regardless) of what the critics have said about it,
————————— Dad is (enthused, enthusiastic) about the new mystery series on
KWGK.

————————— 16. If this is (all the faster, as fast as) you intend to drive, we'll be
————————— (plenty, very) late for the party.

————————— 17. (That, That there) new fullback on the football team (sure,
————————— surely) can move fast for such a heavy person.

————————— 18. An officer stopped our car and said, "You can't go (anywhere,
————————— anywheres) (farther, further) than this point—there's been a
mudslide."

————————— 19. I hope that we will receive an (invitation, invite) to another of
————————— Sue's parties; we had (a very, such a) good time at the one last
week.

————————— 20. (Inside of, Within) ten hours the police had rounded up (almost,
————————— most) all of the escapees.

Directions: Each sentence contains two italicized words or expressions. If you think that a word or expression is inappropriate in serious writing, write an acceptable form in the space at the left. If an expression is correct, write C in the space.

_____ 1. *Due to* the bad weather, *fewer* people than expected came to the auction.

_____ 2. I have no doubt *but what* Mary will do a *swell* job as the new chairperson.

_____ 3. "*In regards to* your uncle's health," said the nurse, "I am happy to report that his condition has improved *somewhat.*"

_____ 4. "I *can't hardly* believe that those car keys aren't *somewheres* in this purse," said Mrs. Wayland.

_____ 5. For patrons who are not *enthused* about Indonesian cooking, the menu offers *plenty of* standard American dishes.

_____ 6. The House resolution is *different from* the Senate version in a *couple* minor details.

_____ 7. "I harbor a tiny *suspicion* that some of *them* jewels his wife is wearing are fakes," said Mr. Kemper.

_____ 8. As I *should of* known, *a lot of* the old landmarks in my hometown were no longer standing.

_____ 9. "Your mother and I *figured* that you would be *awful* tired after your long flight from Tokyo," said Dad.

_____ 10. In those days we kids *used to* swim in the creek on New Year's Day, *irregardless* of the weather.

_____ 11. Eddie acted *like* he thought I *had ought to* apologize to our host for what I had said.

_____ 12. An oddly dressed *party* near the rear of the bus shouted that he *wanted off* at the next stop.

_____ 13. *Being that* Ben spoke no German, he was *sorta* reluctant to sign up for the walking tour of Bavaria.

_____ 14. The reason I declined the invitation is *that* I am *not all that* excited about modern ballet.

_____ 15. The temperature was *so* low that *almost all* of our outdoor water
_____ pipes froze.

_____ 16. The scuffling youngsters bumped into an old *gent* who nearly fell
_____ *off of* the subway platform.

_____ 17. *Those kinds* of friends are *sure* a great help to a person in an
_____ emergency.

_____ 18. In her speech the governor was *real* critical of the Senate's action,
_____ and several legislators were *aggravated* by her remarks.

_____ 19 Just *between* you and me, most of the errors in your term paper
_____ are *due to* your careless proofreading.

_____ 20. The man sitting *besides* me said, "Pardon me, but *can* I borrow
_____ your knife for a moment?"

6 Spelling and Capitalization

Lessons, Practice Sheets, and Exercises

Lesson 27 *Spelling Rules; Words Similar in Sound*

This lesson presents spelling rules that will help you improve your written work.

Rule 1: A word ending in silent *e* generally drops the *e* before a suffix beginning with a vowel and retains the *e* before a suffix beginning with a consonant.

After *c* or *g*, if the suffix begins with *a* or *o*, the *e* is retained to preserve the soft sound of the *c* or *g*.

Drop E before a Vowel

become	+ ing	—becoming	hope	+ ing	—hoping
bride	+ al	—bridal	imagine	+ ary	—imaginary
conceive	+ able	—conceivable	noise	+ y	—noisy
desire	+ able	—desirable	remove	+ able	—removable
fame	+ ous	—famous	white	+ ish	—whitish
force	+ ible	—forcible	write	+ ing	—writing

Retain E before a Consonant

excite	+ ment	—excitement	life	+ like	—lifelike
force	+ ful	—forceful	pale	+ ness	—paleness
hope	+ less	—hopeless	sincere	+ ly	—sincerely

Retain E after C or G if the Suffix Begins with A or O

advantage	+ ous	—advantageous	notice	+ able	—noticeable
change	+ able	—changeable	outrage	+ ous	—outrageous
manage	+ able	—manageable	service	+ able	—serviceable

(See Supplement 1.)

Rule 2: In words with *ie* or *ei* when the sound is long *ee*, use *i* before *e* except after *c*.

Use I *before* E

apiece	frontier	priest
belief	grieve	reprieve
fiend	niece	shriek
fierce	pierce	thievery

Except after C

ceiling	conceive	perceive
conceited	deceit	receipt

The common exceptions to this rule may be easily remembered if you memorize the following sentence: Neither financier seized either species of weird leisure.

Rule 3: In words of one syllable and words accented on the last syllable, ending in a single consonant preceded by a single vowel, double the final consonant before a suffix beginning with a vowel.

Words of One Syllable—Suffix Begins with a Vowel

ban	—banned	hit	—hitting	rid	—riddance
bid	—biddable	hop	—hopping	Scot	—Scottish
dig	—digger	quit	—quitter	stop	—stoppage
drag	—dragged	["qu"-consonant]		wet	—wettest

Accented on Last Syllable—Suffix Begins with a Vowel

abhor	—abhorrence	equip	—equipping
acquit	—acquitted	occur	—occurrence
allot	—allotted	omit	—omitted
begin	—beginner	prefer	—preferring
commit	—committing	regret	—regrettable
control	—controlled	repel	—repellent

Not Accented on Last Syllable—Suffix Begins with a Vowel

differ	—different	open	—opener
happen	—happening	prefer	—preference
hasten	—hastened	sharpen	—sharpened

Suffix Begins with a Consonant

allot	—allotment	mother	—motherhood
color	—colorless	sad	—sadness
equip	—equipment	sin	—sinful

(See Supplement 1.)

An apparent exception to this rule affects a few words formed by the addition of *ing, ed,* or *y* to a word ending in *c*. To preserve the hard sound of the *c*, a *k* is added before the vowel of the suffix, resulting in such spellings as *frolicking, mimicked, panicked, panicky, picnicked,* and *trafficking.*

Another irregularity applies to such spellings as *quitting* and *equipped.* One might think that the consonant should not be doubled, reasoning that the final consonant is preceded by two vowels, not by a single vowel. But because *qu* is phonetically the equivalent of *kw,* the *u* is a consonant when it follows *q.* Therefore, because the final consonant is actually preceded by a single vowel, the consonant is doubled before the suffix.

Rule 4: Words ending in *y* preceded by a vowel retain the *y* before a suffix; most words ending in *y* preceded by a consonant change the *y* to *i* before a suffix.

Ending in Y *Preceded by a Vowel*

boy	—boyish	coy	—coyness	enjoy	—enjoying
buy	—buys	donkey	—donkeys	stay	—staying

Ending in Y *Preceded by a Consonant*

ally	—allies	easy	—easiest	pity	—pitiable
busy	—busily	icy	—icier	study	—studies
cloudy	—cloudiness	mercy	—merciless	try	—tried

The Y *Is Unchanged in Words Like the Following:*

baby	—babyish	lady	—ladylike
carry	—carrying	study	—studying

Words Similar in Sound

Accept. I should like to accept your first offer.

Except. He took everything except the rugs.

Advice. Free advice [noun] is usually not worth much.

Advise. Ms. Hull said she would advise [verb] me this term. (Similarly, devi*c*e [noun] and devi*s*e [verb], prophe*c*y [noun] and prophe*s*y [verb].

Affect. His forced jokes affect [verb] me unfavorably.

Effect. His humor has a bad effect [noun]. Let us try to effect [verb] a lasting peace.

All ready. They were all ready to go home.

Already. They had already left when we telephoned the house.

All together. Now that we are all together, let us talk it over.

Altogether. They were not altogether pleased with the results.

Altar. In this temple was an altar to the Unknown God.

Alter. One should not try to alter or escape history.

Canvas. We used a piece of canvas to shelter us from the wind.

Canvass. The candidate wanted to canvass every person in her precinct.

Capital. A capital letter; capital gains; capital punishment; state capital.

Capitol. Workers are painting the dome of the Capitol.

Cite. He cited three good examples.

Site. The site of the new school has not been decided on.

Sight. They were awed by the sight of so much splendor.

Coarse. The coarse sand blew in my face.

Course. We discussed the course to take. Of course he may come with us.

Complement. Your intelligence is a complement to your beauty.

Compliment. It is easier to pay a compliment than a bill.

Consul. Be sure to look up the American consul in Rome.

Council. He was appointed to the executive council.

Counsel. I sought counsel from my friends. They counseled moderation. He employed counsel to defend him.

Decent. The workers demanded a decent wage scale.

Descent. The descent from the mountain was uneventful.

Dissent. The voices of dissent were louder than those of approval.

Desert. Out in the lonely desert [noun— desert], he tried to desert [verb—desert] from his regiment.

Dessert. We had apple pie for dessert.

Dining. We eat dinner in our dining room. Dining at home is pleasant.

Dinning. Stop dinning that song into my ears!

Formerly. He was formerly a student at Beloit College.

Formally. You must address the presiding judge formally and respectfully.

Forth. Several witnesses came forth to testify.

Fourth. We planned a picnic for the Fourth of July.

Incidence. Better sanitation lowered the incidence of communicable diseases.

Incidents. Smugglers were involved in several incidents along the border.

Instance. For instance, she was always late to class.

Instants. As the car turned, those brief instants seemed like hours.

Its. Your plan has much in its favor. [Possessive of *it*.]

It's. It's too late now for excuses. [Contraction of *it is, it has.*]

Later. It is later than you think.

Latter. Of the two novels, I prefer the latter.

Lead. Can you lead [lēd—verb] us out of this jungle? Lead [lĕd—noun] is a heavy, soft, malleable metallic element.

Led. A local guide led us to the salmon fishing hole.

Loose. He has a loose tongue. The dog is loose again.

Lose. Don't lose your temper.

Passed. She smiled as she passed me. She passed the test.

Past. It is futile to try to relive the past.

Personal. Write him a personal letter.

Personnel. The morale of our company's personnel is high.

Pore. For hours they pored over the mysterious note.

Pour. Ms. Cook poured hot water into the teapot.

Precedence. Tax reform takes precedence over all other legislative matters.

Precedents. The judge quoted three precedents to justify his ruling.

Presence. We are honored by your presence.

Presents. The child received dozens of Christmas presents.

Principal. The principal of a school; the principal [chief] industry; the principal and the interest.

Principle. He is a man of high principles.

Quiet. You must keep quiet.

Quite. The weather was quite good all week.

Rain. A soaking rain would help our crops greatly.

Reign. Samuel Pepys was briefly imprisoned during the reign of William III.

Rein. Keep a tight rein when you ride this spirited horse.

Shone. The cat's eyes shone in the dark.

Shown. He hasn't shown us his best work.

Stationary. The benches were stationary and could not be moved.

Stationery. She wrote a letter on hotel stationery.

Statue. It was a statue of a pioneer.

Stature. Athos was a man of gigantic stature.

Statute. The law may be found in the 1917 book of statutes.

Than. She sings better than I.

Then. He screamed; then he fainted.

Their. It wasn't their fault. [Possessive pronoun.]

There. You won't find any gold there. [Adverb of place.]

They're. They're sure to be disappointed. [Contraction of *they are.*]

Thorough. We must first give the old cabin a thorough [adjective] cleaning.

Through. The thief had entered through [preposition] a hole in the roof.

To. Be sure to speak to her. [Preposition.]

Too. He is far too old for you. [Adverb.]

Two. The membership fee is only two dollars. [Adjective.]

Whose. Whose book is this? [Possessive pronoun.]

Who's. I wonder who's with her now. [Contraction of *who is.*]

Your. I like your new car. [Possessive pronoun.]

You're. You're not nervous, are you? [Contraction of *you are.*]

Supplement 1

(Rule 1): A few common adjectives with the suffix *able* have two correct spellings:

likable/likeable, lovable/loveable, movable/moveable, sizable/sizeable, usable/useable.

(Rule 3): Dictionaries show two spellings for the *-ed* and *-ing* forms (and a few other derived forms) of dozens of verbs ending in single consonants preceded by single vowels. In general, the single-consonant spelling is usually found in American printing; some of the dictionaries label the double-consonant spelling a British preference.

biased/biassed, canceling/cancelling, counselor/counsellor, diagraming/diagramming, equaled/equalled, marvelous/marvellous, modeled/modelled, totaling/totalling, traveler/traveller.

NAME _____ SCORE _____

Directions: Each of the following sentences contains three italicized words, one of which is misspelled. Underline each misspelled word and write it, correctly spelled, in the space at the left.

_____ 1. Professor Alberts *complimented* Edward on the *improvement* in his *writeing.*

_____ 2. The *principal admited* that his school had only limited *offerings* in chemistry and physics.

_____ 3. Last week representatives of nearly *ninety companys* attended a *conference* on our campus.

_____ 4. I'm unhappy about the new neighbors; I'm *beginning* to *believe* that *their* compulsive borrowers.

_____ 5. The accident *occurred* very quickly; *fortunately,* there was no *noticable* damage to either of the cars.

_____ 6. Jeff is having *difficulties* in an introductory mathematics *course* that is a *requirment* in his degree program.

_____ 7. We had a hard time *controlling* our giggles when the *frightened* bride-to-be lost a shoe on her way to the *alter.*

_____ 8. "I have *already* notified the proper *authoritys* about the problem," the *priest* replied calmly.

_____ 9. Several *donkeys* were *noisily* cavorting in an enclosed *feild* behind the barn.

_____ 10. "Can you tell me *whose* responsible for this display of *tasteless* advertising?" asked the enraged *financier.*

_____ 11. The natives earn a barely adequate *livelihood,* the *principle industries* being fishing and mining.

_____ 12. The children became *quiet* again after one of the *ladies openned* the kitchen door.

_____ 13. One of the *attorneys forcefully* argued that the old law has outlived *it's* usefulness.

_____ 14. Three of the managers are *threatening* to resign if they do not *recieve* higher *salaries.*

277

_____ 15. "I am *hoping* that *later* this week I'll be able to interview a *fameous* surgeon who will be on campus," said Ethel.

_____ 16. "My *presence* in the courtroom tomorrow will be *absolutly* necessary," said the *chief* of police.

_____ 17. "The *effect* of these changed *policies* is that our business is no longer *profittable*," complained Mr. Benton.

_____ 18. After a *fierce* contest with a much *wealthier* opponent, Jenny was finally elected to the city *consul.*

_____ 19. Toward the end of the *Fourth-of-July* picnic, some of the exhausted children were *becomeing* almost *unmanageable.*

_____ 20. "My experience has *shone* me that these new tools are *entirely serviceable,*" said the salesperson.

_____ 21. The imposing *statue* in the village square honors the *courageous* men and women who survived the *seige* of the city in World War I.

_____ 22. Mrs. Thompson's young *niece* left the *dining* room with three *peices* of pie on her plate.

_____ 23. The sluggish economy has *adversely effected* the earnings of these *companies.*

_____ 24. "It is *outragous* that this person, after *committing* these crimes, was *acquitted* by the jury," said the judge.

_____ 25. After moving to the state *capital,* Benny found a job that presented him with many *challengeing opportunities.*

_____ 26. "These grades are alarming," said Dean Hawkins; "*your* obviously spending *too* much time on outside *activities.*"

_____ 27. My three roommates usually give me good *advice,* but in this particular *instants,* they are *completely* wrong.

_____ 28. *There* is a good sale in progress at the drug store; I bought some monogrammed *stationary* and some household *supplies.*

_____ 29. Remember, you will *loose* weight only if you count *calories carefully.*

_____ 30. "The new *personnel* manager is a *conceited* young whippersnapper no older *then* I am," said Campbell bitterly.

NAME _____   SCORE _____

Directions: Each of the following sentences contains three italicized words, one of which is misspelled. Underline each misspelled word and write it, correctly spelled, in the space at the left.

_____ 1. It was *altogether inexcuseable* for you to be *ninety* minutes late for the interview.

_____ 2. The four *monkeys* were *peaceably* resting in *they're* enclosure.

_____ 3. *Regrettably,* Fred and his *buddies* did not follow your *advise.*

_____ 4. It is my *belief* that people in their *eightys* are *too* old to take up bungee jumping.

_____ 5. In his *brief* speech the *principal* of the school discussed other *possibilities* for solving the problem.

_____ 6. The *courageous* fireman broke down the door and *lead* the children to *safety.*

_____ 7. Jim *preferred* to spend his *liesure* time in outdoor *activities.*

_____ 8. Mrs. Dale *carried* the bowl of *raspberries* into the *dinning* room.

_____ 9. "My work load is certainly *heavier then* yours is," complained the new *cashier.*

_____ 10. In these *emergencies* the desperate man sometimes felt *compelled* to resort to *theivery.*

_____ 11. The rumor is that representatives of *management* will soon be *quitting* the *conferrence.*

_____ 12. The lawyer apologized to the members of the city *council* for those *deploreable incidents.*

_____ 13. Some of his listeners *inferred* from the *financier's* remark that he might *loose* money on his latest venture.

_____ 14. With great *presents* of mind, the *chief* of police *seized* the fleeing culprit.

_____ 15. The two *attorneys* finally *admitted* that they had *excepted* bribes from underworld figures.

_____ 16. "I consider your list of *grievances outragous*," said the indignant *personnel* manager.

_____ 17. "My *studies* demand that I spend *entirely* too much time *pouring* over these dull textbooks," complained Leroy.

_____ 18. In all *likelihood* these outside *duties* will have a bad *affect* on your grades.

_____ 19. "The situation is *hopeless*," said Mrs. Jackson's *niece*. "I'll never understand the basic *principals* of algebra."

_____ 20. *Earlier* that afternoon we had picked out a *desireable site* for our overnight camp.

_____ 21. Are you *quiet* sure the men are *receiving* the *salaries* they were promised?

_____ 22. The *conceited* young man always writes his letters on *extremely* expensive *stationary*.

_____ 23. Several local *ladies* sent in *entries* in the contest. I wonder *who's* will be judged best.

_____ 24. In that particular *instance* the *famous* lecturer made three errors in English *useage*.

_____ 25. *Its unlikely* that the new manager will be able to correct these *difficulties* in a few months.

_____ 26. I want to *complement* you on the *noticeable improvement* in your class work.

_____ 27. During the riots many of the *frightened* and poorly *equipped* guards *desserted* their posts.

_____ 28. "Of *course*," said the broker, "it is *conceiveable* that the annual *yield* from these bonds may change."

_____ 29. By these *achievements* she has *shone* us that she is seriously *committed* to improving the environment.

_____ 30. "Nothing will *altar* my decision to find the most *advantageous retirement* program for our workers," said the boss.

Lesson 28 *Plurals and Capitals*

This lesson covers the formation of plurals, and the conventions for using capitals.

Plurals

Plurals of most nouns are regularly formed by the addition of *s*. But if the singular noun ends in an *s* sound *(s, sh, ch, x, z)*, *es* is added to form a new syllable in pronunciation:

crab, crabs	foe, foes	kiss, kisses	tax, taxes
lamp, lamps	box, boxes	church, churches	lass, lasses

Nouns ending in *y* form plurals according to the spelling rule. (See Lesson 27.)

toy, toys	army, armies	fly, flies	attorney, attorneys
key, keys	lady, ladies	sky, skies	monkey, monkeys

Some words ending in *o* (including all musical terms and all words having a vowel preceding the *o*) form their plurals with *s*. But many others take *es:*

alto, altos	folio, folios	tomato, tomatoes
piano, pianos	hero, heroes	potato, potatoes

For several nouns ending in *o*, most modern dictionaries give both forms. Here are some examples; they are printed here in the order found in most dictionaries. The first spelling is the more common one:

banjos, banjoes	frescoes, frescos	lassos, lassoes	volcanoes, volcanos
buffaloes, buffalos	grottoes, grottos	mottoes, mottos	zeros, zeroes
cargoes, cargos	halos, haloes	tornadoes, tornados	

Some nouns ending in *f* or *fe* merely add *s*; some change *f* or *fe* to *ves* in the plural; and a few *(hoofs/hooves, scarfs/scarves, wharves/wharfs)* use either form. Use your dictionary to make sure:

leaf, leaves	life, lives	half, halves	wolf, wolves
roof, roofs	safe, safes	gulf, gulfs	elf, elves

A few nouns have the same form for singular and plural. A few have irregular plurals:

deer, deer	ox, oxen	child, children	goose, geese
sheep, sheep	man, men	foot, feet	mouse, mice

Many words of foreign origin use two plurals; some do not. Always check in your dictionary:

alumna, alumnae
alumnus, alumni
analysis, analyses
appendix, appendixes, appendices
basis, bases
beau, beaus, beaux
curriculum, curriculums, curricula
memorandum, memorandums, memoranda
tableau, tableaus, tableaux

bon mot, bons mots
crisis, crises
criterion, criteria
datum, data
thesis, theses
focus, focuses, foci
fungus, funguses, fungi
index, indexes, indices

Note: Do *not* use an apostrophe to form the plural of either a common or a proper noun.

Wrong: Our neighbor's, the Allen's and the Murray's, recently bought new Honda's.
Right: Our neighbors, the Allens and the Murrays, recently bought new Hondas.

Capitals

A capital letter is used for the first letter of the first word of any sentence, for the first letter of a proper noun, and often for the first letter of an adjective derived from a proper noun. Following are some reminders about situations that cause confusion for some writers.

1. Capitalize the first word of every sentence, every quoted sentence or fragment, and every transitional fragment. (See Lesson 14.)

   The building needs repairs. How much will it cost? Please answer me.
   Mr. James said, "We'll expect your answer soon." She replied, "Of course."
   And now to conclude.

2. Capitalize proper nouns and most adjectives derived from them. A proper noun designates by name an individual person, place, or thing that is a member of a group or class. Do not capitalize common nouns, which are words naming a group or class:

   Doris Powers, woman; France, country; Tuesday, day; January, month; Christmas Eve, holiday; Shorewood High School, high school; Carleton College, college; *Mauretania*, ship; Fifth Avenue, boulevard; White House, residence

   Elizabethan drama, Restoration poetry, Chinese peasants, Indian reservation, Red Cross assistance

3. Do not capitalize nouns and derived forms that, although originally proper nouns, have acquired special meanings. When in doubt, consult your dictionary:

   a set of china; a bohemian existence; plaster of paris; pasteurized milk; a mecca for golfers; set in roman type, not italics

4. Capitalize names of religions, references to deities, and most words having religious significance:

   Bible, Baptist, Old Testament, Holy Writ, Jewish, Catholic, Sermon on the Mount, Koran, Talmud

5. Capitalize titles of persons when used with the person's name. When the title is used alone, capitalize it only when it stands for a specific person of high rank:

I spoke briefly to Professor Jones. He is a professor of history.
We visited the late President Johnson's ranch in Texas.
Jerry is president of our art club.
Tonight the President will appear on national television.

6. Capitalize names denoting family relationship but not when they are preceded by a possessive. This rule is equivalent to saying that you capitalize when the word serves as a proper noun:

At that moment Mother, Father, and Aunt Lucy entered the room.
My mother, father, and aunt are very strict about some things.

7. Capitalize points of the compass when they refer to actual regions but not when they refer to directions:

Before we moved to the West, we lived in the South for a time.
You drive three miles west and then turn north on the Pacific Highway.

Do not capitalize adjectives of direction modifying countries or states:

From central Finland the group had emigrated to northern Michigan.

8. Capitalize names of academic subjects as they would appear in college catalog listings, but in ordinary writing capitalize only names of languages:

I intend to register for History 322 and Sociology 188.
Last year I took courses in history, sociology, German, and Latin.

9. In titles of books, short stories, plays, essays, and poems, capitalize the first word and all other words except the articles *(a, an, the)* and short prepositions and conjunctions. (See Lesson 19 for the use of italics and quotation marks with titles.)

Last semester I wrote reports on the following: Shaw's *The Intelligent Woman's Guide to Socialism and Capitalism,* Joyce's *A Portrait of the Artist as a Young Man,* Pirandello's *Six Characters in Search of an Author,* Poe's "The Fall of the House of Usher," Yeats's "An Irish Airman Foresees His Death," Frost's "Stopping by Woods on a Snowy Evening," and Muriel Rukeyser's "The Soul and Body of John Brown."

Note: Traditionally, a capital letter begins every line of poetry. This convention, however, is not always followed by modern poets; when you quote poetry, be sure to copy exactly the capitalization used by the author.

NAME _____ SCORE _____

Directions: Write the plural form or forms for each of the following words. When in doubt, consult your dictionary. When two forms are given, write both of them.

1. ally _____ _____

2. alumna _____ _____

3. axis _____ _____

4. beau _____ _____

5. box _____ _____

6. cameo _____ _____

7. cookie _____ _____

8. cupful _____ _____

9. diagnosis _____ _____

10. handkerchief _____ _____

11. lackey _____ _____

12. lasso _____ _____

13. louse _____ _____

14. man-of-war _____ _____

15. memento _____ _____

16. mongoose _____ _____

17. princess _____ _____

18. referendum _____ _____

19. saleswoman _____ _____

20. scarf _____ _____

21. sheaf _____ _____

22. Thomas _____ _____

23. tomato _____ _____

24. turkey _____ _____

25. wolf _____ _____

Directions: The following sentences contain fifty numbered words. If you think the word is correctly capitalized, write C in the space at the left with the corresponding number. If you think the word should not be capitalized, write W in the space.

_____ _____ _____
1   2   3

_____ _____ _____
4   5   6

_____ _____ _____
7   8   9

_____ _____ _____
10   11   12

_____ _____ _____
13   14   15

_____ _____ _____
16   17   18

_____ _____ _____
19   20   21

_____ _____ _____
22   23   24

_____ _____ _____
25   26   27

_____ _____ _____
28   29   30

_____ _____ _____
31   32   33

_____ _____ _____
34   35   36

_____ _____ _____
37   38   39

_____ _____ _____
40   41   42

_____ _____ _____
43   44   45

_____ _____ _____
46   47   48

_____ _____
49   50

(1) The Secretary of the local Chamber Of Commerce directed us to the Museum Of Business And Industry, telling us to go through Prospect Park, turn left on Underwood Avenue, and walk three blocks North.
[1 = Secretary, 2 = Chamber, 3 = Of, 4 = Commerce, 5 = Museum, 6 = Of, 7 = Business, 8 = And, 9 = Industry, 10 = Prospect, 11 = Park, 12 = Underwood, 13 = Avenue, 14 = North]

(2) Ms. Edith Leary, who taught me Latin and Social Studies at North Bend Junior High School, is engaged to marry a young Professor of Journalism at the local Community College; he recently earned a Ph.D. degree from Princeton.
[15 = Latin, 16 = Social, 17 = Studies, 18 = North, 19 = Bend, 20 = Junior, 21 = High, 22 = School, 23 = Professor, 24 = Journalism, 25 = Community, 26 = College, 27 = Ph.D, 28 = degree, 29 = Princeton]

(3) On New Year's Day Uncle Frank and two of my Cousins joined us, and we watched the broadcast of the Tournament Of Roses parade and the Rose Bowl football game.
[30 = New, 31 = Year's, 32 = Uncle, 33 = Frank, 34 = Cousins, 35 = Tournament, 36 = Of, 37 = Roses, 38 = Rose, 39 = Bowl]

(4) Before dismissing the class, Professor Bacon told us that over the Christmas Holiday we should all read Joyce's *Portrait Of The Artist As A Young Man.*
[40 = Professor, 41 = Christmas, 42 = Holiday, 43 = Portrait, 44 = Of, 45 = The, 46 = Artist, 47 = As, 48 = A, 49 = Young, 50 = Man]

Exercise 28   *Plurals and Capitals*

NAME _____ SCORE _____

Directions: Write the plural form or forms for each of the following words. When in doubt, consult your dictionary. When two forms are given, write both of them.

1. alley _____ _____

2. alumnus _____ _____

3. basketful _____ _____

4. battery _____ _____

5. brother-in-law _____ _____

6. cherry _____ _____

7. crisis _____ _____

8. folio _____ _____

9. fowl _____ _____

10. freshman _____ _____

11. gaff _____ _____

12. half _____ _____

13. index _____ _____

14. loaf _____ _____

15. mango _____ _____

16. mass _____ _____

17. moose _____ _____

18. oaf _____ _____

19. placebo _____ _____

20. potato _____ _____

21. Smith _____ _____

22. tableau _____ _____

23. terminus _____ _____

24. volley _____ _____

25. waitress _____ _____

Directions: The following sentences contain fifty numbered words. If you think the word is correctly capitalized, write C in the space at the left with the corresponding numbers. If you think the word should not be capitalized, write W in the space.

1	2	3
4	5	6
7	8	9
10	11	12
13	14	15
16	17	18
19	20	21
22	23	24
25	26	27
28	29	30
31	32	33
34	35	36
37	38	39
40	41	42
43	44	45
46	47	48
49	50	

(1) The Librarian told me that, although there are other good
1
Encyclopedias, the *Britannica* and the *Americana* are the
2 3 4
ones most often used by Juniors and Seniors at our High
5 6 7
School.
8

(2) The speaker continued: "The Polynesians of the South
9 10 11
Pacific were responsive, for the most part, to the teach-
12
ings of the early Christian Missionaries."
13 14

(3) At Horace Mann Junior High School I first read Frost's
15 16 17 18 19
Stopping By Woods On A Snowy Evening in an eighth-
20 21 22 23 24 25 26
grade Literature class.
27

(4) Last weekend I took a bus to the Twin Cities and visited
28 29
Aunt Laura, Uncle Winston, and two Cousins I had never
30 31 32
met before.

(5) Following Professor Logan's advice, I registered for
33
English 67, Zoology 132, and an introductory course in
34 35
Journalism.
36

(6) A retired Professor whom Father knows recommended that
37 38
I go to some small College in the East and concentrate on
39 40
Liberal Arts courses during my first two years.
41 42

(7) At our Girl Scout meeting last week, Amy Jenkin's Mother
43 44 45
showed us a beautiful blanket she had bought last Winter
46
in Southwestern Arizona at a store that sells products made
47 48
by Native Americans.
49 50

Lesson 29 *Spelling List*

This list includes words frequently misspelled by high school and college students. Each word is repeated to show its syllabic division. Whether this list is used for individual study and review or in some kind of organized class activity, your method of studying should be the following: (1) Learn to pronounce the word syllable by syllable. Some of your trouble in spelling may come from incorrect pronunciation. (2) Copy the word carefully, forming each letter as plainly as you can. Some of your trouble may come from bad handwriting. (3) Pronounce the word carefully again. (4) On a separate sheet of paper, write the word from memory, check your spelling with the correct spelling before you, and, if you have misspelled the word, repeat the learning process.

abbreviate	ab-bre-vi-ate	audience	au-di-ence
absence	ab-sence	auxiliary	aux-il-ia-ry
accidentally	ac-ci-den-tal-ly	awkward	awk-ward
accommodate	ac-com-mo-date	barbarous	bar-ba-rous
accompanying	ac-com-pa-ny-ing	basically	ba-si-cal-ly
accomplish	ac-com-plish	beneficial	ben-e-fi-cial
accumulate	ac-cu-mu-late	boundaries	bound-a-ries
acknowledge	ac-knowl-edge	Britain	Brit-ain
acquaintance	ac-quaint-ance	bureaucracy	bu-reauc-ra-cy
acquire	ac-quire	business	busi-ness
across	a-cross	calendar	cal-en-dar
additive	ad-di-tive	candidate	can-di-date
admissible	ad-mis-si-ble	cassette	cas-sette
aggravate	ag-gra-vate	category	cat-e-go-ry
always	al-ways	cemetery	cem-e-ter-y
amateur	am-a-teur	certain	cer-tain
among	a-mong	chosen	cho-sen
analysis	a-nal-y-sis	commission	com-mis-sion
analytical	al-a-lyt-i-cal	committee	com-mit-tee
apartheid	a-part-heid	communicate	com-mu-ni-cate
apparatus	ap-pa-ra-tus	communism	com-mu-nism
apparently	ap-par-ent-ly	comparative	com-par-a-tive
appearance	ap-pear-ance	competent	com-pe-tent
appreciate	ap-pre-ci-ate	competition	com-pe-ti-tion
appropriate	ap-pro-pri-ate	completely	com-plete-ly
approximately	ap-prox-i-mate-ly	compulsory	com-pul-so-ry
arctic	arc-tic	computer	com-put-er
argument	ar-gu-ment	concede	con-cede
arithmetic	a-rith-me-tic	condominium	con-do-min-i-um
association	as-so-ci-a-tion	conference	con-fer-ence
astronaut	as-tro-naut	confidentially	con-fi-den-tial-ly
athletics	ath-let-ics	conscience	con-science
attendance	at-tend-ance	conscientious	con-sci-en-tious

conscious	con-scious	foreign	for-eign
consistent	con-sist-ent	forty	for-ty
continuous	con-tin-u-ous	frantically	fran-ti-cal-ly
controversial	con-tro-ver-sial	fundamentally	fun-da-men-tal-ly
convenient	con-ven-ient	generally	gen-er-al-ly
counterfeit	coun-ter-feit	ghetto	ghet-to
criticism	crit-i-cism	government	gov-ern-ment
criticize	crit-i-cize	graffiti	graf-fi-ti
curiosity	cu-ri-os-i-ty	grammar	gram-mar
curriculum	cur-ric-u-lum	grievous	griev-ous
decision	de-ci-sion	guarantee	guar-an-tee
definitely	def-i-nite-ly	guerrilla	guer-ril-la
describe	de-scribe	harass	ha-rass
description	de-scrip-tion	height	height
desperate	des-per-ate	hindrance	hin-drance
dictionary	dic-tion-ar-y	humorous	hu-mor-ous
difference	dif-fer-ence	hurriedly	hur-ried-ly
dilapidated	di-lap-i-dat-ed	hypocrisy	hy-poc-ri-sy
dinosaur	di-no-saur	imagination	im-ag-i-na-tion
disappear	dis-ap-pear	immediately	im-me-di-ate-ly
disappoint	dis-ap-point	impromptu	im-promp-tu
disastrous	dis-as-trous	incidentally	in-ci-den-tal-ly
discipline	dis-ci-pline	incredible	in-cred-i-ble
dissatisfied	dis-sat-is-fied	independence	in-de-pend-ence
dissident	dis-si-dent	indispensable	in-dis-pen-sa-ble
dissipate	dis-si-pate	inevitable	in-ev-i-ta-ble
doesn't	does-n't	influential	in-flu-en-tial
dormitory	dor-mi-to-ry	initiative	in-i-ti-a-tive
during	dur-ing	intelligence	in-tel-li-gence
efficient	ef-fi-cient	intentionally	in-ten-tion-al-ly
eligible	el-i-gi-ble	intercede	in-ter-cede
eliminate	e-lim-i-nate	interesting	in-ter-est-ing
embarrass	em-bar-rass	interpretation	in-ter-pre-ta-tion
eminent	em-i-nent	interrupt	in-ter-rupt
emphasize	em-pha-size	irrelevant	ir-rel-e-vant
enthusiastic	en-thu-si-as-tic	irresistible	ir-re-sist-i-ble
entrepreneur	en-tre-pre-neur	irritation	ir-ri-ta-tion
environment	en-vi-ron-ment	knowledge	knowl-edge
equipment	e-quip-ment	laboratory	lab-o-ra-to-ry
equivalent	e-quiv-a-lent	laser	la-ser
especially	es-pe-cial-ly	legitimate	le-git-i-mate
exaggerated	ex-ag-ger-at-ed	library	li-brar-y
exceed	ex-ceed	lightning	light-ning
excellent	ex-cel-lent	literature	lit-er-a-ture
exceptionally	ex-cep-tion-al-ly	livelihood	live-li-hood
exhaust	ex-haust	loneliness	lone-li-ness
existence	ex-ist-ence	maintenance	main-te-nance
exorbitant	ex-or-bi-tant	marriage	mar-riage
experience	ex-pe-ri-ence	mathematics	math-e-mat-ics
explanation	ex-pla-na-tion	memento	me-men-to
extraordinary	ex-traor-di-nar-y	miniature	min-i-a-ture
extremely	ex-treme-ly	miscellaneous	mis-cel-la-ne-ous
familiar	fa-mil-iar	mischievous	mis-chie-vous
fascinate	fas-ci-nate	misspelled	mis-spelled
February	Feb-ru-ar-y	mortgage	mort-gage

mysterious	mys-te-ri-ous	remembrance	re-mem-brance
naturally	nat-u-ral-ly	repetition	rep-e-ti-tion
necessary	nec-es-sar-y	representative	rep-re-sent-a-tive
ninety	nine-ty	respectfully	re-spect-ful-ly
ninth	ninth	respectively	re-spec-tive-ly
nowadays	now-a-days	restaurant	res-tau-rant
nuclear	nu-cle-ar	rhetoric	rhet-o-ric
obedience	o-be-di-ence	rhythm	rhythm
oblige	o-blige	ridiculous	ri-dic-u-lous
obstacle	ob-sta-cle	robot	ro-bot
occasionally	oc-ca-sion-al-ly	sacrilegious	sac-ri-le-gious
occurrence	oc-cur-rence	sandwich	sand-wich
omission	o-mis-sion	satellite	sat-el-lite
opportunity	op-por-tu-ni-ty	satisfactorily	sat-is-fac-to-ri-ly
optimistic	op-ti-mis-tic	schedule	sched-ule
original	o-rig-i-nal	scientific	sci-en-tif-ic
pamphlet	pam-phlet	secretary	sec-re-tar-y
parallel	par-al-lel	separately	sep-a-rate-ly
parliament	par-lia-ment	sergeant	ser-geant
particularly	par-tic-u-lar-ly	significant	sig-nif-i-cant
partner	part-ner	similar	sim-i-lar
pastime	pas-time	sophomore	soph-o-more
performance	per-form-ance	spaghetti	spa-ghet-ti
permissible	per-mis-si-ble	specifically	spe-cif-i-cal-ly
perseverance	per-se-ver-ance	specimen	spec-i-men
perspiration	per-spi-ra-tion	speech	speech
persuade	per-suade	strictly	strict-ly
politics	pol-i-tics	successful	suc-cess-ful
possession	pos-ses-sion	superintendent	su-per-in-tend-ent
practically	prac-ti-cal-ly	supersede	su-per-sede
preceding	pre-ced-ing	surprise	sur-prise
prejudice	prej-u-dice	suspicious	sus-pi-cious
preparation	prep-a-ra-tion	syllable	syl-la-ble
prevalent	prev-a-lent	synonymous	syn-on-y-mous
privilege	priv-i-lege	synthetic	syn-thet-ic
probably	prob-a-bly	technology	tech-nol-o-gy
procedure	pro-ce-dure	temperament	tem-per-a-ment
proceed	pro-ceed	temperature	tem-per-a-ture
processor	pro-ces-sor	together	to-geth-er
professional	pro-fes-sion-al	tragedy	trag-e-dy
professor	pro-fes-sor	truly	tru-ly
pronunciation	pro-nun-ci-a-tion	twelfth	twelfth
propaganda	prop-a-gan-da	unanimous	u-nan-i-mous
psychiatrist	psy-chi-a-trist	undoubtedly	un-doubt-ed-ly
psychological	psy-cho-log-i-cal	unnecessarily	un-nec-es-sar-i-ly
pursue	pur-sue	until	un-til
quantity	quan-ti-ty	usually	u-su-al-ly
questionnaire	ques-tion-naire	various	var-i-ous
quizzes	quiz-zes	vegetable	veg-e-ta-ble
realize	re-al-ize	video	vid-e-o
really	re-al-ly	village	vil-lage
recognize	rec-og-nize	villain	vil-lain
recommend	rec-om-mend	Wednesday	Wednes-day
regard	re-gard	whether	wheth-er
religious	re-li-gious	wholly	whol-ly

NAME _____ SCORE _____

Directions: Each sentence contains two words from the first half of the spelling list. In each one of these words at least one letter is missing. Write the words, correctly spelled, in the spaces at the left.

_____ 1. This election our can—date for mayor is facing very weak
_____ comp—tition.

_____ 2. The cost of the new equip—ent for the factory will be
_____ ex—rbitant.

_____ 3. Excessive cutting of the forests has had a disast—us effect on the
_____ envi—nment.

_____ 4. Our tourist group was dis—pointed with the ac—modations
_____ provided at the resort.

_____ 5. The workmen did an excel—nt job of removing the graf—ti that
_____ had been spray-painted on the bare wall.

_____ 6. After two lengthy confe—nces the representatives of the two war-
_____ ring tribes settled their main dif—nces.

_____ 7. All of us are enthus—tic about the new series of for—gn films
_____ being shown at the local cinema.

_____ 8. Martha was slightly embar—sed by her husband's attempt to tell
_____ the group what he thought was a hum—us story.

_____ 9. A person is not elig—ble for this position if he or she is more
_____ than fo—ty years old.

_____ 10. In a bus—ess letter ordinary words will be written out in full, not
_____ ab—viated.

_____ 11. Many local residents crit—ized the mayor for his appear—nce at
_____ an environmental rally.

_____ 12. In her younger days she had participated in many ath—etic
_____ events, at a strictly amat—r level, of course.

_____ 13. Jerome counted am—ng his a—uaintances several actors and
_____   writers.

_____ 14. We had several severe snowstorms dur—ng the month of
_____   Feb—ary.

_____ 15. I al—ays try to attend every meeting of the hospitality com—tee.
_____

_____ 16. In the ab—ence of the regular teacher, dis—pline in the class-
_____   room became quite lax.

_____ 17. Many members of the aud—nce were clearly dis—tisfied with
_____   the performance of the substitute singers.

_____ 18. In the seventh grade Tidwell's favorite subjects were arith—tic
_____   and English gram—r.

_____ 19. The ambassador im—diately notified her gover—ent of the new
_____   development.

_____ 20. Ms. Cromwell gives her students contin—us practice in using the
_____   unabridged diction—y.

_____ 21. Ms. Lee closed her remarks with an approp—ate reminder:
_____   "Remember, children, curi—ity has killed many a cat."

_____ 22. You will find this free desk calen—r very conv—nt for recording
_____   your appointments.

_____ 23. The foreman conc—ded the fact that Lucas had been a hard-
_____   working and comp—tent assistant.

_____ 24. The clumsy, a—ward boy accident—y dropped the heavy wrench
_____   on his foot.

_____ 25. Draper used nothing except famil—r, worn-out argu—ents in
_____   his debate with the reigning champion.

Exercise 29   *Spelling*

NAME _____   SCORE _____

Directions: Each sentence contains three italicized words from the first half of the spelling list. One of the three words is misspelled. Underline the misspelled word and write it, correctiy spelled, in the space at the left.

_____ 1. The side wall of the *delapidated* shed was almost *completely* covered with *graffiti.*

_____ 2. Any *conscientious* student realizes that a *dictionery* is a *convenient* source of useful information.

_____ 3. *Attendance* at our lectures in *February* is *allways* quite low because of the bad weather.

_____ 4. *During* the demonstration an *awkward* lab assistant dropped a piece of *equiptment* and broke it.

_____ 5. Dr. Albertson *acknowledged* that some students find *compulsery* military training *beneficial.*

_____ 6. A *foreign* student told the *conferrence* participants of the *experiences* she had when the rioting began.

_____ 7. All of us were *fascinated* by the *impromtu* speech given by the *eminent* critic.

_____ 8. The *harassed* teacher was making a *desparate* attempt to maintain *discipline* in his overcrowded classroom.

_____ 9. The *embarrassed entrepreneur* gave the stockholders an unsatisfactory *explaination* for the decline in profits.

_____ 10. *Generally* speaking, Mark's father *dosen't* approve of any new *government* regulation.

_____ 11. Cynthia's *heighth certainly* should make her *eligible* to be a member of the junior-class basketball team.

_____ 12. Mr. Conway *hurriedly* explained that he has never numbered the accused man *among* his *acquaintances.*

295

_____ 13. His main *arguement* is that *athletic competition* between the two schools is a good thing.

_____ 14. The *audiance,* I'm afraid, did not fully *appreciate* the work done by the *amateur* actors.

_____ 15. Craig's *conscience* should bother him because of the many *absence* reports he has *accummulated* this semester.

_____ 16. The youngsters *especially* enjoyed Ms. Lane's *humorous discription* of her broken-down cabin at Lake Wilderness.

_____ 17. *Approximately* three hundred students live in the *dormitory,* although it was designed to *accomodate* only two hundred.

_____ 18. The publisher is *franticly* trying to locate *forty* pages that mysteriously *disappeared* from the manuscript.

_____ 19. *Apparently* someone had *accidently* spilled some ink on Ms. Singer's new *calendar.*

_____ 20. Mr. Linden *finally* managed to *aquire* the vacant lot *across* the street from his house.

_____ 21. The owner of the *computer* store reports that *business* this year has been mildly *dissappointing.*

_____ 22. "The *committee* members thank you for your *competant analysis* of the problem," said the chairperson.

_____ 23. Some of the parents are *extreamly dissatisfied* with the *curriculum* recently adopted by the school.

_____ 24. I will *concede* that the *commission accompolished* much good at its last meeting.

_____ 25. Linda *immediately* accepted the offer to teach *arithemetic* in an *excellent* school district in Alaska.

NAME _____ SCORE _____

Directions: Each sentence contains two words from the second half of the spelling list. In each of these words at least one letter is missing. Write the words, correctly spelled, in the spaces at the left.

_____ 1. Tomorrow you will have an op—tunity to interview the new
_____ sup—tendent of schools.

_____ 2. Several mischiev—us students were being noisy in the school
_____ lib—ry.

_____ 3. Ben decided that he couldn't write an orig—al short story
_____ because he was lacking in im—gination.

_____ 4. Prof—sor Salyer said that it should be clear to anyone that
_____ par—lel lines will never meet.

_____ 5. At the first class session I met my new lab—atory par—ner.
_____

_____ 6. "We prob—ly won't be able to get a decent meal in this tiny
_____ vil—ge," complained Sue.

_____ 7. The committee chairperson has sched—led a meeting for next
_____ We—sday.

_____ 8. Having been suc—sful in business, she decided to enter pol—tics
_____ and seek election to the Senate.

_____ 9. Ms. Stanwood's sec—tary rarely mi—pells a word in a business
_____ letter.

_____ 10. Allan said that he could not rec—mend a rest—rant in his
_____ hometown.

_____ 11. The clerk informed Beth that it is not permis—ble for a freshman
_____ or a soph—ore to register for Physics 344.

_____ 12. At the company picnic more than ni—ty tuna fish sand—ches
_____ were eaten.

_____ 13. In my lit—ature class this term we studied four Shakespearean
_____ comedies and three tra—dies.

297

_____ 14. This kind of prop—anda plays upon people's pre—udices.
_____

_____ 15. "Your interp—tation of the poem is most int—esting," Ms. Stan-
_____ wood said to Bruce.

_____ 16. When their house burned, the family lost pract—ly all of their
_____ pos—sions.

_____ 17. Stan admitted that his knowl—ge of math—atics is limited.
_____

_____ 18. The director finally p—rsuaded Andy to play the part of the
_____ vil—n in the next production of the Drama Club.

_____ 19. Last winter the temp—ture oc—sionally dropped below the
_____ freezing level.

_____ 20. Jane's birthday is the nin—h of February; her brother's birthday
_____ is the twel—h of June.

_____ 21. The new radio announcer made a few r—diculous errors in his
_____ pron—ation of foreign place names.

_____ 22. A few malcontents repeatedly inter—pted the mayor's welcom-
_____ ing spe—ch.

_____ 23. "Perhaps I am unduly opt—mistic, but I believe this problem will
_____ soon be solved satisfact—ly," said the chairman.

_____ 24. To our great su—prise, the waiter then proc—ded to remove all
_____ of the dishes from our table.

_____ 25. Luke's free time is often devoted to crossword puzzles, word
_____ games, and simi—r pa—times.

NAME _____ SCORE _____

Directions: Each sentence contains three italicized words from the second half of the spelling list. One of the three words is misspelled. Underline the misspelled word and write it, correctly spelled, in the space at the left.

_____ 1. A *representative* of the Red Cross spoke to our class; her *speech* was *truely* inspirational.

_____ 2. The Swansons *usually* do not remove their Christmas tree *untill* *Twelfth* Night.

_____ 3. You are *liable* to get a parking ticket, because *paralell* parking is not *permissible* on this street.

_____ 4. This *pamphlet* contains a *particularly* *intresting* chapter on public school financing.

_____ 5. *Together* they visited a *psychiatrist* who *pursuaded* them to work out a compromise.

_____ 6. In *politics* many discussions are made up of equal parts of *rhetoric* and *propoganda*.

_____ 7. The *sergeant* then *proceeded* to return to the *villiage*.

_____ 8. Mario now *recognizes* the fact that he was unduly *predjudiced* against the institution of *marriage*.

_____ 9. To our great delight and *surprise*, we were allowed to make a tour of the *nuclear* *labratory*.

_____ 10. Bertha brought home with her two *miniature* silver teapots as *momentos* of the exciting *occasion*.

_____ 11. Our neighborhood *restaurant* makes excellent *sandwitches* but badly overcooks most *vegetables*.

_____ 12. Entering students fill out *various* *questionaires* that presumably reveal their *knowledge* of basic subjects.

299

_____ 13. On *Wednesday* Lorraine had her first *oppertunity* to serve as a substitute teacher in a *ninth*-grade class.

_____ 14. Many *influential* leaders of *religious* groups consider the novel offensive, even *sacreligious.*

_____ 15. The *temperature* continued to rise, and I noticed beads of *prespiration* on my *partner's* forehead.

_____ 16. After reading several *specimans* of Laura's poetry, *Professor* Ashton *recommended* that she sign up for his advanced class.

_____ 17. "Any *repetition* of this kind of *mischievious* behavior will result *inevitably* in your dismissal," warned the foreman.

_____ 18. "I'm *naturally optomistic,* and I *really* believe that I can do a good job," said Barry.

_____ 19. The dean's *secretary* asked me *wheather* I was a junior or a *sophomore.*

_____ 20. My *original schedual* left me with *practically* no time for recreation.

_____ 21. The *preceeding* semester Ben had taken two *literature* courses that required much research in the *library.*

_____ 22. The men were warned *specifically* to say nothing in *reguard* to the *preparations* being made for the invasion.

_____ 23. "That young man shows that he has *initiative* and *intelligence,* "said the boss, "but I fear that he lacks *preserverance.*"

_____ 24. "I also have in my *possesion* a limited *quantity* of used word *processors* to sell at bargain prices," he concluded.

_____ 25. The manager of the theater *interrupted* the *performance* to announce that *lightening* had struck a car in the parking lot.

NAME _____ SCORE _____

Directions: A sentence may have no misspelled words, one misspelled word, or two misspelled words. Underline the misspelled words and write them, correctly spelled, in the spaces at the left.

_____ 1. If the apparatus in the laboratory has been damaged, some
_____   arrangment should be made to have it replaced.

_____ 2. The new dormatory will accommodate approximately ninety
_____   girls in a very pleasant enviomment.

_____ 3. The commission, meeting in continuous session for seven hours,
_____   accompolished an extraordinary amount of work.

_____ 4. Its apparent that the new law supersedes the original one, which
_____   had been ignored by practically everyone.

_____ 5. Our candidate is a man who has spent over fourty years in
_____   national politics.

_____ 6. The president of the sophomore class conferred with Professor
_____   Haley in regard to the mysterious occurrence.

_____ 7. The woman who lives across the street from the restaurant is an
_____   acquaintance of mine.

_____ 8. The retiring superintendent made his usual speach in which he
                     recommended continued studying of reading, writeing, and
_____   arithmetic.

_____ 9. Undoubtedly the members of the committee will be unanimous
_____   in their voting on the proposed pay raise.

_____ 10. Wednesday is the twelfth day of below-freezing temperatures,
_____   and the village is completely isolated.

_____ 11. Nowdays a high-school diploma is certainly no guarantee of an
_____   adequate livelihood.

_____ 12. The enthusastic support of the principal of the school was par-
_____   ticularily significant in the light of later events.

_____ 13. "If you cannot subdue the mischievious boys by peaceable
_____   means, a little force is permissible," said Sergeant Loomis.

_____ 14. You should seize this opportunity to continue your education
_____   and to travel in foreign lands.

_____ 15. The constant interruptions from disatisfied members of the
_____   audience finally forced us to postpone the preformance.

_____ 16. I acknowledge the fact that your acheivement has been an
_____   extremely admireable one.

_____ 17. For settling questions of grammar and pronunciation, you will
_____   find this dictionary absolutely indispensable.

_____ 18. On the ninth day of February my pardner and I found a desire-
_____   able vacant building for our new video store.

_____ 19. The propaganda in that pamphlet should appear ridiculous to
_____   any moderatly intelligent reader.

_____ 20. Durring the prolonged applause the athelete maintained his awk-
_____   ward position on the parallel bars.

Writing Paragraphs and Essays

Section 1 An Overview of College Writing

Although it may come as a surprise to you, you will be called on to do a great deal of writing in college and in your career. Lecture notes, essays, research papers, and tests are the very stuff of which college courses are made. Memorandums, letters, reports, and proposals are basic tools in almost any career you can name. And all this writing, whether in or out of college, is in great measure a key to your progress and success. In fact, in many large organizations, people are known to those in other areas more through their written work than through personal contact, and progress and promotion ride as much on the quality of that written work as on any other factor. Writing skills will be a major factor in your success.

Beyond such practical benefits, writing is a very effective tool for learning. Writing about a subject produces two good results: greater understanding and control of the material itself, and new connections to other facts and concepts. Writing out lecture notes and textbook materials in your own words will give you better control of those materials and will help you to connect the new materials with facts and concepts you learned earlier.

In the previous sections of this book, you examined the operating principles of the language and applied those principles to writing correct, effective sentences. Now you need to learn to combine those sentences into paragraphs, and the paragraphs into papers that will fulfill your college writing assignments.

The assignments you receive in college may be widely varied, ranging from a single paragraph narrating an event in your life to a complex research paper. Look briefly at a list of these possible assignments:

1. *Personal Essays*
   - Recount an event in your life, explaining its importance.
   - Discuss your position on the approaching presidential election.
2. *Essay Tests*
   - Answer two of the following three questions, using well-developed paragraphs and complete sentences in your answer.
3. *Essays and Discussions*
   - Explain the causes of structural unemployment in our country today.
   - Discuss the work of Jonas Salk in disease prevention.

4. *Critical Papers*
   - Evaluate the enclosed proposal for the construction of a new dam.
   - Assess the work of the Thatcher administration in Britain.
5. *Persuasive or Argumentative Papers*
   - Argue for or against the use of government spending to retrain displaced workers.
   - Discuss the arguments against universal military training in the United States.
6. *Documented Papers*
   - After thorough research into the subject, write a paper discussing the use of nuclear power in this country. Be sure to discuss the history, the current situation, and the arguments for and against continued use and further development.

Although this list seems extremely diverse and the types of writing quite varied, you can take comfort in the fact that underneath this diversity and complexity lies a fairly straightforward process that can be applied to all types of writing. You need only to learn one set of steps, the basic writing process, in order to deal effectively with any writing project you might face.

The Writing Process

Writing is a process, a set of steps, not a project that is started and finished in a single session. Often people believe that successful writers have in some way happened onto a secret method of production that allows them, almost by magic, to sit down and write out a nearly perfect draft on the first try. This happens only rarely, and always to writers with long experience; most people can assume that good writing always rises out of slow, painstaking, step-by-step work.

The steps in the writing process group themselves naturally into two phases, and each phase requires an approach, a mind-set, that is quite different from the other.

In the first phase, composing, you should be very free and creative. Think of this phase as a search, an adventure, an opportunity to try out many possibilities for ideas, content, and strategies.

In the second phase, editing, you must be very critical of the materials you composed earlier. This is the time when you must evaluate, rewrite, reject, and correct the materials you developed while composing.

You must be careful not to mix the modes of operation. Don't edit when you should be composing. Don't delete materials, or decide not to pursue an idea, or ponder the correctness of a mark of punctuation. Such distractions will almost certainly stop your flow of ideas.

But don't allow yourself to be free and creative when you are working as an editor. Keeping a word that is not quite right or failing to cut out a section that does not fit will produce papers that lack focus and are full of distractions.

Remember that each phase in the process is separate and distinct. Each one requires separate and distinct attitudes toward the work at hand.

The following brief explanation provides a general introduction to the steps in the writing process. In later sections you will see these steps applied to different types of writing; those applications will illustrate minor changes to suit specific types of writing.

Composing

Step 1. *Select or identify the subject.*

Basic Question: What should I write about? Or (if the assignment is very specific): What does the assignment require me to write about?

Strategy: Select the subject on the basis of these questions:
- Are you and your reader interested in it?
- Do you have enough knowledge to write on it? If not, can you locate enough?
- Can you treat the subject completely within the length allotted for the assignment?

Step 2. *Gather information about the subject.*

Basic Question: What do I know about the subject? More importantly, what do I need to know to write about this subject fully and effectively?

Strategy: Record what you know, whether the information comes from recollection or research. Seek more information where necessary. ("A Few Words Before Starting" (pages 309–313) will give you some helpful hints about this process.) Continue research and writing until you arrive at Step 3.

Step 3. *Establish a controlling statement or thesis for the paper.*

Basic Question: Exactly what can I say about this subject on the basis of the information and ideas I developed in Step 2?

Strategy: Continue to gather information and write about the subject until a specific idea develops. Write out that idea in a single sentence.

Step 4. *Select specific items of support to include in the paper.*

Basic Question: What ideas, facts, and illustrations can I use to make the thesis completely clear to the reader?

Strategy: Review the stockpile of materials gathered in Step 2. Select from these materials only those ideas, facts, and illustrations that will develop and support the thesis.

Step 5. *Establish an order for presenting the materials you have selected.*

Basic Question: What is the most effective order for presenting the materials that I have selected?

Strategy: Choose an order of presentation that offers your reader a logical progression for the development of your idea. The orders used in paragraph development are sometimes useful in developing an order for an essay. (See pp. 329–339.) Write the draft in any order you choose, starting with the easiest section. Assemble the draft in the order you have selected.

Step 6. *Write the first draft.*

Basic Question: What will the materials look like when presented in the order I have chosen?

Strategy: Write out a complete version of the paper, following the plan developed in the first five steps.

Editing

Before you begin to edit the first completed draft of the paper, be sure that you shift from the role of composer/writer to the role of editor. You have before you a completed product, not a perfect product. You must examine that product with a very critical eye, testing and weighing each part to be sure that it is as good as it can be.

Step 7. Assess the thesis of the draft.

Basic Question: Is the thesis a proper expression of your knowledge on the subject?

Strategy: Read each paragraph or section of the essay individually and write a topic sentence for each one. From the topic statements produce a thesis statement for the draft. Compare it to the original thesis. If there are differences between the two, create a new, better thesis.

Step 8. Assess the content.

Basic Question: Does each paragraph or section offer genuine support for the thesis?

Strategy: Check the topic statement for each paragraph or section to be sure each one supports the new thesis. Remove and replace any paragraph or section that does not support the thesis.

Step 9. Assess the order of presentation.

Basic Question: Does the order of presentation provide the reader with a logical progression or pathway through the essay?

Strategy: Try different orders of presentation, shifting sections around to see if you can find a better order than the one you used for the first finished draft.

Step 10. Assess the paragraphs.

Basic Question: Is each paragraph unified and complete? Is each paragraph developed following the best possible method of development?

Strategy: Read each paragraph separately and write a topic statement for it. Check the content of the paragraph to be sure it develops one idea and only one idea. Check the content to be sure that the paragraph contains enough specific, concrete details to make the topic statement clear to the reader.

Step 11. Correct the mistakes in the draft.

Basic Question: What errors in grammar and mechanics do I need to correct?

Strategy: Reach each sentence as an independent unit, starting at the end of the paper and working to the beginning. Reading "backward" in this fashion assures that you will not make mental corrections or assumptions as you read.

Step 12. Write the final draft.

Basic Question: What form shall I use for the final copy of the paper?

Strategy: Follow the guidelines for manuscript preparation specified by your teacher, printing or typing the final copy on plain white paper. Be sure to read the final copy carefully for errors.

This process can be followed with only minor changes for any writing assignment. Study it carefully as we apply it to various types of assignments. Make the process second nature to you, a set of habits followed anytime you write. The more you practice, the greater will be your facility in writing.

Before we begin to examine the writing process as it applies to specific projects in college writing, take a few moments to study the results that a professional writer can achieve using this process—or a similar one—in writing a publishable article about a personal experience.

The setting for the experience and the article is Australia; the writer is an editor of *Car and Driver,* a magazine for auto enthusiasts. The occasion is a trip across the Outback, a sparsely settled region in the interior of Australia. The author and a passenger are driving on a 1,500-mile trip to survey Australian methods of improving auto safety. They have been driving in desolate country almost all day when, late in the afternoon, they encounter a washed-out bridge and must double back to find a new route. They have been driving fast; the detour seems to urge them to increased speed.

A Drive in the Outback, with Second Chances

DAVID ABRAHAMSON

It took less than two seconds. The stab of oncoming headlights, a blur of looming sheet-metal in the center of the windshield, a jabbing reaction at the steering wheel and then that awful, indelible noise. And then an unearthly silence, as if nature itself knew that something irrevocable had happened and that a moment—maybe much more—was needed for the reality to be dealt with.

I had been driving fast most of the afternoon. Not really at the car's limit, but well above the posted speed. I enjoy fast driving for its own sake, and this new and isolated environment seemed to urge me on. After all, Australia's wide open spaces are exactly that, and we'd encountered less than one car an hour in either direction of the towns. And besides, Baker, my passenger, didn't seem to mind. We were in the middle of a long, sweeping right-hander when suddenly the windshield was filled with another set of headlights. Coming at us, in the middle of the road, was a monstrous truck. The left front corner of the truck cab buried itself in the left front door of our car. The sound was absolutely deafening. Bits of metal and glass were everywhere. The impact ripped the watch off my wrist and the lenses out of my glasses. But I was lucky. Because it was a righthand-drive car, as the driver I was at least three feet away from the point of impact. Passenger Baker, however, was not.

The true violence of the crash took place almost in his lap. Part of his seat was torn up and out of its mount. The door and a section of the roof were battered in toward his head and left shoulder. We were both wearing lap-and-shoulder seat belts at the time. Mine saved my life. Baker's did too, but in the process broke his collarbone and badly bruised a few essential internal organs. A grisly tradeoff.

How and why had the accident happened? What exactly had been my mistake? Long after I'd returned to the United States, long after Baker had recovered from his injuries, I was still asking myself those questions. Now, almost a year later, the answers are clear. And they go far beyond any chance encounter on a strange road in a strange land, even beyond the crushing sense of remorse I felt at the time. And they tell me something about who I was and what I might be. I enjoyed driving, and a big part of that enjoyment came from taking a number of risks. Risks I thought were calculated, but in truth were not. Rather they were part of a glorious game, imbued with notions of independence, willful mobility and a heavy dose of virility. I'd had more than my share of near misses, but they merely served to prove the range of my skills at the wheel—my ability to judge relative speed and distance, the speed of my reflexes, the correctness of my kinesthetic instincts. In my car at speed, there was never any hint of my own mortality. Or of anyone else's. So the accident had to happen. Maybe not with that truck on that blind curve on the far side of the Earth, but somewhere. It has less to do with the law of averages than the laws of physics. Roads are a decidedly hostile environment, peopled with an unknown number of other drivers who are certain to do the wrong thing at the wrong time. And no amount of skill, real or imagined, can save you. Sweet reason is the only defense. Prudence, moderation and caution are not the stuff of grand illusions, unbridled exuberance and youthful panache. But they're great for survival.

And that, in the end, is what my experience boils down to. I now see, as I did not before, that my survival (and that of others who choose to ride with me) is at stake. I've never seen myself as a particularly courageous person, but I've always enjoyed sports containing an element of risk: parachuting, scuba-diving, alpine skiing and the like. Strange that something as mundane as an auto accident should, at age 30, give me my first glimpse of my own mortality. Thinking back to that evening south of Bombala, I am certain that I never want to hear that awful sound again. But I also never want to forget it.

Following the process as we have outlined it, the writer would have asked himself these questions:

1. What should I write about?

My Australian trip, or some part of it. The most memorable and important part of the trip was the terrible accident near Bombala, in which my passenger Bill Baker was injured.

2. What do I know or remember about the trip and, more specifically, about the accident?

Beginning with the plane ride from San Francisco, I can record as background material all the things we did on the flight, in Sydney, and on the trip itself. I will record in greatest detail the auto trip, focusing as closely as possible on the moments before and after the crash. I'll continue to write until I reach a statement or conclusion about that accident and its meaning to me now.

3. Exactly what can I say about this subject, the accident? What impression has it made on me?

The accident changed my view of my driving skills and the importance of those skills in preserving my safety while I drive. I never want to hear the awful sound of the crash again, but I never want to forget it, either.

4. What details, facts, illustrations, and observations can I use to make that thesis clear to my reader?

I will use visual details and facts surrounding the crash itself. I'll include the aftermath of the crash, the time while we wait to take Baker to the hospital. Finally, I'll record my thoughts on and impressions of the importance and meaning of the accident.

5. What order will most effectively present these supporting materials?

Because this piece is basically a narrative, I'll follow chronological order, but I'll use a few details of the actual crash to catch my readers' interest in the introduction.

6. What will the materials look like when I actually write out a first completed version of the article? [You have read the final version of the essay. The rough draft contained much more material.]

I will cut out distracting material that weakens my statement.

A Few Words before Starting

Getting started is often the most difficult part of writing. We all have a tendency to avoid the blank page and the work involved in filling it meaningfully. Writing will always be hard work, but a few preliminary exercises will help make getting started a little easier.

First: Strengthen your muscles so that you can write with ease. You would not go mountain climbing or run a marathon without getting in shape; you should not expect writing to be enjoyable unless you are in shape for it. Do the following exercises once each day:

- Sit in a place where you can watch people passing by. Writing as rapidly as possible, jot down a description of all that occurs, noting sizes, shapes, descriptions, and other visual details.
- Writing continuously, sign your name or copy other words down as many times as you can in two minutes.
- Without stopping, write everything that comes into your head when you read the following words:

submarine

photosynthesis

chocolate milkshake

The goal of these exercises is to be able to write for fifteen minutes without any discomfort and for an hour with two short breaks.

Second: Free your mind to write without constraints. As you work in the first phase of the writing process, composing, you need to learn to write freely without editing what you write. This "free writing," or "stream-of-consciousness writing," will allow you to record at random all the ideas that come to mind on your subject. In fact, you will probably bring to mind ideas that are technically off the subject of your paper. Don't be afraid to record these stray ideas, as they will often lead in circular fashion back to the subject from a direction you had not imagined before. Writing in this free way becomes a way of learning about your subject, a way of making new connections within it.

Free writing is especially valuable when you are writing a paper based on personal experience because it allows you to make something important out of that experience. It is also valuable in writing papers of opinion or papers stating a personal position on a controversial subject. Only through extensive writing can you define your opinion or position clearly and firmly. A would-be comic once said, "I don't know what I think until I see what I've written." He probably intended the statement as a joke, but it is, in fact, the truth. Writing about opinions and ideas forms the ideas as you write about them. Be sure to write extensively, randomly, freely, on all such writing assignments before you formulate your thesis.

Free writing also has an important place in writing more objective papers, papers based on research and written notes. After you have completed your research and put your note cards in reasonably good order, you should read through them two or three times to get a sense of the content. After reading the notes, set them aside and begin to write freely about the subject.

At least two good things should come out of this free writing. First, free writing on the subject will help you to formulate a position on the subject that is specially your own and not the opinion of the writers you covered in your research. You learn about your subject when you write about it.

Second, free writing will allow you to write about your subject in your own voice rather than in the voices of the writers you read during your research. Without this free writing, your writing will sound like every other research paper ever written because we tend to take on the tone and style of the writers we have recently read. Through free writing you can move away from the voices of those other writers and into your own voice. Free writing will allow you to produce a paper that is uniquely "you," rather than a generic, sounds-like-all-the-other-papers-ever-written sort of production.

Free writing will develop both ideas and a voice that are uniquely yours.

Third: Explore your topic extensively. You can employ specialized techniques to help you gather information and formulate your ideas on your writing projects.

Brainstorming

One technique most closely allied to free writing is called **brainstorming** or **clustering.** Clustering is a *nonlinear, free association* drill. In this drill, the writer sits quietly with pen and pencil, or at a typewriter, and records words and phrases as they come to mind. Write the name of the subject

American Politics

and then record the words and ideas that come to mind—without editing or limiting the list.

American Politics

Democrat   Republican   liberal   conservative   neo-liberal
Constitution   Bill of Rights   John F. Kennedy
radicalism   William F. Buckley   The Boston Tea Party
The Sixties   The Civil Rights Movement

Brainstorming will not work in a vacuum. If you have never studied, or even thought about, American politics, you will not have any associations to make. But you will have a store of ideas and concepts to work on if you have been studying U.S. history or political science.

If you have the background to make constructive associations, clustering or brainstorming can help you in two ways.

Brainstorming can help to isolate a manageable topic within a subject area. An assignment in an American history course that simply says: "Write a paper on American politics."

requires a good deal of probing and restriction before a workable topic for a paper emerges. Clearly, you can't write a paper fully exploring American politics in ten pages, or even in a whole semester. To write a successful paper, you will need to restrict and focus your thinking to a single aspect of the subject area. Brainstorming can help to make that restriction.

> Thus you can move from John F. Kennedy to the idea that he became president in 1960 to the idea that the Civil Rights Movement began in the late fifties and early sixties to the idea that there must have been some relationship between his administration and the Civil Rights Movement. At that point you might suspect that you have hit on a workable topic and move off to the library to do some preliminary work on bibliography and some background reading.

Brainstorming can also help you to make connections between ideas within a subject area. Writing about one concept causes you to remember a second concept. Writing about the second concept can lead to a third and then a fourth.

> So you might begin to think on a general subject—grades
> and then about grades in high school
> and then about your greater motivation in college
> and then about your lack of real effort in high school
> and then about your much better grades in college
> and then about the marked improvement in your grades

Then you can make a connection between better grades and greater motivation. From there you might move to a possible comparison between low motivation in high school and higher motivation in college, and then, **by brainstorming again on that concept,** you might develop several reasons why those conditions existed.

At that point, you can choose a direction for the paper, depending on the focus required in the assignment. If the assignment asks for a personal paper—observations on your grades and experiences in high school and college—then you must continue into additional brainstorming and then into free writing and other techniques on gathering information on the topic.

If, on the other hand, you can move into an objective examination of motivation and grades in high school and college, you can go to the library for bibliography work and preliminary reading.

For papers on personal experience, you can employ the five questions used by journalists to develop articles:

1. **WHO** is involved?
2. **WHAT** happens?
3. **WHEN** does it happen?
4. **WHERE** does the event occur?
5. **WHY** does it happen?

In this exercise, don't limit yourself to one-word or brief answers. Employ free writing techniques when you answer the questions. Don't answer the question "Who?" by saying,

"John and Mr. Smith." Write about John and Mr. Smith. Explore the answers to each question extensively in a free writing mode.

Next, you can explore your topic by asking questions that focus on parts and relationships that exist in and around your topic. Suppose your assignment asks you to explore some aspect of business in modern Japan. After examining the general subject, you discover that Japanese business executives use a special style of management that has sparked considerable interest among managers in the United States. You might begin your exploration by looking at the topic in three ways.

> Examine the discrete parts of the topic itself:
> What are the *distinctive features* of Japanese management style?
>
> Examine the topic as a whole.
> How do these features *work together as a system?*
>
> Examine the place of the topic within the general subject matter.
> How does Japanese management style *fit into the overall subject* we call management?

Or, phrased in a different way,

> How do we identify this subject?
> How do we differentiate it from others in the same general area?
> What are the important parts or aspects of this subject?
> What is the physical appearance of these parts?
> What examples of this subject occur in real life?
> How does this subject compare and/or contrast with others of the same general type?

Some writers find it useful to construct *analogies* and *metaphors* on a subject. When you make an analogy, you examine ways in which an unknown concept is like a well-known concept.

> My brother, who plays Little League baseball, is a ballplayer out of the Rickey Henderson mold: he is quick on his feet, aggressive, a singles hitter most of the time, and, above all, he loves the game more than anything else in his life.

This brother is unlike Rickey Henderson in a thousand ways, including age, size, and success in the game. But a person who knows a little bit about Rickey Henderson will be able to know a little more about your brother. And so will you, when you recognize the similarities between the two people.

In the same way, on personal topics, it is possible to construct metaphors and similes, figures of speech that establish comparisons.

> Red Grange was *like a will-o'-the-wisp,* dancing and dodging his way through opposing teams to become the greatest running back in the early history of football.
>
> The invading army *was a tornado,* moving where it wished and destroying everything in its path.

Sometimes even metaphors that seem ridiculous can be productive.

> If your father were an automobile, what make and model would he be?
> He might be a 1938 Cadillac, very classy, but a trifle old-fashioned in some ways.

Images such as these can provide insight that can lead to new information and new insights, **if you follow them up with additional reading and writing on the subject.**

Certain subjects can be explored by **approaching them through the senses.** Recording visual aspects (shapes, sizes, and colors, for example) or recording words that describe sounds, smells, and textures might offer insights into the subject.

All these methods of exploring a subject and refining a subject into manageable parts simply open areas for reading and writing on a subject. They help you with Step 2 of the writing process, gathering materials. The resulting notes and written materials must not be confused with a first, complete draft or the final draft of a paper. They constitute the raw material of a paper, material that must be evaluated, accepted, rejected, placed in order in the draft, and written out for revision. They are not the finished product; they are background to help with production of that finished product.

So don't wait for inspiration or good beginnings. Write what you can write as well as you can write it. If you can't think of a good way to start, start any way you can. If you can't think of exactly the right word, use a close approximation. Time and condition and the freedom to write without editing will improve your ideas; careful attention to revision and correction will improve the quality of your written expression. Practice and more practice will lead to success.

In the next section you will closely examine a very important type of college writing, the essay test.

Writing Exercises for an Overview of College Writing

1. Each day for the first two weeks of your experience in using the writing sections of this book, follow the instructions for getting in shape to write.

2. Follow the steps in the writing process illustrated with "A Drive in the Outback, with Second Chances," and write about an experience in your own life.

3. Find an example of personal writing about an experience or an attitude. Read it to locate the thesis statement or core idea (Step 3 in composing). Then outline the supporting details to show how they develop (or fail to develop) the core idea.

Essay tests provide an excellent opportunity to apply your writing skills to college writing assignments. Working on test taking is very practical; success on tests will improve your grades. Beyond that practical consideration, and perhaps more important, essay test answers require you to work within a very narrow subject area to produce a concise, complete written statement. These tight limitations of time and space require you to be very precise in the formulation of a topic statement and to distinguish carefully between materials essential to your answer and those that are only related to it. Finally, essay tests often require that you present your answer in a single well-developed paragraph. Practice in writing essay test answers will develop your ability to write successful paragraphs.

Getting Ready

The best preparation for taking any test is consistent, effective study throughout the term. In addition, however, you need special strategies for the last few days before the test to improve your chances of success. Begin your final preparations for the test a few days in advance so that you will have ample time to study and assimilate the material. Follow these suggestions as you study.

Step 1. Make an overview or survey of the materials you have covered for the test. Look for periods, trends, theories, and general conclusions. Try to pinpoint important concepts and basic ideas in the materials. You may find it useful to consult a general encyclopedia for an overview or a summary of the subject areas to be covered by the test. If the subject is technical or complex or is part of an advanced course, consult an appropriate specialized encyclopedia or reference work in that field.

Step 2. Write a series of questions encompassing the major items that you have located. Cover broad areas of material. Try to concentrate on questions that begin with such words as *compare, trace, outline,* and *discuss.* (See the discussion of Instruction Words on pages 318–320.) In six to ten broad-scope questions of your own, you can cover all the possible questions that the teacher may ask. If you have covered all the material in your own questions, you will not be surprised by any questions on the exam.

Step 3. Read your outline, notes, and other materials, looking for answers to the questions you have composed. As you read and review, outline the answers, commit the outlines to memory, and use them as guides during the test. Write out answers to any questions that are difficult for you.

Step 4. Review the outlines, the materials, and the answers to your questions the afternoon before the test. Then put the whole thing aside and get a good night's rest.

Final Preparation

Just before going in to take the test:

- Eat a high-energy snack; fruit is a good choice. Coffee or tea will also help. Do some calisthenics or whatever else is necessary to make you alert.
- Get your equipment ready: pens, pencils, erasers, paper or examination booklets, and scratch paper. Take what you will need so that you will not worry about supplies once you enter the room.
- Arrive two minutes early for the test. Get yourself and your equipment arranged. Relax for a few seconds before the work begins.

Taking the Test

Your success in taking tests depends on your study habits and preparation; no student—or at least not very many students—can earn a high grade on a test without proper preparation. But good preparation alone will not guarantee success. You need a strategy for taking tests, a strategy that will help you to decide which questions to answer, what order to use in answering the selected questions, and what organization to use for each question.

When you have made the best possible preparations for taking the test and are in the classroom with the test in your hands, do two things before you write:

First, read the test from start to finish, beginning with the directions. Decide which questions you know the most about. Determine the point value of each question. Answer first the questions you know the most about. Answering them first will ease you into the test, develop your confidence, and keep you from wasting time on questions you can't answer well anyway. Do first what you can do best. Use the remaining time to do the best you can on the rest of the questions.

Be sure to select the most valuable questions from among those you can answer. Don't waste time on a question of low point value when you could be answering a question with a high point value.

Always follow the directions. If options allow you to choose certain questions from a group, be sure you understand the options and make your choices based on your knowledge and on the point value of the questions. Invest your time wisely.

Second, make careful preparations before you write. Adapt the first four steps in the writing process to guide you in writing the answers.

Step 1. Identify the subject. The first step in the writing process is the selection of a subject. On a personal paper narrating an event in your life, your range of choices is wide. On a test, clearly, you have no such choice. The teacher has selected the subject for each question. Your job is to identify that subject correctly. A question that asks for a discussion of the causes of the Great Depression is not properly answered by a discussion of the characteristics of the Roaring Twenties. Make sure you answer the question that is asked.

Step 2. Review what you know about the question. Recall your outlines and notes. Bring to mind the practice answers you wrote in your review exercises. Make notes of these on a sheet of paper. Try to remember as much material as you can. List any special or technical words related to the subject.

Step 3. Decide exactly what the question asks for and what overall statement you are able to make and support in response to the question. Before you write, construct a specific statement of the idea or concept that you intend to develop in writing your answer. This point, or main idea, will come out of the materials you reviewed in Step 2.

Step 4. Carefully select supporting materials, examples, explanations, and other data that will serve to establish and clarify the main idea. You will have pulled together a considerable amount of material in your quick mental review. Not all of it will fit exactly the statement you are making; not all of it will be especially effective in your answer. Select materials that will establish and reinforce your point as effectively as possible within the constraints of time and space.

Now that you have looked at the basic steps in writing essay test answers—or any paragraph, for that matter—let us examine each of these steps in greater detail. Assume that you have read the test carefully, have selected your questions, and are now ready to start on the question you'll answer first.

Let us set up a brief example and follow it through these steps. Suppose you pick up a test and find on it a problem such as this:

Select one of the seven species of sea turtles and discuss its physical appearance, its habitat and geographic distribution, and its status in both present numbers and population trends.

Step 1 requires careful identification of the subject matter covered in the question. The sample question refers to sea turtles, not to all kinds of turtles. It also asks for a discussion of just one of the seven species of sea turtles. It asks for only three rather simple pieces of information about that species:

1. What is the physical appearance of that species?
2. In what type of habitats is the species found, and where are these habitats located?
3. How many individuals of this species are estimated to be alive, and is that number increasing or decreasing?

Only the last point is at all tricky. *Status* has in this question a somewhat specialized meaning referring to the species' survival potential based on what the estimated living population is and on whether it is increasing or decreasing worldwide. So the subject of that question is information about a particular species of sea turtle.

Step 2 is to collect material, to recall what you know about one species of sea turtle. From the textbook, your lecture notes, and a brief outside reading assignment, you remember this about sea turtles and jot down the following notes:

Actually 7 species—only three much covered in class. One stood out because commercial importance (food & other products)—green turtle.

Large: 3 to 6 feet from front to back over curve of upper shell (carapace; lower shell, plastron).

Weighs 200–300 lb. average but reaches 850 lb. some specimens. Color from green-brown to near black.

Scutes (bony plates) clearly marked. Head small compared to body.

Occurs almost worldwide in warmer waters shallow enough to allow growth of sea grass turtles eat.

Present status questionable. Not endangered because lrg. pops. in remote areas—under pressure and declining in pop. areas. Needs protection. First protective law in Caribbean, passed 1620. Used extensively for food by early sailors, who killed mainly females coming on shore to lay eggs. Now used for cosmetics and jewelry.

Large green turtles make good zoo exhibits. W. Indian natives make soup of them.

Nesting habits: Female beaches and lays approx. 100 eggs in shaped hole. First hatchlings on top of nest push out sand covering them and leave. Those on bottom crawl out using sand first hatchlings displaced and crushed shells of vacated eggs as platform. 100 eggs right number—fewer places top of nest too low in hole, more requires nest too deep for last hatchling to escape. Recent increase in ecological pressure because women use more cosmetics based on turtle oil.

This quick mental review, jotted down hastily (perhaps more sketchily on an actual test than in the example), has produced enough information to allow you to move to the next step.

Instruction Words

In Step 3 you must determine what you can say in response to the question. Before you can make that determination, you must know exactly what the question directs you to do. These directions are usually given at the beginning of the question, and, although their exact wording may vary, they generally fall into one of several categories.

The following list of instruction words covers most standard types of essay questions. Read this list carefully; note that each type of instruction requires a different type of answer.

- **List, name, identify**
  These words require short-answer responses that can be written in one or two complete sentences. Do exactly what the question asks; don't try to expand the scope of the question.

  Example: Name the presidents who served in the military prior to becoming president.

  The word *identify* suggests that you ought to mention the two or three most important facts about a person or a subject area, not just any facts that come to mind. You would thus identify Eisenhower as a military commander and U.S. President, not as a West Point graduate who played golf.

- **Summarize, trace, delineate**
  An instruction to *summarize* asks that you give an overview or a capsule version of the subject.

  Example: Summarize Senator Smith's position on tax reform.

An answer to this question would provide a three- or four-sentence statement of the main points of Smith's position. The words *trace* and *delineate* usually ask that you describe the steps or process that brought some event to pass.

Example: Trace the life cycle of the monarch butterfly.

The answer requires a listing of the steps in the development of the butterfly from egg to adulthood.

- **Define**
  The instruction *define* usually asks that you establish the term within a class and then differentiate it from the other members of the class. "A parrot is a bird" establishes the word *parrot* in a class, and "found in the tropics and capable of reproducing human speech" is an attempt at differentiation. You should be careful to add enough elements of differentiation to eliminate other members of the class. For instance, as the myna is also a tropical bird capable of reproducing speech, you must complete your definition of *parrot* by specifying such items as size, color, and habitat.

- **Analyze, classify, outline**
  These command words imply a discussion of the relationship that exists between a whole and its parts. *Analyze* asks that you break an idea, a concept, or a class down into its integral parts.

Example: Analyze the various political persuasions that exist within the Republican party.

This question asks that you look at the party and identify the various categories of political belief ranging from right to left. *Classify* asks that you position parts in relation to a whole.

Example: Classify the following parts of an automobile as to location in engine, steering, or
            drive shaft:
            1. Ball joint
            2. Piston ring
            3. Pinion gear

Outline requires that you break down an idea or a concept into its parts and show how the parts support and reinforce each other. Whether you arrange your sentences in the form of a whole paragraph or in a listing of main headings and subheadings, your outline must show how the idea or concept is made up of smaller parts and how these parts relate to the idea and to each other.

Example: Outline Senator Random's position on emission controls for automobiles.

This question requires that you state the position and its supporting points.

- **Discuss, explain, illustrate**
  This type of command word is probably the most general of all the possible directions for essay tests. The request here is that you expose, in detail, the idea, concept, or process

in question. Single simple sentences will not suffice to answer such instructions. You must provide all pertinent information and write enough so that your readers have no questions, no gaps left in their information, when they've finished reading. Often such questions can be answered by making a statement of the idea or process and providing examples to illustrate your statements. In fact, if the instruction is *illustrate*, examples are required.

Example: Discuss the effect of depriving a child of physical affection in the first three years of its life.

The answer could be given by making a statement or statements of the effects and giving examples of each.

- **Compare, contrast**

A question that asks you to compare, or to compare and contrast, is simply asking that you discuss the similarities and differences between two or more subjects.

Examples: Compare the military abilities of Grant and Sherman.
Make a comparison between Smith's plan and Jones's plan for shoring up the value of the dollar overseas.
What are the similarities and differences between racketball and squash?

All these example questions ask you to establish categories—for example, skill in tactics, ability to motivate, and so on, as they relate to Grant and Sherman—and to explain how the subjects are alike or different in the areas you establish.

- **Evaluate, criticize**

This type of question is probably the most difficult because it requires that you know what is correct or best or ideal and that you assess the assigned topic against that ideal. So you must know the subject *and* the ideal equally well.

Example: Evaluate Eisenhower as a leader in foreign affairs.

The question is, then, "What are the characteristics of a leader in foreign affairs and how does Eisenhower measure up in each of these categories?"

Focus on the Subject

When you have clarified the instruction for a question, determine exactly what subject you must deal with in your answer. Focus on the limited area of the subject specified by the question.

A question asking you to deal with *the qualities of Willa Cather's prose* does not ask for a discussion of her life or her early efforts at poetry. The question asks for treatment of a limited area: *the qualities of Willa Cather's prose.*

Examine the subject area and the instructions of the question very carefully. Be sure to get both clear in your mind before you begin to write. An answer that *evaluates* will get little credit if the question says *define.* A discussion of the care and feeding of peregrine falcons will get few points if the question asks for a classification of birds of prey in North America. Now examine the sample problem presented earlier:

Select one of the seven species of sea turtles and discuss its physical appearance, its habitat and geographic distribution, and its status in both present numbers and population trends.

The direction, the instruction word, is *discuss,* which means make a statement and support it. The subject area is clear: any one of the seven species of sea turtles. The direction is clear: discuss

- the physical appearance
- the habitat and general distribution
- the current status

You have collected information on the subject. Now determine exactly what you can say on that subject. For this sample question, your statement might read:

The green turtle is a large green-to-black sea turtle residing in warm, shallow waters all over the world; it is numerous but is declining in populated areas.

Keep the statement simple and direct. It need not state all the facts and details; indeed, it should not try to. It is designed to serve only as a guide for the development of your answer. If you follow the outline of the answer suggested by this controlling statement, you will select in Step 4 only the materials that serve to answer the question, and you will not be tempted to add irrelevant materials. When you have completed a controlling statement for the answer, move to the next step.

Step 4 requires that you select from the collected materials those items that will develop the statement. Select specific details to explain each area within the statement. For the first section, physical appearance, your notes contain the following concrete details:

1. Size—three to six feet from front to back over the shell; average weight—200–300 pounds, record is 850 pounds.
2. Coloration—greenish brown is lightest color, almost black when splotches are close together.
3. Shape of flippers, head, tail. [Note that these items are not in the original list. New materials often come to mind during preparations.]

You can fill in the other sections by selecting from the collection of materials. Do not include any materials that do not specifically develop or illustrate the statement that controls the answer. Provide ample development, but do not pad.

In the collection of supporting materials for the sample question, the long discussion of the nesting habits and the number of eggs ordinarily laid by the green turtle does not fit into the answer. The material is interesting, it is concerned with the green turtle, but it does *not* fit any of the three categories in the question. Don't use materials simply because they relate to the general subject. Use only materials that support the answer to the specific question.

Writing the Answer

At this point you have before you on scratch paper:

1. A basic idea.
2. Supporting materials for that basic idea.

These will be useful in writing the answer, but they are not the answer. They are the *content* for the answer. The answer requires content, but it also requires form: grammatically correct, complete sentences that present the material in a logical, relevant order.

The best way to provide order for your answer is to modify your controlling statement to suggest the order that you intend to follow. This modification will help your reader to follow your answer. A sentence combining elements of the question with a suggestion of your answer's focus offers a good beginning and adequate control:

> Of the seven species of sea turtles, the green turtle is the largest and the most widely distributed, but it is nearing endangered status because it has commercial value.

Note that the sentence establishes your topic, the green turtle, and defines the aspects that you will discuss by using key words from each of those areas:

1. *Largest* leads to a physical description.
2. *Most widely distributed* leads naturally to a discussion of habitat and distribution.
3. *Nearing endangered status* opens the discussion of population size and trends.

The sentence relates your answer to the question and will keep you from wandering into irrelevancy. Try to make your first sentence as specific as possible, but be sure that you can expand on it. A statement that the green turtle is "an interesting species" is little help in controlling the answer because it does not focus on the question. You are not concerned with how interesting the species is; you are concerned with its appearance, its habitat and distribution, and its status. The entire answer to this sample question might read as follows:

> Of the seven species of sea turtles, the green turtle is the largest and the most widely distributed, but it is nearing endangered status because it has commercial value. It is a large turtle, measuring between 3 and 6 feet in length over the top of the shell and weighing on the average 200–300 pounds. The largest specimens are over 5 feet in length and weigh 800–1000 pounds. The upper shell (carapace) is light to dark brown, shaded or mottled with darker colors ranging to an almost black-green. The lower shell (plastron) is white to light yellow. The scales on the upper surface of the head are dark, and the spaces between them are yellow; on the sides of the head, the scales are brown but have a yellow margin, giving a yellow cast to the sides of the head. The shell is broad, low, and more or less heart-shaped. The green turtle inhabits most of the warm, shallow waters of the world's seas and oceans, preferring areas 10–20 feet deep where it can find good sea grass pastures for browsing. The turtles prefer areas that have many potholes, because they sleep in the holes for security. In numbers and population trends, the status of the green turtle is in doubt. It is under great pressure in highly populated areas such as the Caribbean Sea, where it is avidly hunted for food and for use in making jewelry and cosmetics. However, because it occurs in large numbers in remote areas, it is not technically an endangered species at this time. It needs better protection in populated areas so that its numbers will not decline any further.

Assignments and Exercises

The suggestions offered in this section will not improve your ability to take tests unless you practice applying them in your own work. Here are some suggested exercises to apply the principles:

1. Analyze your performance on a recent essay test and discuss the ways in which following the suggestions in this chapter might have improved your performance.

2. Assume that you are enrolled in a course in American history and must take an essay test on the Revolutionary War. The materials covered include the textbook, your lecture notes, your outside readings, and two films. Write a paragraph describing your preparations for the test.

3. As a practice test, write answers to the following questions on the chapter you have just read on essay-test taking.

   • Discuss the preparations for taking a test up to the point where you enter the test room.

   • Describe the process by which you would decide which questions to answer (if given options) and in which order you would answer them.

   • Name and define four of the seven command-word categories often found in test questions, discussing the kinds of materials that each word requires in its answer.

   • Describe the final form of the answer, including a discussion of thesis statement and development as it occurs in this chapter.

The Paragraph

A paragraph is a group of sentences (or sometimes just one sentence) related to a single idea. Each paragraph begins on a new line, and its first word is indented a few spaces from the left margin. The last line of a paragraph is blank from the end of the last sentence to the right margin.

The function of a paragraph is to state and develop a single idea, usually called a **topic.** The topic is actually the subject of the paragraph, what the paragraph is about. Everything in the paragraph after the statement of the topic ought to **develop the topic.** *To develop* means to explain and define, to discuss, to illustrate and exemplify. From the reader's point of view, the content of the paragraph should provide enough information and explanation to make clear the topic of the paragraph and the function of the paragraph in the essay or the chapter.

The Topic Sentence

The first function of the paragraph is to state what it is about, to establish its topic; therefore the first rule of effective paragraph writing is as follows:

Usually, declare the topic of the paragraph early in a single sentence (called the *topic sentence*). You remember that the first sentence of our sample answer to an essay test question related the answer to the question by paraphrasing a significant part of the question. This sentence also provided direction for the answer by telling briefly what the answer would contain. Each paragraph should contain such a point of departure, a sentence that names what the paragraph is about and indicates how the paragraph will proceed. It may do so in considerable detail:

Although the green turtle—a large, greenish-brown sea turtle inhabiting warm, shallow seas over most of the world—is not yet generally endangered, it is subject to extreme pressure in populated areas.

or rather broadly:

The green turtle is one of the most important of the seven species of sea turtles.

Both statements name a specific topic: the green turtle. But neither sentence stops with a name. A sentence that reads:

This paragraph will be about green turtles.

is not a complete topic sentence because it does not suggest the direction that the rest of the paragraph will take. Note that both the good examples are phrased so that a certain

325

type of development must follow. The first sentence anticipates a discussion that will mention size, color, habitat, and distribution but will focus on the green turtle's chances for survival. The second sentence will develop the assertion that the species is one of the most important of the sea turtles. Note that neither example tries to embrace the whole idea of the paragraph. The topic sentence should lay the foundation for the paragraph, not say everything there is to be said.

As a general rule, make the topic sentence one of the first few sentences in the paragraph. Sometimes a paragraph has no topic sentence; occasionally the topic sentence occurs at the end of the paragraph. These exceptions are permissible, but the early topic sentence is more popular because it helps in three ways to produce an effective message:

1. It defines your job as a writer and states a manageable objective—a single topic.
2. It establishes a guide for your development of the basic idea. You must supply evidence of or support for any assertion in the topic sentence. The topic sentence is only a beginning, but it predicts a conclusion that the paragraph must reach.
3. It tells your reader what the paragraph is going to contain.

Notice how the topic sentence (italicized) in the following paragraph controls it and provides clear direction for the reader:

Of all the inventions of the last one hundred years, *the automobile assembly line has had the most profound effect on American life.* The assembly line provided a method for building and selling automobiles at a price many could afford, thus changing the auto from a luxury item owned by the wealthy few to an everyday appliance used by almost every adult in America. Universal ownership and the use of the automobile have opened new occupations, new dimensions of mobility, and new areas of recreation to everyone. In addition, the automobile assembly line has provided a model for the mass production of television sets, washing machines, bottled drinks, and even sailboats. All these products would have been far too expensive for purchase by the average person without the introduction of assembly-line methods to lower manufacturing costs. With the advent of Henry Ford's system, all Americans could hope to possess goods once reserved for a select class, and the hope changed their lives forever.

The italicized sentence states the topic and the purpose of the paragraph: The paragraph is going to argue that the assembly line, more than any other invention, changed America's way of life. The writer is controlled by this sentence because everything in the paragraph should serve to support this argument. Readers are assisted by the sentence, for they know that they can expect examples supporting the position stated in the sentence.

Develop Each Paragraph

Writing a good topic sentence is only the first step in writing an effective paragraph, for an effective paragraph provides complete development of the topic; that is, it tells the readers all they need to know about the topic for the purposes at hand. This principle is the second basic rule of effective paragraph writing:

Always provide complete development in each paragraph. Complete development tells the readers all that they need to understand about the paragraph itself and the way the paragraph fits into the rest of the essay or chapter. Complete development does not necessarily provide all the information the reader *wants* to know; rather, the reader receives what is *needed* for understanding the internal working of the paragraph (the topic and its development) and the external connection (the relationship between the paragraph and the paper as a whole). As an illustration of that rather abstract statement, read the following paragraph, which gives a set of instructions for a familiar process:

> Another skill required of a self-sufficient car owner is the ability to jump-start a car with a dead battery, a process that entails some important do's and don't's. First, make certain that the charged battery to be used is a properly grounded battery of the same voltage as the dead one. Put out all smoking material. Connect the first jumper cable to the positive terminal of each battery. Connect one end of the second cable to the negative terminal of the live battery, and then clamp the other end to some part of the engine in the car with the dead battery. DO *NOT* LINK POSITIVE AND NEGATIVE TERMINALS. DO *NOT* ATTACH THE NEGATIVE CABLE DIRECTLY TO THE NEGATIVE TERMINAL OF THE DEAD BATTERY. Choose a spot at least 18 inches from the dead battery. A direct connection is dangerous. Put the car with the live battery in neutral, rev the engine, and hold it at moderate rpm while starting the other car. Once the engine is running, hold it at moderate rpm for a few seconds and disconnect the NEGATIVE cable. Then disconnect the positive cable. It is wise to take the car to a service station as soon as possible to have the battery checked and serviced if necessary.

The instructions in this paragraph are clear, and they will enable anyone to start a car with a dead battery. The curious reader, however, will have certain questions in mind after reading the paragraph:

1. What is a properly grounded battery?
2. Why is it necessary to extinguish smoking materials?
3. To what parts of the engine may one attach the negative cable?
   [After all, attaching it to the fan will have exciting results.]
4. What is the danger of making a direct connection?

Also, there are at least two important steps left out of the process:

> Before connecting the two batteries,
> 1. Remove the caps to the cells of both batteries.
> 2. Check the fluid levels in the cells of both batteries.
> Without these steps in the process, the car with the dead battery will start, but there is still a chance of explosion.

A paragraph that lacks material, that is not fully developed, probably won't explode. But it probably won't succeed, either. Questions raised in the mind of the reader will almost always weaken the effect of the paragraph. Sometimes the omissions are so important that the reader will miss the point or give up altogether in frustration. Remember the second rule for writing effective paragraphs:

Always provide complete development in each paragraph. Never leave your reader with unanswered questions about the topic.

Three Simple Steps

Most of the time, you can write a well-developed paragraph by following three very simple steps:

1. Make the topic statement one clear, rather brief sentence.
2. Clarify and define the statement as needed.
3. Illustrate or exemplify the topic statement concretely where possible.

As an example of the use of this three-step process, follow the development of a paragraph in answer to the question, "What is the most important quality that you are seeking in an occupation?" The student's answer, found after much preliminary writing and a good bit of discussion, led to the following topic sentence:

> Above all other qualities, *I want to have variety in the tasks I perform and in the locations where I work.*

Clarification and Definition	I know I must do the general line of work for which I'm trained, but I want to do different tasks in that work every day if possible. Repeating the same tasks day after day must be a mind-numbing experience. Our neighborhood mechanic does one tune-up after another, five days a week. A doctor friend tells me that 90 percent of her practice involves treating people ill with a virus, for which she prescribes an antibiotic against secondary infection. I want no part of that sort of humdrum work. Variety means doing a different part of a job every day, perhaps working on the beginning of one project today and the completion of another tomorrow, or working on broad concepts one day and details the next. I'd also like to work at a different job site as often as possible.
Concrete Example	The field of architecture is one area that might suit me. I could work in drafting, and then switch to field supervision, and move from that task to developing the overall concepts of a large project. By doing this, I could vary my assignments and the locations of my work.

A revised version of such a paragraph might read this way:

Topic Sentence	Some people want salary and others want big challenges, *but in my career I want variety, in both assignment and work location,* more than any other single quality.
Clarification and Definition	As much as possible, I want to do a different part of a job every day. Perhaps I could work on the beginning of one project and shift to the completion of another, or work on details for a while and then shift to broad concepts involved in planning. For this reason architecture looks like a promising field for me.
Concrete Example	I could work in drafting and detailing, move next to on-site supervision, and then shift to developing the design concepts of a major project. I know that doing the same task in the same place would be a mind-numbing experience for me. Our family doctor says that 90 percent of her practice consists of treating patients who have a routine virus infection, for which she routinely prescribes an antibiotic against secondary infection. Our neighborhood mechanic spends all his time doing tune-ups. I want none of that humdrum sort of work. Variety is the spice of life; it is also the ingredient that makes work palatable for me.

These general guidelines will he lp you to provide complete development of your paragraphs:

1. Write a topic sentence.
2. Define and clarify that statement.
3. Provide concrete examples and illustrations.

Patterns for Paragraphs

In addition to the method of development by topic sentence/discussion/example, writers over the years have developed several recognizable patterns for paragraphs. These patterns are useful for presenting certain types of information for specialized purposes within an essay. You should recognize and practice these patterns so that you can use them in your own writing.

Comparison/Contrast

When you are asked to compare, to contrast, or to compare and contrast two or more people, ideas, attitudes, or objects, you are being asked to examine items that fall within the same general group or class and, after this examination, to point out ways in which the items are similar and dissimilar. Common test questions read as follows:

> Compare the attitudes of General Patton and Bertrand Russell toward war and the maintenance of a standing army.

> Compare the effects of heroin and marijuana on the human body.

> Compare orange juice and lemon juice in respect to taste, vitamin C content, and usefulness in cooking.

Note that in each question there is a large class that includes the subjects of the comparison:

> Patton and Russell were both famous people who held carefully developed attitudes toward war. [If one had no attitude on war, the comparison couldn't be made.]

> Heroin and marijuana are both drugs that act on the human body.

> Orange juice and lemon juice are both citrus products.

The point of comparison/contrast is that the items share certain qualities but can be separated or distinguished by other qualities that they do not share. The identification of these like and unlike qualities is the aim of comparison/contrast. One of the most useful ways to employ comparison/contrast is to create an understanding of an unfamiliar concept by showing how that concept is like or unlike a more familiar concept.

> If you know the stereotype of the Texan—loud, boisterous, bragging about his state and his own possessions—you could appreciate my friend Jack because he is the exact antithesis of that stereotype. He is quiet. . . .

In a course in business or investments you might be asked to compare stocks and bonds as investment instruments. Begin by listing the qualities of a common stock and the qualities of a bond side by side.

A bond is	A stock is
1. an instrument used by investors.	1. an instrument used by investors.

Note how this first point in each list establishes that the two objects of comparison are members of the same large class and can therefore be compared and contrasted.

2. a certificate of indebtedness.	2. a representation of ownership of a fraction of a company.
3. a promise to repay a specific number of dollars.	3. worth the selling price on any day, whether more or less than the purchase price.
4. payable on a specified date.	4. sold anytime, but not ever payable as is a bond.
5. sold at a specific rate of interest.	5. not an interest-drawing instrument; rather, it earns a share of profits.

Or consider such a list for a geology course.

In geology, rocks can be divided into three groups:

Igneous	*Sedimentary*	*Metamorphic*
Formed when molten rock material called *magma* cools and solidifies.	Formed from deposits of older rocks or animal or plant life. Are deposited on each other and jointed by pressure or natural chemicals.	Formed when old rocks change under heat or pressure. They do not divide easily into subgroups.
One type (extrusive) is forced out by pressure from within the earth; for example, a volcano erupts and spews out lava, which, if cooled quickly, becomes glassy or forms small crystals such as obsidian or pumice.	Three types: *Classic*—formed of older rock pieces. *Chemical*—formed of crystallized chemicals. *Organic*—formed of plant and animal remains.	

However, a detailed comparison of the three basic types of rocks is impossible in a single paragraph because of the enormous complexity of the subject. Certain qualities exist in each of the three groups—smooth surfaces, for example—but what caused the smooth surfaces in one case or another may not be particularly relevant to the factors that determine what group a rock belongs to. About all that can be dealt with in a single paragraph is a very broad comparison of the three major groups of rocks.

In the study of human anatomy, the two muscle groups—skeletal and smooth—offer a sufficient number of common points to make the exercise of comparison possible. The two groups can be compared on the basis of:

	Skeletal	*Smooth*
1. Location	Attached to skeleton.	Found in blood vessels, digestive system, and internal organs.
2. Function	To move legs, arms, eyes, and so on.	To move food for digestion, contract or expand blood vessels—varies by location.
3. Structure	Long, slender fibers bundled together in parallel, contain many nuclei.	Arranged in sheets or in circular fashion, contain one nucleus.
4. Contraction	Rapid, only when stimulated by nerve; stimulus can be voluntary or involuntary.	Slow, rhythmic; cannot be controlled consciously (voluntarily); stimulated by nerves or by hormones.

It is possible to develop a paragraph of comparison/contrast in two different ways. The first pattern is clearly illustrated in the list of muscle characteristics: The qualities of both muscle groups are listed numerically in the same order. This pattern is useful if you are comparing only a limited number of characteristics. A second pattern, because it focuses the comparison point by point, provides better control of longer or more complicated topics. A paragraph comparing stocks and bonds in this way might read as follows

Although stocks and bonds are both common investment instruments, they differ in several important aspects and thus appeal to different types of investors. A bond is a certificate of indebtedness; a share of stock represents ownership of a percentage of a company. A bond involves a promise to repay a specified amount of money on a day agreed on in advance. Because it represents ownership, stock must be sold to obtain its value, and it is worth only the selling price on a given day, never a guaranteed amount. A bond earns money in the form of interest at a fixed rate, but stocks share in the profits, partial distributions of which are called *dividends*. Thus the value of a bond, if held to its date of maturity, is fixed, and the periodic interest paid by many bonds is relatively secure. A stock, on the other hand, changes its value on the basis of market conditions and its rate of return on the basis of the profitability of the company. The risk in a bond is the risk that inflation will reduce the value of its fixed number of dollars and its fixed rate of return; stocks risk a possible decline in the general market and a possible reduction of profits that might erode the sale price and the dividends. So bonds are useful where security of investment is a high priority and protection against inflation is not vital. Stocks fit an investment portfolio in which some risk is acceptable and a hedge against inflation is very important.

So in this pattern we see bonds and stocks compared in respect to the following categories:

1. The nature of the instrument itself
2. The way the value of the instrument is established
3. The method of earning money
4. The relative security of the two instruments

5. The risks inherent in each one
6. The situations in which each might be useful as an investment

As an exercise in comparison/contrast, you might try following each of the two patterns in writing a paragraph on the two groups of muscles described earlier.

Definition

We have all read definitions; they are the subject matter of dictionaries, which we customarily use to find the meaning of an unfamiliar word. But definition, as a process, is also a useful device in writing; it can serve to establish meaning for words, concepts, and attitudes. You have often written paragraphs of definition on tests and in essays. On tests, you might find instructions such as these:

> Define the *sonata-allegro form* and give examples of it in twentieth-century music.
> Define *conservatism* as it is used in American politics.
> Define a *boom-vang* and say how it is used in sailing.

The correct responses to such instructions are paragraphs of definition. Such paragraphs ought to follow the same rules of presentation and development that the dictionary does. Let's examine two definitions in the pattern used in dictionaries and discover how they are formed.

> Basketball is a game played by two teams on a rectangular court having a raised basket at each end. Points are scored by tossing a large round ball through the opponent's basket.

> Football is a game played with an oval-shaped ball by two teams defending goals at opposite ends of a rectangular field. Points are scored by carrying or throwing the ball across the opponent's goal or by kicking the ball over the crossbar of the opponent's goalpost.

These two definitions concern games familiar to most of us. Notice that they both follow the same pattern. First, they identify both words as the names of games. Second, they specify the:

• Number of teams in a game
• Number of players on each team
• Type of playing area
• Way in which scoring occurs
• Shape of the ball

The examples illustrate the classic pattern of definition: The first step is to classify the word within a class or group; the second step is to differentiate the word from other members of its class:

> Football is a game ... [Establishes in a class.]
> played by two teams
> of eleven players each
> on a rectangular field.   [Differentiates from other games.]
>
> Scoring occurs by crossing
> opponent's goal in a special way.

When you write a paragraph of definition, follow the same method: Classify the term, then distinguish it from other members of its class.

Provide Examples

Your paragraph of definition ought to offer more than just the basic points of differentiation. You should also provide illustrations, examples, and comparisons of the term being defined to terms that might be familiar to your reader. This additional information helps your reader to understand and assimilate the information that you are offering. The process is often called **extending the definition.** Examine the following paragraph defining football and note how basic definition and extension are combined to make an effective presentation:

> On any Saturday or Sunday afternoon in the fall, hundreds of thousands of Americans travel to stadiums, and millions more sprawl out in front of television sets to witness the great American spectator sport, football. In simplest form, a definition of football states that it is a game played on a large field by two teams of eleven players and that scoring is accomplished by carrying or throwing an oval ball across the opponent's goal line or by kicking the ball between two uprights called *goalposts.* But such literal definition scarcely does justice to the game or to its impact on Americans. For it is more than a game or a sport; it is a happening, a spectacle, a ritual that is almost a religious experience for its devotees. The game catches them with its color: a beautiful green field surrounded by crowds dressed in a galaxy of hues, teams uniformed in the brightest shades ever to flow from the brush of deranged artists. It holds these fans with its excitement: the long pass, the touchdown run, the closing-minutes' drive to victory. But above all the game seems to captivate them with its violence, with dangers vicariously experienced, with a slightly veiled aura of mayhem. This element of danger draws casual viewers and converts them into fanatic worshippers of the great American cult-sport, football.

Finally, a word of warning about constructing definitions: A fundamental rule is that a definition must not be circular. A useful definition does not define a term by using a related form of the term itself. To define the word *analgesic* by saying that it causes analgesia means nothing unless the reader knows that *analgesia* means absence or removal of pain. To define *conservatism* as a philosophy that attempts to conserve old values doesn't really add much to a reader's understanding. Thus the rule:

Do not construct circular definitions; in other words, do not use in the definition a form of the word being defined.

Analysis

Chemists analyze compounds to isolate and identify their components. Economists analyze the financial data of the nation to determine the factors contributing to recessions. Sports commentators analyze games to explain the strengths leading to a victory.

Analysis is the act of breaking down a substance or an entity into its components. It is possible to analyze a football team and to point out the various positions: ends, tackles, guards, and the rest. An army can be broken down into infantry, artillery, and engineers. A piano is made up of parts: keys, strings, sounding board, and so on.

A paragraph of analysis provides information derived from this act of breaking down into parts, usually by listing, defining, and explaining the parts of the whole in question.

As an example, take the elements or characteristics that make up that rarest of animals, the good driver.

The good driver possesses:
- Technical competence
- Physical skills
- Sound judgment
- Emotional stability

A paragraph analyzing the qualities of a good driver might read this way:

Every American over age fourteen wants to drive, does drive, or just stopped driving because his or her license was revoked. Not every American—in fact, only a very few Americans—can be counted in the ranks of good drivers. Good drivers must possess technical competence in the art of driving. They must know the simple steps, starting, shifting, and braking, and the highly sophisticated techniques, feathering the brakes and the power slide, for example. In addition they must possess physical skills, such as exceptional eye–hand coordination, fast reflexes, outstanding depth perception, and peripheral vision. They must also possess good judgment. What speed is safe on a rain-slick highway? How far can a person drive without succumbing to fatigue? What are the possible mistakes that the approaching driver can make? And besides the answers to these questions and the technical and physical skills listed above, good drivers possess steel nerves to cope with that potentially lethal emergency that one day will come to everyone who slips behind the wheel of a car. Only with these qualities can a person be called a good driver and be relatively sure of returning home in one piece.

Establish Parallel Categories

A suggestion about analysis: When you divide or break down an entity into its elements, be sure that you establish parallel categories. It is not proper, in analyzing an automobile's main systems, to list

Frame
Body
Drive train
Engine
Piston rings

Although the first four items could possibly be called major systems in an automobile, piston rings are a small part of a large system, the engine, and cannot be included in a list of major systems. The rule for analysis is: **Keep categories parallel.**

Process Analysis

A process paragraph is a form of analysis that examines the steps involved in an action or a sequence of actions. The most common sort of process analysis is the recipe: To make a rabbit stew, first catch a rabbit, and so forth. Instructions for building stereo receivers or flying kites or cleaning ovens are all process analyses. In addition to instructions, process analysis can be used to trace the steps involved in a historical event. Such analysis would be required to answer an essay test question that begins with the word *trace* or *delineate*. The following paragraph provides a set of instructions:

Changing the oil and the filter in your car is a simple process, and "doing it yourself" can save several dollars every time you change the oil. First, go to an auto parts store or a discount store and buy the oil and the oil filter specified for your car. At the same time, buy an oil filter wrench, the only specialized tool necessary for this job. Don't buy these items at your gas station; prices are lower at the other stores. In addition, you will need an adjustable wrench and a pail or bucket low enough to fit under the car to catch the old oil as it drains from the crankcase. Don't lift the car on a bumper jack. Simply crawl under the car and locate the drain plug for the crankcase. From the front of the car the first thing you see underneath will be the radiator— the thing with the large hose running from the bottom. That hose runs to the engine, the next piece of equipment as you work your way back. On the bottom surface is the drain plug, usually square with a few threads visible where it screws into the oil pan. Place the pail or bucket beneath this plug. Fit the wrench to the plug by adjusting its size. Turn the plug counterclockwise until it falls out of its hole into the pail. Don't try to catch it; the oil may be hot. While the oil drains into the pail, find the oil filter on one side of the engine, usually down low. (It will look exactly like the one you bought.) Reach up (or perhaps down from the top, whichever is easier) and slip the circle of the filter wrench over it. Pull the wrench in a counterclockwise direction and take off the old filter. Put the new filter on in exactly the opposite way, tightening it clockwise by hand until it is snug. Put the drain plug back in place, tightening it firmly with the adjustable wrench. Now find the oil filler cap on the top of the engine and pour in the new oil. Tighten the filler cap firmly. Dispose of the old oil at a collection station and wipe your hands clean. Finally, record the mileage for this change somewhere so that you will know when the next change is due.

A process paragraph that traces a historical development might be somewhat more difficult to write than a set of instructions. Essentially, however, tracing the steps in a historical process follows the same form as instructions; the major difference is that the historical event has already occurred and the paragraph is written in the past tense. Examine the following paragraph, which traces the transformation of the computer from mainframe to microcomputer, and notice how its pattern (this happened, then that, then another thing) follows very closely the pattern of the instructions in the previous example (do this, then that, then the other thing):

The first computer was made from vacuum tubes about as big as a bread box, and the collection of them filled up a room the size of a classroom. The tubes were inordinately sensitive to changes in temperature and humidity, and the smallest speck of dust caused them to go berserk. They were expensive to build and expensive to maintain; therefore they were operated only by highly trained technicians. Anyone who wished to use the computer was forced to deal with the people in the white lab coats, an inconvenient arrangement at best. The first step in reducing the size and increasing the reliability of the computer was the invention of transistors, small, inexpensive devices that control the flow of electricity. They are solid and durable, and, most important, they can be made very small. Scientists soon discovered that they could also be hooked together into integrated circuits known as *chips*; the chips could contain tremendous amounts of circuitry, an amount comparable to the wiring diagram of an office building, on a piece of silicon no bigger than your thumbnail. Finally, scientists and computer experts developed the microprocessor, the central works of a computer inscribed on a chip. Presto! The way was opened for the development of a microcomputer about the size of a bread box.

Causal Analysis

Causal analysis, as the name implies, is a discussion of the causes leading to a given outcome. On an essay test, you might be asked to explain or discuss the reasons for a lost war, a victory in an election, a depression, or the collapse of a bridge. In your life outside school, you might be called on to explain why you have selected some occupation or particular college or why you wish to drop out of school to hike the Appalachian Trail for four or five months.

Causal analysis differs from process analysis in that it does not necessarily involve a chronological sequence. Instead, it seeks the reasons for an outcome and lists them (with necessary discussion) in either ascending or descending order of importance. A process analysis concerned with the growth of inflation in the last seventy-five years might trace the fall of the dollar's value and the actions and reactions of government and consumers at intervals of ten years. On the other hand, a causal analysis on the same subject would give the reasons why the dollar has declined in value and why the reactions of government and consumers have produced progressively worse conditions. Causal analysis might also be used to explain why a course of action has been taken or ought to be taken.

It is important that the United States curb inflation over the next few years. Inflation at home is reducing the value of the dollar overseas, making it very difficult for Americans to purchase products from other countries. German automobiles, even those that once were considered low-cost transportation, have increased in price dramatically in the last few years. At home, rapid price increases have made it very difficult for salary increases to keep pace with the cost of living. In spite of large pay increases over the past few years, factory workers have shown little or no gain in buying power; prices have climbed as their wages have increased, leaving them with nothing to show for a larger paycheck. Inflation has been especially hard on retired people who live on a fixed income. They receive only a set number of dollars and do not benefit from pay increases as do wage earners. But while their income has remained the same, prices have increased; thus they cannot buy the same amounts as they could previously. Unchecked inflation works a hardship on all of us, but it is especially hard on those whose income does not increase to match the increases in prices.

Causal analysis might also be used to explain the reasons why someone holds a particular position or opinion. A student explained her love of sailing as follows:

A sailboat, a broad bay, and a good breeze form the most satisfying combination in the world of sport. To be sailing before a brisk wind across an open expanse of water allows—no, requires—cooperation with the forces of nature. Working with the wind in moving the boat provides us one of the few times when we are not forced to ignore, or work against, or even overcome the natural rhythms and functions of the universe. Too much of daily life pits us against those forces; finding them on our side, aiding us in a worthwhile project, is indeed a pleasure. The boats used are in themselves very pleasant. They do not bang or clank, nor do they spout vile fumes or foul the air, suddenly explode, or cease to function altogether. Instead, they offer the soft, sliding sounds of the bow slipping through the sea, the creak of ropes and sails, and the gentle, soothing hum of the standing rigging pulled tight by the pressure of wind on sails. Most important, sailing puts us in close contact, in communion, with that most basic element, the sea. The sea remains constant; winds or storms may stir the surface, but the depths are never moved. The sea always has been and always will be, or so it seems. It offers constancy and permanence in the midst of a world where flux and change are the only constants. Is it any wonder that sailing is such a delight, such a joy?

Use of Examples

One of the simplest yet most effective paragraphs states an idea and uses examples to illustrate and explain the idea. The following paragraph explains an idea by using examples:

Youth and beauty are grand attributes, and together they are a wonderful possession. But television commercials and programs extol youth and beauty to such an extreme that those not so young and less than beautiful are made to feel inferior. Cars, beer, clothes, and even lawn mowers are almost always pictured with lithe, beautiful women of tender age or well-muscled young men with luxuriant, well-groomed hair. Cosmetics are always portrayed in use by people who have almost no need of them. Beauty, and especially youthful beauty, sells goods, we surmise, and those who do not become young and beautiful after buying the car or ingesting the iron supplement are obviously unfit to share the planet with the favored ones. And the programs themselves emphasize youthful beauty. There are few homely, few truly decrepit people who play regularly in any series. Any family, and any individual, who cannot compare with those perfect people ought to be exiled from the land of the lovely. We are left to believe that only the beautiful young are acceptable.

Description and Narration

Two important orders of development remain: development by space and development by time, more commonly called *description* and *narration*. Each of these patterns involves a direction or a movement. Description requires that you move your writer's eye through a given space, picking out selected details in order to create an effect. Narration demands that you create a progression through time, providing details selected to convey a story and its impact. The success of each pattern depends on the careful selection of details of physical qualities or of action and on the vivid presentation of these details.

In *Huckleberry Finn* Mark Twain has Huck give a beautiful description of a sunrise on the Mississippi:

. . . we run nights, and laid up and hid daytimes; soon as night was most gone, we stopped navigating and tied up—nearly always in the dead water under a tow-head; and then cut young cottonwoods and willows and hid the raft with them. Then we set out the lines. Next we slid into the river and had a swim, so as to freshen up and cool off; then we set down on the sandy bottom where the water was about knee deep, and watched the daylight come. Not a sound, anywhere—perfectly still—just like the whole world was asleep, only sometimes the bull-frogs a-cluttering, maybe. The first thing to see, looking away over the water, was a kind of dull line—that was the woods on t'other side—you couldn't make nothing else out; then a pale place in the sky; then more paleness, spreading around; then the river softened up, away off, and warn't black any more, but gray; you could set little dark spots drifting along, ever so far away— trading scows, and such things; and long black streaks—rafts; sometimes you could hear a sweep screaking; or jumbled up voices, it was so still, and sound come so far; and by-and-by you could see a streak on the water which you know by the look of the streak that there's a snag there in a swift current which breaks on it and makes that streak look that way; and you see the mist curl up off the water, and the east reddens up, and the river, and you make out a log cabin in the edge of the woods, away on the bank on t'other side of the river, being a wood-yard, likely and piled by them cheats so you can throw a dog through it anywheres; then the nice breeze springs up, and comes fanning you from over there, so cool and fresh, and sweet to smell, on account of the woods and the flowers; but sometimes not that way, because they've left dead fish laying around, gars, and such, and they do get pretty rank; and next you've got the full day, and everything smiling in the sun, and the song-birds just going it!

Two qualities of this description are important to your writing. Note first the direction or movement of the unfolding picture. Beginning with the dim view of the far bank, the narrator observes traces of paleness in the sky. He then notes that the river has softened up "away off"; notice the logical progression from sky to horizon to river. After he gives details of the changing sights and sounds at river level, the mist curling up from the river focuses his attention again on the sky as the "east reddens up." Then he returns to the river and develops the picture as new details become visible in the light of morning. This movement from mid-picture to background to foreground to background to foreground follows a sensory logic, an order of increasing visibility as the sun rises and the light increases. It is important to select an order of presentation (or, as here, a logic) and to stick with the order, whether it be left-to-right, right-to-left, middle-to-left-to-right, or any other easily followed combination. Second, Twain provides details that appeal to the senses:

Color:	dull line of woods
	pale sky
	river changing from black to gray
	dark spots and black streaks
	east reddening
Sound:	complete absence of sound
	bullfrogs a-cluttering
	sweep screaking
	jumbled up voices
	song birds
Smell:	woods
	flowers
	dead fish
Motion:	dark spots drifting
	snag in swift current
	mist curling up off the water
Touch:	cooling off in water
	sitting on sandy bottom of river
	cool breeze springing up

Supply your reader with sensory appeal. Keep your description lively and colorful.

Twain provides us with a heart-stopping piece of narration in *Huck Finn,* the killing of the old drunk, Boggs.

So somebody started on a run. I walked down the street a ways, and stopped. In about five or ten minutes, here comes Boggs again—but not on his horse. He was a-reeling across the street towards me, bareheaded, with a friend on both sides of him aholt of his arms and hurrying him along. He was quiet, and looked uneasy; and he warn't hanging back any, but was doing some of the hurrying himself. Somebody sings out—"Boggs!"

I looked over there to see who said it, and it was that Colonel Sherburn. He was standing perfectly still, in the street, and had a pistol raised in his right hand—not aiming it, but holding it out with the barrel tilted up towards the sky. The same second I see a young girl coming on the run, and two men with her. Boggs and the men turned round, to see who called him, and when they see the pistol the men jumped to one side, and the pistol barrel came down slow and steady to a level—both barrels cocked. Boggs throws up both of his hands, and says, "O Lord, don't shoot!" Bang! goes the first shot, and he staggers back clawing at the air—bang goes the second one, and he tumbles backwards onto the ground, heavy and solid, with his arms spread out. That young girl screamed out, and comes rushing, and down she throws herself on her father, crying, and saying, "Oh, he's killed him, he's killed him!" The crowd closed up around them, and shouldered and jammed one another, with their necks stretched, trying to see, and people on the inside trying to shove them back, and shouting, "Back, back! give him air, give him air!"

Colonel Sherburn he tossed his pistol onto the ground, and turned around on his heels and walked off.

Again, two aspects of the narrative are important. The order is simple, straight chronology. But notice the action words. The girl comes on the run, the men jump, Boggs staggers. Few forms of the verb *to be* intrude to slow the action, and no statements of thought or emotion stop the progression. All of the impact and emotion is conveyed through action, and that use of action is the essence of good narrative.

A Final Note

Good paragraphs are not necessarily restricted to a single pattern of development. Quite often it is useful to combine patterns to produce a desired effect. The following paragraph on spider webs illustrates such a combination of patterns. The predominant device used here is analysis: The larger unit, spider webs, is broken down into three separate types or categories. But the writer uses an additional strategy; he clarifies his analysis by comparison/contrast, pointing out like and unlike details of the three kinds of spider webs:

Web-spinning spiders construct three kinds of webs. The first type is the tangled web, a shapeless helter-skelter jumble attached to some support such as the corner of a room. These webs are hung in the path of insects and serve to entangle them as they pass. The second type of web is the sheet web. This web is a flat sheet of silk strung between blades of grass or tree branches. Above this sheet is strung a sort of net, which serves to knock insects into the sheet. When an insect hits the sheet, the spider darts out and pulls it through the webbing, trapping the insect. Finally, perhaps the most beautiful of the webs, is the orb. The orb web consists of threads that extend from a center like a wheel's spokes and are connected to limbs or grass blades. All the spokes are connected by repeated circles of sticky silk, forming a kind of screen. Insects are caught in this screen and trapped by the spider.

Unity

An essential quality that you need to develop in good paragraphs is unity. A very simple rule says everything necessary to make clear the concept of unity in paragraph writing:

Handle only one idea in the paragraph. Second and subsequent ideas should be handled in separate paragraphs.

The paragraph originated as a punctuation device to separate ideas on paper and to assist readers in keeping lines separate as they read. Introducing more than one idea in a paragraph violates the basic reason for the existence of the paragraph.

It would seem to be easy to maintain unity in a paragraph, but sometimes ideas can trick you if you don't pay close attention to your topic sentence. A student wrote this paragraph on strawberries some years ago:

> Strawberries are my favorite dessert. Over ice cream or dipped in powdered sugar, they are so good they bring tears to my eyes. My uncle used to grow strawberries on his farm in New Jersey. Once, I spent the whole summer there and my cousins and I went to the carnival. . . .

Things went pretty far afield from strawberries as the paragraph continued, and you can see how one idea, "used to grow strawberries on his farm," led to a recollection of a delightful summer on that farm and opened the door to a whole new idea and a change in form from discussion to narration. "Strawberries" and "that summer on the farm" are both legitimate, interesting, and perfectly workable topics for a paragraph. But they are probably not proper for inclusion in the same paragraph. Unity demands that each topic be treated in a separate paragraph. One paragraph handling one idea equals unity.

Coherence

Coherence is another important quality that you need to develop in your paragraphs. The word *cohere* means "to stick together," "to be united." It is a term used in physics to describe the uniting of two or more similar substances within a body by the action of molecular forces. In paragraph writing, the term *coherence* is used to describe a smooth union between sentences within the paragraph. In other words, the sentences in a coherent paragraph follow one another without abrupt changes. A good paragraph reads smoothly, flowing from start to finish without choppiness to distract the reader.

The first step in establishing coherence occurs when you select a pattern for developing the paragraph. The selection of a pattern is based on the assignment that the paragraph is going to fulfill. You learned in the study of essay test answers that a question asking for discussion requires one sort of development and a question asking for comparison demands another. Review the discussions of essay tests and of paragraph patterns to keep this idea fresh in your mind.

Note, however, that it is sometimes necessary to include more than one pattern of development in a paragraph. A narration, for example, may demand a passage of description. Don't hesitate to shift methods where a switch is useful. Do so with care, and with the possibility in mind that a new method of development might suggest the need for a new paragraph.

The pattern you select will help to establish coherence because it produces a flow and a movement in the paragraph and because it serves as a frame for providing details of development. Select the pattern according to the demands of the assignment and follow that pattern through the whole paragraph.

The selection of a development pattern is perhaps the most important step in achieving a coherent paragraph. There are, however, various other writing strategies contributing to the same end. Three of these strategies are discussed next.

Strategy 1. Repetition of Nouns and Use of Reference Words

My father asked me to dig some postholes. After I finished that, he told me the truck needed washing. It is Father's pride and joy, but I'm the one who has to do such jobs.

These three short sentences show a fairly clear pattern of development that in itself establishes coherence. There is the beginning of a story, suggesting that narration will carry the paragraph further. Events occur one after another, setting a pattern of straight chronology. But note how strongly the repeated nouns and reference words knit the sentences together:

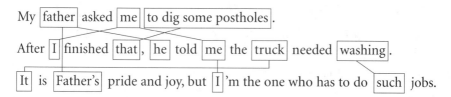

Strategy 2. Use of Temporal Words: Conjunctions and Adverbs

A series of short, abrupt sentences, although following a rigid chronological pattern, does not read as though it has coherence:

I drove to the corner. I stopped for a light. A car smashed into the back of mine. I got out rubbing my neck. The driver of the other car sat behind the wheel and wept. I realized that the other driver was an elderly, gray-haired man.

The writer, sensing that something is lacking from the paragraph, might revise it this way:

I drove to the corner. *While* I was stopped for a light, a car smashed into the back of mine. *As* I got out, rubbing my neck, the driver of the other car sat behind the wheel and wept. Only *then* did I realize that the other driver was an elderly, gray-haired man.

Two features of the revision have improved on the original draft. The first and most obvious is the addition of the words *while, as,* and *then* to connect the sentences by declaring the chronological sequence. Second, *while* and *as* convert short sentences into dependent clauses, thus replacing four choppy sentences with two longer ones and eliminating the jog-trot rhythm that gave the reader hiccups.

Strategy 3. Transitional Words and Phrases
At or Near the Beginning of Sentences

The coordinating conjunctions*; adverbs like *however, moreover, therefore, consequently, similarly,* and *thus;* and expressions like *on the other hand, in addition,* and *for example*— all can produce a subtle transitional effect rather like that of reference words. They force the reader to recollect the preceding material, thus making a tie between the thoughts they introduce and what has already been stated. When you read *But* at the beginning of a sentence, the author is declaring to you in loud tones, "You are to interpret the forthcoming statement as being in opposition or in contrast to what you have just read." *Moreover,* in the same place, suggests that what is coming is an addition to the last remarks; *consequently* means "as a result of what I have just stated."

The ploy of cementing the parts of a paragraph together with these words and phrases is used by nearly every writer. It is a perfectly good device, but unfortunately it is also a seductively easy one. The unwary writer larding sentences with *however*'s and *therefore*'s in search of elegance and poise may get into trouble with logic. "Sam drank too much on our dinner date. Consequently he threw up," may leave one wondering whether the nausea stemmed from the liquor or the date.

Exercises for Patterns for Paragraphs

1. Examine the following facts and observations about two methods for recording and playing music and other sound:

   - Cassette tapes can stretch and lose sound quality.
   - Compact discs are resistant to damage.
   - Compact discs maintain their sound quality.
   - Cassette tapes are less expensive than compact discs.
   - Cassette tapes can be damaged by tangling or unwinding.
   - In general, sound quality on compact discs is higher than sound quality on cassette tapes.

   Write a paragraph of comparison/contrast discussing the merits of these two media.

2. Write a paragraph giving directions for preparing your favorite dessert. Include every step and provide enough detail and information for a beginning cook to be able to make the dessert successfully. Check your work by preparing the dessert following your instructions.

3. Write a description of one of the buildings on your campus. Provide sufficient detail so that a person can identify the building that you are describing. Do not use the name, the location, or any identifying colors in the description.

---

*Disregard the myth that there is something wrong with starting a sentence with *and, but, for, or,* or *nor.* Do realize, however, that these words at the opening of a sentence provide a special effect and call attention to themselves and to what follows them. Don't overuse them, and be sure of your purpose when you do launch a statement with one.

Once you have mastered the steps in the writing process by creating paragraphs, you will need to make only a few adjustments to follow that same process in writing a longer essay, the sort of essay you might be assigned in a college class in biology, business, or English.

In earlier sections you have practiced writing essay tests and special paragraph arrangements; each piece of writing required the use of the writing process applied to a rather short project. In each case the process was the same. Considered as a series of questions, the process looks like the following:

Composing

1. What is my subject? What is the assignment, or what do I wish to write on?
2. What do I know, what can I learn, about that subject?
3. What can I say about that based on what I know or can learn?
4. Of all I know on the subject, what specific items will best support and illustrate that specific statement?
5. What is the best order for presenting the support and illustration?
6. What does a first attempt (draft) at writing that paper produce?

Revising

7. What changes must be made in content and organization to improve the draft and make it acceptable to my reader?
8. What corrections must be made in grammar, mechanics, and usage to make the paper acceptable to my reader?
9. What form must the final version take?

The same writing process works well on a structured class assignment or on an assignment in which some leeway is given on topic selection. Here is how you might develop a paper assigned in your English class.

Step 1. Select the Subject

Because this paper is a class assignment, the first step requires a look at the nature of class assignments and the problems of defining the subject and limiting it to an appropriate, manageable length.

The nature of an assignment for a paper can vary, but you will find that writing assignments usually fall into one of three categories.

1. **Very General:** Write a two-page paper on something we've covered in this course.
2. **Somewhat Specific:** Write a two-page paper on some aspect of the novel *Huckleberry Finn*.
3. **Very Directive:** Write a two-page paper explaining why Huck Finn's experiences led him to make his final statement: "Aunt Sally's going to adopt me and sivilize me and I can't stand it. I been there before."

The first example, the general assignment, grants considerable latitude in the selection of a subject for your paper. Often this latitude will provide more of a problem than a blessing because it is necessary to find something to write about that you *and* the teacher consider interesting and worthwhile. It is of little value to write a fine paper and find that the teacher (the grader) thinks the topic so insignificant that the whole effort can't be worth more than a C. The best approach here is to review the textbook, your lecture notes, and previous tests (if any); to select from these an important content area, concept, or personality; and to use that selection as a starting point for your work. Be sure to choose an area that interests you, an area about which you have some knowledge and some readily accessible sources of information. Once you have made this initial selection, you have converted the type of assignment from "general" to "somewhat specific." Next, you need to restrict the area you selected or were assigned so that you can develop it fully within the assigned length of the paper. Suppose, for example, the assignment names the novel *Huckleberry Finn* as the subject for a two-page paper. Several areas are open to you:

1. Autobiographical aspects of the novel
2. Problems of plot and structure
3. Problems of characterization
4. Philosophical aspects of the novel

For the selection or restriction process, choose one of the areas and make a final selection of a topic within that area. The final selection should be fairly small in scope, something manageable within two pages. In the example of *Huckleberry Finn,* the process of restriction might look like this:

1. Philosophical aspects of the novel
2. The relationship between individuals and society
3. Huck Finn's attitude toward the world as he saw it
4. Why Huck's experiences led him to say that he couldn't stand to be "sivilized"

The final version of the topic (Number 4) is probably limited enough for it to be treated adequately within the assigned length. The topic asks a single question about one person, and that question—"Why?"—can be answered: "because his experiences with civilization were unpleasant or terrifying." That statement and the unpleasant or terrifying experiences can be illustrated efficiently by the use of three or four examples. The statement of this restricted topic results in a "very directive" assignment and provides the basis for organizing and writing a two-page paper.

Pinpoints a Topic

The process just detailed is designed to help you derive a topic that is manageable within the scope of a given assignment. There are three stages in this restriction process.

• Selection of a general subject area
• Selection of a portion or phase of this general area to form a limited subject area
• Final selection of a specific limited topic within the limited subject area

Note that the way in which your teacher states the assignment dictates the starting point for your work. A general assignment requires that you go through all three stages. A somewhat specific assignment completes the first two stages for you by limiting you to a general area. You need deal with only the third stage to complete the restriction process for this assignment. A very directive assignment accomplishes all three stages and leaves you free to begin work on the organization of the paper itself.

The final version of the restricted topic is the same as that "very directive" assignment already listed:

> Explain why Huck's experiences led him to make his final statement: "Aunt Sally's going to adopt me and sivilize me and I can't stand it. I been there before."

Step 2. Gather Materials

You need to establish what you know about this particular topic. What were Huck's experiences? Why did they make him want to avoid Aunt Sally's attentions? List some of the experiences he had in the "sivilized" world. Here are some possibilities:

1. The confining life at the Widow Douglas's home and Miss Watson's efforts to teach Huck manners and religion
2. The brutal shooting of Boggs by Colonel Sherburn and the mob violence of the attempted lynching that was faced down by Sherburn's single-handed capacity for even greater violence
3. The Grangerford—Shepherdson feud
4. Huck's obvious pleasure at living outside civilization with Jim on Jackson's Island and on the raft

Others may come to mind as you work on the paper. The immediate conclusion that you can draw from these experiences is that all of what Huck saw of civilization was unpleasant or bad or dangerous. The list of experiences leads directly to Step 3.

Step 3. Establish a Controlling Statement

The thesis serves the longer essay much as the topic sentence serves the paragraph. The topic sentence states the subject of the paragraph and tells what will be said about it. The thesis statement does exactly the same thing for the longer paper. The statement controls the writer by defining the subject and what is to be said about the subject. It keeps the writer from wandering away from the subject; sometimes it is so specific that it establishes the order in which the essay will be arranged. The thesis statement for the *Huckleberry Finn* paper is obvious:

> Huck could not stand to be "sivilized" because his experiences in civilization were frightening, dangerous, or confining.

Step 4. Select Specific Items of Support

Keeping the thesis statement in mind, you need to select from the book experiences and observations that will clearly illustrate the conditions in civilization. All the possible pieces of evidence listed above can be used to point out the conditions that Huck wanted to avoid. Even the pleasant experiences with Jim on Jackson's Island serve to make the bad experiences more vivid. The strange episode at the end of the book, dealing with the mock freeing of Jim, who is being held as a runaway slave at the home of Tom Sawyer's Aunt Sally, is pretty clear evidence that civilized people often act in an uncivilized fashion.

Step 5. Establish an Order of Presentation

Several orders are possible, but the easiest one to follow is to take the materials in the order in which they occur in the book.

Step 6. Write the First Draft

Begin by writing an introduction and continue into the supporting paragraphs. The introduction might read this way:

> At the close of the novel *Huckleberry Finn,* Huck concludes his story by saying that he intends to "light out for the Territory" because Aunt Sally intends to "sivilize" him, and he feels that he can't stand any more efforts to make him an upstanding, moral, and religious citizen. His attitude is understandable, for his experiences in society as it existed along the Mississippi were confining, unpleasant, or downright terrifying.

We will discuss introductions again in the second example in this section.

Development

Continue now to the paragraphs of development. The paragraphs of development might read this way:

> Huck's experiences of "home," or at the two places where he lives at the opening of the novel, are decidedly unpleasant. The home of Widow Douglas and Miss Watson tends to oppress and constrict a boy's natural energy and interests. Regular meals eaten with careful manners and polite small talk work against Huck's tendency to roam at will through the woods. Lectures on morality and religion tend to confuse him. If one can obtain his or her desires through prayer, why are folks poor, or sick, or crippled? If being good makes one blessed, why is Miss Watson so sour and seemingly unhappy? Life with Pap may be more free from the repressions of etiquette, but it also has its frightening side of drunkenness, violence, and delirium tremens. So Huck decides to leave these situations behind to look for something better.
>
> Something better turns out to be life on the river with Jim, the runaway slave. They meet on Jackson's Island and camp there for a time. Their experiences on the island are mostly pleasant: loafing, camping, fishing, and generally hanging out, all of which suit Huck just fine. The idyll is interrupted by a snakebite (from which Jim recovers) and is ended by the threat of a search party coming out to find Jim. Jim is a slave and, by all the measures of that day, less than human, but in reality he is the only truly civilized person Huck meets in his travels. Jim loves Huck and cares for him, in spite of Huck's tendency to play cruel jokes on him. He shelters Huck from the knowledge of Pap's death and doesn't reject Huck after he discovers the hoax of Huck's dream fabrication when they have been separated in a fog. It is ironic that the only civilized person Huck meets is not considered truly human by those who regard themselves as civilized.
>
> The other people Huck meets in his travels do very little to improve his suspicious view of the world. He and Jim happen upon some fairly terrible people as soon as they venture out on the river: slave hunters, the gamblers who are trying to kill their partner, and a nonhuman agent of

civilization, a steamboat that runs them down and puts Huck back on shore. There he meets the Grangerfords, gentlemen and ladies all, living in a fine house and enjoying prosperity. The Grangerfords are aristocrats and moral churchgoing people who have only one fault: They are engaged in a murderous, generations-old feud with the Shepherdsons. One Sunday afternoon Huck witnesses an outbreak of this feud that leaves most of the people from both families dead.

Fleeing from the killing, Huck returns to the river and finds Jim. They continue down the river. Later they meet the King and the Duke, two great con artists who dupe the people in a nearby town and are eventually tarred and feathered for their efforts. During the adventures with the King and the Duke, Huck witnesses the shooting of the harmless drunk Boggs and the attempted lynching of Colonel Sherburn, the man who shot him. Taken on balance, most of Huck's experiences on shore are grim and frightening, good reasons for his lack of enthusiasm for civilization.

Even the last episode of the book does little to increase Huck's desire to live in the civilized world. Huck comes by chance on the home of Tom Sawyer's Aunt Sally and adopts Tom's identity. When Tom shows up, he is introduced as Cousin Sid. Jim is also on the plantation, being held as a runaway slave. The two boys, with Tom leading, enter an incredible plot to free Jim, although, as Tom knows but conceals, Jim has already been freed. After a series of cops-and-robbers antics, the plot resolves into what looks like a happy ending. It is revealed that Jim is free, Pap is dead, and Huck's personal fortune, presumed lost, is intact. Aunt Sally offers to adopt Huck and raise him properly so that he can become a successful, civilized adult. At this point Huck reviews his situation. Life in town and his misadventures on shore with the Grangerfords, the King and the Duke, Sherburn, and others suggest only bad experiences to come if he accepts Aunt Sally's offer. His time with Jim, living free and easy on the river, seems wonderfully pleasant, compared to those recollections. Little wonder, then, that he decides to "light out for the Territory."

This completes the writing process through the writing of the rough draft. The remaining steps in the process will be covered in the second example of this section.

Sample Business Paper Development

With this review of the process fresh in your mind, follow how you might want to apply it in writing a paper of six to eight paragraphs that might be assigned in a business course.

Your class has been studying business leaders, past and present, and the assignment is to write a paper of about eight hundred words discussing the contributions of one of these leaders to American business.

1. Select the Subject. Several names come to mind from the history of American business: F. W. Taylor, Thomas Watson, Douglas McGregor, Alfred Sloan, Frederick Herzberg. But perhaps the most interesting and certainly one of the most important contributors to the theory and practice of business in America is Peter F. Drucker. His contributions are famous and respected in this country and abroad, and they have been cataloged and discussed in two well-respected books. Thus Drucker's contributions meet the criteria for selection as a subject. They are important and interesting, and information on them is readily available.

2. Gather Materials. What is there to know about Peter Drucker?

He has written twenty-seven books and many articles on business. He was born in Vienna, Austria. Father was a college teacher in America. Drucker started his career as a bookkeeper and a writer. He left Germany early in WWII. Went to London and worked in a bank. Then worked for

American newspapers as a British correspondent. Worked for the U.S. government during the war, then taught at two colleges, moving in 1950 to New York University, where he taught till 1970.

His first consulting job was a massive study of General Motors Corporation, a study highly critical of its management systems. From this work he wrote *The Concept of the Corporation,* a book that was the beginning of management thought in the modern sense of the word. His latest book, *Management: Tasks—Responsibilities—Practices,* is a very broad study of modern management philosophy and practices.

He continues to consult for major corporations, but he requires that the client come to him in California. He charges $1,500 a day and still manages to stay booked up far in advance.

Drucker is well-known as a teacher. He taught first at NYU in a special program for active business people. He now teaches in the Claremont Graduate School in California, a position he has held since 1971. Drucker loves teaching so much that some believe he would pay to do it if necessary. He especially enjoys teaching those who are currently employed in management positions. He uses a case-study method of his own invention, not following accepted case-study methods from other colleges. His case studies are short and are not loaded with data and statistics. Instead they concentrate on analysis and on finding the right questions to ask in a given situation. Often high-level executives attend his classes for enrichment and pleasure, even though they do not need any further course work or degrees to augment their careers. His associations in the classroom often ripen into rich and enduring friendships.

Much more information could be collected about Drucker, and more probably would be needed to fill an essay of eight hundred words. But this is enough material to allow us to move to the next step.

3. *Establish a Controlling Statement.* It is clear from the information gathered about Peter Drucker that he is active in three general areas of business: as a teacher, consultant, and writer. But it is important to note that the key word in the assignment is not *activity;* rather, it is *contributions.* The fact that Drucker has been active as a writer does not automatically mean that he has made a contribution to the theory and practice of American business in his writings. That remains to be determined; you must return to the information gathered in Step 2 to see what is known about his *contributions.* (**Note:** It is not uncommon to discover that writing the statement for a paper [Step 3] requires a return to the information-gathering stage [Step 2] to find additional information to use in formulating the thesis statement.)

The information already collected provides only a suggestion of Drucker's contributions: the phrase that says he wrote a book that was the "beginning of management thought in the modern sense of the word." Now the job is to collect much information directly related to that idea.

Further reading in books and articles about Peter Drucker indicates two very important areas of contribution, one theoretical and the other practical.

In the theory of management, Drucker was the first to identify the corporation as a whole as something that needed management and that could be managed. Prior to his work, discussions of corporation management were rather fragmented, dealing with isolated problems such as accounting and materials handling. Drucker developed a theory for the operation of the entire corporation.

On the practical side, Drucker developed the concept of the manager and his or her role in the corporation, and he has written guides to the day-to-day functions of those in management. He has worked as a consultant for major corporations, and the solutions to their problems have filtered to other companies and influenced institutions such as schools and hospitals. He also did initial work on ideas that later were more fully developed by others: The "hygiene" theory of the effects of wages on motivation and the theories of motivation often labeled X and Y were initially discussed in Drucker's works, at least in concept, and were developed by other writers, Herzberg and McGregor in particular.

The addition of these ideas to the information collected provides a solid basis for working on Step 3, establishing the statement.

The nature of Drucker's contributions is now clear enough for you to try writing a statement about them. Such a statement might read:

> Peter Drucker has made both a theoretical and a practical contribution to American business.

or

> Peter Drucker was the first to develop a theory of the nature and function of the corporation, and he has made practical application of that theory to the day-to-day work of the manager through his writings and his work as a consultant. He also did initial work on concepts fully developed by others.

The second version captures most of what needs to be said, but the order is jumbled and the statement is too wordy. A better version is

> Peter Drucker developed the overall concept of the corporation, its place in society, and its operation; he also began work on specific concepts that were later developed by other men. His practical work as writer and consultant has provided direction to many managers.

You can shape that statement into a general outline for a paper and get an idea of the kinds of materials you will need to support the statement.

Drucker's Contributions

1. Developed theory and concept of the corporation.
2. Began work on concepts later fully developed by others.
3. Provided practical applications of those theories in writings and in consulting work.

Now you are ready to move to Step 4.

4. Select Specific Items of Support. To develop the first point in the outline, you will need to discuss the state of management theory when Drucker began his work. Then you will need to explain how he developed his theory, where he first began to publish it, and, in general terms, what that theory of the corporation and its management is. For the second point, you need to identify the concepts that Drucker began to develop, the people who completed that development, and the name or the final form of those concepts. A discussion of his more practical books and some of the guidelines in them can be joined with a brief discussion of his work as a consultant to present the third point in the outline.

5. Establish an Order of Presentation. There is an order already built into the outline from the materials collected in Step 2: first, theories and concepts of the corporation as a whole, then specific theories, and then practical applications of those theories. This order also seems to arrange the contributions in descending order of importance, taking the larger, more global contributions first and moving to less important theories and practical matters next. It would be possible to reverse that order and work from least important to most important, from practical to theoretical. But such a progression does not seem to suit the materials as well as the first order, so you should present the materials in the draft in the order suggested by the outline.

6. Write the First Draft. It might seem logical to begin writing a draft of a paper with the beginning, the introduction. If a clear, effective introduction comes to mind rather handily, begin with the introduction. But do not wait with pen in hand for the perfect introduction to appear on the page. Make one attempt at an introduction; if nothing comes of that first attempt, begin to write the body of the paper wherever you find the writing easiest, even if you begin with what is actually the last paragraph in the essay. Get the material written and *then* put the paper in the proper order. Write, don't wait for the inspiration.

When you do write the introduction, be sure to make it serve the two important functions of an introduction. First, and more important, an introduction must catch the interest of the reader. Second, the introduction must give the reader an idea of the direction the paper will take. This sense of direction may come from an explicit statement of the core idea or thesis of the paper, a paraphrase of the result of your work in Step 3. On the other hand, it may be given as a general identifying statement of the topic. For the paper on Peter Drucker a paraphrase of the Step 3 statement might read:

> Peter Drucker developed a philosophy of the corporation, devised specific concepts within that philosophy, and showed managers how to make a practical application of that philosophy.

Identifying the topic and making a general statement of the ideas to be covered might produce:

> Of all those who have helped to develop our ideas of the nature and workings of the corporation, Peter Drucker is among the most important.

With this effort to provide a sense of direction, you must also catch the reader's interest. If you have trouble thinking of methods for developing introductions, you might try one of the following strategies:

- Use a quotation or a paraphrase of a striking statement:

  > Peter Drucker is, in the words of C. Northcote Parkinson, "preeminent among management consultants and also among authors of books on management."

- Cite an important fact or statistic:

  > Prior to the writing of *The Concept of the Corporation,* the idea of the corporation as an entity that needed management did not exist. Drucker invented the corporate society.

- Recount an anecdote:

  > "What *is* your business?" the famous consultant asked the directors of a firm that made bottles. "Everyone knows," responded the chairman, "that we make bottles for soft drinks and other

foods." "I disagree," replied the consultant to the astounded board. After a pause to let his words sink in, he continued, "Your business is not the making of bottles; you are in the packaging business." With that one question Peter Drucker, America's foremost business consultant, opened the board's eyes and provided new direction for a foundering company.

- Use a dictionary definition:

  The dictionary defines a corporation as a group of individuals legally united to conduct business. Peter Drucker defines the corporation as the cornerstone of our society.

- Set up a contrast between two ideas:

  The original management consultant was really an efficiency expert, timing workers on an assembly line and suggesting ways of improving their speed and productivity. Peter Drucker's work is as far removed from that practice as the supersonic transport is from the Wright brothers' first plane.

As you become a more experienced writer, you will find less and less need for those strategies. Use them now, but feel free to experiment as your confidence grows.

Conclusions

Always provide a conclusion for your paper. As a rule, a short sentence of summary or a restatement of the topic will suffice. The function of a conclusion for a short paper is to let the reader know that the paper has been completed, to provide a sense of "finishedness." Don't leave the reader with the impression that he or she ought to be looking for more material. Don't try to provide an extensive restatement or summary for a short paper. And be very careful that you never use the conclusion to introduce a new point or add additional information. A one-sentence conclusion should be ample for most college essays.

First Draft

The first completed draft of the paper on the contributions of Peter Drucker might read this way:

> Of the business people, scholars, and writers who have attempted to analyze and influence the business world of the twentieth century, none has made a greater contribution or been more interesting to observe than Peter Drucker. Drucker is a teacher, a consultant, and a writer who has drawn from each role to construct a philosophy or theoretical concept of the corporation and a workable application of the theory to actual business problems and challenges. In theory and in practice, Drucker has been a major influence on American business for the last fifty years.
>
> In the minds of many, Drucker is the person who almost single-handedly invented the idea of the corporation. Prior to Drucker's introduction of the idea in *The Concept of the Corporation*, the study of business management was the study of individual problems such as accounting or materials handling. Drucker changed that view and suggested that the corporation was an entity, a whole, and needed to be managed as a whole, not as a series of isolated services or problems. Much of this book, and the ideas within it, arose from a massive study of General Motors undertaken in 1943. Having examined the operation of that company in great detail, and having reported that he thought it was managed chaotically, he set about developing a unified view of

the corporation and its management. He did develop such a view and, in the process, suggested that the key institution and the chief influence on the future of the Western world would be the corporation, complete with assembly lines. This view of the corporation as a whole and his real-ization that the corporation was a major political, social, *and* economic force have made Drucker a major contributor to the present-day theory of business.

Drucker has written extensively in the area of management and has been a leader in the development of important concepts in specific areas of management. He was a leader, or at least an important forerunner, of the management system commonly called *management by objec-tives* (MBO). He first used the term in his book *The Practice of Management* and says he first heard it used by Alfred Sloan in the 1950s. Essentially, MBO tries to focus the attention of man-agers on their objectives. Managers of the old school had always asked themselves, "What do I do?" Drucker turned their attention from the process to the product or objective and said that the proper question is "What do I wish to accomplish?" That principle of management is now so commonplace in business and government that it seems always to have existed. Two concepts in the area of motivation were suggested by Drucker and developed by others. The first is the now famous "hygiene" theory of compensation, which says that wages and certain other condi-tions of employment do not cause high morale and motivation; instead they prevent low morale and allow other positive motivators to have an impact on the workers. These *hygiene factors* do not increase motivation and production, but motivation and the accompanying higher pro-duction cannot occur without them. Drucker also was an early contributor to the theories of motivation commonly called *Theory X* and *Theory Y*, which are widely discussed by writers such as Douglas McGregor. Theory X says that people are motivated best by threat and fear, by neg-ative or extrinsic motivation; Theory Y counters that people are better and further motivated by satisfaction of their basic needs and by appeals to their sense of participation and involve-ment. These ideas are well known and widely used today; Drucker was a major contributor to their early development.

But Drucker is no airy theorist incapable of practical work. He is a consultant whose services are heavily sought by industry and government. He is in such demand that he can charge $1,500 a day for his services and never lack clients. He is a consultant who does not try to provide clients with an answer to their problems. Rather, he tries to point out what the proper questions are and to help the clients find the answers. In early work with a manufacturer of glass bottles, he shocked the executive committee by asking them what business the firm was in. Silence followed the question, and then the chairman replied with a hint of anger in his voice, "We make glass bottles for soft-drink makers and others." "No," replied Drucker, "your business is not making bottles. You are in the packaging business." That answer, coming from an unusual perspective, greatly altered the executives' view of the company and its problems and led to solutions never suspected by the executive committee. Drucker constantly advises his clients to build from strength, to use the abilities that each person possesses, and to structure assignments so that no manager is forced to work long in an area where she or he is weak. Managers of the old school always looked at weaknesses and worked for their correction. Drucker said, "Forget the weak-nesses. Put the person in a position where his weaknesses will not matter; use and develop the strengths of each employee."

Drucker has raised the art of consulting to new heights, making practical applications of the theories of management he developed. As a writer he has been an important contributor to the practical side of management. *The Effective Executive* is full of good advice to managers, advice useful on a day-to-day basis. His later book, *Management: Tasks—Responsibilities—Practices*, has in it long sections that are intensely practical. Even his more theoretical works have a practical bent. Arjay Miller, former president of Ford Motor Company, says that *The Concept of the Cor-poration* was "extremely useful in forming my judgments about what was needed at Ford. It was, by considerable margin, the most useful and pragmatic publication available and had a definite impact on the postwar organizational development within the Ford Motor Company" (*Drucker:*

The Man Who Invented the Corporate Society, 1976, p. 32). Peter Drucker, philosopher, theorist, and practical authority, is, without doubt, a major figure in the history of American business and a man who helped to shape and form the corporation as we know it today.

Materials for this essay were taken from John J. Tarrant, *Drucker: The Man Who Invented the Corporate Society* (Boston: Cahners Books, Inc., 1976) and from Tony H. Bonaparte and John E. Flaherty, eds., *Peter Drucker: Contributions to Business Enterprise* (New York: New York University Press, 1970). Drucker's latest book is *Managing for the Future* (Truman Talley Books/Dutton, 1992).

The completed version of the paper that comes out of Step 6 is *not*—repeat, *not*—the version of the paper that you ought to turn in. Step 6 produces a rough draft, a version suitable for revision and not much else. Think of that draft as a good start, but remember that it is still a long way from completion. Use the remaining steps of the writing process in revising your draft. Wait a day or two (if possible) between completing the draft and undertaking the revision.

7. Revise the Rough Draft. Read the draft all the way through twice. Then ask the following questions:

- Will the introduction interest the reader? Does it provide a sense of direction for the paper?
- Does the Step 3 statement in the introduction accurately reflect what you intend to say on the topic?
- Does the rest of the paper, does each supporting paragraph, serve to develop the statement you intend to make in the paper?
- Are the supporting points presented in the best order?
- Is there an adequate conclusion?

Read each paragraph of support very carefully.

- Is the point of support developed completely? Will readers have any questions on the point when they finish reading the paragraph? Is the paragraph *complete*?
- Is each paragraph unified? Does any paragraph treat more than one idea?
- Is each paragraph coherent? Does it read smoothly, tying the sentences together with transitional devices?

8. Correct the Draft. Check the paper sentence by sentence to improve its style and to correct errors.

- Check each sentence for errors in completeness (Lesson 13), subject–verb agreement (Lesson 22), pronoun–antecedent agreement (Lesson 23), pronoun case (Lesson 24), dangling or misplaced modifiers (Lesson 14), and the use of prepositions (Lesson 25). (**Note:** As you find errors in your papers and as marked errors appear on papers returned to you, keep a record of them—either by putting a check in the appropriate lessons of this book or by marking your reference handbook. You will soon discover whether you have a tendency to repeat certain kinds of errors, and you can simplify your proofreading by checking first for these errors. In a short time, you should be able to eliminate repeat faults from your writing.)

- Check each sentence for errors in punctuation; check for missing punctuation marks *and* for unneeded marks.
- Check for errors in mechanics, capitalization, and spelling.

9. Write the Final Draft. Copy the paper in its final, corrected form. Be sure to observe correct margins, and to write or type neatly. Make a copy of the paper before you turn it in.

8

Progress Tests

355

Subjects and Verbs; Parts of Speech
(Lessons 1, 2)

NAME _____ SCORE _____

Directions: Copy the subject of the sentence on the first line at the left and the verb on the second line.

_____ 1. Our first sight of the dilapidated house depressed us.
_____

_____ 2. There was no sign of life about the farm.
_____

_____ 3. Each of the tourists carried a small camera.
_____

_____ 4. Beyond the pines grew a few dwarf junipers.
_____

_____ 5. This was only the first of a long series of interruptions.
_____

_____ 6. Close to the summer camp is a nine-hole golf course.
_____

_____ 7. He's the only one of my teenage friends with an unlisted phone
_____   number.

_____ 8. By this time next week most of the vacationers will have left The
_____   island.

_____ 9. Not one of the villagers had received the proper legal notice.
_____

_____ 10. One of the bored clerks perfunctorily rubber-stamped Jane's
_____   passport.

_____ 11. Moments later a covey of quail rose from the large patch of
_____   weeds.

_____ 12. Next on the program will be three songs by the junior-high
_____   mixed chorus.

_____ 13. Finally, shortly before midnight, the last of the guests drove away.
_____

_____ 14. On the kitchen table lay the remnants of a quick lunch.
_____

_____ 15. Behind the shed was a short row of plum trees in full bloom.
_____

Directions: Each sentence contains two italicized words. In the space at the left, write one of the following numbers to identify the part of speech of each italicized word:

1. Noun	3. Verb	5. Adverb
2. Pronoun	4. Adjective	6. Preposition

—————— 1. The *address on* the letter was almost illegible.

—————— 2. The general *addressed* the troops and urged them *on*.

—————— 3. More money will be available at *some later* date.

—————— 4. *Later, some* of the guests washed the dishes.

—————— 5. In a firm *voice*, the sergeant demanded an *apology*.

—————— 6. The teacher *voiced* the opinion that Joe's speech was needlessly *apologetic*.

—————— 7. *Beyond* a doubt, the *arrival* of the Marines saved the day.

—————— 8. *Doubtlessly* a large crowd will await the candidate's *arrival*.

—————— 9. A *lovely* park is *close* to the campus.

—————— 10. The *alert* dog guarded the prisoner *closely*.

—————— 11. The sentinel was commended *for* his *alertness*.

—————— 12. *Everyone* thinks your action deserves a *reward*.

—————— 13. *Every* member of the squad must work *harder*.

—————— 14. The children *like* an *occasional* visit to the zoo.

—————— 15. *Occasionally* Julia's practical jokes *annoy* me.

—————— 16. We consider these interruptions only a *minor annoyance*.

—————— 17. We *worked throughout* the hot afternoon.

—————— 18. You should be commended for your *enthusiastic work* on the project.

—————— 19. *This* plan sounds completely *workable*.

—————— 20. *This* improvement cannot be made *without* additional funds.

NAME _____ SCORE _____

Directions: Identify the italicized word by writing one of the following abbreviations in the space at the left:

S.C. [subjective complement]   I.O. [indirect object]
D.O. [direct object]   O.C. [objective complement]

If the italicized word is *not* used as one of these complements, leave the space blank.

_____ 1. Next Thursday afternoon might be a good *time* for our next meeting.

_____ 2. You should have looked up the correct *spelling* of the word in your dictionary.

_____ 3. I can have your meal *ready* for you in half an hour.

_____ 4. The truck had been standing out in the sub-zero *weather* all week.

_____ 5. One in high political office must avoid even a *hint* of scandal.

_____ 6. In a hard-fought eighteen-hole playoff, Jeremy emerged the *winner*.

_____ 7. The injured woman could give the *police* only a sketchy account of the accident.

_____ 8. You should send the personnel *officer* a list of your previous employers.

_____ 9. These vacuum-packed bags will keep the potato chips *crisp*.

_____ 10. How *old* is that noisy, gas-guzzling car of yours?

_____ 11. How many *miles* per gallon do you get from your car?

_____ 12. The children were happily making sand *castles* on the beach.

_____ 13. Henry made *me* an attractive offer for my used camcorder.

_____ 14. A fresh coat of paint would make this dingy room more *attractive*.

_____ 15. In Chinese cooking, dried sea cucumber is an important *ingredient*.

_____ 16. When will you send *me* a bill for your professional services?

———— 17. Our new state officers are taking on an awesome *responsibility*.

———— 18. "I want every one of these windows *spotless* by noon," said the sergeant.

———— 19. "I want every one of these *windows* spotless by noon," said the sergeant.

———— 20. Later the picture frames will be given three *coats* of varnish.

———— 21. In his youth he had been looked upon as the town *buffoon*.

———— 22. How *certain* can we be of the mayor's support for our project?

———— 23. Which of these three samples do you consider the best *buy*?

———— 24. *Which* of these three samples do you consider the best buy?

———— 25. During the cook's testimony the accused man appeared *worried*.

———— 26. After a noticeable pause the umpire called the pitch a *strike*.

———— 27. All of us wish *you* a prosperous New Year.

———— 28. The influx of refugees brought our *city* new problems.

———— 29. How *wide* should we make the new path?

———— 30. How wide should we make the new *path*?

———— 31. Susan had been putting off a *visit* to her dentist.

———— 32. Did Mrs. Camp offer you *any* of her famous blueberry pie?

———— 33. Did Mrs. Camp offer *you* any of her famous blueberry pie?

———— 34. I now feel *rested* enough for the climb to the summit.

———— 35. How *cold* do the winters get in Anchorage?

———— 36. *Whom* has the chairwoman chosen as her assistant?

———— 37. This dessert must be kept very *cold* until serving time.

———— 38. First of all, someone will give *you* an aptitude test.

———— 39. First of all, you will be given an aptitude *test*.

———— 40. You will find the climate here quite *moderate*.

NAME _____   SCORE _____

Directions: Each of the following sentences contains one subordinate clause. Use square brackets ([ ]) to mark the beginning and the end of each subordinate clause. Circle the subject and underline the verb of each subordinate clause. Identify the clause by writing in the space at the left one of the following abbreviations:

Adv. [adverb clause]   Adj. [adjective clause]   N. [noun clause]

_____ 1. As the chorus marched onto the stage, a small dog followed.

_____ 2. There is much merit in what you propose.

_____ 3. The scenery collapsed at the moment when Gene stepped out from the wings.

_____ 4. Have you told your family of the plans you have made?

_____ 5. Anyone as old as your niece should know the alphabet.

_____ 6. Were I you, I'd apply for the scholarship.

_____ 7. It's unfortunate that you missed the class picnic.

_____ 8. We had nothing to eat except what was left over from lunch.

_____ 9. Theodore Roosevelt did several things that restored presidential leadership over Congress.

_____ 10. According to the legend, Medusa could change a man to stone as he was looking at her.

_____ 11. The dormitory where Julie lived housed several students from India.

_____ 12. This pamphlet explains on what bases the student essays should be judged.

_____ 13. The diamond ring Alice is wearing came originally from her aunt in Holland.

_____ 14. Do you sometimes wonder if you could handle a confining job in an office?

_____ 15. Beth looks after two small children whose mother works afternoons on the campus.

_____ 16. Mark's lawyer argued that his client was not financially liable for the damages.

_____ 17. An argument that Mark's lawyer presented questioned the financial liability for the damages.

_____ 18. Mark's lawyer's argument was that his client was not financially liable for the damages.

_____ 19. Mark's lawyer's argument that his client was not financially responsible for the damages impressed the jury.

_____ 20. Some of us wonder if you would be interested in the job.

Directions: The italicized material in each of these sentences is a subordinate clause. In the first space at the left, write Adv., Adj., or N. to identify the clause. Within the italicized clause the word printed in boldface type is a complement. Identify it by writing in the second space at the left one of the following:

S.C.	[subjective complement]	I.O.	[indirect object]
D.O.	[direct object]	O.C.	[objective complement]

———— 1. One of Jeff's difficulties is *that he is painfully **shy** in the presence of strangers.*
————

———— 2. *If you follow these **directions**,* you will avoid really heavy traffic.
————

———— 3. After you leave this class, I hope that you will practice ***what** you have learned*
———— *here.*

———— 4. The letter of introduction *that you sent **me*** proved very helpful.

———— 5. The car was registered in the name of Charles Albertson, a Britisher ***whom***
———— *the FBI had been investigating.*

———— 6. Beth has as yet told no one ***who** her bridesmaids will be.*

———— 7. We are living in a period *when crises are almost daily **occurrences**.*

———— 8. I'm afraid *that I caused my **parents** some real embarrassment.*

———— 9. The substitute teacher devised some activities *that kept the youngsters **busy***
———— *for half an hour.*

———— 10. Uncle Jake sputtered indignantly *when the waiter reminded **him** that the cus-*
———— *tomary gratuity is fifteen percent.*

———— 11. The first fish ***that** Laura caught* was only five inches long.

———— 12. Several friends commented on *how **happy** Elaine looked.*

———— 13. I am sure *that the best seats for the concert are no longer **available**.*

———— 14. I think you should tell the mechanic *that you consider his bill unreasonably*
———— ***high**.*

———— 15. Although Sue has shown me *where I had been making **mistakes**,* I'm still not
entirely comfortable with my new computer.

———— 16. The board approved Mr. Barnes' suggestion *that the club make Ms. Thomp-*
———— *son an honorary **member**.*

———— 17. An actress ***whom** none of us had ever seen before* played the part of the pros-
———— ecuting attorney.

———— 18. The contractor could only guess at ***what** the total cost will be.*

———— 19. Ted has been studying the pamphlet *the traffic officer gave **him**.*
————

———— 20. Your theme will be improved, I think, *if you make your introductory para-*
———— *graph somewhat **shorter**.*

NAME _____   SCORE _____

Directions: Each sentence contains one verbal phrase. Underline the phrase and, in the space at the left, write one of the following letters to identify the phrase:

G. [gerund phrase]   P. [participial phrase]
I.   [infinitive phrase]   A. [absolute phrase]

_____ 1. It might be a good idea to look into the Acme Company's offer more carefully.

_____ 2. Tomorrow being a holiday, I shall loaf most of the day.

_____ 3. Wayne's daily chores included looking after the boss's collection of African violets.

_____ 4. Do you think that granting Larsen another extension on the loan is wise?

_____ 5. I'll send you a ten-page brochure describing this tremendous real-estate opportunity.

_____ 6. Dad would sometimes let me sit on his lap while he was steering the car.

_____ 7. Troubled by these inaccuracies, one board member demanded that new auditors be hired.

_____ 8. Hatchwood was found guilty of sending an abusive, threatening letter to the mayor.

_____ 9. Can you show me how to put this new cartridge into my printer?

_____ 10. Over the weekend I did little except review my geology notes for the midterm examination.

_____ 11. Dad has done most of the cooking this week, Mother having been called for jury duty.

_____ 12. Perhaps your client might consider buying a somewhat larger piece of property.

_____ 13. The substitute teacher's first mistake was assigning the class some additional homework.

_____ 14. Another possibility would be to rent a car at the airport.

_____ 15. Three men found guilty of espionage were deported.

_____ 16. One of Paula's unusual hobbies is collecting old theater programs.

_____ 17. Keeping the younger children quiet during the long ceremony will tax your ingenuity.

_____ 18. One of the ushers will tell you when to march to the platform for your diploma.

_____ 19. Johnson returned to Memphis, having been unsuccessful in his search for a job in Atlanta.

_____ 20. Being a charitable person, Bascom graciously accepted the apology.

Directions: Each of the italicized words in the following sentences is used as a complement within a verbal phrase. In the first space at the left, write one of the following letters to identify the phrase:

        G. [gerund phrase]   P. [participial phrase]
        I. [infinitive phrase]   A. [absolute phrase]

In the second space, write one of the following numbers to identify the complement:

        1. Subjective complement   3. Indirect object
        2. Direct object   4. Objective complement

———————   1. You can help the committee most by providing *transportation* for the out-of-town delegates.

———————   2. It might be to our advantage to make *Chapman* a second offer for his property.

———————   3. There will be celebrating in Coalville this week, the local baseball team having won the league *pennant.*

———————   4. The excited children raced to the backyard, leaving the kitchen door wide *open.*

———————   5. These graphic pictures succeeded in making the legislators *aware* of the need for immediate action.

———————   6. The clerk, looking extremely *annoyed* by our insistence, finally summoned his supervisor.

———————   7. How may *signatures* were you able to get for our petition?

———————   8. "Remember, jurors," said the attorney, "that no one actually heard my client threaten the police *officer.*"

———————   9. Beth's aunt looked after the children yesterday, our regular sitter being *unavailable.*

———————   10. A new regulation making students *eligible* for membership on college committees is being considered.

———————   11. Having already sent the *bank* the February payment, Tracy was puzzled by the delinquent notice.

———————   12. Spending time with Uncle Josh is almost as unpleasant as visiting the *dentist.*

———————   13. Feeling *sorry* for the embarrassed clerk, Mother paid for the broken cookies.

———————   14. Have you ever thought of becoming an airline flight *attendant?*

———————   15. I must find a new handball partner, Jeff Toner having left *town.*

NAME _____ SCORE _____

Directions: If a sentence is correct, write C in the space at the left. If you find a dangling modifier, underline it and write W in the space.

_____ 1. In purchasing a dog for a family pet, its background is as important to consider as its appearance.

_____ 2. A boat as light as this one can be upset by sitting on the side the way you are doing now.

_____ 3. Turning the car into the driveway, my purse fell to the floor and the contents scattered all over.

_____ 4. Dad is certainly busy enough this morning without asking him to drive us to the gym.

_____ 5. Dad is certainly busy enough this morning without being asked to drive us to the gym.

_____ 6. Upon reaching nine years of age, my family moved again, this time to Omaha.

_____ 7. Having bruised her ankle while taking inventory this morning, the boss told Edith to take the afternoon off.

_____ 8. I think I'll splurge tonight and order an expensive dessert, tomorrow being payday.

_____ 9. The tapes may be used again after rewinding them.

_____ 10. The tapes may be used again after being rewound.

_____ 11. After filing away all the loose magazines and pamphlets that I have acquired this year, my shelves look quite tidy.

_____ 12. To be assured of a capacity audience, the price of the tickets must be kept low.

_____ 13. The weather having turned cold and windy, we decided to take along our parkas.

_____ 14. Exhausted after the long hours of studying, Luke's head slowly nodded and finally came to rest on the open book.

_____ 15. Notice also that, by being reversed, this coat can be used in rainy weather.

_____ 16. Notice also that, by reversing it, this coat can be used in rainy weather.

_____ 17. Notice also that, by reversing it, you can use this coat in rainy weather.

_____ 18. Meeting Lois after work, she suggested that we see a movie.

_____ 19. Yesterday, while eating lunch on the patio, a flock of crows made a raucous racket.

_____ 20. Instead of leaving the lawn mower out in the rain, it should be put away in the carport.

Directions: Rewrite each of the following sentences twice:
    a. Change the dangler to a complete clause with subject and verb.
    b. Begin the main clause with a word that the dangler can logically modify.

1. Having been in the army for five years, my serious reading has been neglected.

    a. _____

    b. _____

2. While mowing the grass, the long-lost gold chain was found.

    a. _____

    b. _____

3. Before applying the first coat of paint, the surface should be sanded well.

    a. _____

    b. _____

4. To be assured of a successful cake, the flour must be sifted thoroughly.

    a. _____

    b. _____

5. Having turned the horses loose, they raced for the cool, inviting stream.

    a. _____

    b. _____

NAME _____ SCORE _____

Directions: Study these paired sentences for incompleteness, misplaced modifiers, faulty parallelism, and faulty comparisons. In the space at the left, write the letter that identifies the correct sentence.

_____ 1. A. Our service department uses only factory-approved materials.
   B. Our service department only uses factory-approved materials.

_____ 2. A. One of the laboratory assistants having had enough presence of mind to rush the injured student to the infirmary.
   B. One of the laboratory assistants had enough presence of mind to rush the injured student to the infirmary.

_____ 3. A. Although a sergeant's pay is lower than a commissioned officer, an officer has several additional expenses.
   B. Although a sergeant's pay is lower than a commissioned officer's, an officer has several additional expenses.

_____ 4. A. Our company specializes in cars of conservative design and which get good gas mileage.
   B. Our company specializes in cars that are conservatively designed and get good gas mileage.

_____ 5. A. Last semester Johnny had a better grade-point average than any other fellow in his fraternity.
   B. Last semester Johnny had a better grade-point average than any fellow in his fraternity.

_____ 6. A. Gladys only approves of a movie if it has a gloriously happy ending.
   B. Gladys approves of a movie only if it has a gloriously happy ending.

_____ 7. A. What started the argument was Fran's casual remark that hers was the fastest of any speedboat on the lake.
   B. What started the argument was Fran's casual remark that hers was the fastest of all the speedboats on the lake.

_____ 8. A. Jan had to reluctantly admit that all college students are not vitally interested in modern dance.
   B. Jan had to admit reluctantly that not all college students are vitally interested in modern dance.

_____ 9. A. It was one of the greatest thrills, if not the greatest thrill, of my life.
   B. It was one of the greatest, if not the greatest thrill of my life.

_____ 10. A. Minnesota, I have been told, has more lakes than any state in the Union.
 B. Minnesota, I have been told, has more lakes than any other state in the Union.

_____ 11. A. The road is wide, hard-surfaced most of the way, and very few sharp curves.
 B. The road is wide and hard-surfaced most of the way and has very few curves.

_____ 12. A. The survey revealed that the salaries of the janitors were equal, and in some cases higher than the beginning teachers.
 B. The survey revealed that the salaries of the janitors were equal to, and in some case higher than, those of the beginning teachers.

_____ 13. A. The receptionist told me to return the questionnaire to her as soon as I finished it.
 B. The receptionist told me to, as soon as I finished the questionnaire, return it to her.

_____ 14. A. Some of the more vocal fans, still complaining about Coach Driscoll's lack of imagination and new ideas.
 B. Some of the more vocal fans are still complaining about Coach Driscoll's lack of imagination and new ideas.

_____ 15. A. "I admire neither the mayor's politics nor the people he associates with," said Ms. Ames.
 B. "I neither admire the mayor's politics nor the people he associates with," said Ms. Ames.

_____ 16. A. The predicted rainfall will be as heavy as that of the last few days, if not heavier.
 B. The predicted rainfall will be as heavy, if not heavier than, the last few days.

_____ 17. A. One unusual bit of information being that Hong Kong boasts of more Rolls Royces per square foot than any city on earth.
 B. One unusual bit of information is that Hong Kong boasts of more Rolls Royces per square foot than any other city on earth.

_____ 18. A. Danny managed by December to pay off nearly half of his father's debts.
 B. Danny managed to by December nearly pay off half of his father's debts.

_____ 19. A. The accident happened because the street was icy and the other driver was inexperienced and careless.
 B. The accident happened because the street was icy and because of the other driver's inexperience and carelessness.

_____ 20. A. Whose ACT scores were best, yours or your twin brothers?
 B. Whose ACT scores were better, yours or your twin brother's?

NAME _____ SCORE _____

Directions: Change the italicized sentence to the form indicated in the parentheses and rewrite enough of the new sentence to illustrate the construction.

1. *The Jensens were in Hawaii on vacation.* They missed the dedication of the new courthouse. (adverbial clause of reason) _____

    _____

2. *The Jensens were in Hawaii on vacation.* They missed the dedication of the new courthouse. (absolute phrase) _____

    _____

3. *Brush the movable metal parts lightly with oil.* This will protect them against rust. (gerund phrase)_____

    _____

4. Brush the movable metal parts lightly with oil. *This will protect them against rust.* (infinitive phrase) _____

    _____

5. The survivors were flown to Ellertown by Ben Towle. *He is a local helicopter pilot.* (adjective clause) _____

    _____

6. The survivors were flown to Ellertown by Ben Towle. *He is a local helicopter pilot.* (appositive) _____

    _____

7. *I had read the editorial.* I decided to write a letter to the editor. (adverbial clause of time) _____

    _____

8. *I had read the editorial.* I decided to write a letter to the editor. (participial phrase)

    _____

    _____

9. *I had read the editorial.* I decided to write a letter to the editor. (prepositional phrase with gerund phrase object) _____

    _____

10. With our sandwiches we drank warm ginger ale. *Our meager supply of ice had melted.* (absolute phrase)_____

    _____

Directions: Rewrite each of the following numbered sections as one complex sentence; show enough of the new sentence to illustrate the construction. In each case use the italicized subject and verb for the main clause. Use a variety of the subordinating units listed on the first page of Lesson 15.

1. I knew Stan Whipple in college. He is now a successful art auctioneer. *I was surprised* to learn this. _____

   _____

2. I spent five hours typing my research paper and *I was* exhausted and so I went to bed before nine o'clock. _____

   _____

3. This *quilt* has been in our family for over sixty years. It *was made* by my grandmother. She was twenty years old when she made it._____

   _____

4. I finished high school in June. I didn't find a job that I liked. *I returned* to summer school for a course in word processing. Word processing is a valuable skill for anyone.

   _____

   _____

5. The recipe called for chopped pecans. *I used* chopped peanuts instead. Chopped peanuts are more fitted to my limited budget. _____

   _____

6. Hank and I attended college together. That was twenty years ago. *He seemed* completely lacking in ambition. But he was intelligent. _____

   _____

7. Jackson is not a very strong student, but he is a good basketball player and so *I suppose* he'll have no trouble getting into college somewhere._____

   _____

8. Mother is usually easygoing. She rarely raises her voice. *She surprised* the family. She announced that this year she was not cooking a big Thanksgiving Day dinner. _____

   _____

9. Duncan graduated from college in pharmacy. But now *he manages* a seed company. The company is large. It is located near Lompoc, California._____

   _____

10. Laura's uncle learned that she was majoring in journalism. *He sent* her a letter. It was stern and unequivocal. It ordered her to change her major to law. _____

    _____

*Commas and Semicolons:
Compound Units (Lessons 7, 17)*

NAME _____ SCORE _____

Directions: In each sentence a *V* marks a point of coordination between (1) two verbs with a coordinating conjunction, (2) two independent clauses with a coordinating conjunction, or (3) two independent clauses without a coordinating conjunction. In the space at the left, write one of the following:

    0 (no punctuation is needed)
    C (a comma is needed)
    S (a semicolon is needed)

_____ 1. "I have a new machine here," said the mechanic *V* "in two minutes it will analyze your car's exhaust."

_____ 2. Dr. Ellis's lecture must have impressed her audience *V* for dozens of people with questions crowded around her after she finished.

_____ 3. Many years ago Jerome had fished for bass and muskellunge in northern Minnesota *V* in those days no one worried about polluted lakes and streams.

_____ 4. Ms. Brady's comments on student themes were sometimes cruel *V* and did not endear her to the students in pre-engineering.

_____ 5. The living conditions of the people are improving slowly *V* but there is little hope for significant change.

_____ 6. The party must have been rather unexciting *V* for my roommate was home and in bed by ten o'clock.

_____ 7. The day-long meeting was routine and uneventful *V* for the visiting students from India it must have seemed quite dull.

_____ 8. Under the new law automobile drivers over seventy years of age must pass a test *V* otherwise their current licenses will be revoked.

_____ 9. This set of matched golf clubs normally sells for $350 *V* but during our anniversary sale it is available for only $265.

_____ 10. This set of matched golf clubs normally sells for $350 *V* during our anniversary sale, however, it is available for only $265.

_____ 11. This set of matched golf clubs normally sells for $350 *V* but during our anniversary sale is available for only $265.

_____ 12. A teenager carrying a noisy boom box lurched past Mrs. Howe *V* and sat down in the only unoccupied seat in the bus.

_____ 13. For several months General Benham had been receiving anonymous threats over the telephone *V* but had not reported them to the police.

_____ 14. For several months General Benham had been receiving anonymous threats over the telephone *V* but he had not reported them to the police.

_____ 15. The ill-mannered guard neither answered Marcy's question *V* nor invited her to step inside out of the rain.

_____ 16. The ill-mannered guard did not answer Marcy's question *V* nor did he invite her to step inside out of the rain.

_____ 17. The ill-mannered guard did not answer Marcy's question *V* moreover, he did not invite her to step inside out of the rain.

_____ 18. This television by itself sells for $672 *V* with its matching stand the price is $730.

_____ 19. The advertised price is $730 *V* but without the matching stand the price is only $672.

_____ 20. Ms. Shaw has used these videos in her seventh-grade class *V* she reports that the student response was good.

_____ 21. Ms. Shaw has used these videos in her seventh-grade class *V* and reports that the student response was good.

_____ 22. Ms. Shaw has used these videos in her seventh-grade class *V* the student response, she reports, was good.

_____ 23. Our special this week is the four-head video receiver pictured in our advertisement *V* we are offering it at the low price of $299.

_____ 24. You'll like its on-screen menu system *V* and inexperienced users will appreciate its easy-to-understand panel display.

_____ 25. Ms. Stern comes to our firm well-recommended *V* for the past four years she headed a work force of nearly seventy people.

_____ 26. Ms. Stern should go far with our firm *V* for she is intelligent and hard-working.

_____ 27. Dean Lewis accepted the students' petition *V* and promised that he would study it carefully.

_____ 28. *Ilex opaca* is an American holly with glossy leaves and red berries *V* the foliage and berries are often used for Christmas decorations.

_____ 29. Juniors in this program normally take History 350 *V* however, Dean Tate has allowed me to substitute Political Science 107.

_____ 30. A limited number of viewers have called this movie a masterpiece *V* but many others are bothered by its ambiguities.

NAME _____ SCORE _____

Directions: The following sentences contain fifty numbered spots between words or beneath words. (The number is beneath the word when the punctuation problem involves the use of an apostrophe in that word.) In the correspondingly numbered spaces at the left, write C if the punctuation is correct or W if it is incorrect.

1. _____   (1) Had we known that the lecture would attract such a large audience; we

2. _____   would have scheduled it for Farwell Hall, which has three hundred seats.

3. _____   (2) The average tourists' equipment consists of: a camera, a raincoat, dark

4. _____   glasses, and a guidebook.

5. _____   (3) Geoffrey Chaucer, who wrote *The Canterbury Tales,* is known for his

6. _____   realism, his humor, and his accurate observation.

7. _____   (4) The 1928 Olympic Games, by the way, made history for competitive

8. _____   events for women were introduced.

9. _____   (5) Mother was not amused when she discovered that the children had made

10. _____   a snowman and had used one of her new golf balls for it's nose.

11. _____   (6) Frank Duveneck, a portrait painter who was born in Kentucky on

12. _____   October 9, 1848, eventually settled in Cincinnati where he died in 1919.

13. _____   (7) "I distinctly heard someone say, 'What's that guy talking about?' " said the

14. _____   new teacher.

15. _____   (8) If you didn't draw this hilarious caricature of me, I wonder who's

16. _____   responsible for it?

17. _____   (9) "Please remember, my dear Miss. Scroggs," said the secretary, "that a

18. _____   neat tidy appearance is one of the best recommendations."

19. _____   (10) Dark clouds crept up from the west, and the hot, sultry air was ominously

20. _____   quiet.

21. _____   (11) When Mr. Davis finally does resign the position will probably be filled

22. _____   by one of the boss's nephews.

373

23. _____ (12) When we lived there, the village was peaceful and restful, now it has been
23

24. _____ ruined by noisy ill-mannered tourists.
24

25. _____ (13) Mr. Oldham's assessment for the new paving on Elm Street being, in his

26. _____ opinion, too high; he protested to Ned Lane, a member of the Council.
25   26

27. _____ (14) "Responsibility for the seating arrangement at the banquet will be

28. _____ someone else's, not your's," the chairperson told Edith.
27   28

29. _____ (15) A short, quite pathetic appeal was made to the mayor by an elderly
29

30. _____ woman whose property tax had been nearly doubled.
30

31. _____ (16) A fiery, political speech was made by our senior county commis-
31

32. _____ sioner who hopes to be reelected.
32

33. _____ (17) "This car seems to be pulling slightly to the left, I wonder if one of the
33

34. _____ tires is going flat?" said Marge.
34

35. _____ (18) Epictetus, a Greek Stoic who was originally a slave, taught in Rome until
35

36. _____ 90 A.D. when the emperor Domitian banished all philosophers.
36

37. _____ (19) This week you'll find real bargains at Shops-Mart in: light fixtures, paint,
37

38. _____ linens, and childrens' shoes.
38

39. _____ (20) "My briefcase isn't here in the car," said McCall; "I wonder if I could have
39

40. _____ left it in your office."
40

41. _____ (21) "We had a bad storm when I was out fishing in the bay two week's ago,"
41

42. _____ said Mark, who knew that Jo was a nervous landlubber.
42

43. _____ (22) The last bus from Lawrenceville having arrived with no passengers, Jim
43

44. _____ and Trudy walked slowly to their car and drove back to the farm.
44

45. _____ (23) "Let's drop the matter," said Anne impatiently. "After all these problems
45

46. _____ are nobody's business but mine."
46

47. _____ (24) Louisa is writing a book about her paternal grandmother who was a
47

48. _____ vigorous worker for womens' rights.
48

49. _____ (25) From the very first difficulties beset the planned expansion; finally
49   50

50. _____ resulting in the withdrawal of funds by the two principal backers.

NAME _____ SCORE _____

Directions: The following sentences contain fifty numbered spots between words or beneath words. (The number is beneath the word when the punctuation problem involves the use of an apostrophe in that word.) In the correspondingly numbered spaces at the left, write C if the punctuation is correct or W if it is incorrect.

1. _____   (1) The treasurer's report was so long, so disorganized, and so dull that some

2. _____   of the listeners dozed off at times.

3. _____   (2) At daybreak a crow parked itself outside our balcony and kept us awake

4. _____   with it's loud   raucous scolding.
                                    3   4

5. _____   (3) The dodo and the roc, both commonly found only in crossword puz-

6. _____   zles, are similar in some respects, and different in others.
                          5   6

7. _____   (4) The dodo, a bird that is now extinct, actually lived in Mauritius but the
                                                              7

8. _____   roc lived only in people's imagination.
                                    8

9. _____   (5) Rotary International was founded in Chicago, Illinois, in 1905, it now has
                                                               9   10

10. _____   chapters in more than seventy countries.

11. _____   (6) The Jensens sat in the airport for six long, tedious hours; their flight being
                                                         11   12

12. _____   delayed by what was called an equipment shortage.

13. _____   (7) Your equipment should consist of: heavy hiking boots, a waterproof
                                             13

14. _____   tarpaulin, and plenty of warm clothing.
                      14

15. _____   (8) Today I received from a travel agency a new calendar; on the cover
                                                             15

16. _____   theres a beautiful picture of the Bay of Naples
                     16

17. _____   (9) "A team that wont be beaten can't be beaten," said Coach Wellby, who is
                                    17   18

18. _____   hopelessly addicted to clichés.

19. _____ (10) In the outer lobby is a huge oil portrait of the founder of the firm; his
                                                                       19

20. _____   stern   humorless face adding to the austerity of the surroundings.
                     20

21. _____ (11) The midterm test will cover the following materials: the class lectures to
                                                               21

22. _____   date and chapters 2, 3, 4, and 5 of the text.
                     22

23. _____ (12) The play has received good reviews from the critics, I suppose it's

23 24

24. _____ impossible to get tickets at this late date.

25. _____ (13) "You agree with me, dont you," Jean answered, "that my suggestion was a

25

26. _____ reasonable one."

26

27. _____ (14) For most of this summer Martha has been borrowing one of my

28. _____ bikes; her's is now too old and too rusty to be safe.

27 28

29. _____ (15) Flight 723, which is scheduled to arrive here at 4:12 P.M. has been delayed

29

30. _____ at Topeka, Kansas, because of bad weather.

30

31. _____ (16) Coleman, the third baseman, threw down his glove, and screamed that the

31

32. _____ runner hadn't touched the base.

32

33. _____ (17) The art teacher, Miss. Philbrick, asked Janey if she had ever done any

33

34. _____ professional modeling?

34

35. _____ (18) Our neighbors, the Thomas's, have a new television set that has a much

35

36. _____ larger picture than our's.

36

37. _____ (19) The notice on the bulletin board announced the new schedule: breakfast

37

38. _____ at six-thirty, lunch at eleven-thirty, and dinner at six.

38

39. _____ (20) "After all my friends will help me out of this, they know that my word is

39 40

40. _____ as good as my bond," said Mr. Winther.

41. _____ (21) Julia's cousin Larry studied at Heidelberg, where he became well

41

42. _____ acquainted with Judge Coleman's only grandson Herman.

42

43. _____ (22) "Judd shouldn't have taken offense at my remark, I merely asked him if he

43

44. _____ was made up for a masquerade party?" said Eugene.

44

45. _____ (23) Dr. Andrews has written articles about child psychology but his own

45

46. _____ childrens' behavior in a group is far from admirable.

46

47. _____ (24) "The story line, the costumes, the music—everything must be changed,"

47

48. _____ said Cecil Burbank, the new director.

48

49. _____ (25) Laura is the kind of person who shops downtown until five oclock, and

49 50

50. _____ then complains about the crowded condition of the bus on her ride

home.

NAME _____ SCORE _____

Directions: Study these sentences for (1) the correct form of a principal part of a verb, (2) the correct subject–verb agreement, and (3) the correct tense of a verb. Underline every incorrect verb and write the correct form in the space at the left. No sentence contains more than two incorrect verb forms. Some sentences may be correct.

_____ 1. After setting in the hot sun all day, every one of the petunia plants
_____   I put out this morning has wilted badly.

_____ 2. Neither Dr. Alterton nor his assistant were able to make sense of
_____   the peculiar symbols written on the wooden slab.

_____ 3. Has either of your two roommates begun to be interviewed for a
_____   job after graduation?

_____ 4. One story that I've heard is that Judge Trowbridge payed back to
_____   the bank all of the money that his nephew had stole.

_____ 5. The mayor, along with three of her top aides, has been asked to
_____   set at the head table with the visiting dignitaries.

_____ 6. "I been hunting in these woods for fifty years but never before
_____   seen a critter like that one," said the guide.

_____ 7. Stan walked into the principal's office, laid his books on the table,
_____   and says, "I've come to the end of my rope."

_____ 8. There was only seven seconds left in the game when Pete West let
_____   fly from midcourt and sank the game-winning three-pointer.

_____ 9. A news story reports that the appearance of mysterious patterns
_____   in wheat fields have become a summer diversion in southern
_____   England.

_____ 10. After the eight-o'clock bell had rang, Mr. Towle said, "The fact
_____   that the weather is bad don't mean that we won't hold classes
_____   today."

_____ 11. I would have liked to have gone to the movie with you, but I saw
_____   that show last month in Dallas.

_____ 12. Don't it worry you that the price of your shares of stock have
_____   fallen by nearly thirty percent in four months?

_____ 13. Seated behind us were a woman with four children who noisily
_____   ate candy and drunk pop during the entire movie.

_____ 14. After the other officers had given their reports, the colonel said,
_____   "The evidence has shown that neither of the two incidents were
_____   the result of equipment failure."

_____ 15. There's been so many improvements made at the Lakeside Inn
_____ that it has became one of the most popular resorts in the state.

_____ 16. As we rose to leave the auditorium, Bart remarked, "I think our
_____ speaker could have chose a livelier topic to discuss."

_____ 17. In July heat records were broke on two days, but during August
_____ the range of temperatures were normal for the season.

_____ 18. Julie had just lain down for a short rest when her neighbor came
running over and tells her that there was a couple of raccoons in
_____ her vegetable garden.

_____ 19. The Associated Press reports that the search for possible survivors of the earthquake have been slowed because of repeated
_____ aftershocks that have shaken the area.

_____ 20. The magnitude of our budgetary problems have left a shadow
across the legislative process; no wonder that the confidence in
_____ our lawmakers has sank to new low levels.

_____ 21. The advertisement announcing that our entire stock of Nature's
_____ Own Vitamins are on sale has drawn huge crowds.

_____ 22. "It's been a hectic day," said Beth. "The two-o'clock bell has
_____ already rung, and I haven't eaten a bite of lunch yet."

_____ 23. "Commissioner Bunker's standards for the behavior of public
servants, including himself," the editor had written, "has always
_____ been minimal."

_____ 24. "Neither of the two Ford trucks in our lot have been drove more
_____ than forty thousand miles," said the salesperson.

_____ 25. The number of fatal accidents at the corner of Fifth and Oak has
_____ risen alarmingly over the past two years.

_____ 26. In the lobby there is a sofa and several overstuffed chairs where
_____ patients can set and read while waiting to see the dentist.

_____ 27. The leader of the gang, along with two of his followers, were lying
_____ wounded on the floor of the garage.

_____ 28. Not one of the paintings that were taken from the museum dur-
_____ ing the robbery last summer have been recovered.

_____ 29. The girls abandoned the sinking canoe and swam safely to shore,
_____ but unfortunately their pet dog was drownded.

_____ 30. Has either your teacher or the school counselor spoke to you
_____ about applying for a scholarship?

NAME _____ SCORE _____

Directions: Study the following sentences for poorly used pronouns. Look for wrong case forms, misspelled possessives, vague or inexact references. Circle each incorrect pronoun. In the space at the left of each pair of sentences, write the letter that identifies the correct sentence.

_____ 1. A. In years past, the personnel director of the laboratory would inquire about an applicant's personal life, including such things as whom were your associates.
   B. In years past the personnel director of the laboratory would inquire about an applicant's personal life, including such things as who were his or her associates.

_____ 2. A. Every guy at the dorm except Jacobs, Peterson, and me has already had his spring-term class schedule approved.
   B. Every guy at the dorm except Jacobs, Peterson, and I has already had their spring-term class schedule approved.

_____ 3. A. Four of us girls got in line for the ticket sale at seven in the morning, and then we were told that the office wouldn't open until noon.
   B. Four of we girls got in line for the ticket sale at seven in the morning, and then they told us that the office wouldn't open until noon.

_____ 4. A. "I'm supposed to ride in Phil's car," said Lew, "but, just between you and I, I'd prefer to ride in someone elses."
   B. "I'm supposed to ride in Phil's car," said Lew, "but, just between you and me, I'd prefer to ride in someone else's."

_____ 5. A. "I plan to become a forester," said Tom, "because it allows you to do your bit for saving the environment."
   B. "I plan to become a forester," said Tom, "because work in forestry allows a person to do his or her bit for saving the environment."

_____ 6. A. It said on television that the finalists, whomever they are, will meet for five games in Las Vegas.
   B. According to a television report, the finalists, whoever they are, will meet for five games in Las Vegas.

_____ 7. A. Ginny told her best friend, Marge, that she should lose at least five pounds.
   B. Ginny told her best friend, Marge, "I should lose at least five pounds."

_____ 8. A. "Dad is a dedicated fisherman, and he keeps trying to get my sister and me interested in fishing," said Mary Jane.
   B. "Dad is a dedicated fisherman, and he keeps trying to get my sister and I interested in it," said Mary Jane.

_____ 9. A. Mr. Capri's lawyer produced two witnesses who he said had been present when the alleged bribe offer was made.
   B. Mr. Capri's lawyer produced two witnesses whom he said had been present when the alleged bribe offer was made.

379

_____ 10. A. "All of us administrators are pleased," said Dean Powers, "that the college is attracting many adults into its Retraining Program."
   B. "The college is attracting many adults into their Retraining Program, which pleases all of we administrators," said Dean Powers.

_____ 11. A. A tourist whom we met at a filling station in Plainview told us that the highway for the next two miles is being resurfaced.
   B. A tourist who we met at a filling station in Plainview told us that they are resurfacing the highway for the next two miles.

_____ 12. A. My younger brother is a better mathematician than me, principally because he has taken several courses in it.
   B. My younger brother is a better mathematician than I, principally because he has taken several courses in mathematics.

_____ 13. A. It clearly states in the application form that you must provide a recent three-by-five picture of yourself.
   B. The application form clearly states that applicants must provide three-by-five pictures of themselves.

_____ 14. A. The person whom the Speaker of the House appoints to make this investigation must reconcile himself or herself to a thankless chore.
   B. The person who the Speaker of the House appoints to make this investigation must reconcile themself to a thankless chore.

_____ 15. A. The car ahead of our's was weaving so erratically that I didn't want to try to pass him.
   B. The car ahead of ours was weaving so erratically that I didn't want to try to pass it.

_____ 16. A. At the first pep rally the cheerleaders told we freshmen to wear our green T-shirts at every game.
   B. At the first pep rally the cheerleaders told us freshmen to wear our green T-shirts at every game.

_____ 17. A. "Is there anyone who you really think might get more votes than I in the primary election?" asked ex-Senator Wiley.
   B. "Is there anyone whom you really think might get more votes than me in the primary election?" asked ex-Senator Wiley.

_____ 18. A. The three new owners of the Busy Bee Store maintain that you can't find another merchant in town who's prices are lower than their's.
   B. The three new owners of the Busy Bee Store maintain that there isn't another merchant in town whose prices are lower than theirs.

_____ 19. A. Your brother likes to tease you. If it wasn't he who sent you the comic valentine, who do you think it might have been?
   B. Your brother likes to tease you. If it wasn't him who sent you the comic valentine, whom do you think it might have been?

_____ 20. A. "This notebook must be someone else's," said Martin. "Mine has an American flag stenciled on its cover."
   B. "This notebook must be someone elses," said Martin. "Mine has an American flag stenciled on it's cover."

NAME _____   SCORE _____

Directions: In the space at the left, write the *number* of the correct form given in parentheses.

_____ 1. I (1. couldn't have   2. couldn't of) finished typing my term paper even if I
_____   had worked on (1. steady   2. steadily) until midnight.

_____ 2. (1. Let us   2. Let's us) put in an extra hour on this project and finish it
_____   (1. faster   2. more faster) than in the time allotted for it.

_____ 3. "(1. Where   2. Where at) can I buy some of (1. them   2. those) huge sun-
_____   glasses like the ones you are wearing?" Ms. Tower asked Letty.

_____ 4. "I have no doubt," said Mrs. Lathrop, "(1. but what   2. that) my daughter
_____   will finally select the (1. more   2. most) expensive of the two dresses."

_____ 5. Our committee got a (1. real   2. really) early start, and by noon we had
_____   addressed (1. most   2. almost) all of the political pamphlets.

_____ 6. Coach Treadwell is (1. sure   2. surely) happy about the large (1. amount
_____   2. number) of junior-college transfers who turned out for the team.

_____ 7. "Old Hank Jones (1. use to   2. used to) appear (1. regular   2. regularly) at
_____   our church functions," said Mrs. Walker, "but I haven't seen him in months."

_____ 8. Frankly, I am (1. kind of   2. rather) surprised that our girls' team did as
_____   (1. good   2. well) as they did in the regional tournament.

_____ 9. As I stood up ready to get (1. off   2. off of) the bus, a fire engine swerved
_____   around the corner and came (1. awful   2. very) close to us.

_____ 10. (1. Due to   2. Because of) his bad eyesight, Mel didn't do very (1. good
_____   2. well) on the map-reading part of the test.

_____ 11. "I know that your uncle will feel (1. bad   2. badly) if he doesn't receive an
_____   (1. invite   2. invitation) to the wedding," said Aunt Yolanda.

_____ 12. "I think (1. this   2. this here) purple scarf would look (1. good   2. well)
_____   with your new suit," said the salesperson.

_____ 13. Judged on (1. this   2. these) new and stricter criteria, Ludlow's essay is
_____   clearly the (1. better   2. best) of the two finalists.

381

_____ 14. From his report, Jack sounded (1. as if   2. like) he had a (1. real   2. really)
_____   good time on his trip to Florida.

_____ 15. I wish Professor Lynn would talk (1. more slower   2. more slowly); I (1. can
_____   hardly   2. can't hardly) take notes when he is racing to finish his lecture.

_____ 16. The thing (1. that   2. what) really surprised the fire fighters is that no one
_____   was injured (1. bad   2. badly) in the spectacular fire.

_____ 17. A (1. couple   2. couple of) friends and I work out (1. regular   2. regularly)
_____   at the company's gymnasium.

_____ 18. (1. Lots of   2. Many) of the native people have (1. emigrated   2. immi-
_____   grated) because of the crop failures in their homeland.

_____ 19. That flower that you call an evening primrose (1. sure   2. surely) smells
_____   (1. sweet   2. sweetly).

_____ 20. The reason the deal fell through is (1. because   2. that) at the last minute
_____   the seller increased the price (1. considerable   2. considerably).

_____ 21. (1. Light-complexioned   2. Light-complected) people like you and me
_____   (1. shouldn't   2. hadn't ought to) stay out in the hot sun on a day like today.

_____ 22. (1. Because of   2. Due to) the infection in his eye, Darrell hasn't been able
_____   to study very (1. good   2. well) this week.

_____ 23. Now that he has lost weight, Graham looks quite (1. different   2. differ-
_____   ently) (1. from   2. than) the way he looks in these old photographs.

_____ 24. "I'm (1. enthused   2. enthusiastic) about my new job," said Malcolm. "It is
_____   interesting, and, best of all, it pays (1. good   2. well)."

_____ 25. By your answer to Mike's question, did you mean to (1. imply   2. infer) that
_____   you feel (1. bad   2. badly) about the election results?

NAME _____ SCORE _____

Directions: Each sentence has two italicized words or expressions. If you think that a word or expression is inappropriate in serious writing, write a correct form in the space at the left. If a word or expression is correct, write C in the space.

_____ 1. *Lying* at the side of the road was a plastic bag full of garbage that
_____   some tourist had apparently thrown from *their* car.

_____ 2. In this senior class there *are* only four or five people *whom* I think
_____   are capable of successful work at the graduate level.

_____ 3. The reward money was divided *among* four of *we* hikers who had
_____   turned in the fire alarm.

_____ 4. The mechanic *lay* down the wrench and explained to Roger and
_____   *I* what had to be done and what it would cost.

_____ 5. We were *plenty* surprised when we learned that there *was* only
_____   one teacher and eighteen pupils in the entire school.

_____ 6. "I doubt that fellows as short as you and *me* can play basketball
_____   *good* enough to earn a letter," Al said to Jeremy.

_____ 7. No one at headquarters was *suppose to* know *who* the new agent
_____   was reporting to in Berlin.

_____ 8. Sergeant Gross did not *suspicion* that quite a few of *we* men had
_____   been sneaking off to the movies in the village.

_____ 9. A gregarious person like Andy seems able to make *themself* feel
_____   right at home almost *anywheres.*

_____ 10. By the end of the second week every freshman should have *cho-*
_____   *sen* which social club *they* will join.

_____ 11. "Who can be *enthused* about *those kind* of video games?" asked
_____   Claire.

_____ 12. Just *like* I had predicted, after the speech there *wasn't* more than
_____   three or four questions from members of the audience.

383

_____ 13. Dan was *sure* surprised to learn that everyone in class except
_____ Marcia Lerner and *him* would have to take another test.

_____ 14. The reason there is a critical shortage is *because* neither of the two
_____ state-supported universities *is* turning out qualified engineers.

_____ 15. The thief, *whoever* he was, had apparently left the warehouse
_____ parking lot in a small truck that he had *stolen* earlier in the day.

_____ 16. "These people speak a language that is strange to us," said the
_____ guide, "but in truth they are really not much different *from* you
and *I.*"

_____ 17. *Has* either of the two plum trees you planted *began* to bear fruit
_____ yet?

_____ 18. *Due to* the icy condition of the roads, all of *we* latecomers were
_____ given excuses today.

_____ 19. The sale of season tickets for basketball games this year *has*
_____ declined *considerable.*

_____ 20. The missing climber's backpack was found *lying* at the bottom of
_____ a small crevasse, where it had apparently *lain* for several days.

_____ 21. Every one of the stocks that you recommended to my wife and
_____ *me* last year *has* declined in value.

_____ 22. All of us agree that *whoever* took the money from the Christmas
_____ Fund was *real* desperate.

_____ 23. The committee's choice for chairperson was Marge Bingham, not
_____ *I,* in spite of the fact that my experience is much broader than
her's.

_____ 24. Just between you and *me,* my parents don't approve of *rue* post-
_____ poning my senior year of college.

_____ 25. *Whom* do you suppose could have written *them* insulting anony-
_____ mous letters to the superintendent?

NAME _____ SCORE _____

Directions: In the spaces at the left, copy the correct forms given in parentheses.

_____
_____ 1. We took a cab to the auditorium, but when we arrived the (con-ference, conferrence) had (already, all ready) begun.

_____
_____ 2. The homemade warning device, although far from perfect, is (quiet, quite) (servicable, serviceable).

_____
_____ 3. The fast-talking salesman maintained that he was a (personal, personnel) friend of several New York (financeirs, financiers).

_____
_____ 4. "In my lifetime I (seized, siezed) many golden (opportunities, opportunitys) but couldn't hold on to them," Mr. Caldwell answered.

_____
_____ 5. "I'd hardly call this an (unforgetable, unforgettable) (dining, dinning) experience," said Sal as she set aside the bowl of luke-warm soup.

_____
_____ 6. "(Neither, Niether) of your two laboratory experiments was (completely, completly) satisfactory," said the lab assistant.

_____
_____ 7. The Acme Corporation has donated to the city a very (desirable, desireable) building (cite, sight, site) for the proposed convention center.

_____
_____ 8. "Just to be in the (presence, presents) of such a (fameous, famous) basketball star is a great honor," said the youngster.

_____
_____ 9. I haven't seen my neighbors lately; in all (likelihood, likelyhood, liklihood, liklyhood) (their, there, they're) out of town.

_____
_____ 10. Some people (beleive, believe) that the city engineer will (altar, alter) the specifications in order to attract more bidders.

_____
_____ 11. Remember, (its, it's) considered good manners to (complement, compliment) the hostess after a good meal.

_____
_____ 12. With my two time-consuming jobs, I assure you that I have no (leisure, liesure) time (activities, activitys) to speak of.

_____ 13. "Our negotiators managed to (affect, effect) an (advantageous,
_____ advantagous) settlement with the union," said Mr. Siebert.

_____ 14. (Unfortunately, Unfortunatly), similar (incidence, incidents) are
_____ being reported to the police with increasing frequency.

_____ 15. The judge (adviced, advised) the quarreling neighbors to settle
_____ their problem (peacably, peaceably) without outside help.

_____ 16. This semester Sherwood's work in mathematics has (shone,
_____ shown) a (noticable, noticeable) improvement.

_____ 17. The (principal, principle) of the school was not (deceived,
_____ decieved) by young Thompson's outlandish story.

_____ 18. After confessing to the theft, the man (lead, led) the officers to the
_____ place in the barren (desert, dessert) where he had buried the loot.

_____ 19. "I think (your, you're) being very (courageous, couragous)," said
_____ Belinda to the young fire fighter.

_____ 20. "Frankly, Alice," said Marlene, "I think that your new friend is
_____ (outrageously, outragously) (conceited, concieted)."

_____ 21. The three (attornies, attorneys) representing our competitor
_____ were much younger (than, then) I had expected.

_____ 22. The bank president rewarded the (casheir, cashier) (who's,
_____ whose) quick thinking had thwarted the holdup.

_____ 23. For her (neice's, niece's) birthday Ms. Simpson sent her a box of
_____ monogrammed (stationary, stationery).

_____ 24. "I predict that our (cheif, chief) of police will (loose, lose) his job
_____ after the next election," said Alderman Whiteside.

_____ 25. After (poring, pouring) over dozens of books in the library, I feel
_____ that I have done a (thorough, through) job of researching the
matter.

NAME _____ SCORE _____

Directions: Each sentence contains two words from the first half of the spelling list. In each of these words at least one letter is missing. Write the words, correctly spelled, in the spaces at the left.

_____   1. The new dorm—tory, which will be finished by next fall, will
_____   ac—modate three hundred students.

_____   2. I am cer—n that you and your family will enjoy your tour of
_____   Great Brit—n.

_____   3. The results of most of our school's ath—tic contests for the past
_____   two seasons have been dis—pointing.

_____   4. In class were between thirty-five and fo—ty enthu—tic students.

_____   5. The careless, a—ward boy accident—y broke one of the jars.

_____   6. The new clerk in the office is sometimes embar—sed by his glar-
_____   ing mistakes in gram—r.

_____   7. We were dis—atisfied with the poor service and the ex—rbitant
_____   price of the meals.

_____   8. Caldwell is building a large apartment complex ac—oss the street
_____   from a large cem—tery.

_____   9. Janice is an exception—y good student of for—n languages.

_____ 10. Delegates are arriving for an international confer—nce con-
_____   cerned with protecting the env—nment.

Directions: These sentences contain thirty italicized words from the first half of the spelling list. A sentence may have no misspelled words, one misspelled word, or two misspelled words. Underline each misspelled word and write it, correctly spelled, in a space at the left.

_____
_____
1. *Confidentially,* Mr. Burke's resignation *dosen't* make any real *difference* in our company's long-range plans.

_____
_____
2. Although only an *amateur,* Ms. Davis has *aquired* a collection of early-American pewter that is *amoung* the best in the nation.

_____
_____
3. *Finally,* late in *Febuary,* an *eminent* retired general spoke out strongly against the proposed treaty.

_____
_____
4. One of the *candidates* for mayor gave the *committee* a lengthy *explaination* of his financial dealings.

_____
_____
5. This applicant is an *efficient* worker whose wide *experience* makes her *especialy* well equipped to replace Thornton.

_____
_____
6. *Apparently* the new *apparatus* will cost the county *approximately* three thousand dollars.

_____
_____
7. *During* your college days, ownership of an *excellent dictionary* is a necessity.

_____
_____
8. The visitor's harsh *criticism* of our *goverment* was, we all agreed, not *appropriate.*

_____
_____
9. "I *allways* went to chapel when I was in school," said Uncle James. "*Attendance,* I might add, was not *compulsory.*"

_____
_____
10. *Accompaning* the letter was a brochure with a *discription* of the proposed *condominium.*

NAME _____   SCORE _____

Directions: Each sentence contains two words from the second half of the spelling list. In each of these words at least one letter is missing. Write the words, correctly spelled, in the spaces at the left.

_____   1. Densmore found it nec—sary to borrow money in order to fin-
_____   ish his sop—ore year of college.

_____   2. I can rec—mend Ms. Lukens highly; I am sure that she will do
_____   the work satisfa—ly.

_____   3. After speaking to Prof—r Quigley, I felt more opt—tic about
_____   being able to finish the course.

_____   4. The secr—ry of the local chamber of commerce ordered a large
_____   quan—ty of the booklets.

_____   5. Leonard's parents lost pract—ly all of their pos—sions in the fire.

_____   6. The three of us left the chemistry lab—atory and walked to a
_____   nearby rest—nt for lunch.

_____   7. The superinten—nt ordered me to return all of the books to the
_____   school lib—ry.

_____   8. The teacher said that Angela's interp—tation of the poem was
_____   highly orig—nal.

_____   9. Oc—sionally Jenny would su—prise the family by offering to
_____   plan and cook a meal for them.

_____   10. The spe—ch instructor criticized my pron—ciation of a few his-
_____   torical place names.

Directions: These sentences contain thirty italicized words from the second half of the spelling list. A sentence may have no misspelled words, one misspelled word, or two misspelled words. Underline each misspelled word and write it, correctly spelled, in a space at the left.

_____
_____

1. You must admit that our Drama Club has put on several *really successful preformances.*

_____

2. Some people look upon *politics* as a somewhat *rediculous pastime.*

_____
_____

3. Last month I worked overtime on *Wednesday* the *ninth* and Saturday the *twelfth.*

_____
_____

4. In his writings one can find many *specimans* of *propaganda* that play upon racial *prejudices.*

_____
_____

5. The *sergeant* and I often go to the gym to exercise on the *parallel* bars to develop grace and *rythm.*

_____
_____

6. My lack of *preserverence* can *undoubtably* be explained in impressive sounding *psychological* terms.

_____
_____

7. I *regard* it a *privilege* to interview such a prominent member of the British *Parliament.*

_____
_____

8. My *pardner's schedual* is so full that he never has time for more than a hurried *sandwich* at noon.

_____

9. "I *usualy* avoid parsnips and *similiar vegetables*," said Mr. Jefferson.

_____
_____

10. I *recognize* the fact that a person of my *temperment* should *probably* avoid being around small children.

Progress Test 18

Plurals and Capitals (Lesson 28)

NAME _____   SCORE _____

Directions: Write the plural form or forms for each of the following words. When in doubt, consult your dictionary. If two forms are given, write both of them.

1. beef   _____   _____

2. child   _____   _____

3. curio   _____   _____

4. donkey   _____   _____

5. fox   _____   _____

6. graffito   _____   _____

7. handkerchief   _____   _____

8. hippopotamus   _____   _____

9. knife   _____   _____

10. mouse   _____   _____

11. oasis   _____   _____

12. opportunity   _____   _____

13. phenomenon   _____   _____

14. portico   _____   _____

15. process   _____   _____

16. roomful   _____   _____

17. species   _____   _____

18. stadium   _____   _____

19. syllabus   _____   _____

20. trout   _____   _____

21. valley   _____   _____

22. variety   _____   _____

23. waltz   _____   _____

24. witch   _____   _____

25. workman   _____   _____

Directions: The following sentences contain fifty numbered words. If a word is correctly capitalized, write C in the space with the corresponding number. If a word should not be capitalized, write W in the space.

1	2	3
4	5	6
7	8	9
10	11	12
13	14	15
16	17	18
19	20	21
22	23	24
25	26	27
28	29	30
31	32	33
34	35	36
37	38	39
40	41	42
43	44	45
46	47	48
49	50	

(1) My advisor, Professor Samuels, suggested that during my Sophomore year I take Accounting 194 and elective courses in Economics, English History, Sociology, and German.

(2) On their recent trip to the East, Mother and Aunt Lydia visited the Museum Of The City Of New York, which is on Fifth Avenue at 104th Street.

(3) Bob's native American fishing guide gave him a photograph of Mount Baker, a snow-capped Mountain of the Cascade Range Northeast of Seattle.

(4) The day after the Fourth Of July holiday the Professor of my class in American Literature tested us on our reading of Poe's *Fall Of The House Of Usher.*

(5) Formerly a Captain in the United States Coast Guard, Linda's Father is now an assistant to Secretary Watkins of the Department Of The Interior.

NAME _____ SCORE _____

Directions: If you find a misspelled word, underline it and write it correctly at the left. (Consider an omitted or misused apostrophe a punctuation error, not a spelling error.) In the column of figures at the left, circle numbers that identify errors in the sentence. Each sentence contains at least one of the following errors:

1. The group of words is a sentence modifier.
2. There is a dangling or misplaced modifier.
3. There is a misused verb (wrong number, tense, or principal part).
4. There is a poorly used pronoun (wrong number or case form, or inexact reference).
5. There is an error in punctuation.

_____
1 2 3 4 5

(1) A car that was backing out of the restaurant parking lot had a breifcase setting on its top but when I tried to signal them they just waved and drove off.

_____
1 2 3 4 5

(2) Last Sunday, while looking out the window of my new condominium, an ugly rat come out from some bushes and ran across the lawn.

_____
1 2 3 4 5

(3) "The simple construction of the five opening lines of the poem result in an especially pleasing rythm," Professor Quigley told his class of literature majors.

_____
1 2 3 4 5

(4) The boss's inability to make quick decisions, as well as her often faulty judgment, have certianly brought about most of our companys really serious problems.

_____
1 2 3 4 5

(5) The chair of the board, to use an obvious example, a person with admireable instincts and real dedication but little skill in management.

_____
1 2 3 4 5

(6) "The fact that advance ticket sales have been dissappointing don't mean that the concert will be postponed, does it," the worried young sophomore asked.

_____
1 2 3 4 5

(7) "The preformance of our defensive backs in the last three games have been less than outstanding," said our head coach who sometimes uses understatement to emphasize his points.

_____
1 2 3 4 5

(8) Trying to decide on our route, it was pointed out that the shorter one was quite hilly and winding, therefore the shorter one would very likely take more time than the longer one.

_____
1 2 3 4 5

(9) Theres not more than three or four people in this entire city goverment whom I'd say are capable of leadership in difficult times.

_____
1 2 3 4 5

(10) The three older women always arrived at the class earlier than the other students, they also managed to quickly, carefully, and throughly complete every assignment.

393

1 2 3 4 5   (11) Assembling in the superintendent's office at ten o'clock, Mr. Swift asked we seven freshmen if we wanted to form an honors class?

1 2 3 4 5   (12) My neighbor's oldest son, for example, who confidently selected a course in engineering, in spite of the fact that his knowledge of mathmatics and physics were slight.

1 2 3 4 5   (13) Apparently the mischievous youngsters choice of companions have given him many oppertunities to get into real trouble.

1 2 3 4 5   (14) Although both Thelma and Mary Lou were named in the grandmother's will neither one of them have as yet received their share of the inheritance.

1 2 3 4 5   (15) How can you maintain that this dictionery is yours when someone else's name and address is stamped on its inside cover.

1 2 3 4 5   (16) Their delay in making shipments, in addition to their higher prices, have lost business for them, they're no longer serious compitition for us.

1 2 3 4 5   (17) "Just between you and I," said Eddie, "there's to many people in this elevator; let's wait for the next one."

1 2 3 4 5   (18) The amateur entrepreneur explained to my partner and I that the influx of orders from small investors have undoubtedly effected the market unfavorably.

1 2 3 4 5   (19) Bruce's face turned flaming red upon hearing that his grade on the literature midterm test was higher then anyone elses.

1 2 3 4 5   (20) I'm quiet sure that I won't get the job, I was told that to be hired a person either had to be a union member or have their apprentice card.

1 2 3 4 5   (21) The article concluded with the following sentence; "Part of the credit should go to whomever supplies the restaurant with its incredibly fresh vegetables."

1 2 3 4 5   (22) People in our neighborhood are extremely dissatisfied with the maintainence work of the Highway Department, there's still several deep chuckholes in our street.

1 2 3 4 5   (23) We were unhappily supprised to hear the mayor say, "Neither of these projects, although desperately needed, have been funded, our repair fund only has four thousand dollars left in it."

1 2 3 4 5   (24) There having been, if I remember correctly, two or three productions of our drama association that many in the audience nearly thought were of professional quality.

1 2 3 4 5   (25) After crossing the boundary into the next country, bad driving conditions can be expected for approximately fourty miles; the government having neglected the roads and bridges outrageously.

Progress Test 20

General Review: Proofreading

NAME _____ SCORE _____

Directions: If you find a misspelled word, underline it and write it correctly at the left. (Consider an omitted or misused apostrophe a punctuation error, not a spelling error.) Circle at least one of the numbers at the left:

1. The sentence is correct.
2. There is a dangling or misplaced modifier.
3. There is a misused verb.
4. There is a misused pronoun.
5. There is an error in punctuation.

_____
1 2 3 4 5

(1) While walking down the slippery wooden steps to the beach, a most embarassing thing happened to my escort and I.

_____
1 2 3 4 5

(2) In the margin of my theme Professor Jenkins had written this note: "You can now see, can't you, that the omission of two commas from this sentence have produced a humerous effect."

_____
1 2 3 4 5

(3) The eminent critic nearly spent forty-five minutes giving us an extraordinary explaination of one of the short poems we had read.

_____
1 2 3 4 5

(4) Clancy, a chunky, pleasant sophomore whom I had known in high school, stopped me and said, "Tell me, friend, what you thought about that last test we took in mathematics."

_____
1 2 3 4 5

(5) "The usual procedure," explained the receptionist, "is that Ms. Stanton's secretary or one of her assistants are on duty until five oclock on Wednesdays."

_____
1 2 3 4 5

(6) I could hardly believe what I had just heard, the superintendent had never before ever spoke so harshly to any of we students.

_____
1 2 3 4 5

(7) The frightened little boy told Mother and me that he had become separated from his parents, had wandered away from the other picnickers, and had been chased by a fierce dog.

_____
1 2 3 4 5

(8) Beyond the village of Greenville the motorist must procede cautiously, I have been told that they are resurfacing the highway for approximately ninety miles.

_____
1 2 3 4 5

(9) If anyone tells me that any child can learn to, with patient teaching, play a musical instrument, I'll give them a real arguement.

_____
1 2 3 4 5

(10) On the last night of Homecoming Week there is usualy a banquet at which the college president or the football coach give the alumni an inspirational speech.

_____
1 2 3 4 5

(11) Apparently every guy in our dorm except you and I has already had a conferrence with their academic adviser.

_____ (12) "The *Santa Maria* wasn't Columbus's favorite ship," explained
1 2 3 4 5   Dr. Slade. "After its destruction he is quoted as saying that it was
                          'too weighty and not suitable for making discoveries.' "

_____ (13) "There's probably only three or four boys on this team whom I
1 2 3 4 5   think stand a chance of receiving college athletic scholarships,"
                          said Coach Wills who is normally quite optimistic.

_____ (14) "I'm absolutely sure that the suspected troublemakers about
1 2 3 4 5   whom the principal of the school has been talking are not you
                          and I," Jacklin confidently told his pal Barnhart.

_____ (15) After reading the pamphlet you brought me from the library,
1 2 3 4 5   my understanding of the history, purpose and accompolish-
                          ments of the United Nations have been broadened.

_____ (16) Unfortunately, many intelligent and conscientious high school
1 2 3 4 5   graduates lack enough funds to go directly to college, which is
                          an outrageous situation.

_____ (17) The person whom I was referred to told me that I would have
1 2 3 4 5   to only wait a few more days before learning whether I or one
                          of the other contestants have won the first prize.

_____ (18) Having paid my fine at the local sheriff's office, our next desti-
1 2 3 4 5   nation was Centerville where I understand they also have
                          extreamly strict laws relating to speeding.

_____ (19) The personnel director replied, "Our company plans to within
1 2 3 4 5   a month or so hire a new financial adviser whom we all hope
                          will solve these troublesome problems for us."

_____ (20) "Dont it seem unusual that every one of us five trainees received
1 2 3 4 5   the same letter of recommendation from the boss?" asked Stan.

_____ (21) The police sergeant approached my roommate and me, opened
1 2 3 4 5   his notebook, and asked, "Has either one of you ever before seen
                          the hammer that was found lying near the front door?"

_____ (22) Miss Perkins was a truely dedicated teacher, she seemed always
1 2 3 4 5   ready to graciously and uncomplainingly give her time to
                          whomever came to her for help.

_____ (23) The members of the planning committee have studied these
1 2 3 4 5   problems and have become convinced that neither of the two
                          suggested remedies has been satisfactorily researched.

_____ (24) This applicant has only been studying Russian for three semes-
1 2 3 4 5   ters, his knowledge of the grammar, literature, and pronounci-
                          ation are quite limited.

_____ (25) The fact that your niece's careless handling of money could
1 2 3 4 5   result in her loosing the property to the mortgage holder don't
                          seem to trouble either she or her husband.

Appendix A

Study Skills: Basic Tools for College Work

The ability to write well is a great advantage to a college student. But there are other skills that you should master early in your college career. Using the dictionary, outlining, paraphrasing, and summarizing written material will be necessary almost from the first day of class. Managing your time is extremely important for success in college. The following sections will serve as an introduction to these very important skills.

Use of the Dictionary

You will soon find that a desk dictionary is as necessary to your writing as pen and paper. A good one is worth every cent of its cost; don't economize on a paperback pocket version and expect it to serve you adequately. Your instructor will probably recommend any of the following:

The American Heritage Dictionary, Third Edition
The Random House *Webster's College Dictionary*
Webster's Tenth New Collegiate Dictionary
Webster's New World Dictionary of the American Language, Third College Edition

Make your dictionary earn its price. Use it. Keep it near you when you study or write. It's a trove of information and will tell you much more than the mere meanings of words. Before you begin to use your dictionary, look inside the covers to see what is printed on the endpapers. It may be something you'll want to refer to often. Browse through the first few pages—especially those that explain the dictionary's system of pronunciation symbols, indication of preferred spellings and pronunciations, treatment of alphabetical order, usage notes, arrangement of multiple meanings, and notation for parts of speech. Then turn to the back pages. Does the dictionary have separate listings for geographic and biographical names? Does it give tables of weights and measures, rules for punctuation and mechanics? If you know what extra content your dictionary holds, you may be able to save yourself time, bother, and even cold cash when the need arises for some odd little fact.

1. Spelling. The dictionary will, of course, give the correct spelling of a word—sometimes two correct spellings, of which the first entry is usually the more widely used spelling.

---

high profile to **H.I.M.**

hi·jack or **high·jack** (hi´ jak´), *v.,* **-jacked, -jack·ing,** *n.* —*v.t.* **1.** to seize (an airplane or other vehicle) by threat or by force, esp. for ransom or political objectives. **2.** to steal (cargo) from a truck or other vehicle after forcing it to stop: *to hijack a load of whiskey.* **3.** to rob (a vehicle) after forcing it to stop: *They hijacked the truck outside the city.* —*n.* **4.** an act or instance of hijacking. [1920-25, *Amer.;* of uncert. orig.]
hi·jack·er or **high·jack·er** (hi´ jak´ ər), *n.* a person who hijacks. [1920-25, *Amer.*]

The *Random House Webster's College Dictionary* by Random House, Inc. Copyright © 1996 by Random House, Inc. Reprinted by permission of Random House, Inc.

The dictionary will also give you information on how compounds or near-compounds should be written. Of the ten entries in the following excerpt, four are written as one word, one may be solid or hyphenated, three are hyphenated, and two appear as two separate words.

> **fly´ ball´**, *n.* a baseball batted up into the air. [1860–65, *Amer.*]
> **fly·belt** (flī´belt), *n.* an area overrun with tsetse flies. [1890–95]
> **fly·blow** (flī´blō´), *v.*, **-blew, -blown, -blow·ing**, *n.* —*v.t.* **1.** to deposit eggs or larvae on (meat or other food). —*n.* **2.** one of the eggs or young larvae of a blowfly, deposited on meat or other food. [1550–60]
> **fly·blown** (flī´blōn´), *adj.* **1.** covered with flyblows: *flyblown meat.* **2.** tainted or contaminated; spoiled. [1565–75]
> **fly´ book´**, *n.* a booklike case for artificial fishing flies. [1840–50]
> **fly·boy** (flī´boi´), *n. Slang.* a member of the U.S. Air Force, esp. a pilot. [1945–50, *Amer.*]
> **fly´-by´** or **fly´-by´**, *n., pl.* **-bys. 1.** the flight of a spacecraft close enough to a celestial object, as a planet, to gather scientific data. **2. a.** a low-altitude flight of an aircraft for the benefit of ground observers. **b.** FLYOVER (def. 1). [1950–55, *Amer.*]
> **fly´-by-night´**, *adj.* **1.** not reliable or well established, esp. in business, and primarily interested in making a quick profit: *a fly-by-night operation.* **2.** not lasting; impermanent; transitory. —*n.* Also, **fly´-by-night´·er. 3.** a debtor who attempts to evade creditors. **4.** a fly-by-night person or business. [1790–1800]
> **fly´-by-wire´**, *adj.* (of an aircraft or spacecraft) actuated entirely by electronic controls. [1970–75]
> **fly´-cast´**, *v.i.* **-cast, -casting.** to fish with a fly rod and an artificial fly as a lure, casting the fly with a whiplike motion of the rod and a length of line pulled from the reel before the cast. [1885–90]

Can you look up the spelling of a word in the dictionary if you can't spell the word to begin with? Yes, almost always. Words like *phobia, pneumatic, rhyme, xylophone,* and a few others in which the first or second letter is the doubtful point may give trouble, but one or two searches under likely combinations will usually turn up the answer.

2. Pronunciation. Before you can use your dictionary effectively, you must understand its pronunciation symbols. In the following entry, the material within parentheses gives other information besides a representation of the sounds of the letters. (1) There is an alternate pronunciation of the second syllable. (2) The primary stress is on the third syllable and the secondary (or lesser) stress is on the first syllable. (3) Although the boldface entry shows that the word has five syllables, the pronunciation transcription shows two hyphens, indicating the two permissible points where the word may be broken at the end of a line.

> **in·di·gest·i·ble** (ĭn´ dĭ-jĕs´ tə-bəl, -dī-) *adj.* Difficult or impossible to digest: *an indigestible meal.* —**in´ di·gest´ i·bil´ i·ty** *n.* — **in´ di·gest´ i·bly** *adv.*

The presence of more than one pronunciation means that different people in different parts of the country pronounce the word differently. It does not mean that one is right and the other wrong. Look up the pronunciations of the following:

1. acclimate
2. adult
3. Caribbean
4. decadent
5. desperado
6. drama
7. exquisite
8. neither
9. pejorative
10. pianist
11. processes
12. sonorous

3. Plurals. If you are not sure about the correct plural of a noun, your dictionary will settle the question.

> **cur·ric·u·lar** \kə-ˈri-kyə-lər\ *adj* (ca. 1909) : of or relating to a curriculum
> **cur·ric·u·lum** \-ləm\ *n, pl* **-la** \-lə\ *also* **-lums** [NL, fr. L, running, course] (1633) **1 :** the courses offered by an educational institution **2 :** a set of courses constituting an area of specialization
> **cur·ric·u·lum vi·tae** \kə-ˈri-kyə-ləm-ˈvē-ˌtī, -kə-ləm-, -ˈwē-ˌtī, -ˈvī-ˌtē\ *n, pl* **cur·ric·u·la vitae** \-lə\ [L, course of (one's) life] (1902) : a short account of one's career and qualifications prepared typically by an applicant for a position

Look up the correct plurals of the following:

1. adieu	4. bus	7. genus	10. radius
2. appendix	5. crocus	8. mother-in-law	11. solo
3. beau	6. cupful	9. ox	12. species

4. Capitalization. Problems of capitalization may also be referred to your dictionary. You know, of course, that proper nouns—that is, names of persons and places—are capitalized. You know that common nouns are not capitalized. But often the real question is whether a noun is used in its proper sense or its common sense. With the help of your dictionary, try to determine whether the italicized words in the following sentences should be capitalized:

1. She ordered *french fries* with her steak.
2. This should be set up in *roman* type.
3. Many students do not understand *roman* numerals.
4. Later in life he was attracted to the *christian* religion.
5. He brought back some very fine *china* from *china*.

5. Principal Parts of Verbs. If you are not sure whether to say, "His coat was laying on the bed" or "His coat was lying on the bed," whether to say, "My sister growed," or "My sister grew," the dictionary will help you.

> **grow** \ˈgrō\ *vb* **grew** \grü\; **grown** \ˈgrōn\; **grow·ing** [ME *growen*, fr. OE *grōwan*; akin to OHG *gruowan* to grow] *vi* (bef. 12c) **1 a :** to spring up and develop to maturity **b :** to be able to grow in some place or situation <trees that ~ only in the tropics> **c :** to assume some relation through or as if through a process of natural growth <ferns *~ing* from the rocks> **2 a :** to increase in size by addition of material either by assimilation into the living organism or by accretion in a non-biological process (as crystallization) **b :** INCREASE, EXPAND <*~s* in wisdom> **3 :** to develop from a parent source <the book *grew* out of a series of lectures> **4 a :** to pass into a condition : BECOME <*grew* pale> **b :** to have an increasing influence <habit *~s* on a person> **c :** to become increasingly acceptable or attractive <didn't like it at first, but it *grew* on him> ~ *vt* **1 :** to cause to grow : PRODUCE <~ wheat> **2 :** DEVELOP **5** — **grow·er** \ˈgrō(-ə)r\ *n* — **grow·ing·ly** \ˈgrō-in-lē\ *adv*

Because *grow* is an irregular verb and does not form the past by adding *ed*, clearly, "My sister *grew*" is the correct choice. Note that *grow* is identified as both *vi* and *vt*, that is, as an intransitive verb and a transitive one. An intransitive verb does not act on an object; a transitive verb does. Now look up *lay* and *lie* in the dictionary. Why is "His coat was *lying* on the bed" the better sentence?

You should know the principal parts of the following troublesome verbs:

1. bring	5. do	9. hang
2. burst	6. drag	10. see
3. buy	7. drown	11. shine
4. dive	8. eat	12. take

6. Meaning. Many words, some of them very ordinary words, have a variety of meanings. The dictionary lists and separates all the definitions and gives their applications.

lead[1] (lēd), *v.,* **led, lead·ing,** *n., adj.* —*v.t.* **1.** to go before or with to show the way; conduct or escort; guide: *to lead a group on a hike.* **2.** to conduct by holding and guiding: *to lead a horse by a rope.* **3.** to influence or induce; cause: *What led her to change her mind?* **4.** to guide in direction, course, action, opinion, etc.; bring: *You can lead him around to your point of view.* **5.** to go through or pass (time, life, etc.): *to lead a full life.* **6.** to conduct or bring (water, wire, etc.) in a particular course. **7.** (of a road, passage, etc.) to serve to bring (a person) to a place: *The next street will lead you to the post office.* **8.** to take or bring: *The visitors were led into the senator's office.* **9.** to be in control or command of; direct: *He led the British forces during the war.* **10.** to go at the head of or in advance of (a procession, list, body, etc.); proceed first in: *The mayor will lead the parade.* **11.** to be superior to; have the advantage over: *The first baseman leads his teammates in runs batted in.* **12.** to have top position or first place in: *Iowa leads the nation in corn production.* **13.** to have the directing or principal part in: *Who is going to lead the discussion?* **14.** to act as leader of (an orchestra, band, etc.); conduct. **15.** to begin a hand in a card game with (a card or suit specified). **16.** to aim and fire a weapon ahead of (a moving target) in order to allow for the travel of the target while the missile is reaching it.
—*v.i.* **17.** to act as a guide; show the way. **18.** to afford passage to a place: *That path leads directly to the house.* **19.** to go first; be in advance. **20.** to result in; tend toward (usu. fol. by *to*): *The incident led to her resignation.* **21.** to take the directing or principal part. **22.** to take the offensive. **23.** to make the first play in a card game. **24.** to be led or submit to being led, as a horse. **25.** (of a runner in baseball) to leave a base before the delivery of a pitch (often fol. by *away*). **26. lead off, a.** to being; start. **b.** *Baseball.* to be the first player in the batting order or the first batter in an inning. **27. lead on,** to mislead.
—*n.* **28.** the first or foremost place; position in advance of others: *to take the lead in the race.* **29.** the extent of such an advance position. **30.** a person or thing that leads. **31.** a leash. **32.** a suggestion or piece of information that helps to direct or guide; tip; clue. **33.** a guide or indication of a road, course, method, etc., to follow. **34.** precedence; example; leadership. **35. a.** the principal part in a play. **b.** the person who plays it. **36. a.** the act or right of playing first in a card game. **b.** the card, suit, etc., so played. **37.** the opening paragraph of a newspaper story, serving as a summary. **38.** an often flexible and insulated single conductor, as a wire, used in electrical connections. **39.** the act of taking the offensive. **40.** *Naut.* **a.** the direction of a rope, wire, or chain. **b.** Also called **leader.** any of various devices for guiding a running rope. **41.** an open channel through a field of ice. **42.** the act of aiming a weapon ahead of a moving target. **43.** the distance ahead of a moving target that a weapon must be aimed in order to hit it. **44.** the first of a series of boxing punches.
—*adj.* **45.** most important; principal; leading; first: *a lead editorial.* **46.** (of a runner in baseball) nearest to scoring.
-*Idiom* **47. lead someone on a (merry) chase** or **dance,** to entice someone into difficulty and confusion by behaving unpredictably. **48. lead up to, a.** to prepare the way for. **b.** to approach (something gradually. [bef. 900; ME *leden,* OE *lǣdan* (causative of *lithan* to go, travel), c. OS *lē djan,* OHG *leiten,* ON *leitha;* akin to LODE]

7. Appropriate Use. A certain word, either in all of its uses or in some of its special meanings, is effective if it is appropriate to the occasion, the purpose, the time, and the place of its use. By means of usage labels, such as *Slang, Colloq., Dial., Archaic, Obs., Illit.,* a dictionary tries to indicate that a certain word has a restricted appropriateness. (Note that dictionaries may vary in their application of these labels.)

Examine this selection from *Webster's New World Dictionary,* in which four uses are labeled *Colloq.,* four *Slang,* and one *Archaic.* Some dictionaries use *Substandard* for *Slang* and *Informal* for *Colloq.* Words without any usage label are usually appropriate at all times, on every occasion, in every situation.

> **good·ly**[1] (good´ ē) *n., pl.* **good´ ies** [Colloq.] **1** something considered very good to eat, as a piece of candy ***2** GOODY-GOODY —*adj.* [Colloq.] GOODY-GOODY —*interj.* a child's exclamation of approval or delight
> **good·ly**[2] (good´ ē) *n., pl.* **good´ ies** [<GOODWIFE] [Archaic] a woman, esp. an old woman or housewife, of lowly social status: used as a title with the surname
> **Good·year** (good´ yir'), **Charles** 1800-60; U.S. inventor: originated the process for vulcanizing rubber
> **goody-goody** (good´ ē good´ ē) *adj.* [redupl. of GOODY[1]] [Colloq.] moral or pious in an affected or canting way—**n.* [Colloq.] a goody-goody person Also **goodly-two-shoes** (-tōō ´ shōōz´)
> ***gooey** (gōō´ ē) *adj.* **goo´ li·er, goo´ li·est** [GOO + -EY] [Slang] **1** sticky, as glue **2** sticky and sweet **3** overly sentimental
> **goof** (gōōf) *n.* [prob. < dial. [goff < Fr goffe, stupid < It goffo] **1** a stupid, silly, or credulous person **2** a mistake; blunder —*vi.* [Slang] **1** to make a mistake; blunder, fail, etc. **2** to waste time, shirk one's duties, etc.: (usually with *off* or *around*)
> ***goof·ball** (-bôl´) *n.* [prec. + BALL[1]] [Slang] a pill containing a barbiturate, or sometimes a stimulant drug, tranquilizer, etc., esp. when used nonmedicinally Also **goof ball**
> **goof-off** (-ôf´) *n.* a person who wastes time or avoids work; shirker
> **goofy** (gōōf´ ē) *adj.* **goof´ li·er, goof´ li·est** [Slang] like or characteristic of a goof; stupid and silly —**goof´ li·ly** *adv.* —**goof´ li·ness** *n.*

Webster's New World Dictionary of the American Language, Third College Edition. Copyright © 1988 by
Simon and Schuster, Inc. Reprinted by permission.

Where the labels *Slang, Colloq.,* and so on are inapplicable, a dictionary may give, at the end of the entry, a short paragraph or two of usage information. (For this purpose *American Heritage* makes use of a panel of consultants.)

> **dec·i·mate** (děs´ ə-māt´) *tr.v.* **-mat·ed, -mat·ing, -mates. 1.** To destroy or kill a large part of (a group). **2.** *Usage Problem.* **a.** To inflict great destruction or damage on: *The fawns decimated my sister's rose bushes.* **b.** To reduce markedly in amount: *a profligate heir who decimated his trust fund.* **3.** To select by lot and kill one in every ten of. [Latin *decimāre, decimāt-,* to punish every tenth person, from *decimus,* tenth, from *decem,* ten. See **dekm** in Appendix.] —**dec´ i·ma´ tion** *n.*
>
> **USAGE NOTE:** *Decimate* originally referred to the killing of every tenth person, a punishment used in the Roman army for mutinous legions. Today this meaning is commonly extended to include the killing of any large proportion of a group. Sixty-six percent of the Usage Panel accepts this extension in the sentence *The Jewish population of Germany was decimated by the war,* even though it is common knowledge that the number of Jews killed was much greater than a tenth of the original population. However, when the meaning is further extended to include large-scale destruction other than killing, as in *The supply of fresh produce was decimated by the accident at Chernobyl,* the usage is accepted by only 26 percent of the Panel.
> **WORD HISTORY:** *Decimate* comes from the Latin word *decimāre,* which meant "to punish every tenth man chosen by lot, as in a mutinous military unit," *dec-*

imāre being derived from *decimus,* "tenth." Our word *decimate* is first recorded in this sense in 1600 in *A Treatise of Ireland,* written by John Dymmok: "All . . . were by a martiall courte condemned to dye, which sentence was yet mittigated by the Lord Lieutenants mercy by which they were onely decimated by lott." *Decimate* then passed beyond the military context and came to be used rhetorically or loosely with reference to more than a tenth. Charlotte Brontë, for example, stated in a letter of 1848 that "Typhus fever decimated the school periodically," although typhus fever certainly did not always kill exactly a tenth of the school's population.

Copyright © 1992 by Houghton Mifflin Company. Reproduced by permission from the *American Heritage Dictionary of the English Language,* Third Edition.

en·thuse \in-´ th(y)üz\ *vb* **en·thused; en·thus·ing** [back-formation fr. *enthusiasm*] *vt* (1827) **1** : to make enthusiastic **2** : to express with enthusiasm ~ *vi* : to show enthusiasm <a splendid performance, and I was *enthusing* over it — Julian Huxley>
> **usage** *Enthuse* is apparently American in origin, although the earliest known example of its use occurs in a letter written in 1827 by a young Scotsman who spent about two years in the Pacific Northwest. It has been disapproved since about 1870. Current evidence shows it to be flourishing nonetheless on both sides of the Atlantic esp. in journalistic prose.

Merriam Webster's Collegiate Dictionary, Tenth Edition. Copyright © 1996 by Merriam Webster, Inc.

8. Synonyms and Antonyms. Although it is impossible for a dictionary to give differentiated synonyms for every word it contains, most dictionaries do group relatively common words that have similar definitions to demonstrate particular qualities and various shades of meaning. Some also give words of opposite meanings (antonyms) as an aid to distinctions in meaning.

mon·strous \´män(t)-strəs\ *adj* (15c) **1** *obs* : STRANGE, UNNATURAL **2** : having extraordinary often overwhelming size ; GIGANTIC **3 a** : having the qualities or appearance of a monster **b** *obs* : teeming with monsters **4 a** : extraordinarily ugly or vicious : HORRIBLE **b** : shockingly wrong or ridiculous **5** : deviating greatly from the natural form or character : ABNORMAL **6** : very great—used as an intensive— **mon·strous·ly** *adv*—**mon·strous·ness** *n*
> **syn** MONSTROUS, PRODIGIOUS, TREMENDOUS, STUPENDOUS mean extremely impressive, MONSTROUS implies a departure from the normal (as in size, form, or character) and often carries suggestions of deformity, ugliness, or fabulousness <the imagination turbid with *monstrous* fancies and misshapen dreams —Oscar Wilde> PRODIGIOUS suggests a marvelousness exceeding belief, usu. in something felt as going far beyond a previous maximum (as of goodness, greatness, intensity, or size) <made a *prodigious* effort and rolled the stone aside> <men have always reverenced *prodigious* inborn gifts— C. W. Eliot> TREMENDOUS may imply a power to terrify or inspire awe <the spell and *tremendous* incantation of the thought of death —L. P. Smith> but in more general and weakened use it means only very large or great or intense <success gave him *tremendous* satisfaction> STUPENDOUS implies a power to stun or astound, usu. because of size, numbers, complexity, or greatness beyond description <all are but parts of one *stupendous* whole, whose body Nature is, and God the soul —Alexander Pope>

Merriam Webster's Collegiate Dictionary, Tenth Edition. Copyright © 1996 by Merriam Webster, Inc.

Note in the example that each synonym is illustrated by a quotation. Not all dictionaries provide this particularly helpful feature.

You can use synonyms in two ways to improve your writing. The first use simply prevents repetition. The same word used again and again may look more important to the message than it really is; it may also make the message dull. The second use of synonyms, possibly the crucial one, is the matter of precision, of discovering just the right word for the sense. By the "right" word we mean no more than a word apt or suitable in its context. There are bookish or literary words that may be suitable in some formal contexts, in serious books. There are simple and homely words that are right in more informal writing. The distinctions between them are learned slowly, it is true, and all we can do here is give a few examples:

Bookish Words	*Simple Words*
impecunious	poor
opulent	rich, wealthy
discoursed	talked, spoke
dolorous	sad, painful, mournful
emolument	pay, wages, salary, fee
sustenance	support, food

9. Denotation and Connotation. A dictionary definition will establish the meaning of a word, but that definition does not necessarily include all the information about meaning that you need to use the word. The first definition in a dictionary for the adjective *fat* could be something like "having an unusual amount of fat" or "made up of too much adipose [fatty] tissue." Definitions such as these, stated in cold, factual, almost clinical analysis, are the *denotative* meanings of the word.

Most dictionaries will also give for such a commonly used word as *fat* a list of synonyms—*American Heritage* gives these: *fat, obese, corpulent, fleshy, portly, stout, pudgy, rotund, plump, chubby.* These words share the same denotative meaning: a fat person, a stout person, and a plump person are all overweight. But words in lists of synonyms are not always interchangeable. They have different emotional weights, different associations with the pleasant and the unpleasant; they express different degrees of positive and negative attitude or appeal. This emotional implication of a word is its *connotation.*

A stout man is an overweight man who gives an impression of solidity, strength, good health, and vigor; *stout* thus has a positive connotation. A plump man is also fat, but in a sense of the ridiculous, as though it were more a question of his being too short for his girth than of his being too broad for his height. *Plump* applied to a woman, on the other hand, is usually a term of approval, implying to many readers that the well-rounded woman thus described is also jovial.

Plump describing a cooked turkey awaiting carving at a holiday feast is effective and appropriate. But, because they normally connote qualities of people, *portly* and *stout* would be wrong if used to describe a cooked turkey. A child could well have *chubby* cheeks and *pudgy* fingers, but *corpulent* cheeks and *obese* fingers verge on the ridiculous. Although careful study of synonyms, their definitions, and illustrative sentences will help you find the word that gives the exact meaning you intend, such study may also help you avoid a completely inappropriate choice.

Study the following words, referring to a dictionary as necessary. Which words are usually positive or neutral by connotation? Which negative? Which words have similar denotative meanings?

1. articulate	6. demure	11. liberal	16. proud
2. blunt	7. eloquent	12. officious	17. prudish
3. candid	8. fussy	13. particular	18. reject
4. credulous	9. garrulous	14. profligate	19. trusting
5. decline (refuse)	10. haughty	15. prolix	20. zealous

10. Derivations of Words. Your dictionary will tell you the derivation or source of any word. Although there is some danger in assuming that the original meaning of a word is still its exact meaning (meanings change, you know, through long use), quite often a knowledge of the source and the original meaning of a word can illuminate it for you and give it a vividness of meaning that you will never forget. Did you know that *salary* comes from the Latin *salarium,* which meant the money given to Roman soldiers to buy salt with? Or that *tribulation* comes from a Latin word meaning a threshing sledge? Hence a man afflicted with tribulation is like a man beaten with the swinging clubs used to pound out grain on a threshing floor. Or consider *recalcitrant.* A recalcitrant child is an obstinate child. But if you look up the original meaning of the word, you find that the child is really "kicking back," like a mule.

The following words have interesting histories. Look them up in your dictionary.

1. bowery	4. carouse	7. hussy	10. panic	13. scuba
2. boycott	5. chortle	8. jeep	11. quixotic	14. tawdry
3. carnival	6. curfew	9. laser	12. sabotage	15. terrier

11. Persons and Places. The most convenient source of information about persons and places is your dictionary. It is true that the information you get there is condensed, but in most cases it is enough to set you on the right track. As a means of finding out where proper names are listed, you might look up some of the names in the following list. Remember that some dictionaries have a special section for geographic names and another for names of persons, whereas others list everything in the regular vocabulary.

1. Boucicault	3. Cassandra	5. Galen	7. Mount Kosciusko
2. Casanova	4. Corday	6. Ganges	8. Poseidon

12. Miscellaneous Information. Finally, the dictionary contains in easily accessible form a large amount of miscellaneous information about science, geography, biography, history, mythology, and so forth. Test this statement by looking up the following:

1. What sort of person would shed crocodile tears?
2. What were the former names of Zimbabwe, Iran, Sri Lanka, and Namibia?
3. What is a Hobson's choice, and how did the expression originate?
4. What is Mrs. Malaprop noted for?
5. Give an example of a spoonerism.
6. Why did the editor object to the reporter's writing about "the Thursday afternoon soiree at the home of . . ."?
7. How do you pronounce *provost* (1) when it refers to a college official, and (2) when it refers to a military officer?
8. Why is *cheeseburger* a totally illogical name?

9. Translate into American English the following: "My last ten bob went for a few litres of petrol for my lorry."
10. What is the most notable characteristic of a Manx cat?
11. Explain this bracketed insertion: One taxpayer wrote that "the schools don't teach enough grammer [*sic*] and spelling."
12. Look up the four italicized words and explain the meaning of this sentence: The word *radar* is probably *unique* in that it is both an *acronym* and a *palindrome*.

Paraphrasing

You will also find it useful to be able to paraphrase short passages that are particularly important or particularly difficult to read. A paraphrase is a rewriting of the original version in your own words—almost a translation. It simplifies, but does not necessarily shorten, the passage. Read the following technical passage on the description and purpose of an automobile turbocharger:

> Basically turbocharging is a system for increasing engine horsepower by using the exhaust gases to drive a turbine connected by a shaft to a compressor which pumps the fuel/air mixture into the engine. With an increase in engine speed, this compressor forces a greater volume of mixture into the combustion chambers, producing more power. During the cruising or light-load conditions, the turbocharger is essentially quiescent and the volume of mixture ingested is about the same as with any normally aspirated engine. The primary benefit of turbocharging, then, is that a fuel efficient small-displacement engine can have increased performance with little or no sacrifice in fuel economy.   (*Road and Track*, February 1978, p. 88)

Two words require immediate definition before any other efforts at simplification can begin:

1. *turbine:* a machine that has a rotor (a system of rotating airfoils) driven by the pressure of moving water, gases, or air. [Sometimes even dictionaries are no help. Picture a set of blades mounted around a shaft, much as the paddles of a water wheel are arranged. These blades—the rotor—are mounted inside a chamber, and water, gas, or even air moving at high speed flows through the chamber and turns the rotor by pressing on the blades.]
2. *compressor:* a pump or other machine for reducing the volume and increasing the pressure of gases. [Again the dictionary is not a great help. This part of the turbocharger pushes more gas–air mixture into the combustion chamber than would enter under ordinary pressure.]

Note: These two definitions offer a classic example of the problems facing a beginner in any field: The dictionary definitions are given in words too technical for a beginner to grasp, forcing the beginner to seek further definitions in the dictionary or to find a person both willing and able to explain the term in simple words. Asking for help from a teacher or a knowledgeable student is the easiest way out of the difficulty.

With these definitions in hand, try the passage in its existing order, making it simpler by substituting simpler words wherever possible.

A turbocharger is a device mounted on an automobile engine to increase the power of the engine. It uses exhaust gases to turn a wheel mounted on a shaft (turbine), which then turns another wheel or pump and forces the fuel–air mixture into the cylinders under pressure. Thus more fuel enters than ordinary pressure would bring in; more fuel mixture produces greater power. At low engine speed the device doesn't turn very fast, and the cylinders receive about as much mixture as they would through an ordinary carburetor. At high speed the compressor greatly increases the efficiency with which the engine uses the fuel–air mixture. The result is that a small engine can produce good performance without sacrificing fuel economy.

Sometimes it is equally useful to shorten a passage and make the basic idea easier to remember. A summary of that same paragraph on the turbocharger might read:

A turbocharger is a compressor driven by a rotor turned by exhaust gases. The compressor forces fuel–air mixture into the cylinders under greater than normal pressure, providing more fuel–air mixture for each detonation; thus the power of a small engine can be increased without a loss of economy.

This new version cuts the number of words in the passage by half and simplifies the wording somewhat. The shorter version ought to prove more manageable during study or review.

Outlining and Taking Notes

As you study, you will need to outline some of the materials you read in order to get an overall view of their scope and direction. Reading, outlining, and taking notes from a chapter of a textbook are not exceptionally difficult, but they constitute a very important skill.

Begin by reading the chapter through once rather quickly, trying to catch the general subject and the direction that the author is taking. Then read the chapter a second time, paying close attention to detail. In this second reading you should look up any words that are unclear to you. Paraphrase short passages that are especially difficult for you to read. This is the time to get complete control of the chapter.

On the third reading, locate the major divisions of the chapter. Note the headings, usually printed in contrasting type; they often indicate major divisions in a chapter. If you do not find headings within the chapter, search the introductory paragraphs for clues or statements that will help you to pick out the major divisions. Quite often the introduction contains some statement of the thesis of the chapter or provides enough direction so that you can find the major divisions.

If the chapter has no headings and the introduction does not offer enough direction to enable you to find the major divisions, work through the chapter paragraph by paragraph, writing a one-sentence summary for each paragraph. Read these sentences and try to group them into topics. If you are able to divide these topics into groups, summarize the ideas in each group and use those summaries as the headings in your chapter outline.

In addition to outlining the chapter, you should take other notes that will give you a complete picture of its content. Write down all the important dates. List the names of people, ideas, and events that figure in the chapter; later on, write out a brief identification of each item in the list. Take from the chapter illustrations and examples that might help to develop an answer on a test or a portion of a paper. Record quotations that seem to state an idea or a concept with exceptional clarity. With an outline and a thorough collection of notes such as these suggested, you should be able to master the material in a chapter without much difficulty.

Planning Your Time and Your Work

Some students do a bare minimum of work during the term and then cram massive amounts of studying into the last few days. Because such cramming requires that you ingest large and potentially harmful doses of coffee, amphetamines, and other stimulants, and because material learned quickly is forgotten quickly, a system of regular, manageable doses of work has much to recommend it.

Such a system of regular work is a necessity for success in college. The time spent in class in a college course is significantly shorter than the class time of a high-school course. New students sometimes fool themselves into believing that this shorter class time means that college is less work than high school. Nothing could be more likely to lead to failure. Many people believe that the average college student ought to spend *at least* an hour in outside work for every hour of class time in a college course. So in a three-credit course you should do three hours of preparation each week. And note that *one hour* is the *minimum* time for an average student. If you wish to make more than an average grade, or if you find a course difficult, you must spend more than the minimum time in outside preparation. Here are a few suggestions that might make your time allotted to preparation more productive:

1. Schedule study (and work, if you have a job) at regular times during the day. Provide enough time to keep up with your course work without cram sessions every two or three weeks to catch up. Allot your time so that the classes needing greater effort will receive extra time. Remember to schedule time regularly for working on long-term assignments and for library work. A large project will be easier and more beneficial if you do it in a number of short sessions than if you cram all the work into one or two marathon sessions.
2. Review your lecture and discussion notes immediately after the class or just before the next session. Consolidate and organize the notes while the material is fresh in your mind.
3. Do outside reading and writing assignments when they are assigned so that work outside the class will relate closely to the lectures and discussions in the class. Use class work and outside preparation to reinforce each other.
4. Work regularly rather than in fits and starts. Your mind needs time to understand new material and to develop new ideas. It does these tasks best in smaller units of time and materials. Trying to pressure-pack four or five weeks of material into a single day's cramming for a test is a very inefficient way to use your time and your mind. The same amount of time, spread out over several weeks, will yield far better results—more learning and better grades—with less strain on you.
5. Work neatly and carefully. Keep your notes and other materials in neat, well-organized folders. Time spent in the regular care and maintenance of these materials will allow you to study productively when test time finally arrives, without the frustration of searching for lost materials and of deciphering unreadable notes.

Regular work, performed with consistent high quality and meticulous care, is the only guarantee of success in college. Good work habits, developed at the beginning of your college career, will pay dividends from the start. It is impossible to emphasize too much the importance of working regularly, as opposed to letting matters slide and trying to catch up in agonized bursts of effort later in the term. A ten-hour project will always take ten hours to complete successfully. You will put in the time one way or another, but ten hours spent in five two-hour sessions will produce far better results than ten hours spent in a single marathon session. Invest your time wisely.

Appendix B

Diagnostic Tests

NAME _____   SCORE _____

Directions: In the space at the left of each pair of sentences, write the letter that identifies the correctly punctuated sentence.

_____ 1. A. "Whenever I try to study my class notes are almost unreadable," complained Ruth, "I must be more careful about my handwriting."
　　　　　　 B. "Whenever I try to study, my class notes are almost unreadable," complained Ruth; "I must be more careful about my handwriting."

_____ 2. A. Some of the stockholders are now wondering if the company has overextended itself by buying the two new ships.
　　　　　　 B. Some of the stockholders are now wondering, if the company has overextended itself by buying the two new ships?

_____ 3. A. Although the Perkinses live less than a block away from us, we hardly feel that we know them well.
　　　　　　 B. Although the Perkins's live less than a block away from us; we hardly feel that we know them well.

_____ 4. A. The following notice recently appeared on the bulletin board; "The editors of this years Senior yearbook have decided to dispense with the so-called humor section."
　　　　　　 B. The following notice recently appeared on the bulletin board: "The editors of this year's Senior yearbook have decided to dispense with the so-called humor section."

_____ 5. A. I scraped the mud and mashed insects from the windshield and Jennie sadly inspected the crumpled, rear fender.
　　　　　　 B. I scraped the mud and mashed insects from the windshield, and Jennie sadly inspected the crumpled rear fender.

_____ 6. A. After they had cleaned the kitchen, put the children to bed, and locked the front door, Pete and Jane looked forward to a quiet, peaceful evening.
　　　　　　 B. After they had cleaned the kitchen, put the children to bed and locked the front door; Pete and Jane looked forward to a quiet peaceful evening.

_____ 7. A. Some neighbors asked questions about Jim's strange friends but Mother told them that it was nobodys concern except our family's.
　　　　　　 B. Some neighbors asked questions about Jim's strange friends, but Mother told them that it was nobody's concern except our family's.

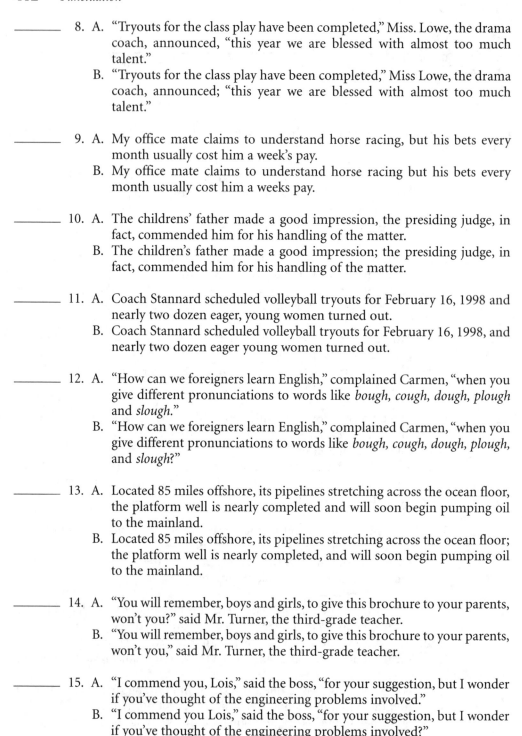

_____ 8. A. "Tryouts for the class play have been completed," Miss. Lowe, the drama coach, announced, "this year we are blessed with almost too much talent."

B. "Tryouts for the class play have been completed," Miss Lowe, the drama coach, announced; "this year we are blessed with almost too much talent."

_____ 9. A. My office mate claims to understand horse racing, but his bets every month usually cost him a week's pay.

B. My office mate claims to understand horse racing but his bets every month usually cost him a weeks pay.

_____ 10. A. The childrens' father made a good impression, the presiding judge, in fact, commended him for his handling of the matter.

B. The children's father made a good impression; the presiding judge, in fact, commended him for his handling of the matter.

_____ 11. A. Coach Stannard scheduled volleyball tryouts for February 16, 1998 and nearly two dozen eager, young women turned out.

B. Coach Stannard scheduled volleyball tryouts for February 16, 1998, and nearly two dozen eager young women turned out.

_____ 12. A. "How can we foreigners learn English," complained Carmen, "when you give different pronunciations to words like *bough, cough, dough, plough* and *slough.*"

B. "How can we foreigners learn English," complained Carmen, "when you give different pronunciations to words like *bough, cough, dough, plough,* and *slough?*"

_____ 13. A. Located 85 miles offshore, its pipelines stretching across the ocean floor, the platform well is nearly completed and will soon begin pumping oil to the mainland.

B. Located 85 miles offshore, its pipelines stretching across the ocean floor; the platform well is nearly completed, and will soon begin pumping oil to the mainland.

_____ 14. A. "You will remember, boys and girls, to give this brochure to your parents, won't you?" said Mr. Turner, the third-grade teacher.

B. "You will remember, boys and girls, to give this brochure to your parents, won't you," said Mr. Turner, the third-grade teacher.

_____ 15. A. "I commend you, Lois," said the boss, "for your suggestion, but I wonder if you've thought of the engineering problems involved."

B. "I commend you Lois," said the boss, "for your suggestion, but I wonder if you've thought of the engineering problems involved?"

_____ 16. A. In a large, antique car collection in California, we saw a one-cylinder car in running condition, it had the starting crank on one side.
　　　　 B. In a large antique car collection in California, we saw a one-cylinder car in running condition; it had the starting crank on one side.

_____ 17. A. "The attendance clerk wasn't impressed by my excuse, and I doubt that she'll find yours very convincing," said Anne.
　　　　 B. "The attendance clerk wasn't impressed by my excuse and I doubt that she'll find your's very convincing," said Anne.

_____ 18. A. "Are you aware of the fact that most of the pistachio nuts sold here, are imported from Greece and Turkey," asked Dr. Ash who is a storehouse of trivia.
　　　　 B. "Are you aware of the fact that most of the pistachio nuts sold here are imported from Greece and Turkey?" asked Dr. Ash, who is a storehouse of trivia.

_____ 19. A. The auto age for America really began in 1908 when Henry Ford, the son of a farmer, produced his Model T which was black, reliable and cheap.
　　　　 B. The auto age for America really began in 1908, when Henry Ford, the son of a farmer, produced his Model T, which was black, reliable, and cheap.

_____ 20. A. The manager smiled faintly and said, "It seems a shame, doesn't it, that a football player of Jake's ability must retire just because someone's spreading ugly rumors?"
　　　　 B. The manager smiled faintly and said, "It seems a shame, doesn't it, that a football player of Jake's ability must retire just because someones spreading ugly rumors."

_____ 21. A. It was four o'clock on a chilly, damp September afternoon, and the beach was deserted except for two bored lifeguards.
　　　　 B. It was four oclock on a chilly, damp, September afternoon and the beach was deserted except for two bored lifeguards.

_____ 22. A. My daughter pulled on her gloves and started to snip off the wilted blossoms, her expression revealing her complete lack of interest in gardening.
　　　　 B. My daughter pulled on her gloves, and started to snip off the wilted blossoms; her expression revealing her complete lack of interest in gardening.

_____ 23. A. Some of the electrical equipment failed, for nearly twenty hour's the explorers had no radio contact with the base.
　　　　 B. Some of the electrical equipment failed; for nearly twenty hours the explorers had no radio contact with the base.

_____ 24. A. If theres one thing today's students don't need; it's more critical, admonitory, or threatening advice hurled at them by long-nosed sanctimonious adults.
B. If there's one thing today's students don't need, it's more critical, admonitory, or threatening advice hurled at them by long-nosed, sanctimonious adults.

_____ 25. A. "A team that won't be beaten can't be beaten," shouted Coach Miller, who had a seemingly endless supply of clichés.
B. "A team that wont be beaten can't be beaten," shouted Coach Miller who had a seemingly endless supply of clichés.

NAME _____ SCORE _____

Directions: Each of the following sentences contains three italicized words, one of which is misspelled. Underline each misspelled word and write it, correctly spelled, in the space at the left.

_____ 1. "There are limitations on the length, breadth, and *heighth* of packages we ship, and the weight must not *exceed forty* pounds," the agent said.

_____ 2. My present was a box of fancy *stationery;* I was *dissappointed* that I didn't *receive* something more practical.

_____ 3. The food served at this rural inn is *becoming fameous* throughout Great *Britain.*

_____ 4. Lathrop sought the *advise* of an *eminent psychiatrist.*

_____ 5. This may sound *unbelievable* to you, but our city *library* has been struck three times by *lightening.*

_____ 6. Jerry is *dissatisfied* with his new *schedual* because it does not allow him time for studying *during* the afternoons.

_____ 7. In her *sophmore* year Joyce took a course in *speech* and two courses in *literature.*

_____ 8. The play had *it's* first *performance* in Hartford last *February.*

_____ 9. "An *acquaintance* of mine *reccommended* your *restaurant* to me," said Mrs. Watkins to the receptionist.

_____ 10. The applicant attempted to flatter the interviewer by saying, "You are *undoubtably knowledgeable* about the latest *technology* in our field."

_____ 11. "Your *humorous* remarks were not *appropriate* for a serious *occassion* such as this one," said the chairperson.

_____ 12. I admit that my new dog behaved *deploreably* last *Wednesday* at *obedience* school.

415

_____ 13. The data we get from these *questionnaires* could have an *effect* on next year's hiring *proceedures*.

_____ 14. *Reference* to a *dictionary* could have quickly settled the *arguement* the two of you were having.

_____ 15. We must all *recognize* the fact that tourism is the *principle* source of income in our quaint *village*.

_____ 16. Yesterday one of the arrested men *lead* the police officers to the place where the *equipment* stolen from the *laboratory* had been hidden.

_____ 17. A *goverment* spokesperson announced that the new *satellite* will provide weather forecasters with *indispensable* data.

_____ 18. The coach happily announced a *noticeable improvement* in batting averages, *especialy* in those of our outfielders.

_____ 19. A serious accident on the highway caused us to *loose approximately ninety* minutes of valuable time.

_____ 20. A senior *pardner* of the firm *conceded* that further meetings would very likely be *necessary*.

_____ 21. "This *pamphlet* is full of the most *rediculous propaganda* I've ever read," shouted the incumbent.

_____ 22. "*Neither* of these two small countries could withstand a long *seige*," replied *Sergeant* Lewis.

_____ 23. As he presented Enid with the award, the *superintendent* said, "Here is a young person *who's courageous* fight has inspired all of us."

_____ 24. When arrested, Elaine had in her *possession* a large *quanity* of *counterfeit* money.

_____ 25. "Serving on this *committee* has been a *priviledge* and a wonderful *experience*," said the retiring chairperson.

NAME _____   SCORE _____

Directions: In the space at the left, copy from within the parentheses the form that would be appropriate in serious writing.

_____ 1. Bert was surprised to learn that everyone in the class except Maria and (he, him) had to take another test.

_____ 2. The thief apparently had crept through the broken ventilator grill and had (laid, lain) quietly in the storeroom until nightfall.

_____ 3. Mary Ellen wasn't at the park yesterday; it hardly could have been (she, her) who tore your scarf.

_____ 4. Anyone selected for the acting presidency must prepare (himself or herself, themself, themselves) for a short and thankless term of office.

_____ 5. The reason I'm looking so pale is (because, that) my sunlamp needs repairing.

_____ 6. Some fellow who had occupied the room before I arrived had left some of (his, their) old clothes in the closet.

_____ 7. I wish someone on the school paper would write an editorial in (regard, regards) to the noise in the library reading room.

_____ 8. Just between you and (I, me), Luke shouldn't expect to get off with only a lecture from the judge.

_____ 9. You're convinced now, aren't you, that you (hadn't ought to, shouldn't) leave your garage unlocked?

_____ 10. My sister once studied the alto saxophone but never played it (good, well) enough to be chosen for the school band.

_____ 11. The robbers, (whoever, whomever) they were, must have known exactly when the workers would be paid.

_____ 12. The school's new program must be effective, for there (has, have) been surprisingly few complaints from parents.

417

——————————— 13. Not many jobs are available, (because, being that) the government has curtailed operations at the navy yard.

——————————— 14. After speaking into the microphone, Laura played back the tape and commented on how (different, differently) her voice sounded.

——————————— 15. "Vote for (whoever, whomever) you think is the best candidate," answered Anita's father.

——————————— 16. In a political campaign every candidate makes promises that (they know, he or she knows) cannot possibly be kept.

——————————— 17. Also included in the packet (is, are) a travel guide, some special trip tips, and two exceptional bonus prizes.

——————————— 18. Someone should have told (we, us) ushers that the main door had not been unlocked.

——————————— 19. Do you know who the man is who is (setting, sitting) at the head table next to the guest speaker?

——————————— 20. As everyone knows, neither DDT nor any other insecticide (has, have) the ability to distinguish between good and bad insects.

——————————— 21. If the helicopter pilot had not dropped blankets to the men stranded on the ice floe, they probably would have (froze, frozen) to death.

——————————— 22. After a few months Carrie (began, begun) to have doubts about her nephew's ability to manage her investments.

——————————— 23. No one could have been more surprised than (I, me) to learn of your recent marriage.

——————————— 24. The gratification resulting from working on the school newspaper and other publications (outweighs, outweigh) the demands on one's time.

——————————— 25. After a person has sat for five hours in the blazing sunlight listening to this kind of music, (he or she feels, they feel) numb and beaten.

NAME _____ SCORE _____

Directions: Study these paired sentences for incompleteness, dangling or misplaced modifiers, faulty parallelism, and faulty comparisons. In the space at the left, write the letter that identifies the correct sentence.

_____ 1. A. The cotton crop this year, we all hope, will be much better than last years.
B. The cotton crop this year, we all hope, will be much better than last year's.

_____ 2. A. Because we are the parents of five active children, our washing machine is running much of the time.
B. Being the parents of five active children, our washing machine is running much of the time.

_____ 3. A. Searching the area carefully, we finally found the tunnel entrance, expertly covered by underbrush and which the other searchers had overlooked.
B. Searching the area carefully, we finally found the tunnel entrance, which had been expertly covered by underbrush and which the other searchers had overlooked.

_____ 4. A. The group's intention, surely a noble one, to constantly and relentlessly encourage the protection of the environment.
B. The group's intention, surely a noble one, is to encourage constantly and relentlessly the protection of the environment.

_____ 5. A. Believing me to be a better public speaker than anyone else in the class, my parents told all the relatives that I would be the valedictorian.
B. Being a better public speaker than anyone in the class, my parents told all the relatives that I would be the valedictorian.

_____ 6. A. Malaysia and other countries proved incapable of sheltering or unwilling to shelter all of the refugees.
B. Malaysia and other countries proved incapable or unwilling to shelter all of the refugees.

_____ 7. A. "I neither intend to withdraw from the race nor to in any degree stop pointing out my opponent's shortcomings," Ms. Hawley replied.
B. "I intend neither to withdraw from the race nor in any degree to stop pointing out my opponent's shortcomings," Ms. Hawley replied.

419

_____ 8. A. When seen from a distance, the white cliffs seem to resemble icebergs.
   B. When seen from a distance, one might think that the white cliffs were icebergs.

_____ 9. A. This popular young actor lives high in the Hollywood hills in a small apartment decorated with posters of auto races and bullfights.
   B. This popular young actor lives in a small apartment decorated with posters of auto races and bullfights high in the Hollywood hills.

_____ 10. A. The relatively small amount of flood water has not and probably won't cause any major damage.
   B. The relatively small amount of flood water has not caused and probably won't cause any major damage.

_____ 11. A. When we replaced the wooden shingles with a composition roof, the insurance company agreed to lower our annual premium quite considerably.
   B. By replacing the wooden shingles with a composition roof, the insurance company agreed to quite considerably lower our annual premium.

_____ 12. A. Commissioner Reed stated that our downtown streets are as clean, if not cleaner than, other cities.
   B. Commissioner Reed stated that our downtown streets are as clean as, if not cleaner than, those of other cities.

_____ 13. A. I already have a full enough schedule of work today without being asked to listen to you practice your speech.
   B. I already have a full enough schedule of work today without asking me to listen to you practice your speech.

_____ 14. A. The reason for our moving being that the security system at Elmhurst Manor is more modern than the old apartment.
   B. The reason for our moving is that the security system at Elmhurst Manor is more modern than that at the old apartment.

_____ 15. A. Sylvia Andrews is a self-sufficient and talented person who, since her parents died, has supported herself and her younger brothers tutoring students in mathematics.
   B. Sylvia Andrews, a self-sufficient and talented person who has supported herself and her younger brothers since her parents died tutoring students in mathematics.

_____ 16. A. My mother's paternal grandmother was one of the very few, if not the only, woman to study veterinary medicine in the early 1900s.
   B. My mother's paternal grandmother was one of the very few women, if not the only woman, to study veterinary medicine in the early 1900s.

_____ 17. A. You must either return these books to the library or pay a substantial fine.
   B. Either you must return these books to the library or pay a substantial fine.

_____ 18. A. I hope that the yield from these tax-free bonds will be equal to, if not more than, the yield from your stocks.
   B. I hope that the yield from these tax-free bonds will be equal, if not more than, your stocks.

_____ 19. A. Albert's plan being to, as soon as he receives his inheritance, retire to some remote island in the South Seas.
   B. Albert's plan is to retire to some remote island in the South Seas as soon as he receives his inheritance.

_____ 20. A. You will be given preferred seating only if you have donated at least two hundred dollars to the Opera Guild.
   B. You will only be given preferred seating if you have donated at least two hundred dollars to the Opera Guild.

_____ 21. A. Ellen hopes that her tax-deductible contributions this year will be equal to, if not more than, last year's.
   B. Ellen hopes that her tax-deductible contributions this year will be equal, if not more than, last year.

_____ 22. A. Pietro maintains that most people in his country are easygoing, warm-hearted, friends to Americans, and having a tolerance for the ideas and ways of foreigners.
   B. Pietro maintains that most people in his country are easygoing and warmhearted, are friends to Americans, and have a tolerance for the ideas and ways of foreigners.

_____ 23. A. Fairhaven has one of the largest airports in the state, if not the largest.
   B. Fairhaven has one of the largest, if not the largest, airport in the state.

_____ 24. A. While just getting nicely adjusted to high-school life, my family moved again, this time to Baltimore.
   B. While I was just getting nicely adjusted to high-school life, my family moved again, this time to Baltimore.

_____ 25. A. Quickly totaling the bills, imagine my dismay on discovering that I nearly owed my entire month's salary.
   B. Quickly totaling the bills, I was dismayed to discover that I owed nearly my entire month's salary.

Appendix C

Answer Key to Practice Sheets

Practice Sheet 1, page 5
1. was
2. were
3. selected
4. hid
5. are
6. comes
7. arrived
8. came
9. is
10. remains
11. rumbled
12. ride
13. (i)s
14. disappeared
15. helped
16. missed
17. covered
18. flies
19. delivered
20. seem

Practice Sheet 1, page 6
1. shorter
2. snake
3. package
4. friend
5. person
6. bat
7. question
8. students
9. hiker
10. skill
11. decrease
12. members
13. few
14. last
15. sources
16. sunflowers
17. Applications
18. alarm
19. trophies
20. assistant

Practice Sheet 2, pages 13, 14
1. 6, 4
2. 1, 3
3. 4, 6
4. 4, 5
5. 4, 3
6. 5, 2
7. 6, 1
8. 4, 4
9. 3, 5
10. 1, 4
11. 4, 2
12. 4, 1
13. 6, 4
14. 1, 4
15. 5, 4
16. 5, 2
17. 4, 6
18. 5, 1
19. 2, 3
20. 2, 5
21. 4, 4
22. 4, 1
23. 3, 1
24. 1, 5
25. 5, 2
26. 1, 4
27. 2, 4
28. 5, 3
29. 4, 1
30. 1, 4
31. 4, 1
32. 4, 1
33. 5, 6
34. 1, 4
35. 5, 4
36. 5, 1
37. 4, 1
38. 4, 4
39. 6, 1
40. 1, 5

Practice Sheet 3, page 25
1. success
2. rivals
3. choice
4. offer
5. favorite
6. way
7. sources
8. winners
9. student
10. source
11. addition
12. member
13. secret
14. appearance
15. part
16. help
17. birthplace
18. success
19. winner
20. player

Practice Sheet 3, page 26
1. tired
2. predictable
3. delighted
4. discouraged
5. faithful
6. hazy
7. restless
8. disappointed
9. peaceful
10. open
11. unmanageable
12. cold
13. ready
14. fruitless
15. clear
16. elated
17. sour
18. sleepy
19. full
20. ill

Practice Sheet 4, page 33
1. textbook
2. paragraphs
3. lumber
4. members
5. assistance
6. top
7. course
8. files
9. hours
10. pages
11. copies
12. story
13. grade
14. fire
15. heater
16. handful
17. all
18. clue
19. idea
20. checks

Practice Sheet 4, page 34
1. I. O.
2. O .C.
3. D. O.
4. O. C.
5. I. O.
6. D. O.
7. I. O.
8. D. O.
9. O. C.
10. D. O.
11. D. O.
12. I. O.
13. O. C.
14. D. O.
15. I. O.
16. D. O.
17. D. O.
18. I. O.
19. O. C.
20. I. O.

Practice Sheet 5, pages 41, 42
1. have, 3
2. will, 3
3. should have, 4
4. would have, 3
5. must, 3
6. might have, 4
7. should have, 5
8. could have been, 1
9. has, 4
10. should have, 1
11. have, 4
12. will have, 3
13. is, 2
14. has, 5
15. should, 3
16. has, 2
17. has been, 1
18. has, 5
19. had, 1
20. could, 2
21. has been, 1
22. should, 1
23. has, 4
24. will have, 3
25. could, 3
26. were, 5
27. has, 4
28. (ha)ve, 3
29. has been, 3
30. will, 3
31. has, 5
32. should be, 1
33. had been, 1
34. does, 4
35. would, 2
36. have been, 1
37. should, 3
38. will, 3
39. has, 3
40. must, 1

423

Practice Sheet 6, page 51

1. 3, was printed
2. 5, is considered
3. 4, will be given
4. 3, were counted

5. 3, must be solved
6. 4, have been offered
7. 5, has been selected
8. 3, should not be cut up

9. 5, was called
10. 4, were sent

Practice Sheet 6, page 52

1. whom
2. what
3. who

4. what color
5. manager
6. who

7. whom
8. assistant
9. paper

10. paper
11. what
12. people

13. children
14. whom
15. who

Practice Sheet 7, pages 59, 60

1. 3;
2. 2,
3. 2,
4. 3;
5. 1

6. 3;
7. 2,
8. 2,
9. 2,
10. 1

11. 3;
12. 2,
13. 1
14. 3;
15. 3;

16. 1
17. 3;
18. 3;
19. 3;
20. 2,

21. 1
22. 2,
23. 1
24. 3;
25. 1

Practice Sheet 8, pages 71, 72

1. Time
2. Concession
3. Time
4. Cause
5. Time
6. Modification
7. Condition
8. Comparison

9. Time
10. Purpose
11. Comparison
12. Condition
13. Result
14. Purpose
15. Manner
16. Time

17. Cause
18. Time
19. Modification
20. Manner
21. Place
22. Cause
23. Time
24. Manner

25. Purpose
26. Concession
27. Comparison
28. Modification
29. Result
30. Condition
31. Condition
32. Condition

33. Place
34. Condition
35. Cause
36. Manner
37. Modification
38. Condition
39. Time
40. Concession

Practice Sheet 9, page 81

1. restaurant
2. Pentagon Restaurant
3. 1989
4. time

5. Jill Wright
6. woman
7. passengers
8. Tom Wilson

9. classes
10. C. L. class
11. girl
12. person

13. anyone
14. car
15. car

Practice Sheet 9, page 82

1. articles, that . . . paper
2. article, which . . . Blows."
3. boys, who . . . jobs
4. James Rogers, who . . . jobs
5. people, to . . . invitations

6. moment, when . . . me
7. person, whose . . . borrowed
8. Paul Rollins, whose . . . missing
9. writer, whose . . . atrocious
10. day, when . . . her

11. place, where . . . found
12. person, who . . . account
13. Jim Shavers, who . . . store
14. car, that . . . inexpensive
15. students, who . . . me

Practice Sheet 10, page 93

1. S. C.
2. Ap.
3. O. P.
4. D. O.

5. D. O.
6. S.
7. S. C.
8. O. P.

9. S.
10. Ap.
11. O. P.
12. S. C.

13. D. O.
14. S.
15. O. P.
16. S.

17. S. C.
18. D. O.
19. D. O.
20. Ap.

Practice Sheet 10, page 94

1. S.
2. O. P.
3. O. P.
4. D. O.

5. Ap.
6. S.
7. D. O.
8. O. P.

9. D. O.
10. D. O.
11. S.
12. Ap.

13. D. O.
14. S.
15. D. O.
16. S. C.

17. D. O.
18. D. O.
19. S.
20. D. O.

Practice Sheet 11, page 105

1. D. O.
2. O. P.
3. S. C.
4. D. O.

5. O. P.
6. S.
7. O. P.
8. S.

9. S. C.
10. S.
11. D. O.
12. O. P.

13. D. O.
14. S.
15. O. P.
16. D. O.

17. O. P.
18. S. C.
19. O. P.
20. S.

Practice Sheet 11, page 106

1. Adv.
2. Adj.
3. N.
4. N.

5. Adj.
6. Adv.
7. N.
8. Adv.

9. N.
10. N.
11. N.
12. Adv.

13. N.
14. Adv.
15. Adj.
16. N.

17. N.
18. N.
19. N.
20. N.

Practice Sheet 12, pages 115, 116

1. –	7. –	13. –	19. numbers	25. Winnie
2. Mike	8. –	14. funds	20. –	26. –
3. cars	9. –	15. Mr. Miller	21. Arnie	27. –
4. payments	10. anyone	16. –	22. man	28. Barbara
5. –	11. –	17. Jennifer	23. –	29. –
6. Jan	12. Mark	18. –	24. textbook	30. rest

Practice Sheet 13, pages 127, 128

1. S	7. S	13. F	19. S	25. F
2. F	8. F	14. S	20. S	26. F
3. F	9. S	15. S	21. S	27. S
4. S	10. S	16. F	22. S	28. S
5. F	11. F	17. S	23. S	29. F
6. S	12. S	18. F	24. F	30. S

Practice Sheet 14, page 137

1. A	3. A	5. B	7. A	9. A
2. B	4. A	6. B	8. B	10. B

Practice Sheet 14A, pages 141, 142

1. B	5. A	9. B	13. B	17. A
2. A	6. B	10. A	14. B	18. A
3. B	7. B	11. A	15. B	19. A
4. B	8. A	12. B	16. A	20. A

Practice Sheet 15, page 149

1. 7	4. 5	7. 1	10. 3	13. 2
2. 1	5. 3	8. 6	11. 5	14. 4
3. 2	6. 4	9. 1	12. 7	15. 7

Practice Sheet 15, page 150

1. Although my entire family is coming to visit this weekend, I am not planning to give any kind of party.
2. Because my entire family is coming to visit this weekend, I am planning to give a huge party.
3. Wanting to watch an old movie on TV, I stayed home last night.
4. You can consult Hugh Johnson, our athletic trainer, about your tennis elbow.
5. You can consult Hugh Johnson, who is our athletic trainer, about your tennis elbow.
6. Installing air conditioning in your office will increase your efficiency.
7. Install air conditioning in your office to increase your efficiency.
8. After washing his car, Jim drove to the game.
9. The last flight having been canceled, everyone in this room needs a new reservation.
10. Since the last flight has been canceled, everyone in this room needs a new reservation.

Practice Sheet 16, page 157

1. A	3. B	5. B	7. B	9. A
2. B	4. A	6. B	8. B	10. A

Practice Sheet 16, page 158

1. B	3. A	5. B	7. B	9. A
2. B	4. B	6. B	8. B	10. A

Practice Sheet 17, pages 165, 166

1. 2, 1 history, . . . math,	8. 5(4), 3 up, . . . leisurely,	15. 2, 1 chairs, . . . , but
2. 3, 4 long, . . . report,	9. 5, 3 that, . . . immediate,	16. 3, 4 cold, . . . rain,
3. 3, 2 handsome, . . . throat,	10. 4, 3 early, . . . short,	17. 2, 3 slowly, . . . quiet,
4. 4, 3 runners, . . . long,	11. 1, 3 car, . . . sleepy,	18. 4(5), 1 mopping, . . . clean,
5. 2, 1 titles, . . . slides,	12. 4, 2 graphics, . . . programming,	19. 2, 1 Robert, . . . Helen,
6. 1, 3 , or . . . noisy,	13. 3, 1 big, . . . tomatoes,	20. 4, 3 questions, . . . last,
7. 4, 2 away, . . . barn,	14. 4, 3 choices, . . . simplest,	

Practice Sheet 18, page 175

1. 3	5. 5	9. 6	13. 1	17. 5
2. 1	6. (OK)	10. 2	14. 3	18. 6
3. 1	7. 1	11. 1	15. 6	19. 4
4. 6	8. 1	12. 2	16. 2	20. 1

Practice Sheet 18, page 176

1. R	5. N	9. R	13. R	17. R
2. R	6. R	10. N	14. N	18. N
3. N	7. N	11. R	15. R	19. N
4. N	8. N	12. R	16. N	20. R

Practice Sheet 19, page 187

1. C	5. W five-dollar	9. W That's	13. W ;
2. W " , "	6. W :	10. W Whose	14. W yours
3. C	7. W yours	11. W ;	15. W hundred-dollar
4. W it's	8. C	12. C	

Practice Sheet 19, page 188

1. The programmer told us, "The new program . . . complicated."
2. Marge said, "I need to take a few days . . . week."
3. Benny said, "I signed up for the course so that I . . . game."
4. One person in the audience announced, "The singer will . . . month."
5. Does our contract . . . say, "Our company must . . . months"?
6. The president's assistant said that they would . . . events.
7. My neighbor said that she needed . . . to paint her house.
8. The little boy responded that he had lost . . . street.
9. Mrs. Williams asked when the repairs . . . would be completed.
10. Did I hear the television meteorologist say that there would be . . . tonight?

Practice Sheet 20, pages 195, 196

1. W	11. W	21. W	31. W	41. C
2. C	12. W	22. C	32. C	42. W
3. C	13. W	23. W	33. C	43. C
4. C	14. W	24. C	34. W	44. W
5. W	15. W	25. W	35. C	45. C
6. C	16. W	26. C	36. C	46. W
7. W	17. C	27. W	37. W	47. W
8. C	18. C	28. W	38. W	48. W
9. W	19. C	29. W	39. C	49. W
10. C	20. C	30. C	40. W	50. C

Practice Sheet 21, pages 207, 208

1. saw, ran	5. sat, risen	9. worn, drank	13. came, stung	17. sunk, drowned
2. fallen, clung	6. known, ridden	10. lay, eaten	14. did, broken	18. hung, drawn
3. began, came	7. shaken, frozen	11. brought, flown	15. bought, stolen	19. spoken, given
4. swam, lay	8. threw, dragged	12. gone, chose	16. became, spent	20. sworn, lent

Practice Sheet 21, pages 209, 210

1. C, worn	5. frozen, C	9. blew, C	13. known, ridden	17. did, drawn
2. C, C	6. C, stole	10. thrown, C	14. laid, hanged	18. came, C
3. saw, became	7. C, C	11. C, flown	15. lying, written	19. C, drowning
4. were, C	8. C, rose	12. began, C	16. C, C	20. sitting, spoken

Practice Sheet 22, page 219

1. was	4. exist	7. were	10. is	13. were
2. are	5. plans	8. is	11. was	14. keeps
3. leave	6. is	9. have	12. was	15. has

Practice Sheet 22, page 220

1. were	4. C	7. C	10. has	13. C
2. was	5. are	8. is	11. tells	14. is
3. doesn't	6. doesn't	9. pays	12. doesn't	15. was

Practice Sheet 23, pages 229, 230

1. B
2. A
3. A
4. B
5. B
6. A
7. B
8. A
9. B
10. A
11. A
12. B
13. B
14. B
15. A
16. A
17. B
18. A
19. B
20. A

Practice Sheet 24, page 239

1. 4
2. 4
3. 1
4. 2
5. 5
6. 4
7. 2
8. 1
9. 1
10. 5
11. 1
12. 1
13. 5
14. 4
15. 4
16. 1
17. 1
18. 1
19. 4
20. 4

Practice Sheet 24, page 240

1. us
2. whoever
3. she
4. whom
5. me
6. she
7. yours
8. us
9. our
10. who
11. whoever
12. she
13. I
14. he
15. me
16. we
17. whom
18. else's
19. us
20. me

Practice Sheet 25, pages 249, 250

1. prices, Adj.
2. flew, Adv.
3. aware, Adv.
4. situation, Adj.
5. job, Adj.
6. will see, Adv.
7. you, Adj.
8. drive, Adv.
9. process, Adj.
10. step, Adv.
11. chance, Adj.
12. he, Adj.
13. will reward, Adv.
14. is trying, Adv.
15. one, Adj.
16. streets, Adj.
17. voters, Adj.
18. helpful, Adj.
19. train, Adj.
20. kicked, Adv.

Practice Sheet 25, pages 251, 252

1. well
2. bad
3. faster
4. carefully
5. better
6. very
7. reasonably
8. good
9. well
10. sad
11. sadly
12. almost
13. more
14. bad
15. conservatively
16. surely
17. considerably
18. independently
19. well
20. badly

Practice Sheet 26, pages 263, 264

1. 1, 2
2. 1, 2
3. 1, 1
4. 1, 1
5. 1, 1
6. 2, 1
7. 1, 2
8. 1, 2
9. 2, 1
10. 2, 2
11. 1, 1
12. 1, 2
13. 2, 2
14. 1, 2
15. 2, 2
16. 2, 1
17. 1, 2
18. 2, 1
19. 2, 2
20. 1, 1

Practice Sheet 26, pages 265, 266

1. shouldn't, that
2. fewer, because of
3. many, C
4. as if, wants to go out
5. somewhat, nowhere near
6. surely, C
7. person, very
8. C, off
9. well, enthusiastic
10. man, this
11. suspect, might have
12. C, that
13. regardless, as far as
14. supposed to, C
15. C, those
16. very, C
17. a couple of, inside
18. in regard to, try to
19. used to, anywhere
20. C, C

Practice Sheet 27, pages 277, 278

1. writing
2. admitted
3. companies
4. they're
5. noticeable
6. requirement
7. altar
8. authorities
9. field
10. who's
11. principal
12. opened
13. its
14. receive
15. famous
16. absolutely
17. profitable
18. council
19. becoming
20. shown
21. siege
22. pieces
23. affected
24. outrageous
25. challenging
26. you're
27. instance
28. stationery
29. lose
30. than

Practice Sheet 28, page 285

1. allies
2. alumnae
3. axes
4. beaux, beaus
5. boxes
6. cameos
7. cookies
8. cupfuls, cupsful
9. diagnoses
10. handkerchiefs, handkerchieves
11. lackeys
12. lassos, lassoes
13. lice
14. men-of-war
15. mementos, mementoes
16. mongooses, mongeese
17. princesses
18. referenda, referendums
19. saleswoman
20. scarfs
21. sheaves
22. Thomases
23. tomatoes
24. turkeys
25. wolves

Practice Sheet 28, page 286

1. W	11. C	21. C	31. C	41. C
2. C	12. C	22. C	32. C	42. W
3. W	13. C	23. C	33. C	43. C
4. C	14. W	24. C	34. W	44. W
5. C	15. C	25. W	35. C	45. W
6. W	16. W	26. W	36. W	46. C
7. C	17. W	27. C	37. C	47. W
8. W	18. C	28. C	38. C	48. W
9. C	19. C	29. C	39. C	49. C
10. C	20. C	30. C	40. C	50. C

Practice Sheet 29, pages 293, 294

1. candidate, competition
2. equipment, exorbitant
3. disastrous, environment
4. disappointed, accommodations
5. excellent, graffiti
6. conferences, differences
7. enthusiastic, foreign
8. embarrassed, humorous
9. eligible, forty
10. business, abbreviated
11. criticized, appearance
12. athletic, amateur
13. among, acquaintances
14. during, February
15. always, committee
16. absence, discipline
17. audience, dissatisfied
18. arithmetic, grammar
19. immediately, government
20. continuous, dictionary
21. appropriate, curiosity
22. calendar, convenient
23. conceded, competent
24. awkward, accidentally
25. familiar, arguments

Practice Sheet 29A, pages 297, 298

1. opportunity, superintendent
2. mischievous, library
3. original, imagination
4. professor, parallel
5. laboratory, partner
6. probably, village
7. scheduled, Wednesday
8. successful, politics
9. secretary, misspells
10. recommend, restaurant
11. permissible, sophomore
12. ninety, sandwiches
13. literature, tragedies
14. propaganda, prejudices
15. interpretation, interesting
16. practically, possessions
17. knowledge, mathematics
18. persuaded, villain
19. temperature, occasionally
20. ninth, twelfth
21. ridiculous, pronunciation
22. interrupted, speech
23. optimistic, satisfactorily
24. surprise, proceeded
25. similar, pastimes

Index

A

a, an, 255

a lot of. **See** *lots of*

Abbreviations
    acceptable, 191
    "alphabet" forms, 191
    period with, 191
    unacceptable, 191

Abrahamson, David, 307

Absolute elements, commas
    with, 163

Absolute phrases
    as method of subordination,
        145
    commas with, 172
    defined, 112
    preceded by *with,* 113

Absolute qualities, adjectives of,
    247

Academic subjects, capital letters
    with, 283

accept, except, 273

accordingly, 57

Accusative case. **See** Objective
    case

Acronyms, 191–192

Active voice
    defined, 45
    forms of, 9–10

A.D., B.C., 191

ad, clipped forms, 255

Addresses, commas with, 173

Adjective clauses
    as method of subordination,
        145
    as reduced sentence, 77
    commas with, 79, 171
    contrasted with appositive
        noun clause, 89
    defined, 77
    subordinating word
        unexpressed, 78
    subordinating words with, 77

Adjectives
    comparison of, 11, 154, 247
    defined, 10, 245
    degree, 11, 155, 247
    double comparison, 154, 247
    misused for adverb, 246

of absolute quality, 247
other words used as, 12
same form as adverb, 245
suffixes that form, 10–11

Adverb clauses
    as method of subordination,
        145
    classified by meaning, 66–67
    commas with, 162–163
    conjunctions with, 66–67
    defined, 65
    elliptical, 67
    modifying adjectives and
        adverbs, 67
    position of, 68

Adverbs
    classified by use, 11
    comparison of, 154, 247
    defined, 11, 245
    forms with and without *ly,*
        245
    misplaced, 133
    misused comparative or
        superlative degree, 155, 247
    misused for adjective, 246
    same form as adjective, 245

advice, advise, 273

affect, effect, 273

after, introducing adverb clause,
    66

aggravate, 255

Agreement, pronoun and
    antecedent
    antecedents differing in
        gender, 226
    basic rule, 225
    collective noun antecedent,
        227
    compound unit antecedent,
        227
    indefinite pronoun
        antecedent, 225
    you referring to third person,
        227

Agreement, subject and verb
    basic rule, 215
    collective noun subject, 217
    compound subjects joined by
        and, 216

compound subjects joined by
    or, nor, 216
indefinite pronoun subject, 216
none as subject, 216
one of those . . . who, number
    of, 217
plural subjects of amount,
    etc., 217
relative pronoun subject,
    217–218
sentences starting with *there,
    here,* 216
verb preceding subject, 216
words intervening between
    subject and verb, 215

ain't, 255

all, singular or plural, 217

all ready, already, 273

all the farther, all the faster, 255

all together, altogether, 273

alright, 255

altar, alter, 273

Alterations of basic sentence
    patterns
    negatives, 49
    passive voice, 45–46
    questions, 46–48

although, introducing adverb
    clause, 67

A.M., P.M., 191

American Heritage Dictionary,
    397

among, between, 255–256

amount, number, 256

Amount, plural nouns of, 217

Analogy, 312

Analysis
    as method of paragraph
        development, 333–334
    causal analysis, 336–337
    process analysis, 334–335

analyze, as instruction word in
    essay test, 319

and
    commas before, 59
    excessive use of, 65, 145
    in compound sentence, 59
    number of subjects joined by,
        216

429

Credits